Mastering Docker

From Basics to Expert Proficiency

Contents

1 Introduction to Docker **13**

1.1 What is Docker? An Overview 13

1.2 The Evolution of Containerization 16

1.3 Benefits of Using Docker 18

1.4 Docker vs Virtual Machines 20

1.5 Key Docker Terminology 22

1.6 Docker Architecture 24

1.7 Understanding Docker Images and Containers 27

1.8 The Docker Ecosystem 29

2 Setting Up Docker **33**

2.1 System Requirements for Docker 33

2.2 Installing Docker on Windows 36

2.3 Installing Docker on macOS 38

2.4 Installing Docker on Linux 40

2.5 Post-Installation Steps 42

2.6 Verifying the Docker Installation 45

2.7 Setting Up Docker Command-Line Interface (CLI) . . . 47

2.8 Configuring Docker Daemon 50

2.9 Managing Docker with Docker Desktop 52

2.10 Upgrading and Uninstalling Docker 56

3 Docker Images **61**

3.1 What are Docker Images? 61
3.2 Understanding Dockerfile 64
3.3 Creating Your First Docker Image 66
3.4 Best Practices for Writing Dockerfiles 68
3.5 Building Docker Images 71
3.6 Managing Docker Images with Docker Hub 73
3.7 Tagging and Versioning Docker Images 76
3.8 Inspecting Docker Images 78
3.9 Optimizing Docker Images 81
3.10 Working with Base Images 83
3.11 Publishing Docker Images 86
3.12 Using Multi-Stage Builds 89

4 Docker Containers **93**

4.1 What are Docker Containers? 93
4.2 Starting Your First Container 96
4.3 Container Lifecycle Management 99
4.4 Running Containers in Detached Mode 102
4.5 Exposing and Mapping Ports 104
4.6 Running Interactive Containers 106
4.7 Working with Container Logs 108
4.8 Accessing Containers via Shell 110
4.9 Stopping and Restarting Containers 112
4.10 Removing Containers 114
4.11 Linking and Networking Containers 116
4.12 Creating Persistent Storage for Containers 119
4.13 Committing Containers to Images 121
4.14 Scaling Containers 123

5 **Docker Networking** **127**
5.1 Introduction to Docker Networking 127
5.2 Types of Docker Networks 129
5.3 Bridge Networks 131
5.4 Host Networks 134
5.5 Overlay Networks 137
5.6 Macvlan Networks 139
5.7 Creating and Managing Custom Networks 142
5.8 Connecting Containers to Networks 145
5.9 Networking in Docker Compose 147
5.10 Service Discovery in Docker 151
5.11 Docker Network Security 154
5.12 Troubleshooting Docker Networking Issues 157

6 **Docker Storage and Volumes** **161**
6.1 Introduction to Docker Storage 161
6.2 Understanding Docker Volumes 164
6.3 Creating and Managing Volumes 166
6.4 Mounting Volumes to Containers 168
6.5 Using Bind Mounts 170
6.6 Volume Drivers and Plugins 173
6.7 Backing Up and Restoring Volumes 176
6.8 Sharing Data Between Containers 179
6.9 Persistent Storage in Docker 181
6.10 Storage Options in Docker Swarm 183
6.11 Optimizing Storage Performance 185
6.12 Troubleshooting Storage Issues 187

7 **Docker Compose and Multi-Container Environments** **191**
7.1 Introduction to Docker Compose 191

7.2 Installing Docker Compose 194
7.3 Understanding the Docker Compose File Structure . . 197
7.4 Creating Your First Docker Compose File 200
7.5 Building and Running Multi-Container Applications . . 203
7.6 Defining Services in Docker Compose 206
7.7 Working with Volumes and Networks in Compose . . . 210
7.8 Scaling Services with Docker Compose 212
7.9 Environment Variables in Docker Compose 216
7.10 Using Docker Compose for Development and Testing 218
7.11 Managing Docker Compose Lifecycle 222
7.12 Using Compose with Docker Swarm 225
7.13 Best Practices for Docker Compose 227

8 Docker Kubernetes Integration 233

8.1 Introduction to Kubernetes 233
8.2 Understanding Kubernetes Architecture 236
8.3 Setting Up Kubernetes with Docker 239
8.4 Deploying Docker Containers on Kubernetes 241
8.5 Kubernetes Pods and Deployments 244
8.6 Service Discovery and Networking in Kubernetes . . . 246
8.7 Managing Storage with Kubernetes 250
8.8 Configuring and Managing Kubernetes Clusters 253
8.9 Using Kubernetes ConfigMaps and Secrets 256
8.10 Scaling Applications in Kubernetes 259
8.11 Monitoring and Logging in Kubernetes 262
8.12 Kubernetes Security Best Practices 265
8.13 Upgrading and Maintaining Kubernetes Clusters . . . 267

9 Docker Best Practices and Security 271

9.1 Introduction to Docker Best Practices 271

9.2 Optimizing Dockerfile Instructions 275
9.3 Image Size Reduction Techniques 278
9.4 Container Resource Management 279
9.5 Using Health Checks 283
9.6 Docker Logging Best Practices 285
9.7 Implementing Docker Security Best Practices 288
9.8 Running Containers with Least Privilege 290
9.9 Isolating Containers 293
9.10 Network Security in Docker 295
9.11 Using Docker Bench for Security 299
9.12 Managing Secrets in Docker 301
9.13 Regular Updates and Patch Management 304
9.14 Auditing and Compliance with Docker 306

10 Advanced Docker Concepts and Techniques 311

10.1 Introduction to Advanced Docker Concepts 311
10.2 Docker Daemon Configuration 313
10.3 Customizing Docker with Plugins 316
10.4 Multi-Stage Builds for Production 319
10.5 Docker Networking Internals 321
10.6 Advanced Volume Management 324
10.7 Docker API and Client Libraries 326
10.8 Automating Docker with Scripts 329
10.9 Integrating Docker with CI/CD Pipelines 332
10.10 Docker Swarm Advanced Features 336
10.11 Using Docker with Other Orchestration Tools 340
10.12 Container Orchestration Strategies 342
10.13 Performance Tuning for Docker 345
10.14 Monitoring and Logging Advanced Techniques 348

11 Troubleshooting Docker **353**
11.1 Introduction to Docker Troubleshooting 353
11.2 Common Docker Installation Issues 356
11.3 Diagnosing and Resolving Container Startup Problems 358
11.4 Managing Container Performance Issues 361
11.5 Analyzing Docker Logs for Troubleshooting 363
11.6 Networking Issues and Solutions 365
11.7 Storage and Volume Troubleshooting 368
11.8 Dealing with Docker Daemon Failures 370
11.9 Debugging Dockerfile Issues 373
11.10 Resolving Docker Build Failures 375
11.11 Troubleshooting Docker Compose Deployments . . . 378
11.12 Using Docker Inspect and Other Diagnostic Tools . . . 380
11.13 Reporting and Seeking Help for Docker Issues 383

12 Real-World Docker Use Cases **387**
12.1 Introduction to Real-World Docker Use Cases 387
12.2 Docker for Development Environments 393
12.3 Docker in Continuous Integration/Continuous Deployment (CI/CD) 396
12.4 Microservices Architecture with Docker 399
12.5 Docker for Database Management 403
12.6 Running Legacy Applications with Docker 406
12.7 Docker for Data Science and ML Workflows 409
12.8 Managing Big Data Applications with Docker 412
12.9 Hosting Web Applications with Docker 416
12.10 Docker for IoT Applications 419
12.11 Cloud Deployment with Docker 422
12.12 Docker in Multi-Cloud Environments 428
12.13 Case Studies: Successful Docker Implementations . . 432

Introduction

Docker has emerged as a leading platform for containerization, revolutionizing the way applications are developed, shipped, and deployed. This book, "Mastering Docker: From Basics to Expert Proficiency," aims to provide a comprehensive guide covering the core concepts, practical techniques, and advanced strategies needed to effectively utilize Docker in various environments.

Containerization is a method that allows developers to package applications and their dependencies into a standardized unit, known as a container. These containers are lightweight, standalone, and executable, ensuring that applications run consistently across different computing environments. Docker, an open-source platform, automates the deployment of these containers, significantly enhancing the efficiency and reliability of the software development and deployment lifecycle.

The rise of Docker is closely tied to the evolution of containerization. Traditional methods of running applications involved complex configurations and dependency management, often leading to compatibility issues when moving applications from development to production. Docker addresses these challenges by providing a unified framework that encapsulates the application along with its dependencies into isolated containers. This standardization simplifies both development and operations, reducing friction between teams and streamlining workflows.

This book is structured to guide readers from understanding the fundamental principles of Docker to mastering advanced concepts and best practices. The initial chapters introduce Docker, highlighting its benefits and distinguishing it from traditional virtual machines. Readers will learn about the key components of Docker's architecture, such as Docker Engine, Docker Images, and Docker Containers. The Docker Ecosystem, which includes tools like Docker Compose, Docker Swarm, and Kubernetes, will also be explored.

Setting up Docker is an essential first step. This book provides detailed instructions for installing Docker on various platforms, including Windows, macOS, and Linux. Readers will be walked through the post-installation steps, configuring the Docker Daemon, and managing Docker using the command-line interface and Docker Desktop.

Subsequent chapters delve into Docker images, a core component of the Docker platform. Readers will learn about Dockerfiles, the blueprint for Docker images, and how to create, build, and manage images effectively. Best practices for writing Dockerfiles, optimizing image size, and leveraging multi-stage builds are thoroughly covered.

The book then transitions to Docker containers, explaining their lifecycle, how to manage them, and how to run applications within them. Key concepts such as exposing and mapping ports, interactive containers, container logs, and persistent storage are discussed in detail. Advanced topics include container linking, networking, and scaling.

Networking is a crucial aspect of any containerized environment. This book provides an in-depth look at Docker's networking capabilities, covering different types of networks, creating and managing custom networks, and networking in Docker Compose. Security aspects and troubleshooting common networking issues are also addressed.

Storage and volumes are equally important in the container ecosystem. Chapters dedicated to Docker storage explain the use of volumes and bind mounts, volume drivers, and plugins. Techniques for backing up and restoring volumes, optimizing storage performance, and managing persistent storage in Docker Swarm are outlined.

Docker Compose is a powerful tool for defining and running multi-container Docker applications. This book guides readers through the composition of Docker Compose files, managing multi-container environments, and using Compose for development, testing, and scaling services.

One of Docker's significant strengths is its integration with Kubernetes, an orchestration system for automating application deployment, scaling, and management. Readers will learn about Kubernetes architecture, setting up and deploying Docker containers on Kubernetes, managing storage, and implementing configuration and security best practices.

Security is a paramount concern in any software environment. This book dedicates a chapter to Docker best practices and security, covering essential topics like image optimization, resource management, container isolation, network security, and using Docker Bench for Security.

Advanced Docker concepts and techniques are also explored, including daemon configuration, custom plugins, multi-stage builds, and integration with Continuous Integration/Continuous Deployment (CI/CD) pipelines. Performance tuning, monitoring, and orchestration strategies are covered to equip readers with the skills needed for complex, real-world scenarios.

Finally, troubleshooting Docker is an essential skill for maintaining a robust containerized environment. This book provides practical advice on diagnosing and resolving common issues related to installation, container performance, networking, storage, and Dockerfile errors.

The concluding chapters illustrate real-world Docker use cases across various domains, from development environments and microservices architectures to data science, big data applications, and cloud deployments. Case studies of successful Docker implementations provide insights into the practical applications of the concepts learned.

Through this structured approach, "Mastering Docker: From Basics to Expert Proficiency" aims to be an authoritative resource for both beginners and experienced practitioners, providing a pathway to mastering Docker and leveraging its full potential in modern software development and deployment practices.

Chapter 1

Introduction to Docker

This chapter provides a comprehensive overview of Docker, including its evolution, benefits, and key differences from virtual machines. It introduces essential Docker terminology, delves into Docker's architecture, and explains the fundamental concepts of Docker images and containers. The chapter also explores the broader Docker ecosystem and guides readers through the initial setup and installation of Docker on various platforms, culminating in running a first container.

1.1 What is Docker? An Overview

Docker is a platform that utilizes containerization technology to help developers and system administrators deploy applications efficiently within any environment. At its core, Docker offers an integrated set of tools and a standardized unit of software, namely containers, which package an application's code along with all its dependencies to run consistently across different computing environments. This package includes libraries, configuration files, and support binaries.

Docker adopts a client-server architecture with three key components: the Docker client, the Docker daemon, and the Docker registry. The Docker client is a command-line interface (CLI) that users can interact with. The Docker daemon listens for Docker API requests and manages Docker objects, such as images, containers, networks, and volumes. Docker registries are repositories where Docker images are stored.

A Docker image is a read-only template that contains the application code and all its dependencies. Each image is built from a series of layers, and each layer represents an instruction in Dockerfile, a script that contains a series of commands for assembling an image. These layers are stacked and represented by a union filesystem, making images lightweight, portable, and shareable.

A Docker container is a runtime instance of an image. It includes the necessary execution environment for applications: operating system binaries, libraries, and an application code image. Containers are isolated but can communicate with each other through well-defined channels. They bring an added advantage of consistency since an application running inside a container behaves the same irrespective of the development, staging, or production environment.

Additionally, Docker's ecosystem comprising Docker Compose, Docker Swarm, and Docker Engine enhances its capabilities. Docker Compose simplifies the definition and multi-container deployment of applications. Docker Swarm provides native clustering and orchestration for Docker containers, turning a pool of Docker hosts into a single, virtual Docker host. Docker Engine is the core containerization capability built into the infrastructure, enabling the management and configuration of Docker containers.

To illustrate how Docker operates, consider the following example of a Docker workflow that builds an image and runs a container.

We start with a Dockerfile which defines the environment in which our application will run:

```
# Use an official Python runtime as a parent image
FROM python:3.8-slim

# Set the working directory in the container
WORKDIR /app

# Copy the current directory contents into the container at /app
ADD . /app

# Install any needed packages specified in requirements.txt
RUN pip install --no-cache-dir -r requirements.txt

# Make port 80 available to the world outside this container
EXPOSE 80

# Define environment variable
ENV NAME World

# Run app.py when the container launches
CMD ["python", "app.py"]
```

The above Dockerfile performs several critical tasks:

- **FROM** – Specifies the base image to use; here, it is a lightweight Python runtime image.
- **WORKDIR** – Sets the working directory inside the container.
- **ADD** – Copies application code into the container.
- **RUN** – Executes a command to install dependencies.
- **EXPOSE** – Declares the port number on which the container's application will listen.
- **ENV** – Sets an environment variable inside the container.
- **CMD** – Defines the command to run within the container.

Next, we build the Docker image from this Dockerfile using the Docker CLI:

```
$ docker build -t my-python-app .
```

The build command constructs a Docker image from the Dockerfile in the current directory. The -t flag tags the image with a name for easier reference.

After building the image, we can instantiate a container using the run command:

```
$ docker run -p 4000:80 my-python-app
```

The run command starts a new container from the specified image. The -p flag maps the container's port 80 to port 4000 on the Docker host, making the application accessible via http://localhost:4000.

The execution and output of the running container can be observed as:

```
* Serving Flask app "app"
* Running on http://0.0.0.0:80/ (Press CTRL+C to quit)
```

The container runs the application server inside the isolated environment while providing access to the application via the host's network interfaces. This process exemplifies how Docker ensures that packaged applications can reliably execute across various host platforms.

By isolating applications from their underlying systems through containers, Docker significantly optimizes development workflows, reduces the chances of deployment failures due to environmental inconsistencies, and enhances scalability and resource efficiency.

1.2 The Evolution of Containerization

Containerization, which encapsulates software applications along with their dependencies into isolated user spaces called containers, has evolved tremendously over the past few decades. This section examines the historical milestones and technological advancements that have shaped the modern containerization landscape.

The concept of containerization traces its roots back to the late 1970s and early 1980s with the advent of the chroot system call introduced in Unix Version 7. The chroot system call remaps the root directory, effectively creating isolated file systems. The isolation provided by chroot jails was rudimentary, focusing primarily on file system isolation without advanced resource control or security mechanisms.

1990s: The early 1990s saw the development of more advanced forms of application isolation. In 1991, Bill Joy developed Solaris Containers (commonly referred to as Solaris Zones), which allowed running multiple secure and isolated applications on a single instance of the Solaris Operating System. These zones provided not just file system isolation but also process and network namespace isolation, which was a significant step forward.

2000s: The early 2000s witnessed significant contributions to container technology, particularly from the open-source community. In 2001, the FreeBSD Project introduced FreeBSD Jails, which extended the capabilities of chroot, adding security enhancements and resource controls. FreeBSD Jails could isolate filesystems, users, networks, and even partition kernel resources.

2005: The Linux-based containerization framework, OpenVZ, emerged. OpenVZ provided operating system-level virtualization and could run multiple isolated Linux containers (referred to as VEs or VPSs). Each container in OpenVZ had its own file system, network devices, process trees, and user IDs. OpenVZ was a prolific stepping stone towards the development of more feature-rich containerization solutions for Linux.

2008: Google launched the process container project, which later evolved into Control Groups (cgroups) in the Linux kernel. cgroups provided fine-grained resource control and accounting, enabling limits and prioritization for CPU, memory, disk I/O, and network bandwidth. This integration into the Linux kernel laid the groundwork for modern container solutions, allowing multiple processes to be isolated and limited individually or in groups, effectively managing their resource usage.

2011: The advent of LXC (Linux Containers) furthered the capability of the Linux kernel in terms of application containerization. LXC utilized cgroups and Linux namespaces to offer a user space interface for running applications within isolated containers. It was the first widely adopted, full-featured container manager for Linux, representing a comprehensive platform bridging multiple preceding advancements.

2013: Docker was released by Solomon Hykes as an open-source project, revolutionizing container technology with several key innovations. Docker introduced an easy-to-use CLI and API, making it accessible to developers and system administrators alike. Some of its most significant contributions included the Dockerfile, which allowed the creation of portable and reproducible images, and the concept of image layering, which optimized storage and bandwidth usage through reusable layers.

2015-2017: The widespread adoption of Docker drove the emergence of orchestration tools such as Kubernetes, developed by Google. Kubernetes automated the deployment, scaling, and operation of containerized applications, addressing the complexity of managing containerized workloads in production. Both Docker Swarm and Kubernetes became integral parts of the Docker ecosystem, enabling scalable and resilient container orchestration.

Present Day: Modern containerization extends far beyond Docker and Kubernetes, with a vibrant ecosystem of tools and platforms, including CRI-O, containerd, and Podman. The Open Container Initiative (OCI), established in 2015, has driven standardization in the container space, ensuring interoperability and fostering innovation across the industry. The standardization of container image formats and runtime specifications has facilitated an ecosystem where various tools and platforms can interoperate seamlessly.

```
docker run -it ubuntu:latest /bin/bash
```

Output:
root@<container_id>:/#This command executes an Ubuntu container interactively, launching the bash shell inside it.

Containerization has matured into a cornerstone of modern software deployment strategies, offering unparalleled efficiencies, scalability, and consistency. Its evolution represents a journey from simple file system isolation towards comprehensive orchestration frameworks like Kubernetes, reshaping the way applications are developed, shipped, and maintained.

1.3 Benefits of Using Docker

Docker stands as a transformative tool in modern software development and deployment practices, delivering various benefits that considerably improve the efficiency, scalability, and reliability of applications. An understanding of these benefits cultivates an appreciation for Docker's extensive adoption in the industry.

One of the most significant advantages of Docker is **environment consistency**. Docker containers encapsulate an application and its dependencies, ensuring that the software runs identically across different environments. This uniformity eliminates the common "works on my machine" problem, where discrepancies between development, testing, and production environments lead to deployment issues. Docker achieves this by packaging the application code, runtime, libraries, and configuration files together into a single container image, providing a standardized environment for application execution.

Resource efficiency is another prominent benefit offered by Docker. Containers share the host system's kernel and resources, enabling multiple containers to run on a single operating system instance. This sharing mechanism results in significantly lower overhead compared to traditional virtual machines, which require separate OS installations for each VM. Consequently, Docker containers start up faster and consume less memory and CPU, facilitating higher application density and better utilization of hardware resources.

Efficiency also extends to **development and deployment workflows**. Docker streamlines continuous integration/continuous deployment (CI/CD) pipelines by allowing seamless building, testing, and deploying of applications. Developers can write Dockerfiles to automate the creation of container images, ensuring reproducibility and version control. These container images can then be stored in registries and easily pulled by downstream processes. The standardized environment provided by Docker enhances the reliability of tests and ensures that deployed applications behave as expected, minimizing the chances of deployment failures.

Scalability is inherently improved with Docker. Containers can be easily scaled up or down according to the demand, without the need for complex reconfigurations. This capability is essential for modern cloud-native applications, which need to handle variable loads dynamically. Tools like Docker Swarm, Kubernetes, and other container orchestration platforms enable automated scaling, load balancing, and failover management, making Docker an integral part of DevOps practices and microservices architectures.

Isolation is a critical feature provided by Docker, enhancing security and stability. Each Docker container operates in an isolated environment, meaning that processes running inside a container do not interfere with other containers or the host system. This isolation limits the impact of potential security vulnerabilities and bugs, as they are confined within the container. It also facilitates running multiple instances of the same service or different versions of software on the same host, without conflicts.

Another key benefit is **portability**. Docker containers are designed to run consistently across various environments, from a developer's local machine to on-premises data centers to cloud platforms like AWS, Google Cloud, and Azure. This portability ensures that applications can be deployed and moved across different environments with minimal changes, fostering a true "build once, run anywhere" paradigm. The widespread support for Docker in various PaaS (Platform-as-a-Service) and cloud environments further underscores its portability advantage.

Docker also enhances **collaboration** among development teams. By encapsulating the entire runtime environment inside a container, team members can share and use the same environment, ensuring consistency. This fosters a more collaborative and integrated development process, where developers, testers, and operations can work more closely and effectively.

The **rapid prototyping** capability of Docker allows developers to quickly spin up containers for new features, experiments, or bug fixes. This accelerates the development lifecycle by enabling fast feedback and iteration, ultimately leading to more robust and feature-rich applications.

Lastly, Docker promotes the principle of **infrastructure as code** (IaC). Dockerfiles, along with other IaC tools, allow infrastructure configurations to be versioned, reviewed, and managed similarly to application code. This practice enhances infrastructure management and operational efficiency, contributing to a more streamlined and automated deployment pipeline.

Overall, Docker's benefits—environment consistency, resource efficiency, improved development workflows, scalability, isolation, portability, enhanced collaboration, rapid prototyping, and support for infrastructure as code—collectively make it a powerful tool for modern software development and operations.

1.4 Docker vs Virtual Machines

Docker and virtual machines (VMs) offer solutions for isolating and managing applications in a portable and efficient manner, but they differ significantly in terms of architecture, resource usage, and performance.

Firstly, let's examine the architectural differences. Virtual machines utilize a hypervisor, which is a software layer that allows multiple operating systems to run concurrently on a single physical machine. Each VM includes a full operating system, the application, and its dependencies. The hypervisor can be of two types: Type 1 (bare-metal) hypervisors such as VMware ESXi and Microsoft Hyper-V, which run directly on the host's hardware, and Type 2 (hosted) hypervisors such as VMware Workstation and Oracle VirtualBox, which run on top of a conventional operating system.

In contrast, Docker employs a containerization approach where containers run on a single shared operating system but provide an isolated user space. This is achieved by leveraging kernel features such as control groups (cgroups) and namespaces. Unlike VMs, Docker does not require a full-fledged operating system for each container; instead, containers share the host system's kernel.

The following diagram illustrates these differences graphically:

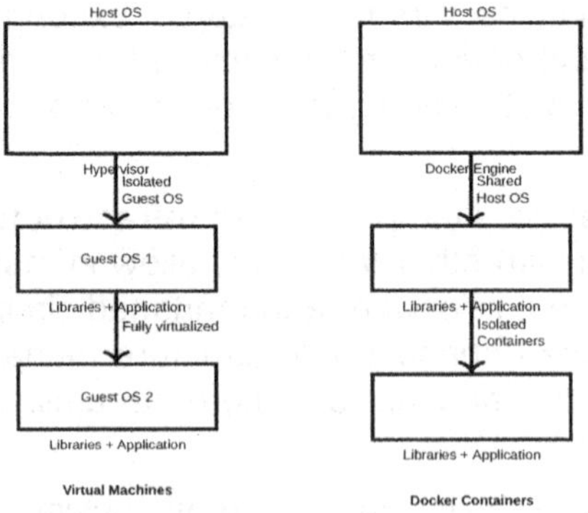

The resource overhead incurred by VMs is significantly higher than that of Docker containers. Each VM needs to allocate a portion of the system's CPU, memory, and storage resources to run the guest OS, thus leading to additional overhead. In contrast, Docker containers share the host OS kernel and therefore require considerably fewer resources, allowing for higher density and efficiency.

Moreover, the boot-up time of VMs is inherently longer than that of Docker containers. This is because VMs must start an entire operating system, whereas Docker containers can start almost instantaneously by creating an isolated process within the existing OS.

Consider the following example where a simple web server is configured and run using both a virtual machine and a Docker container.

Example: Running a web server using VMs and Docker

Virtual Machine setup:

```
# On the host machine
$ vagrant init hashicorp/bionic64
$ vagrant up
$ vagrant ssh

# Inside the VM
$ sudo apt-get update
$ sudo apt-get install -y nginx
$ sudo systemctl start nginx
```

Docker setup:

```
# On the host machine
$ docker run -d -p 80:80 nginx
```

The execution time and resource usage can be compared by inspecting the resource allocation and system logs.

Virtual Machine resource usage:

```
$ top
%CPU  %MEM  TIME+  COMMAND
12.5  2.1   0:00.44  nginx
```

Docker container resource usage:

```
$ docker stats
CONTAINER ID  NAME  CPU %  MEM USAGE / LIMIT  MEM %  NET I/O
cf6e78d7efcd  loving_hypatia  0.25%  1.25MiB / 1.94GiB  0.06%  648B / 0B
```

From the outputs, it is evident that the Docker container consumes less memory and CPU resources compared to a virtual machine running a similar service.

Both VMs and Docker have their respective use cases. VMs are well-suited for running software that requires a complete OS environment or different OS versions. They also offer strong isolation, which is crucial for certain security-sensitive applications. Docker containers, on the other hand, excel in environments where lightweight, fast, and scalable application deployment is required, making them ideal for microservices architecture, CI/CD pipelines, and horizontal scaling scenarios.

Understanding these differences and knowing when to use Docker or VMs allows developers and IT professionals to architect efficient, scalable, and resource-optimized solutions.

1.5 Key Docker Terminology

Understanding the terminology associated with Docker is crucial for comprehending the technology and its application effectively. This section delineates key Docker terms, establishing a foundation for more advanced topics.

Docker Engine: The Docker Engine is the core component of Docker, enabling users to develop, ship, and run applications. It consists of three main parts:

- **Server**: A continuously running daemon (dockerd) that handles all Docker objects.
- **REST API**: Used by applications to interact with the daemon and communicate with the Docker Engine.
- **Client**: A command-line interface (docker) that allows users to interact with Docker and issue commands to the Docker daemon via the REST API.

Docker Daemon: The Docker daemon (dockerd) is a background service responsible for managing Docker containers on the host system. It listens for Docker API requests and acts upon them, such as the creation, execution, and monitoring of containers.

Docker Client: The Docker client (docker) is a command-line tool that communicates with the Docker daemon using REST API commands. It allows users to perform tasks such as building, running, and managing Docker containers.

Docker Image: A Docker image is a lightweight, standalone, executable software package that includes everything needed to run a piece of software: code, runtime, libraries, environment variables, and configuration files. Images are built from instructions contained within a Dockerfile and serve as a blueprint for creating Docker containers.

Docker Container: A Docker container is a runnable instance of a Docker image. Containers are isolated environments that run applications, ensuring compatibility across various computing environments. They are responsible for packaging the application code and dependencies together, offering scalability and easy management.

Dockerfile: A Dockerfile is a text document that contains a series of instructions for building a Docker image. Each instruction in the Dockerfile corresponds to a command that is executed in the terminal to create an image layer.

Docker Hub: Docker Hub is a cloud-based registry service where Docker users can create, test, store, and distribute Docker images. It serves as a central repository for finding and sharing container images.

Docker Compose: Docker Compose is a tool used for defining and running multi-container Docker applications. Using a YAML file, users can configure their application's services, define networks, and specify volumes. Commands such as docker-compose up will start the entire application configuration.

Docker Swarm: Docker Swarm is a native clustering and orchestration tool for Docker. It allows for the grouping of multiple Docker hosts into a single, managed cluster. Docker Swarm enables scaling to multiple nodes and automates the deployment, scaling, and management of containerized applications.

Volume: A Docker volume is a mechanism for persisting data generated by and used by Docker containers. Volumes provide a way to store and share data between containers securely and reliably, and they can be managed independently of the container lifecycle.

Network: Docker networks provide a means for containers to communicate with each other and with external systems. Networks can be configured to ensure secure and efficient communication in a containerized application.

Registry: A Docker registry is a storage and content delivery system that holds named Docker images, available in different tagged versions. Docker Hub is the default registry, but private registries can also be set up for more stringent access control.

Repository: A repository is a collection of related Docker images, typically with multiple versions distinguished by tags. For example, a repository named nginx might have versions tagged 1.19, 1.20, and latest.

Tag: Tags are used to differentiate versions of Docker images within a repository. By default, the `latest` tag is applied when no tag is specified. Tags facilitate version control and easy image management.

Service: In the context of Docker Swarm, a service defines how a Docker container runs in a cluster. It specifies the image, the number of replicas, and the required configuration for the container.

The understanding and utilization of these terms will enable users to navigate and employ Docker technology effectively. Implementing these concepts in Docker operations assures a structured and proficient approach to container management. The previous knowledge will be instrumental in practical applications and further exploration into Docker's capabilities.

```
docker pull ubuntu:latest
```

Corresponding output:

```
latest: Pulling from library/ubuntu
5bed26d33875: Pull complete
3cda6acd42e5: Pull complete
6c40cc604d8e: Pull complete
Digest: sha256:719d4fe818999b348f0bbdcb4cabc23433d9ef686f8f4fdf123e72bc8a75cb94
Status: Downloaded newer image for ubuntu:latest
docker.io/library/ubuntu:latest
```

1.6 Docker Architecture

Docker's architecture is composed of several interrelated components that work together to provide a robust and efficient containerization platform. Understanding these components and their interactions is crucial for leveraging the full potential of Docker.

At a high level, Docker architecture consists of the following key components:

- Docker Client
- Docker Daemon (dockerd)
- Docker Images
- Docker Containers
- Docker Registries

The interaction between these components ensures that Containerization processes are seamless.

Docker Client

The Docker Client is the primary interface through which users interact with Docker. It accepts commands from the user, such as docker run, docker build, and docker pull, and communicates these commands to the Docker Daemon. Typically, the Docker Client is a simple command-line tool that uses REST APIs to communicate with the Daemon. This client can run on the same host as the daemon or connect to a daemon on a remote host.

```
$ docker --version
Docker version 20.10.8, build 3967b7d
```

Docker Daemon (dockerd)

The Docker Daemon (dockerd) is the core component of Docker architecture. It runs on the host machine and listens for Docker API requests from the Docker Client. Upon receiving these requests, the Daemon manages docker objects, including images, containers, networks, and volumes. It also handles the heavy lifting of building, running, and distributing Docker containers.

dockerd manages the creation, running, and monitoring of containers, ensuring resource isolation and efficient resource utilization. For example, when the user executes a command to create a new container, the Docker Daemon creates a container as per the specified image and configurations.

```
$ sudo service docker start
```

Docker Images

Docker Images are immutable templates used to create containers. They represent a snapshot of the application and its dependencies, providing a portable and consistent environment. Images are created using a Dockerfile, which is a plain text file containing instructions for building the image.

A typical Dockerfile consists of a series of commands (keywords), such as FROM, RUN, ADD, COPY, and CMD, that the Docker Daemon executes to assemble the image. Each instruction in a Dockerfile creates a new layer in the image, promoting reuse and efficient storage.

```
# A simple Dockerfile example
```

```
# Use an official Ubuntu base image
FROM ubuntu:20.04

# Set environment variables
ENV DEBIAN_FRONTEND=noninteractive

# Install dependencies
RUN apt-get update && apt-get install -y \
    python3 \
    python3-pip

# Set the working directory
WORKDIR /app

# Copy the application files
COPY . /app

# Run the application
CMD ["python3", "app.py"]
```

Docker Containers

Containers are the runnable instances of Docker images. They provide isolated environments for running applications, ensuring consistency across different deployment stages. While each container runs a single process (or a group of processes) within its isolated environment, it shares the host system's kernel, making it lightweight and fast compared to traditional virtual machines.

When a container is started, it uses the image layers as its file system, and the data created during its runtime is stored in a writable layer above the image layers. Containers can be stopped, restarted, and removed without affecting the underlying image or other containers.

```
$ docker run -d -p 80:80 --name myapp myapp-image
```

ea09b6c9b1b2b3f0828fca821ed86c3a3f97a6e2a9e357dae09c92b4d8b1e9d

Docker Registries

Docker Registries are repositories for Docker images. The most common registry is Docker Hub, a public registry where users can pull and push images. Registries can also be private, allowing organizations to securely store and manage their own images. Docker clients interact with registries to download images or upload their own.

Registries can be configured to run on local servers or cloud services, providing flexible options for image distribution. The use of registries simplifies the deployment process by offering a centralized place to store and retrieve Docker images.

```
$ docker pull ubuntu:20.04
```

```
20.04: Pulling from library/ubuntu
e6ca3592b144: Pull complete
534514c73ba9: Pull complete
c4ff7513909f: Pull complete
Digest: sha256:c95a8e8be6a209ceff38f4fe9c430b11b1d97cfb99d8ace6ad429391cd268cf7
Status: Downloaded newer image for ubuntu:20.04
docker.io/library/ubuntu:20.04
```

The combination of these components creates a powerful and flexible platform for containerized applications. Understanding the architecture and interactions of these elements enables users to design and manage efficient containerized environments with Docker.

1.7 Understanding Docker Images and Containers

Docker images and containers are fundamental elements in the Docker ecosystem. Understanding their distinct roles is crucial for efficient utilization of Docker in diverse scenarios.

A **Docker image** is a read-only template that contains a set of instructions for creating a container that can run on the Docker platform. It provides the skeleton, defining what should be in the container, the configuration settings, and the dependencies needed for execution. Images are built in layers, each representing a set of file changes or additions. This layered approach enables image reusability, efficient storage, and simplified updates:

```
# Example Dockerfile for building an image
FROM ubuntu:20.04
LABEL maintainer="yourname@example.com"
RUN apt-get update && apt-get install -y \
    python3 \
    python3-pip
COPY . /app
WORKDIR /app
RUN pip3 install -r requirements.txt
CMD ["python3", "app.py"]
```

In the above example, the base image is ubuntu:20.04. Subsequent instructions such as RUN, COPY, and CMD build layers on top of the base, each adding specific functionalities or resources to the image.

A **Docker container**, on the other hand, is an executable instance of a Docker image. It comprises all components (code, runtime, system libraries, settings) necessary to run the application. While an image is static, a container is dynamic and provides the runtime environment. Containers utilize the host operating system's kernel, isolated in their own file system, networking, and process space.

To illustrate the relationship, consider the following sequence of commands:

```
# Build the Docker image
docker build -t myapp:latest .

# Run a container using the built image
docker run -d -p 5000:5000 --name myapp-container myapp:latest
```

Output:

```
Successfully built [image-id]
Successfully tagged myapp:latest
[container-id]
```

Here, docker build converts the content defined in a Dockerfile into an image named myapp:latest. The docker run command then instantiates a container from this image, linking the container port 5000 to the host port 5000 in a detached mode.

Each image is identified by a unique hash, serving as an immutable identifier. An image can be stored in repositories and managed via Docker Hub or other container registries, facilitating easy sharing and deployment across different environments.

Repositories on platforms like Docker Hub often employ multiple tags to version a single image. For example, tagging a production-ready image as v1.0 allows precise version control:

```
# Tagging an existing image
docker tag myapp:latest myapp:v1.0

# Pushing the tagged image to Docker Hub
docker push yourusername/myapp:v1.0
```

Containers inherit certain attributes from images but offer a more granular level of customization and ephemeral runtime services. For instance, you can override the default command by using the –entrypoint flag and bind host directories to a container's file system:

```
# Running a container with a different entrypoint and mounted volume
docker run -it --entrypoint /bin/bash -v $(pwd)/data:/app/data myapp:latest
```

Output:

```
root@[container-id]:/app#
```

This flexibility allows developers to tailor containers to specific needs while maintaining consistency in development, testing, and production environments.

Managing containers includes starting, stopping, restarting, and removing them as needed, using explicit commands:

```
# List running containers
docker ps

# Stop a container
docker stop myapp-container

# Remove a stopped container
docker rm myapp-container
```

Output:

```
CONTAINER ID  IMAGE          STATUS      PORTS
[container-id] myapp:latest  Up X mins   0.0.0.0:5000->5000/tcp

myapp-container
myapp-container
```

By emphasizing the separation between images (static) and containers (dynamic), Docker optimizes resource management, ensures consistency across various stages of application development, and facilitates scalability.

1.8 The Docker Ecosystem

The Docker ecosystem comprises a suite of interrelated tools and services that collectively simplify the creation, deployment, and management of containerized applications. This section delves into the key components of the Docker ecosystem, elucidating their purposes and functionalities to provide a comprehensive understanding.

At its core, Docker relies on several foundational elements, such as Docker Engine, Docker Hub, Docker Compose, Docker Swarm, and Docker Desktop. Each tool plays a critical role in the lifecycle of containerized applications.

Docker Engine serves as the underlying client-server application for creating and managing containers. It comprises three main components: a server (dockerd), a REST API interface, and a command-line interface (CLI) client (docker). The server is responsible for managing Docker objects, such as images, containers, networks, and volumes.

The REST API provides programmatic access to communicate with the server, while the CLI enables interaction with the Docker server using commands.

```
# Sample Docker command using CLI to run a container
docker run -it --name myContainer ubuntu /bin/bash
```

In this example, the docker run command is used to start a new container from the Ubuntu image, naming it myContainer and using the /bin/bash shell.

Docker Hub is a public registry where users can publish and share container images. It facilitates Docker's distribution channel, hosting a vast repository of both official and user-contributed images. Using Docker Hub, one can easily find predefined images to reduce the time spent on building from scratch.

```
# Command to pull the latest Ubuntu image from Docker Hub
docker pull ubuntu:latest
```

The command above fetches the latest Ubuntu image from Docker Hub, making it available for local use.

Docker Compose is a tool designed for defining and running multi-container Docker applications. With Docker Compose, users can configure application services in a docker-compose.yml file and manage them with simple commands, ensuring consistent environments in development, testing, and production stages.

```
# Example of a docker-compose.yml file
version: '3'
services:
  web:
    image: nginx:alpine
    ports:
      - "80:80"
  db:
    image: mysql:5.7
    environment:
      MYSQL_ROOT_PASSWORD: example
```

By using the above configuration, deploying a web service using the Nginx server and a MySQL database can be executed with a single command.

```
# Command to start services defined in docker-compose.yml
docker-compose up
```

Docker Swarm provides native clustering functionality for Docker, allowing the management of a group of Docker engines as a single swarm cluster. This tool simplifies workload orchestration and aids in scaling applications efficiently.

```
# Command to initialize a Docker Swarm mode
docker swarm init
```

The initialization command allows the Docker Engine to be transformed into a swarm mode, ready for deploying services across multiple nodes.

Docker Desktop is an application for Mac and Windows users, providing a simple yet powerful interface for managing Docker containers. It includes Docker Engine, Docker CLI client, Docker Compose, Kubernetes, and other essential components. Docker Desktop streamlines the development process for users on local workstations.

These tools and services integrate seamlessly, fostering a robust Docker ecosystem that accelerates containerized application development, deployment, and management. The next critical component in the Docker ecosystem is Kubernetes, which, although not an inherent Docker tool, complements Docker by providing advanced orchestration functionalities.

To illustrate, consider the deployment of a multi-service application utilizing Docker Compose for local development and Docker Swarm for production. Docker Compose helps define and deploy services consistently on a developer's machine, while Docker Swarm ensures scalable deployment across a cluster of nodes. Additionally, Docker Hub serves as the intermediary platform for storing and distributing application images, streamlining the CI/CD pipeline.

```
# Sample workflow using Docker ecosystem tools
# Step 1: Build Docker image locally
docker build -t myapp:latest .

# Step 2: Push image to Docker Hub
docker tag myapp:latest username/myapp:latest
docker push username/myapp:latest

# Step 3: Pull image from Docker Hub on the production server
docker pull username/myapp:latest

# Step 4: Deploy application using Docker Swarm
docker service create --name myservice -p 80:80 username/myapp:latest
```

This example showcases a practical workflow from development to deployment, leveraging various tools within the Docker ecosystem to achieve efficiency and consistency.

Understanding these components and effectively integrating them within your workflow can significantly enhance productivity and agility in managing containerized applications.

Chapter 2

Setting Up Docker

This chapter details the system requirements for Docker and provides step-by-step instructions for installing Docker on Windows, macOS, and Linux. It includes post-installation steps, verification methods, and guidance on configuring the Docker Daemon and Command-Line Interface (CLI). The chapter also covers managing Docker through Docker Desktop, as well as upgrading and uninstalling Docker.

2.1 System Requirements for Docker

Understanding the system requirements is crucial for the successful installation and operation of Docker. System requirements ensure that Docker runs efficiently and without errors. The requirements specify the supported operating systems, hardware specifications, and necessary software dependencies.

Supported Operating Systems

Docker is supported on the following operating systems:

- **Windows:** Docker for Windows runs on Windows 10 64-bit: Pro, Enterprise, or Education (1607 Anniversary Update, Build 14393 or later). Additionally, Windows Server 2016 and Windows Server 2019 are supported.
- **macOS:** Docker for Mac is compatible with macOS versions op-

erating from macOS Catalina 10.15 and newer.

- **Linux:** Docker supports various Linux distributions, including Ubuntu, Debian, Fedora, and CentOS. Specific versions supported include:
  - **Ubuntu:** 20.04 LTS, 18.04 LTS
  - **Debian:** 10 (Buster), 9 (Stretch)
  - **Fedora:** 32, 31
  - **CentOS:** 8, 7

Hardware Requirements

Hardware requirements ensure optimal performance of Docker and include specifications such as CPU, RAM, and disk space. The minimal requirements are:

- **CPU:** A modern processor with virtualization support (Intel or AMD).
- **RAM:** At least 4 GB of RAM is recommended. Systems with 8 GB of RAM or higher will provide a more efficient and responsive Docker engine.
- **Disk Space:** A minimum of 4 GB disk space is required for Docker installation. However, additional disk space is recommended for container storage and Docker operations, especially when dealing with large images and volumes.

Software Requirements

Certain software prerequisites must be met for Docker to function properly. These prerequisites vary depending on the operating system.

For **Windows:**

- **Virtualization Support:** Ensure that Hyper-V and Containers Windows features are enabled. This can be verified and enabled in the Windows Features settings.
- **Windows Subsystem for Linux (WSL 2):** Docker Desktop requires WSL 2 for Windows Home and alternative methods for other editions. Ensure WSL 2 is installed and configured properly.

- **Windows Update:** Ensure the system is up-to-date with the latest Windows updates and patches installed.

For **macOS:**

- **Virtualization Support:** Docker Desktop for Mac uses Apple's built-in Hypervisor framework. Ensure the system supports virtualization.

- **brew (optional):** Homebrew can simplify the installation process of dependencies.

For **Linux:**

- **Kernel Version:** Docker requires a 64-bit version of the OS with a kernel version of 3.10 or higher. Verify the kernel version using the command:

```
uname -r
```

- **Storage Driver:** Docker relies on storage drivers like overlay2, aufs, and devicemapper. Ensure the storage driver is properly configured.

- **Dependencies:** Common dependencies include apt-transport-https, ca-certificates, curl, gnupg-agent, and software-properties-common. These can be installed using:

```
sudo apt-get install apt-transport-https ca-certificates curl gnupg-agent software-
    properties-common
```

Network Configuration

Proper network configuration is essential for Docker to communicate with external networks and manage containers' communication:

- **Firewall Rules:** Configure firewall rules to allow Docker container traffic. Essential ports include:
  - 2375 and 2376 for Docker daemon (unencrypted and encrypted, respectively),
  - 80, 443 for HTTP and HTTPS,
  - 8080 for web applications (varies based on application).

- **DNS Configuration:** Proper DNS settings are required for containers to resolve domain names. This is critical when pulling images from remote registries.

Ensuring your system meets these requirements is fundamental to the seamless operation of Docker. Adequate preparation will streamline installation and usage, preventing potential issues related to system incompatibility or resource constraints.

2.2 Installing Docker on Windows

Docker's functionality on Windows necessitates the installation of Docker Desktop, which provides a seamless and integrated development environment. The following steps are comprehensive and intended to ensure a successful installation on Windows operating systems.

Docker Desktop is available for download on the official Docker website. Before beginning the installation process, ensure that your system meets the necessary requirements, notably:

- Windows 10 64-bit: Pro, Enterprise, or Education (Build 16299 or later).
- Enable the Hyper-V and Containers Windows features.
- The Windows Subsystem for Linux 2 (WSL 2) must be installed and enabled for enhanced performance.
- BIOS-level hardware virtualization support must be enabled in the BIOS settings.
- At least 4 GB of RAM.

First, download Docker Desktop from https://www.docker.com/products/docker-desktop. The downloaded file will be a Docker Desktop Installer.exe executable.

1. **Run the Installer**: Locate the downloaded executable, right-click on the file and select Run as administrator. The installation wizard should start.

2. **Configuration Settings**: During the installation, you will be prompted with configuration settings. Ensure that the boxes for Install

required Windows components for WSL 2 and Use WSL 2 instead of Hyper-V are checked for optimal performance. Click Ok to proceed.

The installer will download required packages, and this might take a few minutes depending on your internet speed and system performance.

3. **Complete Installation**: Follow the on-screen instructions to complete the installation. Once the installation is complete, you will need to log out and log back into Windows to finalize the configuration.

Once the system restarts, you should see the Docker Desktop icon on your desktop or application menu.

4. **First Run and Configuration**: Double-click the Docker Desktop icon to start Docker. A dialog may appear asking if you want to use WSL 2. Confirm this setting to benefit from performance improvements. After a few moments, Docker Desktop should indicate that it is running.

5. **Docker Command-Line Interface (CLI)**: Open a Command Prompt or PowerShell window. You can verify that Docker is correctly installed by executing the following command:

```
docker --version
```

The output should be similar to:

```
Docker version 20.10.7, build f0df350
```

6. **Setting up WSL 2 Backend (Optional but Recommended)**: To use the WSL 2 backend, follow these steps:

1. Open PowerShell as Administrator and set WSL 2 as the default version by running:

   ```
   wsl --set-default-version 2
   ```

2. Install a Linux distribution from the Microsoft Store (e.g., Ubuntu). Once installed, open the distribution from the Start menu. Complete the initial setup.

3. Ensure that Docker Desktop is configured to use WSL 2. Navigate to Docker Desktop settings, select General, and ensure that Use the WSL 2 based engine is checked.

Reload Docker Desktop if necessary to apply changes.

7. **Testing the Installation**: To validate that Docker is up and running correctly, execute the following command to run a test container:

```
docker run hello-world
```

The expected output should resemble:

```
Hello from Docker!
This message shows that your installation appears to be working correctly.
```

These steps ensure a successful setup of Docker on Windows. Subsequent sections will expand on advanced configurations, such as setting up the Docker Daemon and managing Docker via the CLI, thus building a cohesive and integrated Docker environment.

2.3 Installing Docker on macOS

Installing Docker on macOS involves several steps to ensure a smooth setup and optimal performance. This section will guide you through the process, including downloading Docker Desktop, installing it, and configuring the necessary system preferences.

Firstly, verify that your macOS version is compatible with Docker. Docker Desktop for macOS requires macOS 10.14 or newer. To check your macOS version, click on the Apple icon in the upper-left corner of the desktop, and select *About This Mac*.

Downloading Docker Desktop

Docker Desktop is the official Docker application for macOS. It includes Docker Engine, Docker CLI client, Docker Compose, Docker Content Trust, Kubernetes, and Credential Helper. To download Docker Desktop:

1. Open a web browser and go to the Docker Hub website: https://hub.docker.com/editions/community/docker-ce-desktop-mac 2. Click on the *Download from Docker Hub* button. 3. Sign in to Docker Hub. If you don't have an account, you will need to create one.

This will download a .dmg file containing Docker Desktop.

Installing Docker Desktop

Once the download is complete, follow these steps to install Docker Desktop on your macOS system:

1. Open the .dmg file by double-clicking it. This will mount the disk image and open a new Finder window showing the Docker Desktop icon. 2. Drag the Docker icon to the Applications folder. This will copy

Docker Desktop to your Applications directory.

Next, you need to open Docker Desktop and complete the initial setup.

Running Docker Desktop

1. Open the Applications folder and double-click on the Docker icon. This will launch Docker Desktop. 2. Upon first launch, Docker will ask for your system password to proceed with the installation of networking components and privileged access. 3. Enter your password and click OK.

Docker Desktop will then complete the installation of necessary components and start the Docker engine.

Configuring System Preferences

Docker Desktop requires certain system preferences to be configured to function correctly:

1. If you see a request for access to your folders, you must grant it. Docker Desktop needs access to your files to share volumes and install updates correctly. 2. Navigate to System Preferences and select Security & Privacy. Under the General tab, ensure that any permissions relating to Docker are approved. Often, you may see an *Allow* button next to Docker, which you should click to grant necessary permissions.

Verifying Installation

To verify that Docker has been installed successfully, open the Terminal application and execute the following command:

```
docker --version
```

If Docker is installed correctly, you should see an output similar to:

```
Docker version 20.10.7, build f0df350
```

You can also check the status of Docker Desktop by looking at the Docker icon in the status bar at the top of your screen. A successful installation will show a Docker whale icon indicating that the Docker daemon is running.

Another method of verification is to run a simple Docker container. Execute the following command in the Terminal:

```
docker run hello-world
```

This command downloads a test image and runs it in a container. The expected output should be:

```
Hello from Docker!
This message shows that your installation appears to be working correctly.
```

Once these steps are complete, Docker Desktop is fully installed and ready for use on macOS. You can now configure additional preferences or start using Docker to manage containers and images.

2.4 Installing Docker on Linux

Before beginning the installation of Docker on a Linux system, it is imperative to ensure that the system meets the necessary prerequisites. The official Docker documentation recommends using a 64-bit operating system with kernel version 3.10 or higher. Most modern Linux distributions such as Ubuntu, Debian, CentOS, and Fedora conform to these requirements. This section will elucidate the installation steps for various distributions, focusing on Ubuntu/Debian and CentOS/Fedora.

Installation Steps for Ubuntu and Debian

First, Docker requires that some prerequisite packages be installed. Update the package index and install the necessary packages by executing the following commands:

```
sudo apt-get update
sudo apt-get install apt-transport-https ca-certificates curl software-properties-common
```

Next, add Docker's official GPG key to verify the authenticity of the software source:

```
curl -fsSL https://download.docker.com/linux/ubuntu/gpg | sudo apt-key add -
```

You need to set up the stable repository for Docker. Ensure the command corresponds to the correct distribution (Ubuntu or Debian), substituting <distribution> with bionic for Ubuntu 18.04, focal for Ubuntu 20.04, or the corresponding codename for Debian.

```
sudo add-apt-repository "deb [arch=amd64] https://download.docker.com/linux/
    ubuntu <distribution> stable"
```

After adding the repository, update the package index again:

```
sudo apt-get update
```

Now, install Docker CE (Community Edition):

```
sudo apt-get install docker-ce
```

To verify that Docker is installed correctly, run the following command which should return the Docker version:

```
docker --version
```

Installation Steps for CentOS and Fedora

For CentOS and Fedora, the installation steps are different. Start by removing any older versions of Docker that might exist:

```
sudo yum remove docker docker-client docker-client-latest docker-common docker-latest
    docker-latest-logrotate docker-logrotate docker-selinux docker-engine-selinux
    docker-engine
```

Next, install the package that allows your package manager to use repositories over HTTPS:

```
sudo yum install -y yum-utils
```

Add the Docker repository:

```
sudo yum-config-manager --add-repo https://download.docker.com/linux/centos/docker-
    ce.repo
```

Update the package index:

```
sudo yum makecache fast
```

Now, install Docker CE:

```
sudo yum install docker-ce docker-ce-cli containerd.io
```

Start Docker with the following command:

```
sudo systemctl start docker
```

Ensure Docker starts at boot:

```
sudo systemctl enable docker
```

Verify that Docker CE is installed correctly by running:

```
docker --version
```

Running Docker as a Non-root User

By default, Docker commands can only be executed by the root user or by a user in the docker group, which needs to be created. To avoid using sudo with Docker commands, add your user to the docker group.

Create the docker group:

```
sudo groupadd docker
```

Add your user to the docker group:

```
sudo usermod -aG docker $USER
```

Log out and back in so that your group membership is re-evaluated. You can verify that the user has been added properly by executing:

```
groups $USER
```

To confirm that the user can run Docker commands without root privileges, execute a simple Docker command:

```
docker run hello-world
```

```
Output:
Hello from Docker!
This message shows that your installation appears to be working correctly.
```

These steps ensure that Docker is installed on the Linux system and configured to be run by a non-root user. Throughout, the commands and configurations are intended to maintain system security and integrity.

2.5 Post-Installation Steps

Once Docker has been installed on your system, several post-installation steps are crucial to ensure that Docker is functioning as expected and to customize your Docker environment according to your needs. These steps also involve configuring user permissions, setting up Docker to start on boot, and optimizing performance settings to suit your development or production environment.

1. Starting the Docker Service

Depending on your operating system, the Docker service may need to be started manually following installation.

For Unix-based systems (e.g., Linux), you can manage Docker as a systemd service:

```
sudo systemctl start docker
```

To ensure Docker starts automatically on boot:

```
sudo systemctl enable docker
```

For Windows and macOS, Docker usually starts automatically when you launch Docker Desktop. However, you can manually manage this from the Docker Desktop settings.

2. Managing User Permissions

Post-installation, the Docker daemon runs as the root user, and by default, users must have root privileges to employ Docker commands. This can be managed by adding your user to the Docker group:

```
sudo usermod -aG docker $USER
```

After running the above command, log out and log back in for the changes to take effect. Verify the addition by running:

```
groups
```

The 'docker' group should now be listed.

3. Configuring Docker to Start on Boot

For systems using systemd, enabling Docker to start on boot can be achieved using:

```
sudo systemctl enable docker
```

For Windows, you can adjust this setting in the Docker Desktop configurations under the "Settings" menu. Enabling Docker to start on boot ensures your containers and services are restored after a system reboot.

4. Testing Docker Installation

It is essential to verify that Docker is correctly installed and operational. Running the 'hello-world' container is a straightforward way to confirm this:

```
docker run hello-world
```

This command downloads a test image, runs it in a container, prints a confirmation message, and then exits. The expected output should look like this:

```
Hello from Docker!
This message shows that your installation appears to be working correctly.
```

5. Installing Docker Compose

Docker Compose is a tool for defining and running multi-container

Docker applications. To install Docker Compose, follow these steps for Unix-based systems:

```
sudo curl -L "https://github.com/docker/compose/releases/download/1.29.2/docker-
    compose-$(uname -s)-$(uname -m)" -o /usr/local/bin/docker-compose
sudo chmod +x /usr/local/bin/docker-compose
```

After installation, you can test it by running:

```
docker-compose --version
```

On Windows, Docker Compose is included as part of Docker Desktop, and no additional steps are required for its installation.

6. Configuring Docker Daemon Settings

You might need to adjust the Docker daemon settings for your specific requirements, such as logging, storage drivers, and resource limits. Edit the '/etc/docker/daemon.json' file for Unix-based systems:

```
{
  "log-driver": "json-file",
  "log-opts": {
    "max-size": "10m",
    "max-file": "3"
  },
  "storage-driver": "overlay2"
}
```

After making changes to this file, restart the Docker daemon to apply them:

```
sudo systemctl restart docker
```

7. Adjusting Performance Settings

For development environments, you may need to adjust performance settings to optimize Docker's behavior. For example, configuring memory limits for containers can prevent a single container from exhausting the host's resources. Specify memory limits in your container run commands:

```
docker run -m 512m --memory-swap 1g image_name
```

This sets a memory limit of 512MB with a swap limit of 1GB.

By following these post-installation steps, you ensure that your Docker environment is secure, performant, and tailored to your specific use cases.

2.6 Verifying the Docker Installation

Verifying the Docker installation involves a series of simple, yet crucial steps to ensure that Docker is correctly installed and configured on your system. This process can help identify any issues early, allowing for timely resolution before proceeding with more advanced Docker operations.

First, open your terminal (or Command Prompt on Windows). The primary command to verify Docker installation is:

```
docker --version
```

This command will output the installed Docker version. It demonstrates that the Docker binary is correctly installed and accessible through the system's PATH.

```
Docker version 20.10.7, build f0df350
```

If this output or a similar version number is displayed, the Docker client is correctly installed. Next, verify if the Docker daemon is running. The following command should be executed:

```
docker info
```

This command provides detailed information about Docker's configuration and the daemon status. A successful execution indicates that the Docker daemon is operational. The output comprises several sections, including system status, installed plugins, and resource limits. An example output is:

```
Client:
 Context:    default
 Debug Mode: false

Server:
 Containers: 2
  Running: 1
  Paused: 0
  Stopped: 1
 Images: 1
 Server Version: 20.10.7
 Storage Driver: overlay2
 ...
```

For further confirmation, run the hello-world image, which is widely used for Docker installation verification. The command to run this image is:

```
docker run hello-world
```

Docker attempts to find the hello-world image locally. If it is not found,

Docker downloads the image from the Docker Hub. Upon execution, the following output should be expected:

```
Unable to find image 'hello-world:latest' locally
latest: Pulling from library/hello-world
2db29710123e: Pull complete
Digest: sha256:6a65f2f32c255fd805b7ed7a939b25d6c5f6ca8a4f7c8d16380473a727e7d736
Status: Downloaded newer image for hello-world:latest

Hello from Docker!
This message shows that your installation appears to be working correctly.
...
```

This message indicates that Docker can pull images from the Docker Hub and execute containers. If all previous steps have succeeded, Docker is correctly installed and operational on your system.

To ensure complete verification, especially in development environments, you may need to verify Docker Compose installation. Docker Compose is a tool for defining and running multi-container Docker applications. Verify its installation by checking the version:

```
docker-compose --version
```

The output should resemble the following:

```
docker-compose version 1.29.2, build 5becea4c
```

If Docker Compose is installed and correctly configured, this command confirms its presence.

Finally, checking user permissions is vital. Docker commands usually require superuser privileges. For Linux users, ensure that your user account belongs to the docker group to run Docker commands without sudo. Check group membership using:

```
groups
```

If the docker group is not listed, add your user to the docker group:

```
sudo usermod -aG docker $USER
```

You must log out and back in for the changes to take effect. Verify the addition by re-running the groups command.

In summary, verifying Docker installation ensures that Docker and its components are active and accessible, setting a robust foundation for future Docker operations.

2.7 Setting Up Docker Command-Line Interface (CLI)

Setting up the Docker Command-Line Interface (CLI) entails configuring the environment to interact seamlessly with Docker services. This section covers key steps including setting up the environment variables, understanding commonly used Docker CLI commands, and configuring the Docker CLI for optimal performance.

When Docker is installed, the docker command becomes available in your terminal. The Docker CLI is a powerful tool that gives users the ability to create, manage, and inspect containers, images, volumes, and networks. Below are some essential configurations and commands.

Environment Variables

Docker requires certain environment variables to be set for it to function correctly. These include DOCKER_CERT_PATH, DOCKER_HOST, DOCKER_TLS_VERIFY, and DOCKER_MACHINE_NAME. They are particularly useful when working with Docker Machine or Docker Swarm.

To set environment variables in a Unix-like operating system, you can use the export command in the shell. Here is an example:

```
export DOCKER_HOST=tcp://192.168.99.100:2376
export DOCKER_CERT_PATH=/Users/user/.docker/machine/machines/default
export DOCKER_TLS_VERIFY=1
```

On Windows, setting environment variables can be done through the System Properties window or using the setx command in the command prompt. For instance:

```
setx DOCKER_HOST tcp://192.168.99.100:2376
setx DOCKER_CERT_PATH C:\Users\user\.docker\machine\machines\default
setx DOCKER_TLS_VERIFY 1
```

Basic Docker CLI Commands

Once the environment is set up, it is crucial to familiarize with basic commands that are commonly used.

- docker –version Displays the currently installed Docker version.
- docker info Provides detailed information about the Docker installation including the number of containers and images.

- docker run Runs a command in a new container. For example, docker run hello-world starts a new container from the hello-world image.

Executing the command below will confirm the Docker CLI installation and connectivity:

```
docker --version
```

The expected output would resemble:

```
Docker version 20.10.7, build f0df350
```

Next, running the docker info command will yield comprehensive details about the Docker setup:

```
docker info
```

Analysis of the output helps in verifying if Docker is set up correctly:

```
Client:
 Context:    default
 Debug Mode: false

Server:
 Containers: 3
  Running: 1
  Paused: 0
  Stopped: 2
 Images: 5
```

Running and Managing Containers

To get started with Docker containers, the docker run command is often used. Here is a command that pulls the latest Ubuntu image and starts a container from it:

```
docker run -it ubuntu
```

When executed, this command fetches the latest Ubuntu image from the Docker Hub registry and invokes an interactive terminal session inside the new container.

Stopping and starting containers can be managed via the docker stop and docker start commands respectively. If you have a container running and wish to stop it, you can use:

```
docker stop <container_id>
```

To restart the container, execute:

```
docker start <container_id>
```

Listing all running containers can be efficiently managed via:

```
docker ps
```

To list all containers, regardless of their running state:

```
docker ps -a
```

Pulling and Pushing Images

The Docker CLI enables users to pull images from Docker Hub and other repositories. To pull an image:

```
docker pull nginx
```

Pushing an image to a repository is done using the docker push command, but this requires tagging the image properly to link it to your repository:

```
docker tag myimage myrepo/myimage:mytag
docker push myrepo/myimage:mytag
```

The commands above tag an image in the local repository and push it to a remote repository under the specified tag.

Configuring for Optimal Performance

Enhancing the performance of Docker CLI interactions can be accomplished by configuring the CLI settings. The configurations are typically stored in a JSON file located at ~/.docker/config.json.

An example configuration might include setting up experimental features and specifying custom Docker contexts. Here is a sample JSON configuration:

```
{
    "experimental": "enabled",
    "stackOrchestrator": "swarm",
    "detachKeys": "ctrl-e,e"
}
```

These configurations enable experimental features, set Swarm as the stack orchestrator, and customizes the key sequence for detaching from a running container.

Analyzing these configurations and commands provides a comprehensive understanding of setting up and efficiently using the Docker CLI, ensuring streamlined container management and deployment tasks.

2.8 Configuring Docker Daemon

The Docker daemon (dockerd) is the background service responsible for managing Docker containers on your system. Proper configuration of the Docker daemon is crucial for optimizing performance, ensuring security, and customizing Docker's behavior to better fit the needs of your development or production environment. This section elaborates on the various aspects of configuring the Docker daemon, including altering configuration files, setting up logging, managing storage drivers, and adjusting network settings.

Configuration File

The primary method to configure the Docker daemon is by modifying its configuration file. By default, this file is typically located at /etc/docker/daemon.json on Linux and C:\ProgramData\Docker\config\daemon.json on Windows. Here, you can specify a variety of settings in JSON format.

A basic example of a daemon.json file:

```
{
    "debug": true,
    "hosts": ["tcp://0.0.0.0:2376", "unix:///var/run/docker.sock"],
    "log-level": "warn",
    "storage-driver": "overlay2",
    "log-opts": {
        "max-size": "10m",
        "max-file": "3"
    },
    "dns": ["8.8.8.8", "8.8.4.4"]
}
```

Debug Mode

Enabling debug mode can be helpful for diagnosing issues. In the daemon.json file, this is accomplished by setting "debug": true. When enabled, the Docker daemon produces more detailed logs, aiding in troubleshooting.

Host Configuration

The Docker daemon can listen on multiple interfaces, such as a Unix socket and a TCP port. In the example above, the hosts field specifies that the daemon should listen on all network interfaces (via tcp://0.0.0.0:2376) as well as the Unix socket (via unix:///var/run/docker.sock).

Log Level

The log-level directive in daemon.json controls the verbosity of logs generated by the Docker daemon. Possible values include "debug", "info", "warn", "error", and "fatal". Setting the log level to "warn" ensures that only warnings, errors, and critical issues are logged.

Storage Driver Configuration

Docker supports several storage drivers such as overlay2, aufs, btrfs, and zfs. The choice of a storage driver can significantly impact performance and storage efficiency. To specify a storage driver, use the "storage-driver" field.

Example:

```
"storage-driver": "overlay2"
```

Logging Options

The log-opts settings allow you to configure the logging mechanism in greater detail. Options include setting a maximum log size ("max-size") and the number of log files ("max-file") to retain. This prevents logs from consuming too much disk space.

Example:

```
"log-opts": {
    "max-size": "10m",
    "max-file": "3"
}
```

DNS Configuration

For resolving domain names within containers, you can specify DNS servers using the "dns" field. This is particularly useful in environments where custom DNS settings are required.

Example:

```
"dns": ["8.8.8.8", "8.8.4.4"]
```

Restart Policy

Docker provides restart policies to handle container failures. Policies like "no", "on-failure", "always", and "unless-stopped" can be set in the Docker daemon configuration.

Example:

```
"restart-policy": {
    "name": "on-failure",
    "maximumRetryCount": 5
}
```

Reloading Configuration

After modifying daemon.json, the Docker daemon must be reloaded for the changes to take effect. On a Linux system, you can achieve this by restarting the Docker service:

```
sudo systemctl restart docker
```

On a Windows system:

```
Restart-Service Docker
```

Command-Line Options

Besides daemon.json, you can also configure the Docker daemon using command-line options. These options are passed when starting the daemon. For example, to change the logging level, use:

```
dockerd --log-level=warn
```

Securing the Docker Daemon

To secure communication between the Docker client and daemon, you can use TLS. This requires creating and specifying certificates and keys in the daemon.json file.

Example:

```
{
    "tls": true,
    "tlsverify": true,
    "tlscacert": "/etc/docker/ca.pem",
    "tlscert": "/etc/docker/server-cert.pem",
    "tlskey": "/etc/docker/server-key.pem"
}
```

This configuration enforces the usage of TLS for securing the TCP connection, ensuring that only authenticated clients can connect to the Docker daemon.

By meticulously configuring the Docker daemon using the settings discussed, you can enhance Docker's performance, security, and functionality to better align with your operational requirements.

2.9 Managing Docker with Docker Desktop

Docker Desktop is a powerful application that allows developers to quickly and efficiently manage Docker containers, images, volumes, and networks using a graphical user interface (GUI). This section delves into the features and functionalities of Docker Desktop, providing essential knowledge and step-by-step instructions on its effective use.

Launching Docker Desktop

After installing Docker Desktop, launch it by executing the Docker Desktop application from your operating system's application menu. On startup, Docker Desktop initializes the Docker Daemon, making the Docker engine available for container management. The Docker Desktop icon will appear in your system's status area (system tray on Windows, menu bar on macOS), indicating it is running.

Overview of the Docker Desktop Interface

Upon launching Docker Desktop, the main dashboard provides an overview of container metrics, recent activity, and shortcuts to common tasks. The primary sections include:

- **Containers / Apps**: Displays currently running and stopped containers, with options to start, stop, restart, and remove containers.
- **Images**: Shows the list of locally stored Docker images. Allows pulling new images, removing existing ones, and launching containers from these images.
- **Volumes**: Manages Docker volumes, enabling users to view, create, and delete volumes.
- **Development Environments**: Supports setting up isolated development environments, though primarily integrated with Docker's additional premium features.
- **Dashboard**: Provides metrics and logs for active containers, helping in monitoring and troubleshooting.

Managing Containers

To manage containers, navigate to the **Containers / Apps** tab. Here, you can:

- **Start a Container**: Select an existing stopped container and click the start button to run it.

```
docker start <container_name>
```

- **Stop a Container**: To stop a running container, click the stop button.

  ```
  docker stop <container_name>
  ```

- **Restart a Container**: Click the restart button to stop and immediately start the container.

  ```
  docker restart <container_name>
  ```

- **Remove a Container**: To remove a container, ensuring it is stopped first, and then click the remove button.

  ```
  docker rm <container_name>
  ```

Managing Images

In the **Images** tab, Docker Desktop allows the following actions:

- **Pull a New Image**: Use the search bar to find and pull new images from Docker Hub.

  ```
  docker pull <image_name>
  ```

- **Remove an Image**: To remove an image, select it and click the remove button.

  ```
  docker rmi <image_name>
  ```

- **Launch a Container from an Image**: Select an image and click the run button to start a new container.

  ```
  docker run -d <image_name>
  ```

Managing Volumes

The **Volumes** tab is used for data persistence across containers. Actions available include:

- **Create a Volume**: Click on the create volume button.

  ```
  docker volume create <volume_name>
  ```

- **Remove a Volume**: Select and remove unused volumes.

  ```
  docker volume rm <volume_name>
  ```

- **Inspect a Volume**: View details and configurations of a volume.

```
docker volume inspect <volume_name>
```

Development Environments

Docker Desktop's development environments facilitate isolated, consistent setups across development teams. This feature integrates well with Visual Studio Code, providing a seamless development experience. To set up a development environment:

- Click on the **Add Development Environment** button.
- Follow the guided setup to configure source repositories, Dockerfiles, and other environment settings.
- Launch the configured environment, which opens in an integrated IDE workspace.

Settings and Preferences

Docker Desktop settings can be accessed by clicking on the **Settings** (or **Preferences** on macOS) icon. Key configuration areas include:

- **General**: Configure startup behavior, update settings, and send usage statistics.
- **Resources**: Allocate system resources such as CPU, memory, disk space, and configure file sharing.
- **Docker Engine**: Customize daemon configurations, including experimental features.
- **Kubernetes**: Enable or disable Kubernetes, an orchestration tool integrated with Docker Desktop.
- **Proxies and Network**: Define proxies and manage network settings.
- **Software Updates**: Manage Docker Desktop updates.

Using the Docker Desktop CLI Integration

Docker Desktop includes a Command-Line Interface (CLI) integration within its GUI. Users can switch seamlessly between the UI and CLI to perform advanced configurations and troubleshooting:

```
docker ps
docker images
docker network ls
```

Executing the above commands in the terminal integrated with Docker Desktop will provide outputs directly related to Docker Desktop's managed resources.

Monitoring and Logs

The **Dashboard** tab allows real-time monitoring of active containers' performance metrics such as CPU, memory usage, and network I/O. Logs for individual containers can also be accessed, aiding in debugging and system health checks.

```
CONTAINER ID   NAME     CPU %    MEM USAGE / LIMIT    NET I/O
a1b2c3d4e5     webapp   2.34%    85MiB / 2GiB         1MB / 0.5MB
```

Understanding and leveraging these capabilities ensures efficient Docker management, aiding developers in optimizing their containerized applications' deployment and maintenance.

2.10 Upgrading and Uninstalling Docker

Upgrading and uninstalling Docker are critical maintenance tasks that ensure the smooth and secure operation of your containerized applications. This section provides detailed instructions for performing these tasks across different platforms, including Windows, macOS, and Linux.

Upgrading Docker involves updating the software to the latest version, which often includes security enhancements, new features, bug fixes, and performance improvements. Keeping Docker up to date is essential for leveraging the latest advancements and ensuring compatibility with Docker images and containers.

Uninstalling Docker is necessary when you need to completely remove Docker from your system, perhaps for troubleshooting, a clean reinstallation, or migration purposes. This process involves removing all Docker components, including containers, images, volumes, and configuration files.

This section will cover both upgrading and uninstalling Docker in comprehensive detail.

Upgrading Docker on Windows

For Windows users, Docker can be upgraded via Docker Desktop, which simplifies the process and ensures that all related components are updated accordingly.

1. Open Docker Desktop.
2. Click on the *Settings* icon in the top-right corner.
3. Navigate to the *General* tab and check *Automatically check for updates*.
4. If an update is available, you will see a notification. Follow the prompts to download and install the update.

Alternatively, you can manually download the latest version from the Docker website and run the installer. The installer will handle the upgrade process and retain your existing configuration and data.

To verify the Docker version, use the command:

```
docker --version
```

```
Docker version 20.10.8, build 3967b7d
```

Upgrading Docker on macOS

Upgrading Docker on macOS is straightforward with Docker Desktop for Mac.

1. Open Docker Desktop from the Applications folder.
2. Click on the *Preferences* icon.
3. Go to the *Updates* tab.
4. If an update is available, click on *Download update*. Docker Desktop will download and install the update for you.

Manually updating involves downloading the latest Docker Desktop for Mac package from the Docker website and running the installer, which will automatically upgrade your current installation.

To verify the installation, use the following command:

```
docker --version
```

```
Docker version 20.10.8, build 3967b7d
```

Upgrading Docker on Linux

Upgrading Docker on Linux depends on the package manager used by your distribution.

For systems using apt (Debian-based distributions):

```
sudo apt-get update
sudo apt-get install --only-upgrade docker-ce
```

For systems using yum (Red Hat-based distributions):

```
sudo yum update
sudo yum upgrade docker-ce
```

To confirm the Docker version after upgrading:

```
docker --version
```

```
Docker version 20.10.8, build 3967b7d
```

Uninstalling Docker on Windows

To completely uninstall Docker Desktop from Windows:

1. Open the *Control Panel*.
2. Navigate to *Programs and Features*.
3. Locate *Docker Desktop* from the list of installed programs.
4. Right-click on Docker Desktop and select *Uninstall*.
5. Follow the prompts to remove Docker Desktop.
6. Delete remaining Docker files located in C:\Users\YourUsername\.docker.

Ensure that you remove all Docker images, containers, and volumes before uninstalling Docker to avoid orphaned data.

Uninstalling Docker on macOS

To uninstall Docker Desktop on macOS:

1. Open Docker Desktop.
2. Click on the *Docker* icon in the menu bar and select *Quit Docker Desktop*.

3. Open *Finder*, navigate to the *Applications* folder, and drag *Docker.app* to the *Trash*.

4. To remove Docker configuration files, in Terminal, run:

```
rm -rf ~/.docker
sudo rm -rf /var/lib/docker
sudo rm -rf /etc/docker
```

Uninstalling Docker on Linux

The uninstallation process varies by distribution. For Debian-based distributions:

```
sudo apt-get purge docker-ce
sudo apt-get autoremove --purge docker-ce
```

For Red Hat-based distributions:

```
sudo yum remove docker-ce
sudo yum autoremove docker-ce
```

To remove Docker images, containers, and volumes, delete the Docker directory:

```
sudo rm -rf /var/lib/docker
```

Ensure that all configuration files and Docker dependencies are removed to prevent future conflicts.

Regularly upgrading Docker and knowing how to properly uninstall it when necessary ensures a robust and manageable Docker environment across different operating systems.

Chapter 3

Docker Images

This chapter explains what Docker images are and covers the creation and management of Docker images using Dockerfile. It includes best practices for writing Dockerfiles, building and tagging images, and how to optimize and inspect them. The chapter also explores managing images with Docker Hub, using base images, multi-stage builds, and the process of publishing Docker images.

3.1 What are Docker Images?

Docker images constitute the core of Docker's functionality, encapsulating everything needed to run a piece of software—code, runtime, libraries, environment variables, and configuration files. These lightweight, standalone, and executable packages include all dependencies, eliminating discrepancies between different computing environments. Understanding Docker images is essential for leveraging the power of Docker to create reproducible and easily deployable applications.

Each Docker image is built in layers, often referred to as the layered filesystem. These layers are read-only and stacked on top of each other, with each layer representing a change or addition upon the previous one. This design provides several key benefits:

- **Efficiency:** Only the layers that have changed need to be distributed or downloaded.

- **Reusability:** Common layers can be reused across multiple images, optimizing storage and reducing redundancy.
- **Modularity:** Each layer is a self-contained unit of functionality, promoting modular image creation and management.

At runtime, Docker images become Docker containers. Containers are running instances of images that share the same kernel as the host operating system, but run in isolated processes. This isolation ensures consistency and fairness in how computing resources are allotted, enhancing security and efficiency.

Image Layers: Each Docker image starts with a base image. Typically, this base image is an official Docker image representing an operating system like Ubuntu or a language runtime like Node.js. Successive instructions in a Dockerfile form additional layers, each built upon the preceding ones.

```
# Start with a base image
FROM ubuntu:20.04

# Install dependencies
RUN apt-get update && apt-get install -y python3

# Copy application files
COPY . /app

# Set the working directory
WORKDIR /app

# Set the entry point
ENTRYPOINT ["python3", "main.py"]
```

In this example, the base image ubuntu:20.04 is the first layer. Subsequent layers are formed by the RUN, COPY, and WORKDIR instructions. When the Dockerfile is built, Docker applies these layers sequentially, caching intermediate results whenever possible to speed up subsequent builds.

Union Filesystem: Docker uses a union filesystem to manage these layered images. The union filesystem allows multiple filesystems to be overlaid into a single filesystem, creating a unified view. This mechanism underpins Docker's ability to efficiently manage image layers.

Content-Addressable Storage: Docker images are stored using content-addressable storage. Each image layer is identified by a unique SHA-256 digest (hash), ensuring uniqueness and immutability. This approach simplifies the sharing and caching of image layers, as identical layers only need to be stored once, no matter how many images use them.

Docker Image Attributes: Each Docker image is defined by a manifest, which includes metadata such as the image's layers, creation time, and the command to run. One can inspect these attributes using the docker inspect command:

```
docker inspect ubuntu:20.04
```

The output from this command is detailed JSON, which provides a comprehensive look at the image's properties:

```
[
   {
      "Id": "sha256:c53a917048e7b1c8b6abf8e78184511e5a57c1b36b30395a0159974d88d27880",
      "RepoTags": ["ubuntu:20.04"],
      "Created": "2023-01-01T00:00:00Z",
      "Architecture": "amd64",
      "Os": "linux",
      "Size": 725860285,
      ...
   }
]
```

Every Docker image is immutable, meaning once published, it cannot be modified. Any updates or changes result in the creation of a new image with a new identifier.

Docker Hub and Registries: To distribute Docker images, they are uploaded to Docker registries like Docker Hub. Docker Hub, the default registry, acts as a centralized repository where developers can share and access images. Private registries also exist for enterprise use cases, offering controlled access and additional security measures.

Pulling and Running Images: Docker images are pulled from registries using the docker pull command, and they are run using the docker run command. For instance, to run the Ubuntu 20.04 image:

```
# Pull the image from Docker Hub
docker pull ubuntu:20.04

# Run a container from the image
docker run -it ubuntu:20.04 /bin/bash
```

This command sequence first downloads the image locally if it's not already present, and then starts a container instance with an interactive terminal.

Understanding Docker images is crucial for building reliable, portable, and efficient containerized applications. By mastering the concepts of image layers, storage, and registries, one can effectively create, manage, and distribute Docker images, ensuring consistent application behavior across diverse environments.

3.2 Understanding Dockerfile

A Dockerfile is a script containing a series of instructions on how to build a Docker image. Each instruction in a Dockerfile creates a layer in the image, making Dockerfiles essential for constructing portable and reusable software environments. Engineers and developers harness Dockerfiles to automate the assembly of images, ensuring consistency across different environments.

The structure of a Dockerfile is straightforward, consisting of a sequence of commands and arguments. These commands instruct Docker on how to set up the environment and how the application should be built, configured, and run. Understanding each command's role is vital for efficient Dockerfile construction.

Consider the basic structure of a Dockerfile:

```
FROM ubuntu:20.04
LABEL maintainer="example@example.com"
RUN apt-get update && apt-get install -y \
    python3 \
    python3-pip
COPY . /app
WORKDIR /app
RUN pip3 install -r requirements.txt
CMD ["python3", "app.py"]
```

FROM specifies the base image for the build process. In this example, the base image is ubuntu:20.04. The base image lays down the foundation; it is often a minimal Linux distribution, but it can also be a custom image previously built.

LABEL adds metadata to the image, which can be useful for documentation and management purposes. For instance, the maintainer label is used to specify the author responsible for the image.

RUN executes commands in the container during the image build process. This command is used to install software packages. Here, apt-get update updates the package list, and apt-get install -y python3 python3-pip installs Python and pip. Chaining commands with && ensures that if one command fails, the subsequent commands are not executed.

COPY copies files or directories from the host machine to the container filesystem at the specified destination path. In this instance, the current directory (denoted by .) is copied to the /app directory within the image.

WORKDIR sets the working directory for any subsequent RUN, CMD, ENTRYPOINT, COPY, and ADD instructions. This command simplifies path management within the image, making scripts and commands more readable and maintainable.

CMD specifies the instruction that should be executed when the container starts. It is a key aspect of the image as it dictates the primary process of the container. The command ["python3", "app.py"] runs the Python application.

Each command in a Dockerfile introduces a layer to the Docker image. Layers caching optimizes the build process, allowing Docker to reuse unchanged layers from previous builds, resulting in faster image builds and deployments.

Other useful commands and directives enhance the functionality of Dockerfiles:

EXPOSE informs Docker that the container will listen on network ports at runtime. For example:

```
EXPOSE 8080
```

This command does not publish the port; it serves as documentation for users running the container.

ENV sets environment variables within the Docker image. These variables can influence the behavior of software within the container:

```
ENV APP_NAME=MyApp
```

ENTRYPOINT configures a container that will run as an executable. This instruction gives more control over how the command in CMD is executed. ENTRYPOINT can be overridden at runtime:

```
ENTRYPOINT ["python3", "app.py"]
```

Utilizing both ENTRYPOINT and CMD can establish default behavior while still permitting command-line arguments:

```
ENTRYPOINT ["python3"]
CMD ["app.py"]
```

The distinction lies in ENTRYPOINT setting the default executable, whereas CMD defines default parameters. Overriding the CMD at runtime is simpler compared to ENTRYPOINT.

VOLUME creates a mount point in the container and marks it as holding externally mounted volumes from the native host or from other containers:

```
VOLUME /data
```

Volumes are crucial for persisting data beyond the lifecycle of a container, enhancing stateful applications.

Understanding the fundamental commands and best practices in Dockerfile construction is instrumental for creating efficient, maintainable, and scalable Docker images. An adeptly crafted Dockerfile enhances build performance, reduces image size, and ensures consistency across development, testing, and production environments.

3.3 Creating Your First Docker Image

Creating your first Docker image is a fundamental step in grasping the core functionalities Docker offers. Docker images are built from Dockerfiles, which are scripts containing a series of instructions on how to build your image. This section will guide you through creating a basic Docker image, leveraging a Dockerfile to encapsulate the desired environment and application.

We will start by writing a simple Dockerfile to create an image that runs a basic Python application. This practical example will help solidify your understanding of Dockerfile syntax and the image creation process.

First, create a new directory to hold your Dockerfile and the associated application code. This ensures an organized file structure.

```
$ mkdir my-python-app
$ cd my-python-app
```

Next, create a Python script named ‘app.py‘ with the following content:

```
print("Hello, Docker!")
```

Now, create a Dockerfile in the same directory. The Dockerfile will define the steps needed to set up the environment and run this Python script.

```
# Use an official Python runtime as a parent image
FROM python:3.8-slim

# Set the working directory in the container
WORKDIR /usr/src/app
```

```
# Copy the current directory contents into the container at /usr/src/app
COPY . .

# Run app.py when the container launches
CMD ["python", "./app.py"]
```

In this Dockerfile, several essential instructions are used:

1. FROM - Specifies the base image to use for the subsequent instructions. In this case, the Python 3.8-slim image is used, which is a lightweight version of Python 3.8. 2. WORKDIR - Sets the working directory for any COPY and CMD instructions that follow. This command ensures that your commands run in the specified directory. 3. COPY - Copies files from the host machine to the container's file system. Here, it copies the entire current directory content into '/usr/src/app' inside the container. 4. CMD - Specifies the command to run within the container. In this case, it instructs the container to run 'app.py' using Python.

To build the Docker image from the Dockerfile, execute the following command in your terminal:

```
$ docker build -t my-python-app .
```

The docker build command creates the Docker image by following the instructions listed in the Dockerfile. The -t flag allows you to tag the image with a name, here "my-python-app". The dot (.) at the end of the command directs Docker to use the current directory as the build context.

Upon successful execution of the docker build command, you should see an output similar to the following:

```
Sending build context to Docker daemon  2.048kB
Step 1/4 : FROM python:3.8-slim
3.8-slim: Pulling from library/python
...
Step 2/4 : WORKDIR /usr/src/app
 ---> Using cache
 ---> e1a5fc1b9de6
Step 3/4 : COPY . .
 ---> Using cache
 ---> 8827131614aa
Step 4/4 : CMD ["python", "./app.py"]
 ---> Using cache
 ---> 5f70bf18a086
Successfully built 5f70bf18a086
Successfully tagged my-python-app:latest
```

To verify that the image was created successfully, list all Docker images using the following command:

```
$ docker images
```

You should see an entry for 'my-python-app' among the listed images:

```
REPOSITORY       TAG          IMAGE ID        CREATED          SIZE
my-python-app    latest       5f70bf18a086    2 seconds ago    113MB
python           3.8-slim     16bd1c9adc5a    3 days ago       113MB
```

To run the Docker container using the newly created image, use the docker run command as shown below:

```
$ docker run my-python-app
```

The output should display the message from your Python script:

```
Hello, Docker!
```

This example illustrates the fundamental process of creating a Docker image: defining a Dockerfile, building the image, and running a container based on that image. Understanding these basic principles is crucial as you proceed to explore more complex Docker functionalities, such as image optimization, multi-stage builds, and Docker Hub integration.

3.4 Best Practices for Writing Dockerfiles

Writing a Dockerfile efficiently requires adherence to certain best practices that ensure images are secure, small in size, and performant. The structured approach to crafting Dockerfiles not only aids maintainability but also improves the consistency and reliability of Docker images.

Firstly, it is critical to leverage official base images or trusted publishers, as they are maintained and regularly updated. Using a strong and stable base image ensures a solid foundation for your subsequent layers.

Use Specific Version Tags: Always specify a tag for the base image instead of using the latest tag. The latest tag can introduce breaking changes when the base image updates. For instance:

```
FROM python:3.8-slim
```

Minimize the Number of Layers: Each command in a Dockerfile creates a layer. To minimize image size, you should combine commands where possible using shell's && operator. For example:

```
RUN apt-get update && apt-get install -y \
    python3-pip \
    python3-dev
```

This creates a single layer instead of multiple layers for each command.

Leverage Caching: Docker uses a layer caching mechanism to optimize the build process. Reordering commands in the Dockerfile, ensuring that steps which change less frequently are placed earlier, can take full advantage of the cache:

```
COPY requirements.txt /app/
RUN pip install --no-cache-dir -r /app/requirements.txt
COPY . /app/
```

In the example above, the pip install command will be cached until requirements.txt changes, saving time in subsequent builds.

Optimize the Number of RUN Instructions: Group related commands together in a single RUN instruction whenever they can be logically combined. This helps in reducing the number of intermediate layers:

```
RUN apt-get update && apt-get install -y \
    build-essential \
    curl && \
    apt-get clean && \
    rm -rf /var/lib/apt/lists/*
```

Multi-Stage Builds: Use multi-stage builds to reduce image size by separating the build environment from the runtime environment. This is particularly useful for applications requiring compilation or build processes:

```
FROM golang:1.17 as builder
WORKDIR /app
COPY . .
RUN go build -o myapp

FROM alpine:latest
WORKDIR /root/
COPY --from=builder /app/myapp .
CMD ["./myapp"]
```

Using multi-stage builds, the final image only includes the necessary binaries, significantly reducing the final image size.

Security Best Practices: Regular updates to base images and packages are essential. Critical security patches should be included to prevent vulnerabilities. Avoid exposing sensitive information such as credentials in Dockerfiles. If environment variables are necessary, use .env files:

```
ENV DB_PASSWORD=supersecret
```

Instead, consider using Docker secrets or environment variable passing at runtime to manage sensitive data securely.

Utilize .dockerignore File: Similar to .gitignore, .dockerignore excludes unwanted files and directories from the build context, reducing the image size and build time. Common patterns include ignoring local environment files, build artifacts, and version control directories:

```
node_modules
*.log
.git
```

Clean Up After Installation: Temporary files created during installation processes should be removed to keep the image lean. The following example installs packages and subsequently removes cached files:

```
RUN apt-get update && apt-get install -y \
    libexample && \
    apt-get clean && \
    rm -rf /var/lib/apt/lists/*
```

Use LABEL Instruction: Including metadata using the LABEL instruction helps in managing and documenting the image:

```
LABEL maintainer="you@example.com"
LABEL version="1.0"
LABEL description="A sample Python application"
```

Fixed Ports and Volumes: Declare default port mappings and volumes in the Dockerfile to make the containerized application self-documenting and easy to understand:

```
EXPOSE 8080
VOLUME [/app/data]
```

Order of Commands: Proper command sequence can take advantage of Docker's caching mechanism. For example, commands that change frequently should be placed at the end of the Dockerfile.

Minimal Add-ons: Use the smallest possible number of third-party tools and libraries. This not only reduces complexity but also minimizes potential security risks:

```
RUN apt-get update && apt-get install -y \
    --no-install-recommends curl
```

Adherence to these best practices in writing Dockerfiles facilitates creating Docker images that are robust, efficient, and secure.

3.5 Building Docker Images

To build a Docker image, the user needs a Dockerfile. This file contains the commands and instructions required to assemble the image, operating as a script that Docker reads and executes to create the image. A Dockerfile consists of a series of commands that individually add layers to the image. Understanding the components of a Dockerfile and the steps to build an image is crucial for efficient and effective use of Docker.

A basic Dockerfile might look like this:

```
# Use a base image
FROM ubuntu:20.04

# Set environment variables
ENV DEBIAN_FRONTEND=noninteractive

# Run an update and install dependencies
RUN apt-get update && \
    apt-get install -y python3-pip python3-dev

# Copy files into the container
COPY . /app

# Set working directory
WORKDIR /app

# Install Python packages
RUN pip3 install -r requirements.txt

# Define the command to run the application
CMD ["python3", "app.py"]
```

To build the Docker image from this Dockerfile, the command to use is:

```
docker build -t myapp:latest .
```

Here, the '-t' flag tags the image with a name ('myapp') and a version ('latest'). The '.' at the end of the command specifies the build context, which is the current directory in this case.

The build process enumerates the layers each command in the Dockerfile produces, caching intermediate layers to optimize future builds. Here's what each command does:

1. 'FROM' specifies the base image. It is often the first command in the Dockerfile and dictates the operating system and environment. There can be multiple 'FROM' statements for multi-stage builds, which will be discussed in a later section.

2. 'ENV' sets environment variables. These are accessible throughout

the container's lifetime.

3. 'RUN' executes the commands in a new layer and commits the results. This command is used to install packages and utilities or perform other setup tasks.

4. 'COPY' copies files from the local filesystem into the image. This command can increase the build's context size if care isn't taken to exclude unnecessary files via a '.dockerignore' file.

5. 'WORKDIR' sets the working directory for subsequent instructions. If this directory does not exist, it will be created.

6. 'CMD' defines the default command to run when the container starts. It is different from 'RUN' because 'RUN' executes at build time, whereas 'CMD' executes at runtime.

During the build process, Docker provides a log of each step, including cache hits for intermediate layers:

```
Sending build context to Docker daemon  3.072kB
Step 1/7 : FROM ubuntu:20.04
20.04: Pulling from library/ubuntu
2e6e20c8e2e6: Already exists
Digest: sha256:b8e9...
Status: Downloaded newer image for ubuntu:20.04
 ---> 2e6e20c8e2e6
Step 2/7 : ENV DEBIAN_FRONTEND=noninteractive
 ---> Running in 5c150d80dc96
 ---> 47aab366b8e9
Step 3/7 : RUN apt-get update && apt-get install -y python3-pip python3-dev
 ---> Running in 55cf54c57b40
 ...
Step 7/7 : CMD ["python3", "app.py"]
 ---> Running in e045b6b6b086
 ---> 73eab777d7ff
Successfully built 73eab777d7ff
Successfully tagged myapp:latest
```

Each step produces a new image layer, which Docker caches for reuse in future builds to speed up the process.

Developers should strive to use efficient commands and order them in a way to maximize cache hits. For example, placing less frequently changing instructions at the top of the Dockerfile ensures that frequently changing instructions later in the file don't invalidate the cache for the earlier, less volatile layers.

One common pitfall is frequently changing files like source code or configuration files. It's recommended to copy these files after system-level dependencies are installed to leverage the cache effectively:

```
COPY requirements.txt /app/requirements.txt
RUN pip3 install -r /app/requirements.txt
```

```
COPY . /app
```

This way, changes to the codebase do not invalidate the cache established during the installation of dependencies, making rebuilds faster and more efficient.

By carefully structuring Dockerfiles and understanding the build caching mechanism, developers can optimize build times significantly, making the process more efficient and maintaining agile development practices.

3.6 Managing Docker Images with Docker Hub

Docker Hub is a registry service provided by Docker Inc. that allows developers to manage and distribute Docker images. It serves as the central location to store public or private repositories. Understanding how to effectively utilize Docker Hub is essential for sharing images across various environments and collaborating with other developers.

Docker Hub's primary functionalities include pushing and pulling images, managing repositories, automated builds, and integration with third-party services. This section delves into these functionalities, emphasizing practical commands and scenarios.

Pushing and Pulling Images

To upload Docker images to Docker Hub, the image must first be tagged appropriately. Tagging an image typically involves assigning a name that includes the repository and an optional version tag. The default tag is latest if no version tag is specified. For example:

```
docker tag my-local-image:latest username/my-repository:tagname
```

The docker push command is used to upload the tagged image to Docker Hub:

```
docker push username/my-repository:tagname
```

For retrieving images from Docker Hub, use the docker pull command:

```
docker pull username/my-repository:tagname
```

When logging in for the first time, use:

```
docker login
```

This prompts for Docker Hub credentials. Successfully logging in will allow pushing and pulling images without repeating the authentication process.

Managing Repositories

Repositories on Docker Hub can be either public or private. Public repositories are accessible to anyone, while private repositories require granted access. Creating a repository through the Docker Hub web interface involves navigating to the Repositories tab and selecting Create Repository. Add a repository name, description, and specify visibility.

To manage a repository's settings or delete it, use the Docker Hub interface. Addition of collaborators to a private repository is a critical feature for collaborative development. Click on the repository and select Settings. Under Manage Access, add the team members and assign the correct permissions.

Automated Builds

Automated builds simplify the process of creating Docker images from source code. By linking repositories from GitHub or Bitbucket, Docker Hub can automatically build images whenever changes are pushed to version control. This maintains an updated image in line with the associated source code.

To set up an automated build, follow these steps:

- Link your Docker Hub account with your GitHub or Bitbucket account.
- Navigate to Create -> Create Automated Build.
- Select an existing repository or create a new one.
- Choose the source code repository and specify the branch and Dockerfile path.

Docker Hub provides build status updates and detailed logs for debugging build issues.

Access Control and Organizations

Organizations in Docker Hub allow for structured access control, team collaboration, and resource management. By creating an organization, teams can have shared access to repositories while maintaining user-level roles and permissions. This feature is particularly useful in larger teams or corporate environments.

Creating an organization and adding team members involves the following steps:

- Select Organizations in the Docker Hub menu.
- Click on Create Organization.
- Input the organization name and description.
- Invite team members and assign them to teams with varying levels of access.

Each team can be granted different permissions such as read, write, or admin access to repositories.

Webhooks and Third-party Integrations

Webhooks enable Docker Hub to send HTTP POST requests to external services upon specific events such as successful image builds. This allows for continuous integration and deployment workflows by triggering automation tools or notifying project management platforms.

To set up a webhook, follow these steps:

- Navigate to the repository settings in Docker Hub.
- Select the Webhooks tab.
- Add the target URL of the service to notify.

Third-party integrations, such as linking Docker Hub to CI/CD platforms like Jenkins, CircleCI, or GitLab, further extend the capabilities of Docker Hub. These integrations ensure a seamless workflow from code commit to image deployment.

Understanding and leveraging Docker Hub's functionalities optimizes image management and enhances collaborative development effectively.

3.7 Tagging and Versioning Docker Images

Docker tags play a crucial role in identifying and managing Docker images. They provide a means to address specific versions or variants of your images, allowing for greater control and organization within your Continuous Integration/Continuous Deployment (CI/CD) pipelines and deployment strategies. A Docker tag is essentially a mutable alias pointing to a Docker image SHA256 digest which provides immutability and uniqueness to the image.

When you build an image using the Docker CLI, you can assign it one or more tags. Tags are named using the format *repository:tag*. If no tag is provided, Docker defaults to using the `latest` tag. Tags should be chosen carefully to convey meaningful versioning information, facilitating clarity and predictability in your development and deployment workflows.

Creating and Using Tags

To illustrate how to tag Docker images, let's consider a simple example. Suppose you have a Dockerfile for a Node.js application and you want to build an image while tagging it.

```
docker build -t mynodeapp:1.0 .
```

In this command, `-t` is used to specify the tag for the image. `mynodeapp` is the repository name, and `1.0` is the tag. This will produce an image that is referred to as `mynodeapp:1.0`.

You can apply multiple tags to a single image using the Docker `tag` command. For instance, if you want to tag the same image with `stable`:

```
docker tag mynodeapp:1.0 mynodeapp:stable
```

This command takes an existing image tag `mynodeapp:1.0` and creates another tag `mynodeapp:stable` that points to the same image ID.

Pushing Tagged Images to Docker Hub

After tagging, these images can be pushed to Docker Hub or any other Docker registry. This makes them accessible to other team members or deployment environments.

```
docker push mynodeapp:1.0
docker push mynodeapp:stable
```

These commands push the `1.0` and `stable` tags of the `mynodeapp` image to the Docker Hub repository.

Tagging Strategies

A well-defined tagging strategy is imperative for efficient image management. Some common strategies include:

- *Semantic Versioning*: Using tags like 1.0.0, 1.1.0, 2.0.0, where the format is MAJOR.MINOR.PATCH, helps convey the nature of updates and compatibility.
- *Branch Naming*: Tags corresponding to version control branches like develop, feature-xyz, release, etc.
- *Build Metadata*: Incorporating CI/CD build numbers or dates (e.g., v1.0-build45, 2023-10-15) in tags for identifying specific build instances.

Inspecting Tags

To inspect and verify the tags associated with an image, you can use the docker images command.

```
docker images
```

The output provides a list of images with their respective repository names, tags, and image IDs.

```
REPOSITORY      TAG       IMAGE ID        CREATED       SIZE
mynodeapp       1.0       abcd1234efgh    2 days ago    123MB
mynodeapp       stable    abcd1234efgh    2 days ago    123MB
```

It is critical to understand that tags are mutable pointers to images. Therefore, pushing a new image with an existing tag (like latest) can overwrite the previous image associated with that tag.

Best Practices for Tagging

- **Immutability**: Tags should be immutable in production workflows to avoid unintentional overwrites, which can lead to inconsistencies.
- **Clarity**: Use tags that convey clear, meaningful information about the image versions and states.
- **Consistency**: Maintain a consistent tagging scheme across all projects to streamline image management and automation scripts.

- **Documentation**: Document your tagging strategy within your project's version control system to ensure team-wide adherence.

Examples:

```
# Tagging a stable release
docker build -t myapp:2.1.0 .

# Tagging a nightly build
docker build -t myapp:nightly-20231001 .
```

These tagging conventions ensure your Docker images are properly versioned and easier to manage and deploy across various environments.

3.8 Inspecting Docker Images

Inspecting Docker images is a crucial step in Docker image management, as it allows you to examine the metadata associated with an image and verify its integrity. Docker provides several commands and options to facilitate the inspection of images. Understanding these commands and how to interpret their outputs can lead to more efficient debugging, optimization, and overall management of Docker images.

To inspect a Docker image, the primary command used is:

```
docker image inspect <image_name_or_id>
```

This command returns a JSON array that contains detailed information about the specified image. The JSON output includes several key fields such as 'Id', 'RepoTags', 'RepoDigests', 'Created', 'Size', and 'VirtualSize', among others. Below is a detailed explanation of significant fields found in the JSON output:

- **Id**: This is the unique identifier for the Docker image. It is a 64-character hexadecimal string.
- **RepoTags**: This field lists the repositories and tags associated with the image. For instance, '"ubuntu:latest"' indicates that the image is tagged as 'latest' in the 'ubuntu' repository.
- **RepoDigests**: Contains the content-addressable digest (in the form of a checksum) of the image stored in the repository.
- **Created**: The timestamp indicating when the image was created.

- **Size**: The total size (in bytes) of the image on disk.
- **VirtualSize**: The total size of all image layers combined, including those shared with other images.
- **Labels**: A collection of key-value pairs used to add metadata to the image.
- **Config**: Contains the image's configuration, including default command, environmental variables, and network settings. Notable subfields include:
  - **Hostname**: The hostname to use for the container.
  - **ExposedPorts**: Ports that the image exposes, specified as a dictionary.
  - **Env**: Environmental variables set within the image.

A concise example of the output from 'docker image inspect' is as follows:

```
[
  {
    "Id": "sha256:7691a76...",
    "RepoTags": [
      "ubuntu:latest"
    ],
    "RepoDigests": [
      "ubuntu@sha256:eabd36..."
    ],
    "Created": "2023-09-24T11:45:12.123Z",
    "Size": 123456789,
    "VirtualSize": 123456789,
    "Labels": {},
    "Config": {
      "Hostname": "12345abcde",
      "ExposedPorts": {
        "80/tcp": {}
      },
      "Env": [
        "PATH=/usr/local/sbin:/usr/local/bin:/usr/sbin:/usr/bin"
      ]
    }
  }
]
```

Layer Information: Understanding the layering structure of an image is essential. The 'RootFS' object in the output provides insight into the layers that comprise the Docker image. The 'Layers' array lists the filesystem change sets applied in sequence to build the image.

To view a specific layer's information, one might access it using:

```
"RootFS": {
  "Type": "layers",
```

```
    "Layers": [
        "sha256:abc123...",
        "sha256:def456...",
        "sha256:ghi789..."
    ]
}
```

Each layer in the 'Layers' array is identified by its content-addressable hash.

History of an Image: Viewing the history of an image helps decipher the sequence of instructions used to build it. This can be achieved using:

```
docker image history <image_name_or_id>
```

The 'docker image history' command lists all layers that form the image, along with details such as size and command used to build each layer. Here's an example output:

```
IMAGE          CREATED      CREATED BY                                      SIZE     COMMENT
sha256:ghi789  2 days ago   /bin/sh -c #(nop)  CMD ["bash"]                 0B
sha256:def456  2 days ago   /bin/sh -c apt-get update && apt-get install...  105MB
sha256:abc123  3 days ago   /bin/sh -c #(nop) ADD file:abc123 in /           70MB
```

In this example, the history command shows the chronology of commands ('CREATED BY') used to construct the image, starting from the base layer added to the final command executed.

Scanning an Image for Vulnerabilities: Ensuring the security of Docker images is crucial. Tools like Docker's 'docker scan' command (available as part of Docker Desktop) and third-party tools (e.g., Clair, Trivy) can scan images for vulnerabilities.

Using Docker's scan command:

```
docker scan <image_name_or_id>
```

This command integrates with Snyk to provide vulnerability analysis, helping to identify potential security issues in the image layers.

Understanding and implementing these inspection methods allows finer control and greater transparency over Docker image management. Each detailed field in the inspection output provides insights that are invaluable for optimizing, securing, and maintaining Docker images effectively.

3.9 Optimizing Docker Images

Optimizing Docker images is crucial for enhancing performance, reducing image size, and improving deployment efficiency. This section delves into various strategies and methods to optimize Docker images, including minimizing the number of layers, leveraging multi-stage builds, choosing suitable base images, and employing caching mechanisms effectively.

A fundamental principle in Docker image optimization is to create minimal and efficient images. Each command in a Dockerfile produces a layer, contributing to the final image's size. Therefore, reducing the number of layers and removing unnecessary files can significantly decrease the image size.

Minimizing Layers

To minimize layers, it is advisable to combine multiple commands into a single RUN statement whenever feasible. Consider the following suboptimal Dockerfile structure:

```
FROM ubuntu:20.04
RUN apt-get update
RUN apt-get install -y python3
RUN apt-get install -y python3-pip
RUN pip3 install flask
```

This results in five layers. It is more efficient to consolidate these commands:

```
FROM ubuntu:20.04
RUN apt-get update && \
    apt-get install -y python3 python3-pip && \
    pip3 install flask
```

The above notation not only reduces layers but also improves build speed.

Choosing a Suitable Base Image

Another optimization strategy is selecting a lean base image. Comprehensive images like ubuntu or debian offer extensive functionality but are often larger than necessary. For simpler applications, consider using smaller base images like alpine, a minimal distribution optimized for security and efficiency. Here is an example of using alpine as a base image:

```
FROM alpine:3.14
RUN apk add --no-cache python3 py3-pip \
```

```
&& pip3 install flask
```

This provides a significant size reduction while maintaining necessary functionalities.

Employing Multi-Stage Builds

Multi-stage builds provide an advanced mechanism for optimizing Docker images, particularly for large, complex build environments. By separating the build environment from the final runtime environment, multi-stage builds can drastically minimize the resultant image size. Consider a scenario involving a Go application; the build process might involve large compilers and dependencies that are not required in the final image:

```
FROM golang:1.17 as builder
WORKDIR /app
COPY . .
RUN go build -o myapp

FROM alpine:3.14
COPY --from=builder /app/myapp /myapp
ENTRYPOINT ["/myapp"]
```

The first stage (builder) includes a full Go build environment. The compiled binary is then copied to a minimal alpine base in the second stage, resulting in a much smaller final image, devoid of unnecessary build tools.

Using .dockerignore to Exclude Unnecessary Files

Docker's .dockerignore file functions similarly to .gitignore, specifying files and directories to exclude from the build context. This helps avoid bloating the image with redundant files. Below is an example of a .dockerignore file:

```
*.log
node_modules
tmp
```

This ensures logs, dependencies, and temporary files are excluded, conserving space and accelerating build times.

Cleaning Up After Installations

It is important to remove unnecessary package management files post-installation. Package managers such as apt-get and yum often leave residual files that contribute to image size. To mitigate this, cleanup commands can be appended within the same RUN statement as the installations:

```
RUN apt-get update && apt-get install -y \
    python3 python3-pip && \
    pip3 install flask && \
    apt-get clean && \
    rm -rf /var/lib/apt/lists/*
```

The above script installs the necessary packages and immediately removes the package manager's caches and lists, keeping the image lean.

Leveraging Caching

Docker employs a robust caching mechanism to optimize build processes and reduce image size. Understanding and utilizing cache effectively can lead to significant performance improvements. Docker caches image layers and reuses them if the corresponding layer in the Dockerfile hasn't changed.

For example, ordering commands from least to most frequently changing ensures maximum reuse of cached layers. Compare the following two Dockerfiles:

```
# Less efficient
COPY . /app
RUN pip3 install -r /app/requirements.txt

# More efficient
COPY requirements.txt /app/
RUN pip3 install -r /app/requirements.txt
COPY . /app
```

By copying the requirements.txt file first, Docker can cache the installation of dependencies. Thus, if application code changes without modifying dependencies, only the last layer is rebuilt, enhancing build speed.

Through combining these strategies—minimizing layers, selecting appropriate base images, using multi-stage builds, excluding unnecessary files with .dockerignore, cleaning up after installations, and effectively leveraging caching—one can produce significantly more efficient and optimized Docker images.

3.10 Working with Base Images

Docker base images constitute the foundational building blocks upon which custom Docker images are constructed. These images are termed "base" because they furnish the essential environment and tools necessary for application deployment. The astute selection and utilization of base images can profoundly affect the performance, security, and efficiency of the resultant Docker image.

Base images generally fall into two categories: official and custom. Official images are rigorously maintained and verified by the Docker community or Docker, Inc., and are publicly available on Docker Hub. Custom base images, on the other hand, are tailored to meet specific organizational or application requirements.

Choosing the Right Base Image

When selecting a base image, several factors warrant consideration:

- **Compatibility:** Ensure that the base image's operating system and architecture align with the application's requirements.
- **Size:** Smaller base images typically result in more efficient containerization, reducing the disk space consumed and minimizing the attack surface.
- **Security:** Opt for images that are periodically updated and have a strong track record of security practices.
- **Maintenance:** Choose images from reputable sources or maintainers who provide regular updates and patches.

Using Official Images

To leverage an official base image, incorporate its reference in the Dockerfile's FROM directive. Official images are accessible on Docker Hub and include a variety of operating systems, languages, and utilities. For instance, to utilize an official Debian image, the Dockerfile would include:

```
FROM debian:latest
```

This command signifies that the Docker build process should initiate from the most recent Debian image.

Creating Custom Base Images

Custom base images are crafted to satisfy precise specifications that are not met by official images. To develop such an image, commence with an official base image and then add custom layers. Below is an example Dockerfile that constructs a custom image with additional tools:

```
FROM ubuntu:20.04

RUN apt-get update && apt-get install -y \
```

```
    build-essential \
    curl \
    vim
```

This Dockerfile starts with the Ubuntu 20.04 official base image and augments it by installing essential development tools alongside curl and vim.

Optimizing Base Images

Optimization of base images hinges on principles such as minimization, caching, and modularization.

Minimization: Smaller base images accelerate the build process and enhance security. Utilize minimal base images like alpine, which is succinct and purpose-built:

```
FROM alpine:latest
```

Caching: Docker employs a layered architecture to cache builds efficiently. Each Dockerfile instruction creates a new layer. Reordering instructions to maximize cache hits can significantly abbreviate rebuild times:

```
FROM ubuntu:20.04

RUN apt-get update && apt-get install -y \
    nginx \
    python3
COPY . /app
WORKDIR /app
RUN pip3 install -r requirements.txt
```

The COPY command is separated to leverage caching of the apt-get installation step.

Modularization: Multi-stage builds enable separation of build and run environments. This results in smaller, more efficient images by discarding unnecessary artifacts after the build process:

```
FROM golang:1.17 AS builder
WORKDIR /app
COPY . .
RUN go build -o myapp

FROM alpine:latest
WORKDIR /app
COPY --from=builder /app/myapp .
CMD ["./myapp"]
```

The new image only retains the final binary, resulting in a significantly reduced footprint.

Best Practices for Updating Base Images

Regular updates to base images mitigate vulnerabilities and ensure up-to-date dependencies. Utilize the "latest" tag robustly and periodically rebuild and redeploy images:

```
docker pull debian:latest
docker build -t myapp:latest .
```

Thoroughly testing the integrated environment post-update is crucial to preclude regressions and ensure compatibility.

By adeptly combining official and custom base images with optimization strategies, one can craft Docker images that are both performant and secure. These practices facilitate efficient, maintainable, and scalable containerized application deployment.

3.11 Publishing Docker Images

Publishing Docker images is an integral part of the container lifecycle, enabling the distribution and deployment of images across various environments. This process involves pushing Docker images to a registry, making them accessible for pull operations by other users or deployment tools. Efficient management and publication facilitate continuous integration/continuous deployment (CI/CD) pipelines and collaborative development.

To publish a Docker image, follow these steps:

1. Create a Docker Hub account.
2. Tag the Docker image appropriately.
3. Authenticate with Docker Hub.
4. Push the Docker image to the registry.

Begin with creating a Docker Hub account. Docker Hub is a popular public registry, and having an account is necessary for publishing images. Sign up at https://hub.docker.com/ and follow the instructions for account creation.

Next, tag the Docker image adequately. Tagging provides meaningful version identifiers that assist in managing and retrieving specific image versions. If you have an image with the name myapp, tag it using the following command:

```
docker tag myapp:latest username/myapp:1.0
```

Replace username with your Docker Hub username and 1.0 with the version number. The format username/repository:tag ensures the image is identifiable within the Docker Hub repository.

Authenticate with Docker Hub using the docker login command. Enter your Docker Hub credentials when prompted:

```
docker login
```

Successful authentication leads to output indicating login success.

```
Login Succeeded
```

Now, push the image to Docker Hub with the docker push command:

```
docker push username/myapp:1.0
```

Docker uploads the image layers to the registry, and the process concludes with confirmation messages showing uploaded layers. Once pushed, the image becomes available in your Docker Hub repository, which you can verify by visiting your profile on Docker Hub.

Team collaboration and CI/CD pipelines often require automated image publishing. For this, integrate the Docker CLI commands with CI/CD tools like Jenkins, GitHub Actions, GitLab CI/CD, or others. Here is an example GitHub Actions workflow configuration that builds and publishes a Docker image:

```
name: CI/CD Pipeline

on:
  push:
    branches:
      - main

jobs:
  build:
    runs-on: ubuntu-latest

    steps:
    - name: Checkout repository
      uses: actions/checkout@v2

    - name: Set up Docker Buildx
      uses: docker/setup-buildx-action@v1

    - name: Login to Docker Hub
      uses: docker/login-action@v1
      with:
```

```
        username: ${{ secrets.DOCKER_USERNAME }}
        password: ${{ secrets.DOCKER_PASSWORD }}

    - name: Build and push Docker image
      uses: docker/build-push-action@v2
      with:
        context: .
        push: true
        tags: username/myapp:1.0
```

In this configuration, the workflow triggers on pushes to the main branch. The Docker Buildx toolset, essential for advanced Docker build capabilities, is set up. Authentication to Docker Hub uses GitHub secrets for storing sensitive information securely. Finally, the image is built and pushed to Docker Hub, similar to the manual process but automated.

Docker images can also be published to private registries or other public registries like Google Container Registry (GCR), Amazon Elastic Container Registry (ECR), or Azure Container Registry (ACR). The general process remains consistent: tagging the image, authenticating to the registry, and pushing the image. Here is how to push an image to Google Container Registry:

```
# Tag the image
docker tag myapp gcr.io/project-id/myapp:1.0

# Authenticate using Google Cloud SDK
gcloud auth configure-docker

# Push the image
docker push gcr.io/project-id/myapp:1.0
```

And for Amazon ECR:

```
# Create a repository (one-time setup)
aws ecr create-repository --repository-name myapp

# Tag the image
docker tag myapp:latest aws_account_id.dkr.ecr.region.amazonaws.com/myapp:1.0

# Authenticate Docker to the Amazon ECR registry
aws ecr get-login-password | docker login --username AWS --password-stdin
      aws_account_id.dkr.ecr.region.amazonaws.com

# Push the image
docker push aws_account_id.dkr.ecr.region.amazonaws.com/myapp:1.0
```

Publishing Docker images efficiently ensures that the images are accessible, versioned correctly, and can be pulled as needed by different systems. It encapsulates an essential practice for Docker-based workflows, ensuring that images are readily available for deployment and consistent across different environments.

3.12 Using Multi-Stage Builds

Multi-stage builds are an advanced feature in Docker that allow you to create smaller, more efficient container images by using multiple FROM statements in your Dockerfile. This technique can significantly reduce the final image size by excluding unnecessary build and intermediary files, thus improving the speed and security of your applications.

To understand the usability and implementation of multi-stage builds, consider the following example of a Dockerfile designed to build a Go application.

```
FROM golang:1.16 AS builder

# Set the working directory
WORKDIR /src

# Copy the source code
COPY . .

# Fetch dependencies and build the application
RUN go get -d -v ./...
RUN go build -o myapp

# Second stage: Create a minimal runtime image
FROM alpine:latest

# Install necessary dependencies for the runtime
RUN apk --no-cache add ca-certificates

# Set the working directory on the runtime image
WORKDIR /app

# Copy the compiled binary from the builder stage
COPY --from=builder /src/myapp .

# Command to run the application
CMD ["./myapp"]
```

In this Dockerfile, the process is split into two stages:

- **Builder Stage:**
  - The first FROM statement uses the golang:1.16 image to compile the Go application.
  - Commands like RUN go get -d -v ./... and RUN go build -o myapp are executed in this builder context.

  - This stage includes all tools and dependencies required to build the application, which are not needed in the final runtime environment.

- **Runtime Stage:**
  - The second FROM statement uses a minimal alpine:latest image.
  - Only essential runtime dependencies are installed in this stage.
  - The compiled binary is copied from the previous builder stage using the COPY –from=builder directive.
  - The final image size is drastically reduced because it only includes what is necessary to run the application.

```
Step 1/10 : FROM golang:1.16 AS builder
 ---> b1eaga4ec
Step 2/10 : WORKDIR /src
 ---> Using cache
 ---> fddf3a3af
Step 3/10 : COPY . .
 ---> Using cache
 ---> 3b8844gh
Step 4/10 : RUN go get -d -v ./...
 ---> Running in 2a386f4ea
...
Step 7/10 : FROM alpine:latest
 ---> ae690d9..
Step 8/10 : RUN apk --no-cache add ca-certificates
 ---> Using cache
 ---> cf0500f..
Step 9/10 : WORKDIR /app
 ---> Using cache
 ---> d5eee5863f
Step 10/10 : COPY --from=builder /src/myapp .
 ---> 7f4b0f3ad
Successfully built 89c1d4e
```

Multi-stage builds are especially beneficial for complex builds that involve dependencies and multiple build steps. By structuring Dockerfiles in a modular way, using multiple FROM statements, different environments can be leveraged for different steps in the build process—each environment tailored to its specific needs.

Advantages of Using Multi-Stage Builds:

- **Reduced Image Size:** Only includes the final artifacts, excluding development dependencies.
- **Build Separation:** Separates the build environment from the runtime environment, mitigating potential security risks.

- **Maintainability:** Modular Dockerfiles are easier to manage and update.
- **Cost Efficiency:** Smaller images mean faster deployments, lower storage requirements, and reduced transfer times.

Multi-stage builds can also be used in other contexts, such as compiling and bundling assets for front-end applications and performing extensive testing before final building. Consider this example for a Node.js application with build and test stages:

```
FROM node:14 AS build-stage

# Create app directory
WORKDIR /usr/src/app

# Install app dependencies
COPY package*.json ./
RUN npm install

# Bundle app source
COPY . .

# Build the app
RUN npm run build

FROM node:14 AS test-stage

# Create app directory
WORKDIR /usr/src/app

# Copy dependencies and build
COPY --from=build-stage /usr/src/app/node_modules ./node_modules
COPY --from=build-stage /usr/src/app/dist ./dist

# Run tests
RUN npm test

FROM nginx:stable-alpine

# Copy built app to serve
COPY --from=build-stage /usr/src/app/dist /usr/share/nginx/html

# Expose port and run the nginx server
EXPOSE 80
CMD ["nginx", "-g", "daemon off;"]
```

Explanation:

- **Build Stage:** Compiles and prepares the application.
- **Test Stage:** Copies assets from the build stage, runs tests to ensure everything works as expected.
- **Production Stage:** Copies only the necessary build outputs to the minimal nginx:stable-alpine image for serving.

Multi-stage builds enhance efficiency and security by optimizing Docker images through a clear separation of concerns across different stages. This method significantly benefits both development and production environments, proving to be an invaluable tool when creating Docker images for any production-ready application.

Chapter 4

Docker Containers

This chapter delves into Docker containers, covering their lifecycle, management, and practical usage. It includes running containers in different modes, managing container logs, accessing containers via shell, and persistent storage. Additionally, the chapter addresses container networking, linking, scaling, and committing containers to images.

4.1 What are Docker Containers?

Docker containers are lightweight, standalone, and executable packages that include everything needed to run a piece of software, including the code, runtime, system tools, libraries, and settings. Containers leverage operating-system-level virtualization to deploy and run distributed applications without launching an entire virtual machine (VM) for each application.

Conceptually, Docker containers are an abstraction at the application layer that packages code and dependencies together. Multiple containers can run on the same machine and share the OS kernel with other containers, each running as isolated processes in user space. They are designed to be fast and portable from one computing environment to another.

To understand Docker containers more comprehensively, it is useful to explore their defining characteristics and operational insights:

- **Isolation:** Containers provide process and filesystem isolation. Each container operates as if it were an independent machine, ensuring that applications running inside containers do not interfere with each other. This isolation is achieved using Linux kernel features such as namespaces and cgroups (control groups). Namespaces provide isolated system resources, while cgroups manage resource limits, ensuring efficient utilization without conflict.
- **Portability:** Docker containers enable consistent environments across different stages of development and production. Since containers encapsulate their dependencies, the application will run the same regardless of where the container is executed, be it a developer's laptop, a test server, or a production cloud environment.
- **Efficiency:** Containers are more lightweight compared to traditional virtual machines as they share the host system's kernel and do not require a full guest operating system per instance. This reduces the overhead and allows for higher density and efficient use of underlying hardware resources.
- **Immutable Infrastructure:** Containers encourage the practice of immutable infrastructure, meaning once a container is created, it should not be changed. Any update or modification involves creating a new container version, ensuring predictable deployment and minimizing configuration drift.
- **Microservices Architecture:** Containers are particularly well-suited for microservices architectures. Each microservice can be deployed and managed as a container, enabling an agile and scalable solution by making use of container orchestration tools like Kubernetes.

The Docker Engine, which comprises the Docker daemon, Docker client, and REST API, forms the core of container functionality:

- **Docker Daemon:** This is a background service responsible for managing containers on the host. It listens to Docker API requests and manages Docker objects such as images, containers, networks, and volumes.
- **Docker Client:** This is a command-line interface (CLI) tool that users interact with to issue commands to the Docker daemon.

Commands like docker run, docker build, docker pull, and docker push are some examples of client interactions.

- **Docker REST API:** Provides a programmatic way to interface with the Docker daemon. It can be used to develop custom client applications and integrate Docker into various development workflows.

Main Docker commands frequently interact with containers, controlling their lifecycle from creation to removal. Examples include:

```
# Pull an image from Docker Hub
docker pull ubuntu:latest

# Run a container from a pulled image
docker run -it ubuntu:latest /bin/bash

# List all running containers
docker ps

# Stop a running container
docker stop <container_id>

# Remove a stopped container
docker rm <container_id>
```

The output of executing some of these commands can be observed below for better understanding:

```
$ docker ps
CONTAINER ID   IMAGE    COMMAND       CREATED       STATUS     PORTS   NAMES
e7a90e6629bc   ubuntu   "/bin/bash"   2 hours ago   Up 2 hours         goofy_turing

$ docker stop e7a90e6629bc
e7a90e6629bc

$ docker rm e7a90e6629bc
e7a90e6629bc
```

Understanding how Docker manages filesystem layers is also crucial:

- **Union File System:** Docker uses union file systems (UnionFS) to provide a lightweight and high-performance layer. This enables images to be stacked and each layer to add differences compared to the layers below. The built image is a combination of these layers, offering reusability and efficient storage.
- **Layered Images:** Each instruction in a Dockerfile creates a new layer in the Docker image. Layers are cached and reused in subsequent builds, which speeds up the build process significantly. For instance, commonly used base images, such as ubuntu:latest, are downloaded and serve as the foundational layer for other application-specific layers.

Furthermore, containers allow for environment consistency across different deployment stages. By employing containers, developers can ensure that the applications act uniformly across different infrastructures. This is achieved by encapsulating the application and its dependencies within the container, thus eliminating the "it works on my machine" problem often encountered in traditional deployment processes.

The orchestration of containers through systems like Docker Swarm or Kubernetes introduces capabilities for deploying, scaling, and managing containerized applications across clusters of nodes. Such systems can automatically handle the complexity of container management, enhancing the robustness and ease of deploying large-scale microservices architectures.

By exploring these elements, the utility and significance of Docker containers as an essential tool for modern application development and deployment are underscored.

4.2 Starting Your First Container

Starting your first Docker container is a fundamental step towards mastering Docker. This process involves several key commands and concepts that will help solidify your understanding of Docker's core functionality. Generally, running a container requires specifying which image to use, as well as any necessary options like ports to expose or filesystems to mount.

To illustrate this, let's consider an example where we will start a Docker container using the official hello-world image. The hello-world image is a minimal Docker image that is often used to verify a working Docker installation.

First, ensure Docker is installed and running on your system. In a terminal, you can check if Docker is installed by running:

```
docker --version
```

This command should output the version of Docker installed, confirming that Docker is set up. Once Docker is confirmed as running, proceed with starting your first container.

To run a Docker container using the hello-world image, execute the following command:

```
docker run hello-world
```

Upon execution, Docker will search for the hello-world image in the local library. If the image is not available locally, Docker will download it from the Docker Hub. After pulling the image, Docker creates and starts a container from that image, and the container runs the commands specified in the image's configuration. The output will be similar to:

```
Hello from Docker!
This message shows that your installation appears to be working correctly.

To generate this message, Docker took the following steps:
 1. The Docker client contacted the Docker daemon.
 2. The Docker daemon pulled the "hello-world" image from the Docker Hub.
 3. The Docker daemon created a new container from that image which runs the
    executable that produces the output you are currently reading.
 4. The Docker daemon streamed that output to the Docker client, which sent it
    to your terminal.

To try something more ambitious, you can run an Ubuntu container with:
 $ docker run -it ubuntu bash

Share images, automate workflows, and more with a free Docker ID:
 https://hub.docker.com/

For more examples and ideas, visit:
 https://docs.docker.com/get-started/
```

This output delineates the steps Docker took to execute the container:

- **Client-Daemon Communication:** The Docker client communicates with the Docker daemon, requesting it to run a container.
- **Image Retrieval:** If the image isn't locally available, Docker pulls it from Docker Hub.
- **Container Creation:** Docker uses the image parameters to create a new container.
- **Execution and Output:** The container executes its command, and the output is streamed back to the client.

Next, let us delve deeper into starting a container with a more versatile image, such as Ubuntu. By using the Ubuntu image, we can explore more features of Docker containers. The command for running an Ubuntu container interactively is:

```
docker run -it ubuntu bash
```

Here, the options specified are:

- **-i:** Allows for interactive mode, which keeps stdin open even if not attached.

- **-t:** Allocates a pseudo-TTY, which is essential for terminal interaction.
- **ubuntu:** Specifies the image to use.
- **bash:** Specifies the command to run inside the container.

When executed, the terminal will switch to the command line inside the running Ubuntu container. The prompt changes to indicate that you are now working within the container environment:

root@<container_id>:/#

You can now run typical Linux commands inside this container. For example:

```
apt-get update
```

This updates the package lists for available packages in Ubuntu, simulating a scenario where a user may want to install additional software inside the container. To exit from the container's interactive mode, use the exit command:

```
exit
```

Once exited, the container stops. You can list all containers (both running and stopped) using:

```
docker ps -a
```

This command outputs the following information about each container:

- **Container ID:** Unique identifier for each container.
- **Image:** Image used to create the container.
- **Command:** Command that was run when the container started.
- **Created:** Time when the container was created.
- **Status:** Current state of the container (e.g., exited, running).
- **Ports:** Port mappings (if any).
- **Names:** User-defined names for easier container identification.

An example output might be:

```
CONTAINER ID  IMAGE        COMMAND   CREATED          STATUS                     PORTS  NAMES
879c39f36c01  ubuntu       "bash"    10 minutes ago   Exited (0) 5 minutes ago          objective_payne
d27538f3cd01  hello-world  "echo"    20 minutes ago   Exited (0) 15 minutes ago         nifty_blackwell
```

The CONTAINER ID and NAMES fields uniquely identify containers, simplifying management tasks. If you wish to rerun a stopped container, use the start command coupled with the container's ID or name:

```
docker start -i <container_id or name>
```

With this command, the -i flag re-attaches the terminal for interactive input. The foundational skills acquired through starting and interacting with Docker containers are pivotal for advanced Docker functionalities and management.

4.3 Container Lifecycle Management

Effective management of container lifecycles is essential for maintaining a robust and efficient Docker environment. The lifecycle of a Docker container encompasses several stages, including creation, running, stopping, restarting, and removal. Understanding these stages and the associated Docker commands will enable smooth and effective container operations.

A container's lifecycle begins with its creation from a Docker image. The command to create a container is:

```
docker create [OPTIONS] IMAGE [COMMAND] [ARG...]
```

The docker create command initializes a new container but does not start it. This command is useful when you wish to configure the container's settings before its initial run. It returns the unique container ID that can be used for subsequent operations.

Once a container is created, it can be started using the docker start command:

```
docker start [OPTIONS] CONTAINER [CONTAINER...]
```

This command transitions the container from the created state to the running state. Multiple containers can be started simultaneously by specifying multiple container IDs or names.

To run a container immediately from an image in one step, the docker run command can be used:

```
docker run [OPTIONS] IMAGE [COMMAND] [ARG...]
```

The docker run command combines the creation and starting of a container in a single operation. It also supports several options to customize the container's environment, such as setting environment variables, mapping ports, and mounting volumes.

Occasionally, there might be a need to stop a running container. This can be achieved with the docker stop command:

```
docker stop [OPTIONS] CONTAINER [CONTAINER...]
```

The docker stop command sends a SIGTERM signal to the running container, giving it time to gracefully shutdown processes. After the container has been stopped, it transitions to the exited state.

In situations where a quick and forceful stop is required, the docker kill command can be used instead:

```
docker kill [OPTIONS] CONTAINER [CONTAINER...]
```

This command sends a SIGKILL signal, immediately terminating the container's processes and transitioning it to the exited state.

Restarting containers is a frequent operation, especially during development or when applying updates. Docker provides the docker restart command for this purpose:

```
docker restart [OPTIONS] CONTAINER [CONTAINER...]
```

The docker restart command stops and then starts the specified container, allowing you to refresh the application's state or the environment without removing and recreating the container.

To keep track of the containers' states and obtain detailed information about their status, the docker ps command is highly valuable:

```
docker ps [OPTIONS]
```

This command lists all running containers by default, but it can be extended to include stopped containers by adding the -a option. The output includes essential details such as container IDs, images, status, and the commands being executed.

Cleaning up unused or unnecessary containers is crucial for maintaining a tidy environment and freeing up system resources. The docker rm command deletes one or more containers that are no longer needed:

```
docker rm [OPTIONS] CONTAINER [CONTAINER...]
```

The docker rm command requires the container to be in the stopped state before it can be removed. For containers that are still running, the docker rm -f option can be used to forcefully stop and remove them.

Once a container is removed, its data and state are permanently lost unless persistent storage mechanisms, such as volumes or bind mounts, are employed.

One of the key aspects of managing container lifecycles is automating the process. Docker supports several strategies for automated container management, including restart policies. Restart policies ensure that containers are automatically restarted under specified conditions. The policy can be set during the container creation using the –restart option:

```
docker run --restart [Restart Policy] IMAGE [COMMAND] [ARG...]
```

Common restart policies include:

- no: Do not automatically restart the container (default).
- always: Always restart the container if it stops.
- on-failure: Restart the container only if it exits with a non-zero exit code.
- unless-stopped: Restart the container unless it is explicitly stopped or Docker itself restarts.

Another powerful tool for lifecycle management is Docker Compose, which allows for defining and running multi-container Docker applications. With a docker-compose.yml file, you can specify the services, networks, and volumes required by the application, enabling comprehensive lifecycle control through a single command:

```
docker-compose up
```

```
docker-compose down
```

In essence, mastering the lifecycle management of Docker containers is pivotal for orchestrating and maintaining containerized applications efficiently. Through proficient use of Docker commands and automation tools, administrators can ensure that containerized environments remain stable, resilient, and optimized.

4.4 Running Containers in Detached Mode

Detached mode in Docker allows a container to run in the background, decoupled from the terminal. This mode is particularly useful for long-running services or applications that do not require direct interaction after startup. To implement this mode, the -d option is employed during the docker run command invocation.

Basic Usage

The simplest way to run a container in detached mode involves appending the -d flag to your docker run command. An example showcasing the initiation of an NGINX web server in detached mode is provided below:

```
docker run -d --name mynginx nginx
```

This command pulls the latest NGINX image (if not locally available) and starts a container named mynginx in the background. To verify successful startup, utilize the docker ps command:

```
docker ps
```

```
CONTAINER ID   IMAGE   COMMAND                  CREATED          STATUS         PORTS                                NAMES
d3d1fd3195b6   nginx   "/docker-entrypoint...."   10 seconds ago   Up 9 seconds   0.0.0.0:80->80/tcp, :::80->80/tcp   mynginx
```

The output confirms the container is running, with port 80 exposed.

Interacting with Detached Containers

To interact with containers running in detached mode, standard Docker commands can be used. For instance, to view logs generated by the NGINX server, employ the docker logs command:

```
docker logs mynginx
```

Output from this command presents recent log entries, providing insight into the container's operations.

In cases that necessitate command execution within the running container, docker exec proves beneficial. An example involves accessing the NGINX configuration directory:

```
docker exec -it mynginx ls /etc/nginx
```

```
conf.d
fastcgi_params
mime.types
modules
nginx.conf
proxy_params
scgi_params
uwsgi_params
```

This output lists the configuration files and directories within the container, confirming successful execution.

Stopping and Restarting

Managing the lifecycle of detached containers involves their termination and potential reactivation. To stop the mynginx container, execute:

```
docker stop mynginx
```

This command initiates an orderly shutdown, ensuring any ongoing processes are terminated gracefully. To restart the container, use:

```
docker start mynginx
```

These commands facilitate the maintenance of service continuity, crucial for applications requiring high availability.

Benefits and Considerations

Running containers in detached mode offers several advantages. Primarily, it allows the terminal to remain free for other tasks, enhancing multitasking capabilities. Moreover, background execution ensures that services remain operational even if the terminal session is terminated, boosting service reliability.

However, there are considerations to account for. Debugging issues in detached containers can be more challenging, as it necessitates indirect interactions through logs or docker exec. Furthermore, resource consumption by detached containers could be less visible to the operator, necessitating diligent monitoring to prevent system resource exhaustion.

Advanced Configurations

Advanced use cases involve sophisticated options during container startup. For instance, associating a detached container with a specified network, defining environment variables, or mounting volumes. An example configuring a detached MySQL container with an environmental variable for the root password is depicted below:

```
docker run -d --name mymysql -e MYSQL_ROOT_PASSWORD=securepassword
     mysql
```

```
docker network create mynet
docker run -d --name mynginx --network mynet nginx
```

In this scenario, mynet is a user-defined network which the NGINX container utilizes, illustrating the flexibility of Docker's detached mode functionality.

Running containers in detached mode is integral for managing services efficiently. Effectively leveraging this mode optimizes system utilization, ensuring seamless and continuous service delivery. When orchestrated properly, it underpins the reliable operation of containerized applications, indispensable in production environments.

4.5 Exposing and Mapping Ports

Exposing and mapping ports in Docker containers is a fundamental aspect of enabling communication between the containerized application and the outside world. When running applications inside Docker containers, they often need to be reachable from the host machine, other containers, or external networks. Docker provides mechanisms to expose and map ports to facilitate this communication.

By default, Docker containers are isolated from the network of the host machine and other containers. They have their own network namespace that includes their own IP addresses, network interfaces, and routing tables. For outside traffic to reach the container, Docker allows the binding of container ports to the host ports. This can be achieved using the -p or –publish flag during the docker run command. The syntax for this flag is:

```
-p <host_port>:<container_port>
```

Consider an example where an Nginx web server is running inside a Docker container. Nginx's default port is 80. To make this service accessible from the host machine on port 8080, the Docker container can be started with the following command:

```
docker run -d -p 8080:80 nginx
```

In the example above, -d runs the container in detached mode, -p 8080:80 maps port 8080 on the host to port 80 inside the container. The Nginx service inside the container is now accessible on the host machine at http://localhost:8080.

It is also possible to bind a container port to a specific IP address on the host system. This is useful when the host has multiple IP addresses or network interfaces and you want to restrict access to a particular address. The syntax for this is:

```
-p <host_ip>:<host_port>:<container_port>
```

For example, the following command binds the container port 80 to port 8080 on the host's IP address 192.168.1.100:

```
docker run -d -p 192.168.1.100:8080:80 nginx
```

In some scenarios, you might need to expose a range of ports instead of individual ones. Docker supports this by allowing ranges to be specified. The syntax is as follows:

```
-p <start_host_port>-<end_host_port>:<start_container_port>-<
      end_container_port>
```

This allows multiple contiguous ports to be published at once. For instance:

```
docker run -d -p 8080-8085:80-85 some_image
```

This command maps ports 8080 to 8085 on the host to ports 80 to 85 in the container.

Docker also allows the use of the -P or –publish-all flag to publish all exposed ports to random ports on the host machine. Each exposed port will be mapped to a random high-numbered port (generally above 32768) on the host:

```
docker run -d -P some_image
```

The docker ps command shows which ports are mapped:

```
CONTAINER ID   IMAGE        COMMAND    CREATED          STATUS         PORTS                    NAMES
17a0b0c1d2e3   some_image   "/app"     10 seconds ago   Up 8 seconds   0.0.0.0:32770->80/tcp    brave_mayer
```

In the above output, the container's port 80 is mapped to the host's port 32770.

Use cases often require ensuring the container always uses the same port on the host. Specifying explicit port mappings guarantees consistent availability and accessibility for applications.

Furthermore, some applications may need to communicate with each other via specific ports across different containers. Docker networks, which allow containers to discover each other and communicate over custom-defined networks, come into play. Exposing and mapping ports remain relevant when communication needs to extend beyond the Docker network, to the external host or the wider internet.

In practice, it is essential to balance port exposure and security. Exposing numerous ports unnecessarily increases security risks. Only necessary ports should be mapped and firewall rules should be configured appropriately to protect services from unauthorized access.

Understanding and managing the exposure and mapping of ports is critical for successful Docker deployment. It ensures that applications inside containers are accessible and can communicate with other services and users as intended.

4.6 Running Interactive Containers

Interactive containers in Docker are pivotal for various administrative and developmental tasks, including debugging, running tests, or interacting with applications directly. An interactive container provides a way for users to execute commands inside the container, leveraging a shell like bash or sh.

To run an interactive container, the -it options are utilized with the docker run command. The -i flag ensures that the container process is attached to the terminal's standard input (stdin), allowing you to send commands interactively. The -t flag allocates a pseudo-TTY, providing an interactive terminal session within the container. Here is an example of how to run an interactive container:

```
docker run -it ubuntu /bin/bash
```

In this example, the command starts a container based on the ubuntu image and opens a bash shell. Once inside the container, you can execute any command available in the ubuntu image.

```
root@container-id:/#
```

The prompt changes to indicate that you are now operating inside the container. You can then perform various tasks such as updating package lists, installing new software, or even running custom scripts:

```
apt-get update
apt-get install -y python3
```

Exiting the container will stop it unless explicitly run with the –rm option, which automatically removes the container upon exit. If the interactive session is terminated, the container will also cease execution. To exit the shell and stop the container, you can use the exit command:

```
exit
```

Working interactively is not limited to basic shells. Advanced use cases may involve running containers interactively with different images and executing various commands directly. Here is an example of using a Python image to start an interactive Python interpreter session:

```
docker run -it python:3.8 python
```

This command initiates a container from the python:3.8 image and starts the Python interpreter inside it. An essential aspect to note is that the commands and scripts executed within the interactive session are ephemeral unless proper volume mounts or Dockerfile instructions are employed to persist data.

Interactive containers are also beneficial for debugging purposes. Developers can manually intervene and inspect container processes, filesystems, and logs. For instance, after starting a web server in a container, the user might want to check configuration files or logs without restarting the container:

```
docker run -d --name webserver nginx
docker exec -it webserver /bin/bash
```

The docker exec command runs a new command in an already running container. With the -it flags, it attaches an interactive terminal to the running webserver container, providing a bash shell. This approach is crucial for troubleshooting live applications without interrupting their execution.

Interactive containers can be configured to have persistent storage by specifying volume mounts. This functionality is crucial when changes need to be retained beyond the lifespan of the container. By using the -v option, directories on the host can be mounted into the container:

```
docker run -it -v /host/path:/container/path ubuntu /bin/bash
```

This command mounts the directory /host/path from the host machine to /container/path inside the container. Any changes made in /container/path will be reflected in /host/path and vice versa, ensuring data persistence.

To facilitate repetitive tasks, custom entrypoints and command overrides can be configured in Dockerfiles or command lines. This allows containers to start with predefined scripts or commands, creating reproducible and efficient interactive environments. For instance, a Dockerfile with a tailored entrypoint:

```
FROM ubuntu
ENTRYPOINT ["/bin/bash"]
CMD ["-c", "echo Hello, Docker!"]
```

After building this Dockerfile into an image, any container started from this image will directly execute the echo Hello, Docker! command in a bash shell:

```
docker build -t custom-ubuntu .
docker run -it custom-ubuntu
```

As demonstrated, interactive containers offer substantial flexibility and control, allowing users to customize their workflows, debug applications, and persist data efficiently. These features make interactive containers indispensable for both development and operational environments in Docker.

4.7 Working with Container Logs

Logs are essential for debugging, performance monitoring, and ensuring the reliability of software applications. Docker containers generate logs just like traditional applications. By default, Docker captures the standard output (stdout) and standard error (stderr) of processes running inside the container. To access these logs, Docker provides several commands and options.

To access the logs of a running container, the command docker logs is used. This command retrieves the logs from the container specified by its name or ID.

```
docker logs <container_name_or_id>
```

For example, retrieving logs from a container named my_container:

```
docker logs my_container
```

Viewing Real-Time Logs

To view logs in real-time, Docker offers the -follow option. This option keeps the log stream open and continuously displays new log entries as they are generated.

```
docker logs --follow <container_name_or_id>
```

Similar to the tail -f command in Unix-based systems, this is particularly useful for watching live logs during development or troubleshooting.

Time-stamped Logs

Logs can also be prefixed with timestamps using the –timestamps option, providing better context for when log entries were generated. This can be critical for diagnosing issues that are time-dependent.

```
docker logs --timestamps <container_name_or_id>
```

This will result in output similar to:

```
2023-10-15T12:34:56.789Z Container started
2023-10-15T12:35:01.123Z Performing health check
```

Log Output Limits

To limit the number of log entries displayed, the –tail option is used. It allows specifying how many lines from the end of the log to display.

```
docker logs --tail <number_of_lines> <container_name_or_id>
```

For instance, to display the last 50 lines of logs:

```
docker logs --tail 50 my_container
```

Combining Options

Options can be combined to refine log output. To view the last 100 lines of logs in real-time with timestamps:

```
docker logs --tail 100 --follow --timestamps my_container
```

Configuring Logging Drivers

Docker supports multiple logging drivers, enabling integration with logging backends such as Syslog, Fluentd, and AWS CloudWatch. The default logging driver is json-file, which writes container logs as JSON.

To set a specific logging driver, the –log-driver option is used when starting a container.

```
docker run --log-driver syslog <image_name>
```

Moreover, logging options specific to the chosen logging driver can be configured using the –log-opt flag.

```
docker run --log-driver syslog --log-opt syslog-address=tcp://192.168.0.1:514 <
    image_name>
```

This command configures the container to send logs to a remote Syslog server at 192.168.0.1 on port 514.

Inspecting Logging Configuration

To inspect the logging configuration of a running container, the docker inspect command is used. This command provides detailed information about the container, including the logging driver and options.

```
docker inspect --format '{{.HostConfig.LogConfig}}' <container_name_or_id>
```

Rotating Logs

Log rotation is crucial for managing disk space and ensuring log files do not grow indefinitely. Docker provides built-in support for log rotation with the json-file logging driver. To set up log rotation, max-size and max-file options are specified:

```
docker run --log-opt max-size=10m --log-opt max-file=3 <image_name>
```

This command limits each log file to 10 megabytes and retains up to 3 log files.

By carefully monitoring and managing container logs, potential issues can be identified and addressed promptly, contributing to the reliability and robustness of Dockerized applications.

4.8 Accessing Containers via Shell

Interacting with Docker containers often necessitates direct access to their shell environment. This can be indispensable for troubleshooting, configuration, and running directly interactive commands. Accessing the shell of a running container can be accomplished using a few Docker commands, primarily focusing on the docker exec and docker attach commands. Detailed understanding and correct usage of these commands enhance operational efficiency and container management.

The docker exec command allows you to run commands inside a running container. For instance, starting a bash shell session inside an existing container can be achieved with:

```
docker exec -it <container_id_or_name> /bin/bash
```

Here, the -it flag is a combination of two options: -i for interactive mode, and -t for allocating a pseudo-TTY. This permits interactive shell access, enabling command execution as though done directly on a traditional server.

Example output from the above command:

```
root@container_id:/#
```

In cases where containers do not include /bin/bash, such as with minimalist images like alpine, you may need to use an alternative shell:

```
docker exec -it <container_id_or_name> /bin/sh
```

The output is similar:

```
/ #
```

Using docker exec, environment variables, additional options, and specific commands can be specified as needed. For example, to list files in a container's directory interactively:

```
docker exec -it <container_id_or_name> ls /path/to/directory
```

The docker attach command attaches your terminal to a running container's main process. This can be useful when you need to interact with the container's primary process, such as when an application provides a command-line interface:

```
docker attach <container_id_or_name>
```

Unlike docker exec, docker attach connects directly to the input/output streams of the container's primary process, which can be beneficial for monitoring or interactive application sessions. However, it does not provide the same flexibility for executing arbitrary commands.

To detach from a container while using docker attach, the escape sequence Ctrl+P Ctrl+Q can be employed. This keeps the container running without terminating your session or causing container disruptions.

For embedding commands within automated scripts, non-interactive mode with docker exec is advantageous:

```
docker exec <container_id_or_name> command_to_run
```

Output from the above command would be:

```
command_output
```

Additionally, Docker provides options to access container-specific logs, which can complement direct shell access. Commands like:

```
docker logs <container_id_or_name>
```

produce:

```
log_output
```

Integrating direct shell access into regular maintenance tasks is critical, especially for debugging purposes. Understanding and utilizing docker exec and docker attach commands ensures comprehensive management and operational control over Docker containers.

4.9 Stopping and Restarting Containers

Understanding how to stop and restart Docker containers is paramount for effective container lifecycle management. This knowledge enables developers to manage resources efficiently and maintain application availability during development, testing, and deployment phases. Containers can be stopped gracefully, killed, restarted, or paused, each method serving different purposes as needed.

Stopping a Container

Stopping a container is akin to shutting down a computer system; it allows the application running inside to terminate processes gracefully. The primary command to stop a running container is docker stop. When this command is issued, Docker sends a SIGTERM signal to the main process running inside the container. This signal informs the process to shut down cleanly. If the process has not terminated within a specified timeout, Docker then sends a SIGKILL signal, forcing an immediate shutdown.

```
docker stop <container\_id>
```

The <container_id> can be either the container's unique ID or its name. Optionally, a timeout value can be specified:

```
docker stop -t 30 <container\_id>
```

In this example, Docker will wait 30 seconds after sending the SIGTERM signal before sending SIGKILL.

Killing a Container

In cases where a container must be stopped immediately, without waiting for graceful shutdown, the docker kill command can be used. This command sends a SIGKILL signal directly to the container.

```
docker kill <container\_id>
```

The immediate cessation of processes within the container can be critical in scenarios involving malfunctioning or unresponsive applications.

Restarting a Container

Restarting a container stops and then starts the container anew. This action is useful for applying configuration changes, recovering from failure states, or redeploying updated versions of applications. The command to restart a container is:

```
docker restart <container\_id>
```

Similar to the docker stop command, a timeout for the stop phase can be specified:

```
docker restart -t 30 <container\_id>
```

Here, Docker will wait 30 seconds before force-stopping the container if it does not terminate on its own.

Pausing and Unpausing a Container

Pausing a container temporarily suspends its processes without stopping the container. This can be useful for temporarily halting resource usage without terminating the container's state. To pause a container:

```
docker pause <container\_id>
```

To resume the container's processes:

```
docker unpause <container\_id>
```

Checking Container Status

It is essential to verify the status of a container after issuing stop, kill, restart, pause, or unpause commands. The docker ps command lists all running containers, while the docker ps -a command lists all containers, including those that have been stopped. Here is the output you might see for docker ps -a:

```
CONTAINER ID   IMAGE    COMMAND                   CREATED         STATUS                       PORTS     NAMES
e5dd5437e2bc   ubuntu   "/bin/bash"               2 minutes ago   Exited (0) 46 seconds ago              determined_poincare
5d6c7v29d1de   nginx    "nginx -g 'daemon of..."  5 minutes ago   Up 3 minutes                 80/tcp    nostalgic_euler
```

In this example, the container with ID e5dd5437e2bc is in an exited state, indicating it has been stopped.

Practical Example

Consider a scenario where you have an Nginx container running, which needs to be restarted to apply new configuration changes. First, check the running container status:

```
docker ps
```

Expected output:

```
CONTAINER ID   IMAGE   COMMAND                  CREATED          STATUS          PORTS    NAMES
524df2d4ee4e   nginx   "nginx -g 'daemon off;'" 10 minutes ago   Up 10 minutes   80/tcp   vibrant_morse
```

To restart the container:

```
docker restart 524df2d4ee4e
```

Post-restart, verify the container is running correctly:

```
docker ps
```

Expected output:

```
CONTAINER ID   IMAGE   COMMAND                  CREATED          STATUS          PORTS    NAMES
524df2d4ee4e   nginx   "nginx -g 'daemon off;'" 11 minutes ago   Up 5 seconds    80/tcp   vibrant_morse
```

In this example, the Nginx container has successfully restarted and has been running for 5 seconds post-restart. This verification step confirms the successful application of the new configuration.

Meticulous management of container state changes—involving stopping, killing, restarting, pausing, and resuming—enhances Docker's utility in orchestrating robust, reliable applications.

4.10 Removing Containers

Effective management of Docker containers necessitates understanding the process of removing containers, especially when they are no longer needed. Removing containers helps free up system resources and maintain a clean environment. Docker provides several mechanisms for removing containers, including removing individual containers and removing multiple containers simultaneously.

To remove a single Docker container, use the docker rm command followed by the container ID or name. The general syntax is as follows:

```
docker rm <container_id_or_name>
```

For example, to remove a container with the name mycontainer, the command would be:

```
docker rm mycontainer
```

If the container is currently running, you will encounter an error message indicating that the container cannot be removed while it is running. In such cases, the -f option can be utilized to force the removal of the running container. This option stops the container before removing it:

```
docker rm -f mycontainer
```

It is also possible to remove multiple containers simultaneously by listing their IDs or names after the docker rm command. To remove multiple containers, provide a space-separated list of container IDs or names:

```
docker rm <container_id_or_name1> <container_id_or_name2> <
    container_id_or_name3>
```

Sometimes, multiple unused or 'dangling' containers accumulate within the system. Removing all stopped containers can be efficiently accomplished using the docker container prune command. This command removes all containers that are not currently running:

```
docker container prune
```

Executing this command prompts a confirmation request to delete all stopped containers.

```
WARNING! This will remove all stopped containers.
Are you sure you want to continue? [y/N] y
```

After confirming, Docker removes the stopped containers and displays the amount of reclaimed disk space.

To provide more control, Docker enables filtering the containers that should be removed based on specific criteria. For instance, using labels, which are key-value pairs attached to containers and images, allows for selective removal. The following example demonstrates how to remove containers labeled with 'app=web':

```
docker container prune --filter "label=app=web"
```

This command will only remove containers with the specified label that are in a stopped state.

Removing containers that depend on certain volumes or networks can also be managed effectively. However, it is essential to remove the dependent containers before deleting such volumes or networks to avoid dependency issues. This ensures proper cleanup of resources associated with containers.

It is crucial to be aware that removing a container does not delete the associated image. The container removal process does not automatically free up space occupied by the image. Therefore, managing images separately is necessary for optimized disk space utilization.

Understanding the implications of container removal helps maintain a clean Docker environment while efficiently managing resources. Avoid inadvertently removing critical containers by verifying the container IDs or names before executing the removal commands. This practice ensures accuracy and prevents disruption of running applications.

4.11 Linking and Networking Containers

Linking and networking Docker containers effectively allows communication between different containers and external systems. This section addresses methods for linking containers, configuring networks, and ensuring secure and robust inter-container communication.

The traditional method for linking containers is the deprecated –link flag, which, while still functional, has been largely replaced by Docker's network features. Instead, the use of custom networks provides a more flexible and powerful mechanism for container networking.

Creating a Custom Network

A custom network can be created using the Docker CLI. By default, Docker creates a bridge network, but creating a custom bridge network gives more control over communication between containers.

```
docker network create my_custom_network
```

This command establishes a new bridge network named my_custom_network. To validate the creation of the network, the following command can be used:

```
docker network ls
```

The output should list my_custom_network among other networks:

```
NETWORK ID      NAME                DRIVER     SCOPE
f3d7c3d975f4    my_custom_network   bridge     local
```

Connecting Containers to a Network

To connect a container to this network, the network name is specified at the time of container creation.

```
docker run -d --name container1 --network my_custom_network my_image
docker run -d --name container2 --network my_custom_network my_image
```

This attaches both container1 and container2 to my_custom_network. Containers on the same network can communicate by referencing each other by their container names.

Verifying Container Networking

To verify that the containers can communicate, one container can be connected to another. For instance, using a simple CentOS image with a netcat (nc) command to send a ping:

```
docker run -d --name container3 --network my_custom_network centos sleep 1000
docker exec -it container3 /bin/bash
nc -vz container2 80
```

The output should confirm the connection attempt:

```
container2 (172.18.0.2:80) open
```

DNS Resolution

Docker networks are equipped with an embedded DNS server. This server handles container name resolution, allowing containers to find each other using their names. This feature simplifies configuring and maintaining inter-container communication.

Inspecting Networks

The docker network inspect command shows detailed information about the network and connected containers.

```
docker network inspect my_custom_network
```

Typical output includes a representation of the configuration and containers using this network:

```
[
  {
    "Name": "my_custom_network",
    "Id": "f3d7c3d975f4",
    ...
    "Containers": {
      "2c73dcd6355f": {
        "Name": "container1",
        ...
      },
      "ecc70a77af58": {
        "Name": "container2",
        ...
      }
    }
  }
]
```


External Networking

Connecting Docker containers to external networks requires exposing ports. The -p flag in the run command maps container ports to host ports.

```
docker run -d --name web_container -p 8080:80 nginx
```

This command maps port 8080 on the host to port 80 on the web_container, allowing external access via http://host_IP:8080.

Overlay Networks

Docker's overlay networks enable building scalable, multi-host networks, suitable for services in a distributed environment. Creating an overlay network typically involves configuring a Docker Swarm cluster.

Initiate a swarm:

```
docker swarm init
```

Then, create the overlay network:

```
docker network create -d overlay my_overlay_network
```

Services can be deployed to this overlay network for inter-host communication.

```
docker service create --name my_service --network my_overlay_network my_image
```

Multiple hosts in the swarm use this overlay network to manage service discovery and routing transparently.

Security

Security in container networking involves isolation and encryption. Ensuring containers communicate securely often means leveraging encrypted overlay networks and configuring appropriate firewall rules. Docker supports encrypted overlay networks by enabling the –opt encrypted flag.

```
docker network create -d overlay --opt encrypted secure_overlay_network
```

This configuration encrypts all traffic between containers on this network, enhancing security for sensitive applications.

Understanding the basics of Docker container networking combined with secure practices can significantly optimize container deployment and communication, leading to robust and scalable Dockerized applications.

4.12 Creating Persistent Storage for Containers

Persistent storage in Docker is critical for ensuring that data generated and used by containers is not lost when containers stop or are removed. This is particularly important for stateful applications such as databases, where data needs to be preserved across container lifecycles. Docker natively provides two mechanisms to handle persistent storage: volumes and bind mounts.

Volumes manage the storage on Docker's terms. They are completely managed by Docker and are stored in a part of the host filesystem which is managed by Docker ('/var/lib/docker/volumes/' on Linux). **Bind mounts** allow mounting a specific directory on the host filesystem within a container.

To create and use a volume, the following Docker commands are relevant:

- docker volume create
- docker run -v
- docker volume ls
- docker volume inspect
- docker volume rm

The command to create a new volume is:

```
docker volume create my\_volume
```

This creates a volume called my_volume that Docker manages.

To use this volume in a container, the -v flag is used with the docker run command:

```
docker run -d -v my_volume:/path/inside/container --name my_container my_image
```

The flag -v my_volume:/path/inside/container mounts the my_volume volume to the specified path inside the container. This ensures that any data written to /path/inside/container in my_container persists across container restarts or removals.

To list all volumes, the following command is utilised:

```
docker volume ls
```

To inspect a specific volume and get detailed information about it:

```
docker volume inspect my_volume
```

When a volume is no longer needed, it can be removed by using:

```
docker volume rm my_volume
```

When using bind mounts, the directory on the host machine is directly mounted into the container. The following command exemplifies this:

```
docker run -d -v /host/path:/container/path --name my_container my_image
```

Here, the path /host/path on the host machine is mounted to /container/path inside the container. This approach is useful when you need to share the data between the Docker host and containers or when you require absolute control over the directory being shared.

It is important to understand the implications of mounting options. Bind mounts inherently come with the risk of inadvertently exposing sensitive data to containers, or conversely, inadvertently allowing containers to influence the host filesystem. Therefore, the use of volumes or bind mounts should be carefully considered in the context of security and data integrity constraints.

A critical aspect of persistent storage is applying the appropriate access control. When volumes or bind mounts are created, by default they have the same permissions and ownership as the process that starts the container. You can explicitly set read-only flags to a volume to mitigate accidental data corruption:

```
docker run -d -v my_volume:/path/inside/container:ro --name my_container
    my_image
```

Here, the :ro suffix implies that the volume is mounted as read-only.

Persistent storage is also invaluable for complex multi-container applications managed by Docker Compose. Consider the following docker-compose.yaml example:

```
version: '3.8'
services:
  db:
    image: postgres:latest
    volumes:
      - mydbdata:/var/lib/postgresql/data
  web:
    image: nginx:latest
    volumes:
      - ./website:/usr/share/nginx/html
volumes:
  mydbdata:
```

In this configuration, the db service uses a Docker managed volume called mydbdata to persist PostgreSQL data. The web service uses a bind mount to serve static content from the host directory. This ensures that the data persisted by the database container is not lost if the container stops and that web content can be modified directly on the host system.

Understanding these storage mechanisms allows the design of robust Docker-based architectures where data integrity and persistence are maintained across various operational scenarios, facilitating the deployment of stateful applications in stateless environments.

4.13 Committing Containers to Images

Committing containers to images is a fundamental process in Docker, allowing you to save the state of a container as a new image. This is particularly useful when you have made changes to the container's filesystem, environment configurations, or installed new software, and you wish to preserve these changes for future use or distribution.

The command to commit an existing container to a new Docker image is docker commit. The general syntax for this command is:

```
docker commit [OPTIONS] CONTAINER [REPOSITORY[:TAG]]
```

Here, the CONTAINER refers to the ID or name of the container you want to commit, while REPOSITORY[:TAG] optionally specifies the repository and tag for the new image. If not provided, Docker will assign a default repository name and tag.

To illustrate, suppose you have a container with the ID e678d12f7ab0. You can commit this container to an image named my-application with the following command:

```
docker commit e678d12f7ab0 my-application:latest
```

After running this command, you can verify the newly created image using the docker images command:

```
docker images
```

You should see output similar to the following:

```
REPOSITORY       TAG       IMAGE ID       CREATED              SIZE
my-application   latest    dcfeb9294086   About a minute ago   570MB
```

In this output, the IMAGE ID uniquely identifies this image, and the CREATED column reflects the time of its creation.

Options can be passed to the docker commit command to control various aspects of the image creation process. Notable options include:

- -a, –author: Sets the image author.
- -m, –message: Adds a commit message describing the change.
- –change: Applies Dockerfile instructions to the created image.
- -p, –pause: Pauses the container while the image is committed (enabled by default).

For example, to add author information and a commit message, the command would be:

```
docker commit -a "John Doe" -m "Updated application dependencies" e678d12f7ab0 my
    -application:latest
```

The –change option allows you to modify the image configuration using Dockerfile syntax. You can change environment variables, entry points, commands, labels, hosts, and more. For example, to set an environment variable ENV_VAR to value, you would use:

```
docker commit --change="ENV ENV_VAR=value" e678d12f7ab0 my-application:latest
```

Committing changes to a new image is a powerful feature, but it is essential to consider the image's reproducibility and maintainability. Typically, Dockerfiles are preferable for defining images because they provide a clear, versioned, and easily reproducible means of constructing images. While commits are useful for rapid prototyping and capturing the state of a running container, maintaining Dockerfiles ensures a more sustainable and scalable approach.

Therefore, after committing a container to an image, it is a good practice to document the steps taken in a Dockerfile to mirror the committed state. This practice helps automate future builds and provides transparency to the image creation process.

4.14 Scaling Containers

Scaling containers is a crucial aspect of orchestrating applications in a dynamic environment. It enables the deployment of multiple instances of a containerized application to handle varying loads efficiently. Docker provides several tools and techniques to scale containers, ensuring high availability, and optimal resource utilization.

Docker Compose

Docker Compose allows for scaling of containers with simplicity when orchestrating multi-container applications. A docker-compose.yml file defines the services, networks, and volumes for the application. To scale a service up or down, the docker-compose up command is used with the –scale flag.

Here is an example of a docker-compose.yml file:

```
version: '3'
services:
  web:
    image: nginx
    ports:
      - "80:80"
  app:
    image: my_app
    environment:
      - DATABASE_HOST=db
  db:
    image: postgres
```

To scale the app service, use the following command:

```
docker-compose up --scale app=3
```

This command starts three instances of the app service. Docker Compose handles the orchestration and networking, ensuring each container instance runs seamlessly with the required dependencies.

Docker Swarm

Docker Swarm is a native clustering and orchestration tool for Docker. It transforms a group of Docker engines into a single virtual Docker Engine. Services in Docker Swarm can be scaled using the docker service scale command.

First, initialize a Docker Swarm:

```
docker swarm init
```

Create a service:

```
docker service create --name web --publish 80:80 nginx
```

To scale this service, use the following command:

```
docker service scale web=5
```

This command scales the web service to five instances. Docker Swarm manages the distribution and load balancing of these instances across the available nodes.

Kubernetes

Kubernetes, an open-source container orchestration tool, offers advanced scaling capabilities. It uses a declarative configuration to manage scaling via Deployments and ReplicaSets.

Here is an example of a Kubernetes deployment configuration file (deployment.yaml):

```
apiVersion: apps/v1
kind: Deployment
metadata:
  name: web-deployment
spec:
  replicas: 2
  selector:
    matchLabels:
      app: web
  template:
    metadata:
      labels:
        app: web
    spec:
      containers:
      - name: nginx
        image: nginx
        ports:
```

```
        - containerPort: 80
```

Apply the deployment file:

```
kubectl apply -f deployment.yaml
```

To scale the deployment, use:

```
kubectl scale deployment web-deployment --replicas=5
```

This command scales the web-deployment to five replicas. Kubernetes handles the distribution through sophisticated scheduling algorithms, ensuring optimal resource utilization.

Horizontal Pod Autoscaler

Kubernetes also supports Horizontal Pod Autoscaler (HPA), which automatically scales the number of pods in a deployment based on observed CPU utilization or other select metrics.

Enable HPA using:

```
kubectl autoscale deployment web-deployment --cpu-percent=50 --min=1 --max=10
```

This command creates an HPA for the web-deployment, scaling the number of replicas between 1 and 10 based on CPU utilization, with a target value of 50

Scaling Down

Scaling down is as essential as scaling up to free up resources and reduce costs. The methods for scaling down containers follow the same principles as scaling up but with decreased values:

For Docker Compose:

```
docker-compose up --scale app=1
```

For Docker Swarm:

```
docker service scale web=1
```

For Kubernetes:

```
kubectl scale deployment web-deployment --replicas=1
```

These commands reduce the number of container instances to one, ensuring that the application can continue to operate while conserving computational resources.

Through these tools and commands, precise container scaling can be effectively achieved, ensuring applications remain responsive, resilient, and cost-effective.

Chapter 5

Docker Networking

This chapter explores Docker's networking capabilities, discussing the various types of Docker networks such as bridge, host, overlay, and macvlan. It covers creating and managing custom networks, connecting containers to different networks, service discovery, and network security. The chapter also includes networking in Docker Compose and troubleshooting common networking issues.

5.1 Introduction to Docker Networking

Docker networking is a critical component for containerized applications, enabling communication both within and outside the host machine where the containers are running. This section delves into the fundamentals and essential concepts of Docker networking, offering a comprehensive understanding that serves as a foundation for the more advanced topics covered later in the chapter.

By default, Docker provides several network drivers for handling the various networking needs of containers. These drivers facilitate the connections among containers, between containers and the Docker host, and with external systems. The primary types of network drivers in Docker include bridge, host, overlay, and macvlan. Each type of network driver is designed to serve specific use cases, and understanding their differences is crucial for designing robust containerized applications.

Bridge Networking is the default network driver when a Docker container is started. In this mode, Docker creates a private internal network on the host machine where containers are connected using the docker0 bridge. Each container is assigned an IP address from this subnet, allowing the containers to communicate with each other through their IP addresses or exposed ports. This configuration suits scenarios where isolated container networks are required, with optional port forwarding to allow external access to specific services running inside the containers.

Host Networking bypasses the network abstraction layer introduced by Docker for simplicity and performance efficiency when containers need to use the host's networking stack directly. In this mode, the container shares the host's networking namespace, and no network isolation is provided between the container and the host. This configuration can improve performance for certain use cases where network latency and overhead are critical factors, such as high-performance computing or applications requiring low-latency network access.

Overlay Networking is designed to support container networking across multiple Docker hosts, typically used in a Docker Swarm or Kubernetes environment. It allows for the creation of a distributed network that can span across multiple nodes, enabling container-to-container communication even when they are on different physical or virtual machines. Overlay networks simplify the deployment of containerized applications that need to scale horizontally across a cluster of hosts.

Macvlan Networking assigns a unique MAC address to each container, making it appear as a separate physical device on the network. This network driver is useful for legacy applications that rely on MAC address-based network segregation or require direct Layer 2 network access. Macvlan networks can be configured to operate in bridge or passthru modes, providing flexibility in how containers are separated and interacted with on the network.

To illustrate and experiment with these networking concepts, consider the following command examples and their respective outputs. These commands help visualize how Docker networking operates and provide tangible evidence of the network configurations discussed.

```
docker run -d --name my_bridge_container nginx
```

This command starts a new container named my_bridge_container using the Nginx image, which will be connected to the default bridge network. To inspect the network configuration of this container, use the following command:

```
docker inspect my_bridge_container
```

The output would display details similar to the following:

```
"NetworkSettings": {
    "Bridge": "",
    "SandboxID": "abcdef123456",
    "HairpinMode": false,
    "LinkLocalIPv6Address": "",
    "LinkLocalIPv6PrefixLen": 0,
    "Ports": {
        "80/tcp": null
    },
    "SandboxKey": "/var/run/docker/netns/default",
    "SecondaryIPAddresses": null,
    "SecondaryIPv6Addresses": null,
    "EndpointID": "123abc456def",
    "Gateway": "172.17.0.1",
    "GlobalIPv6Address": "",
    "GlobalIPv6PrefixLen": 0,
    "IPAddress": "172.17.0.2",
    "IPPrefixLen": 16,
    "IPv6Gateway": "",
    "MacAddress": "02:42:ac:11:00:02",
    ...
}
```

From this information, it is evident that the container is assigned an IP address in the 172.17.0.0/16 subnet, with 172.17.0.1 as its gateway. This demonstrates the connectivity features and address assignment characteristic of bridge networks.

Understanding these core networking principles is essential as you progress through the following sections, which delve deeper into each network type and its management, as well as Docker's more advanced networking capabilities like custom networks, network security, and troubleshooting techniques.

5.2 Types of Docker Networks

Docker networking is foundational to deploying containerized applications that communicate effectively. Docker provides several network drivers to cater to various use cases, including development, production, and isolated environments. These drivers determine how Docker containers communicate with each other, with other services, and with the outside world. The primary types of Docker networks include bridge, host, overlay, and macvlan networks.

Bridge Networks

A bridge network is the default type of network created by Docker. When Docker is installed, a bridge network named bridge is automatically created. Containers that are started without specifying a network are connected to this bridge network. The bridge network is a private internal network created on the host. When a container is connected to the bridge network, it receives an IP address and can communicate with other containers on the same bridge network using this address.

To create a custom bridge network, use the following command:

```
$ docker network create --driver bridge my_bridge_network
```

This command creates a bridge network named my_bridge_network. You can connect containers to this network using the –network flag:

```
$ docker run -itd --name my_container --network my_bridge_network alpine
```

Bridge networks provide isolation and security, ensuring that containers connected to different bridge networks cannot directly communicate with each other. This makes bridge networks ideal for environments where inter-container communication within a defined boundary is necessary.

Host Networks

A host network removes the network isolation between the Docker container and the Docker host. When a container is run in the host network mode, it shares the network namespace of the host, allowing it to use the host's IP address. This effectively means that the container's networking configuration mirrors that of the host.

To run a container in the host network mode, use the –network host flag:

```
$ docker run -itd --name my_host_networked_container --network host alpine
```

Host networks are particularly useful when high performance is required and when network latency must be minimized. However, it reduces the level of isolation between the container and the host, potentially exposing the host to security vulnerabilities.

Overlay Networks

Overlay networks connect multiple Docker daemons together and allow swarm services to communicate with each other regardless of the node on which they are running. It can span across multiple hosts, thereby enabling distributed systems to communicate transparently.

Create an overlay network using the following command:

```
$ docker network create -d overlay my_overlay_network
```

For Docker Swarm mode, overlay networks are essential as they facilitate container communication across different nodes in a swarm. By connecting services to an overlay network, containers can reach each other regardless of which host they are running on.

Macvlan Networks

Macvlan networks assign a MAC address to each container's virtual network interface, making it appear as a physical device on the network. This allows containers to communicate directly with the physical network as if they were physical devices.

To create a macvlan network, execute:

```
$ docker network create -d macvlan \
    --subnet=192.168.1.0/24 \
    --gateway=192.168.1.1 \
    -o parent=eth0 my_macvlan_network
```

This command sets up a macvlan network named my_macvlan_network on the eth0 interface with the specified subnet and gateway. Containers connected to this network can be addressed just like any other device on the local network.

Each of these Docker network types serves specific purposes and is used based on the requirements of the containerized application being deployed. Bridge networks provide scoped inter-container communication, host networks are suitable for high-performance needs, overlay networks are built for orchestrated environments like Docker Swarm, and macvlan networks enable containers to be treated as physical devices on a network. Understanding these various networks allows for better design and deployment of complex, multi-container applications.

5.3 Bridge Networks

Docker includes an inbuilt networking driver called the 'bridge' driver, which enables the creation of a private internal network for containers to communicate with each other on the same host. By default, Docker creates a 'bridge' network named 'bridge' when the Docker daemon starts, and containers connected to this default network can communicate with each other using IP addresses.

Understanding bridge networks is fundamental for managing container interconnectivity efficiently. This section aims to provide an in-depth look at bridge networks, exploring their configuration, usage, and troubleshooting.

When a new container is created without specifying a network, Docker connects it to the default 'bridge' network. This default network provides network isolation between the container and the host, while still allowing outbound connections.

```
docker run -d --name webserver nginx
```

In this example, an NGINX container ('webserver') is created and connected to the default 'bridge' network. Docker assigns an IP address from the bridge network's subnet to the container.

To inspect the default bridge network and understand its configuration, use the following command:

```
docker network inspect bridge
```

The output of this command provides detailed information about the network, including the subnet, gateway, and connected containers.

```
[
  {
    "Name": "bridge",
    "Id": "e5cf0d369f3b",
    "Created": "2021-08-01T16:42:56.387028837Z",
    "Scope": "local",
    "Driver": "bridge",
    "EnableIPv6": false,
    "IPAM": {
      "Driver": "default",
      "Options": null,
      "Config": [
        {
          "Subnet": "172.17.0.0/16",
          "Gateway": "172.17.0.1"
        }
      ]
    },
    "Containers": {
      "a1031e5153347604424d927aa57d675c81bc55ab4adc41147f3": {
        "Name": "webserver",
        "EndpointID": "c491f3ad96df35c1e1cd512dd1b6561575024aeaf7a2e1db0e90e7e4e4c",
        "MacAddress": "02:42:ac:11:00:02",
        "IPv4Address": "172.17.0.2/16",
        "IPv6Address": ""
      }
    },
    "Options": {
      "com.docker.network.bridge.default_bridge": "true",
      "com.docker.network.bridge.enable_icc": "true",
      "com.docker.network.bridge.enable_ip_masquerade": "true",
      "com.docker.network.bridge.host_binding_ipv4": "0.0.0.0",
      "com.docker.network.bridge.name": "docker0",
      "com.docker.network.driver.mtu": "1500"
    },
    "Labels": {}
  }
]
```


The ‘docker0‘ bridge is crucial in the default setup. It acts as a virtual switch that allows all containers connected to the bridge network to communicate with each other. Any system's IP routing or NAT rules can be configured using ‘iptables‘ to control traffic flow between containers and the outside world.

Users can also create custom ‘bridge‘ networks to override defaults, thereby enhancing security and configuration specificity. Use the following command to create a new bridge network:

```
docker network create --driver bridge my_bridge_network
```

Once the network is created, observe its details using the inspect command:

```
docker network inspect my_bridge_network
```

Adding a container to the new network involves:

```
docker run -d --name webserver_custom --network my_bridge_network nginx
```

Containers in the same user-defined bridge network can talk to each other by their names, facilitating service discovery. The DNS resolution is managed by Docker.

To illustrate connecting multiple containers, consider the following example, which demonstrates creating two containers in the custom bridge network:

```
docker run -d --name webserver_custom --network my_bridge_network nginx
docker run -d --name dbserver --network my_bridge_network mysql
```

These containers can now discover each other by their container names and using internal Docker DNS service. The 'ping' command inside any container can test connectivity:

```
docker exec -it webserver_custom ping dbserver
```

This command will show the IP address assigned to 'dbserver' and provide ICMP echo responses, indicating successful connectivity.

Bridge networks leverage 'iptables' under the hood, ensuring that all packets between containers are appropriately routed. By default, Docker isolates containers from external networks, enforcing security.

```
docker network ls
```

Understanding potential issues in bridge networks starts with these inspection and listing commands. For example, if network connectivity between containers fails, verify they are on the same network and use the 'docker logs' command to inspect service-specific logs.

For more complex setups, network troubleshooting tools like 'tcpdump' or 'traceroute' can be installed in containers to provide further insights into networking issues.

With mastery of Docker bridge networks, one can facilitate seamless and secure inter-container communication, bolstering the reliability and efficiency of containerized applications.

5.4 Host Networks

In Docker, a host network provides near-native performance and direct access to the host machine's network interface. When a container is attached to the host network, it bypasses Docker's network isolation and directly shares the host's network stack. This chapter elaborates on the specifics of host networks, their benefits, and potential drawbacks, as well as examples of how to use them effectively.

Using the host network mode is straightforward with the Docker CLI. To run a container with the host network, the –network host flag is used. The following command illustrates running an Nginx container on the host network:

```
docker run --rm --network host nginx
```

In this example, the Nginx server directly binds to the host's network interface, listening on the same port that the container would if it were running outside Docker.

One of the primary advantages of host networks is the reduction of network latency and overhead since it eliminates the translation between container and host network layers that typically occurs in Docker's bridge networking. This is particularly beneficial for high-performance applications that require low-latency network communication, such as real-time data processing systems.

However, it is essential to consider the implications of using the host network mode. Containers running on the host's network interface have potential security risks since they expose the host's network stack. This configuration can inadvertently share more resources and services than intended. Additionally, port conflicts can arise if multiple services attempt to bind to the same port on the host. Containers on the host network can no longer rely on Docker's isolation to automatically prevent such conflicts.

When using host networking in a Docker Compose file, the network mode is specified within the service definition. Consider the following example, which exhibits a simple Docker Compose setup for running an Nginx server in the host network mode:

```
version: '3.8'

services:
  web:
    image: nginx:latest
    network_mode: host
```

In this configuration, the Nginx container will run on the host network, ensuring direct communication with the host's network stack.

To inspect details about containers running on the host network, Docker provides the network command. Here is how you can list containers connected to the host network:

```
docker network inspect host
```

The output will describe all the containers connected to the host network along with their network settings.

```
[
  {
    "Name": "host",
    "Id": "acc86b5f34...",
    "Created": "2023-10-03T20:09:15.64490989Z",
    "Scope": "local",
    "Driver": "host",
    "EnableIPv6": false,
    "IPAM": {
      "Driver": "default",
      "Config": []
    },
    "Containers": {
      "a131bc0a48...": {
        "Name": "nginx",
        "EndpointID": "a12e23c6ca...",
        "MacAddress": "",
        "IPv4Address": "",
        "IPv6Address": ""
      }
    },
    "Options": {},
    "Labels": {}
  }
]
```

Combining the host network with other Docker features, such as volume mounts and environment variables, can create powerful and efficient application setups. Consider the following example to mount a configuration file and set environment variables for an application running in host mode:

```
docker run --rm \
  --network host \
  -v $(pwd)/config.json:/app/config.json \
  -e ENV=production \
  myapp:latest
```

In this case, the container myapp mounts the config.json file from the current directory to /app/config.json inside the container and runs with the environment variable ENV set to production, all while leveraging the host network.

Considering the trade-offs, it is crucial to use host networks judiciously, especially for applications requiring enhanced isolation and security. For services needing minimal network latency and direct interaction with the host's network, deploying on a host network mode can achieve the required performance levels effectively. However, it mandates careful management of networking configurations to avoid conflicts and unintentional exposure of the host system's networking resources.

5.5 Overlay Networks

Overlay networks facilitate the communication between multiple Docker hosts, enabling containers on different hosts to communicate as if they were on the same local network. This network model abstracts the underlying physical network, providing scalability and isolation for services in a multi-host cluster environment. Overlay networks are integral to Docker Swarm and Kubernetes deployments, where multi-host communication is a necessity.

Fundamental Concepts

The overlay network creates a virtual subnet that is superimposed over an existing physical network infrastructure. Packets within an overlay network are typically encapsulated using tunneling protocols such as VXLAN (Virtual Extensible LAN).

The main concepts involved in overlay networking include:

- **VXLAN Encapsulation**: VXLAN encapsulates Layer 2 Ethernet frames within Layer 3 UDP packets. This allows the creation of a Layer 2 network on top of a Layer 3 infrastructure. It uses a unique 24-bit VXLAN Network Identifier (VNI) to identify overlay networks, supporting up to 16 million unique network segments.

- **Virtual Distributed Router (VDR)**: This acts as a logical router for the overlay network. Each Docker host participating in the overlay network hosts an instance of the VDR, which is responsible for routing traffic between containers.

- **Service Discovery**: Overlay networks integrate with Docker's service discovery mechanism, allowing containers to locate each other via DNS. Docker manages the DNS resolution internally, making service discovery seamless.

- **Encryption**: Enabling IPsec encryption on overlay networks provides secure communication by encrypting packets in transit.

Creating Overlay Networks

Creating an overlay network in Docker requires the use of a key-value store (e.g., Consul, Etcd, or a Docker Swarm manager) to coordinate network state across multiple hosts. Docker handles the complex process of creating and managing the VXLAN tunnels.

To create an overlay network, use the following docker network create command:

```
docker network create -d overlay --attachable my_overlay_network
```

The -d overlay parameter specifies the network driver as overlay, and the –attachable option allows standalone containers to attach to the network in addition to Swarm services.

Example Scenario

Consider a Docker Swarm setup with three nodes: manager1, worker1, and worker2. To create an overlay network named app_network and deploy services:

1. Initialize Docker Swarm mode on manager1:

```
docker swarm init --advertise-addr <manager1-IP>
```

2. Join worker1 and worker2 to the Swarm:

```
docker swarm join --token <swarm-token> <manager1-IP>:2377
```

3. Create the overlay network:

```
docker network create -d overlay app_network
```

4. Deploy a service on the network:

```
docker service create --name web_service --network app_network nginx
```

5. Verify network connectivity among service replicas:

```
docker service ps web_service
docker exec -it <container-ID> ping <another-container-ID>
```

Service Discovery

Docker handles service discovery in overlay networks using an embedded DNS server. Containers can reach services by name, resolving internally managed DNS entries. For instance, if a service named db_service is running on the app_network, containers can connect using db_service:port.

Network Security

Overlay networks can employ IPsec for encryption, ensuring secure communication between Docker hosts. To enable this, configure the overlay network with encryption by setting the -opt flag:

```
docker network create -d overlay --opt encrypted my_secure_overlay
```

This configuration ensures that all traffic on my_secure_overlay is encrypted using IPsec.

Practical Use Cases

Overlay networks are particularly beneficial in scenarios such as:

- **Microservices Architecture**: Each service instance, possibly across multiple hosts, communicates seamlessly.
- **High Availability Setups**: Ensuring containers on different hosts can communicate despite host failures.
- **Multi-cloud Deployments**: Connecting Docker hosts across different cloud providers or data centers.

The overlay network abstracts the complexities of cluster-wide communication, manages routing and service discovery, and provides options for security through encryption, making it a robust solution for orchestrated environments.

5.6 Macvlan Networks

Macvlan networks allow user-created virtual interfaces to be assigned directly to containers. This method provides each container with its own unique MAC address, empowering them to appear as separate physical devices on the network. This network mode is particularly useful for legacy applications that require native Layer 2 functionalities or need direct access to the physical network.

Macvlan networks can operate in several modes, including bridge, private, VEPA (Virtual Ethernet Port Aggregator), and passthru modes. Each mode serves specific purposes and use cases, offering flexibility depending on network requirements.

To create a macvlan network, Docker provides the docker network create command. Below is an example of creating a macvlan network in bridge mode:

```
docker network create -d macvlan \
  --subnet=192.168.1.0/24 \
  --gateway=192.168.1.1 \
  -o parent=eth0 macvlan_bridge
```

In this command:

- -d macvlan: Specifies that the macvlan driver is used.
- –subnet: Defines the subnet address range.
- –gateway: Sets the gateway for the network.
- -o parent=eth0: Indicates the parent interface on the Docker host to which the macvlan will be attached.
- macvlan_bridge: The name of the created network.

Once a macvlan network is created, containers can be connected to it. The following example demonstrates how to create a new container attached to the macvlan network:

```
docker run -itd --name=container1 --network=macvlan_bridge --ip=192.168.1.2 alpine
```

In this command:

- -itd: Runs the container in interactive mode, detached.
- –name=container1: Assigns a name to the container.
- –network=macvlan_bridge: Connects the container to the macvlan network created earlier.
- –ip=192.168.1.2: Assigns a specific IP address to the container within the macvlan network.
- alpine: Specifies the Alpine Linux image to use for the container.

To inspect the network and verify its configuration, we can use the docker network inspect command:

```
docker network inspect macvlan_bridge
```

This command provides detailed information about the macvlan network, including the subnet, gateway, and connected containers. The output details will resemble the following:

```
[
  {
    "Name": "macvlan_bridge",
    "Id": "c3b3e9d38a1b891b5ff34f8980aringoc",
    "Created": "2023-07-01T14:30:00.000Z",
    "Scope": "local",
    "Driver": "macvlan",
    "EnableIPv6": false,
    "IPAM": {
      "Driver": "default",
      "Options": {},
      "Config": [
        {
          "Subnet": "192.168.1.0/24",
          "Gateway": "192.168.1.1"
        }
      ]
    },
    "Internal": false,
    "Attachable": false,
    "Ingress": false,
    "ConfigFrom": {
      "Network": ""
    },
    "ConfigOnly": false,
    "Containers": {
      "d2a1e1b8fantes1d3b7523fhb1b0e6ench": {
        "Name": "container1",
        "EndpointID": "a1f2c1de0e7cd7066ab1b104c3a4aa5c",
        "MacAddress": "02:42:c0:a8:01:02",
        "IPv4Address": "192.168.1.2/24",
        "IPv6Address": ""
      }
    },
    "Options": {
      "parent": "eth0"
    },
    "Labels": {}
  }
]
```


When working with macvlan networks, it's crucial to recognize that communication between containers on the same macvlan network through the parent host interface is disabled by default for security reasons. To enable such communication, configuring special settings at the network interface level on the host system is required, typically by creating a macvlan sub-interface and binding it to a Docker container.

Consider the following steps to create and configure a macvlan sub-interface:

1. Create the sub-interface:

```
ip link add macvlan0 link eth0 type macvlan mode bridge
```

2. Assign an IP address to the sub-interface:

```
ip addr add 192.168.1.100/24 dev macvlan0
```

3. Bring up the sub-interface:

```
ip link set macvlan0 up
```

4. Deploy a container connected to the sub-interface:

```
docker run -itd --network=macvlan_bridge --ip=192.168.1.101 alpine
```

This configuration allows the parent host to communicate with containers on the created macvlan network. However, one must exercise caution and thoroughly review security implications, especially in multi-tenant environments or environments with high-security requirements.

The benefits of using macvlan networks include enhanced network isolation, improved network performance by reducing the overhead of port mappings, and enabling containers to have direct access to the physical network. Such functionality makes macvlan an excellent choice for integrating Docker workloads into existing enterprise networks and legacy systems.

5.7 Creating and Managing Custom Networks

Docker's flexibility in handling networks provides a substantial advantage for creating isolated environments tailored to specific applications. Creating and managing custom networks enables you to define and control the communication landscape of your Docker containers with enhanced precision. This section covers the steps and configurations necessary to create and manage custom networks in Docker.

Docker networks can be created using several drivers, such as bridge, overlay, and macvlan. Each of these drivers provides unique properties suited for different use cases. The default bridge network is suitable for small setups and single-host applications, while overlay networks are designed for scaling across multiple hosts. Macvlan networks allow container interfaces to appear directly on the physical network, offering compatibility with traditional VLAN setups.

```
docker network create --driver bridge my_bridge_network
```

In the example above, the docker network create command initializes a new network called my_bridge_network using the bridge driver. This network naturally facilitates communication between containers on the same host, isolated from the host's network.

To inspect the newly created network, you can use:

```
docker network inspect my_bridge_network
```

The output will display detailed information about the network, including its unique ID, driver, subnet information, and connected containers.

```
[
  {
    "Name": "my_bridge_network",
    "Id": "10d1ecbdf90c0e49cd8fe4d3f8611f47e7d345f409354eb0012a2952d2d91752",
    "Created": "2023-10-12T11:26:42.554149178Z",
    "Scope": "local",
    "Driver": "bridge",
    "EnableIPv6": false,
    "IPAM": {
      "Driver": "default",
      "Options": {},
      "Config": [
        {
          "Subnet": "172.18.0.0/16",
          "Gateway": "172.18.0.1"
        }
      ]
    },
    ...
  }
]
```

When creating containers, you can connect them to a specific network using the –network flag:

```
docker run -d --name web_server --network my_bridge_network nginx
```

In this command, a new container named web_server runs an Nginx instance and joins the my_bridge_network network. The container can communicate with other containers on the same network directly via their container names.

To list all networks on a Docker host:

```
docker network ls
```

```
NETWORK ID      NAME                DRIVER     SCOPE
10d1ecbdf90c    my_bridge_network   bridge     local
f7d61304d237    bridge              bridge     local
8cf4ba634485    host                host       local
d5f4c6a8a14c    none                null       local
```

Custom networks can also be removed when no longer needed using:

```
docker network rm my_bridge_network
```

Be aware that attempting to remove an active network with connected containers will result in an error. Ensure that containers are disconnected before removing a network. Disconnection can be achieved using:

```
docker network disconnect my_bridge_network web_server
```

This command disconnects the web_server from my_bridge_network. The container remains running but loses access to that network segment.

Custom networks can also include specific options. For example, creating a bridge network with custom subnet and gateway settings:

```
docker network create --driver bridge \
  --subnet 192.168.10.0/24 \
  --gateway 192.168.10.1 \
  custom_bridge_network
```

Here, the network custom_bridge_network has a subnet IP range of 192.168.10.0/24 and a gateway of 192.168.10.1. This provides fine-grained control over the IP addressing scheme used within the Docker environment.

Overlay networks are utilized in Docker Swarm mode to enable communication between containers across different Docker hosts. Creating an overlay network requires initializing Docker Swarm:

```
docker swarm init
```

After initializing Swarm, create the overlay network:

```
docker network create --driver overlay my_overlay_network
```

This command creates a new overlay network named my_overlay_network, allowing containers across multiple nodes to interact seamlessly.

Managing custom networks in Docker requires a judicious approach to ensure efficient use of resources and robust network security. Proper segmentation, subnetting, and the use of appropriate drivers tailored to your infrastructure will optimize performance and maintain a secure container environment. Connecting, inspecting, and administrating these networks through Docker CLI provides control necessary to handle complex deployment scenarios.

5.8 Connecting Containers to Networks

When creating Docker containers, specifying their network connectivity is paramount for inter-container communication and access to external resources. This section delves into the mechanisms and commands for connecting containers to different network types in Docker, emphasizing best practices to ensure optimal network performance and security.

The primary command to connect a container to a network during its creation is docker run. By using the –network flag, you can specify the target network. Here is an example:

```
docker run --name my_container --network my_network my_image
```

This command starts a container named my_container based on my_image, and connects it to the my_network network. However, there are scenarios where containers may need to connect to multiple networks or change networks dynamically. The following sections illustrate these complex configurations.

To simplify our discussion, consider two main tasks: connecting a running container to a network and disconnecting a running container from a network.

Connecting a Running Container to a Network

Docker facilitates attaching a running container to an additional network using the docker network connect command. This is particularly useful for containers that need to interact with multiple networks post-deployment.

```
docker network connect my_network my_container
```

Here, my_container will now be able to communicate with other containers or services within my_network. This command does not disrupt the container's current operations, ensuring seamless network integration.

To validate the connection, examine the container's network interfaces and routes. The docker inspect command helps in this regard:

```
docker inspect my_container
```

The output includes the NetworkSettings section, detailing connected networks and associated IP addresses.

```
"NetworkSettings": {
   "Networks": {
      "my_network": {
         "IPAMConfig": null,
         "Links": null,
         "Aliases": [
            "abcdef"
         ],
         ...
      },
      ...
   }
}
```

Having confirmed the container's connectivity, ensure that any necessary configurations, such as DNS settings, are appropriately adjusted. The Docker DNS server automatically resolves service names based on the connected networks, facilitating straightforward service discovery.

Disconnecting a Running Container from a Network

Similar to connecting, Docker allows detaching a container from any network via the docker network disconnect command:

```
docker network disconnect my_network my_container
```

Executing this command removes the container my_container from my_network, effectively isolating it from any services or containers within that network. After disconnection, inspect the container to verify the detached status.

Practical Example: Connecting a Web Server and Database

Consider a common scenario where a web server container needs to interact with a database container securely. Typically, these containers are deployed in separate networks for segregation and security.

First, create the networks:

```
docker network create web_net
docker network create db_net
```

Next, start the database container in db_net:

```
docker run -d --name my_db --network db_net my_db_image
```

Then, start the web server container, initially attaching it to web_net:

```
docker run -d --name my_web --network web_net my_web_image
```

At this stage, the web server and database are isolated. To enable them to communicate, connect the web server to db_net:

```
docker network connect db_net my_web
```

The my_web container is now part of both web_net and db_net, thereby allowing it to access the database securely while maintaining its presence in the web network for front-end communications.

Multihost Networking with Overlay Networks

For Docker Swarm or other orchestration solutions that span multiple hosts, overlay networks enable container-to-container connectivity across different nodes. The process begins by creating an overlay network:

```
docker network create -d overlay --subnet 10.0.0.0/24 my_overlay_net
```

Deploy services or containers onto this overlay network to achieve scalable and distributed networking capabilities.

```
docker service create --name my_service --network my_overlay_net my_service_image
```

Points to Consider

- **IP Address Management (IPAM):** When connecting containers to multiple networks, ensure IP address ranges do not overlap to avoid conflicts.
- **Security:** Deploy appropriate network security measures (e.g., firewalls, security groups) to protect inter-container communication.
- **Performance:** Monitor network performance, especially in overlay networks, to avoid latency or bottleneck issues.

Combining these techniques empowers developers and system administrators to configure network environments that cater to complex application architectures, ensuring flexibility, security, and performance.

5.9 Networking in Docker Compose

Docker Compose simplifies the orchestration of multi-container Docker applications by allowing the definition of services, networks, and volumes in a single YAML file. Networking is a crucial aspect of Docker Compose, as it enables seamless communication between services.

This section delves into the networking features provided by Docker Compose, how to use specific network configurations, and best practices for managing Docker Compose networks.

When defining a Docker Compose file (typically named docker-compose.yml), networks can be specified under the networks key. By default, each service defined in the Compose file is connected to a default network, allowing them to communicate with each other. The network configuration section allows specifying custom driver options and network-specific settings.

Here is an example of a simple Docker Compose file with network configuration:

```
version: '3.8'

services:
  web:
    image: nginx:latest
    ports:
      - "8080:80"
    networks:
      - webnet

  db:
    image: mysql:5.7
    environment:
      MYSQL_ROOT_PASSWORD: example
    networks:
      - webnet

networks:
  webnet:
    driver: bridge
```

In this example: - The services web and db are defined. - Both services are connected to the custom network webnet. - The webnet network is created using the bridge network driver.

By defining the network under the networks key, we explicitly create a network instead of relying on the default network that Docker Compose would create. This approach offers greater control over network settings and is particularly useful for specifying custom network drivers or options.

Services connected to the same Docker Compose network can communicate using their service names as hostnames. For instance, in the above example, the container running the web service can connect to the MySQL database container using the hostname db.

Additional parameters can be configured within the networks section. Here are some common options:

- ipam: Configure IP Address Management settings for custom IP ranges or subnets. - driver_opts: Specify options for the network driver.

Below is an extended example demonstrating the use of IPAM:

```
version: '3.8'

services:
  web:
    image: nginx:latest
    ports:
      - "8080:80"
    networks:
      - webnet

  db:
    image: mysql:5.7
    environment:
      MYSQL_ROOT_PASSWORD: example
    networks:
      - webnet

networks:
  webnet:
    driver: bridge
    ipam:
      config:
        - subnet: 172.16.238.0/24
        - gateway: 172.16.238.1
```

In this example, the webnet network is configured with a custom subnet 172.16.238.0/24 and a gateway 172.16.238.1. This custom IPAM configuration ensures that all services within webnet have IP addresses in the specified range, which is advantageous for network segmentation and avoiding IP conflicts in a more complex network architecture.

Docker Compose also supports specifying external networks. External networks are pre-defined Docker networks that are created outside of the Docker Compose file. This feature is useful when multiple Compose projects should share the same network. Here is an example:

```
version: '3.8'

services:
  web:
    image: nginx:latest
    ports:
      - "8080:80"
    networks:
      - external_network

networks:
  external_network:
    external: true
```

In this example, the service web is connected to an existing network named external_network. The external key indicates that Docker Compose should not create the network but use an existing one.

To enhance network isolation and security in Docker Compose, using network aliases can be beneficial. Network aliases allow services to be reached by alternative hostnames, offering flexibility and granular control over service name exposure. Here is how to define network aliases:

```
version: '3.8'

services:
  web:
    image: nginx:latest
    ports:
      - "8080:80"
    networks:
      webnet:
        aliases:
          - my-web-host
  db:
    image: mysql:5.7
    environment:
    MYSQL_ROOT_PASSWORD: example
    networks:
      webnet:
        aliases:
          - my-db-host

networks:
  webnet:
    driver: bridge
```

In the above example, the web service can be reached by the alias my-web-host and the db service by the alias my-db-host. This is advantageous for scenarios where service hostnames need to be abstracted or when integrating with other networking services.

One advanced feature of Docker Compose networking is the ability to use Docker's overlay network driver. The overlay driver is useful for deploying multi-host networks in a Docker Swarm context. Below is a concise example of integrating an overlay network within Docker Compose:

```
version: '3.8'

services:
  web:
    image: nginx:latest
    deploy:
      replicas: 2
    ports:
      - "8080:80"
    networks:
```

```
      - overlaynet

  db:
    image: mysql:5.7
    environment:
      MYSQL_ROOT_PASSWORD: example
    networks:
      - overlaynet

networks:
  overlaynet:
    driver: overlay
```

In this example, the Compose file specifies an overlay network overlaynet. The deploy key is used to indicate that the Compose file is intended for Docker Swarm mode, with the web service running in two replicas. The overlay network driver facilitates cross-host communication, which is essential for distributed applications.

Lastly, attention to container restart policies, proper use of environment variables for network settings, and understanding potential pitfalls such as network bottlenecks or DNS resolution issues are crucial for effective Docker Compose networking. Each of these elements contributes to building resilient, scalable, and maintainable Docker-based applications.

5.10 Service Discovery in Docker

Service discovery in Docker is a fundamental concept that allows containers to find and communicate with each other, even as they start, stop, or scale dynamically. This is especially crucial in a microservices architecture where services need to interact seamlessly and maintain consistency.

Docker provides built-in support for service discovery through several mechanisms, including DNS-based service discovery and Docker's own internal service registry. Understanding these mechanisms is essential for building resilient and scalable containerized applications.

Docker's default service discovery mechanism uses DNS. When containers are launched within a Docker network, they can resolve each other's names using DNS. Docker automatically configures a DNS server in the network namespace of each container. The following examples illustrate how this works in practice.

First, let's create a custom network:

```
docker network create mynetwork
```

Now, launch two containers within this network:

```
docker run -d --name container1 --network mynetwork busybox sleep 3600
docker run -d --name container2 --network mynetwork busybox sleep 3600
```

You can test service discovery by executing a ping command from one container to another. Connect to container1:

```
docker exec -it container1 sh
```

Once inside container1, ping container2:

```
ping container2
```

You should see similar output indicating successful name resolution and communication:

```
PING container2 (172.18.0.3): 56 data bytes
64 bytes from 172.18.0.3: seq=0 ttl=64 time=0.093 ms
64 bytes from 172.18.0.3: seq=1 ttl=64 time=0.107 ms
```

Another essential aspect of service discovery is using Docker Compose, which simplifies the process by defining multi-container applications. Consider the following example docker-compose.yml file:

```
version: '3.8'

services:
  web:
    image: nginx
    networks:
      - mynetwork
  database:
    image: mysql
    environment:
      MYSQL_ROOT_PASSWORD: example
    networks:
      - mynetwork

networks:
  mynetwork:
```

By using Docker Compose, we can start both the nginx web server and the mysql database in the same user-defined network. Use the following command to bring up the services:

```
docker-compose up -d
```

Running the above command starts the services and connects them to mynetwork, enabling service discovery. To verify, you can enter the web container and ping the database service:

```
docker exec -it <web_container_id> sh
ping database
```

The successful ping demonstrates that Docker Compose has facilitated service discovery within the defined network.

For services running in Docker Swarm mode, Docker offers an advanced service discovery and load balancing mechanism. Here, services are defined at a higher abstraction level, and Docker manages the internal networking, service discovery, and load balancing.

First, initialize a Docker Swarm:

```
docker swarm init
```

Next, deploy a service with replicas:

```
docker service create --name my_web --replicas 3 -p 8080:80 nginx
```

Docker creates an internal DNS entry for the service my_web, which load balances requests among the replicas. Verify the service discovery by inspecting the tasks of the service:

```
docker service ps my_web
```

You will see multiple replicas of the nginx service running across different nodes. Each task has its own IP address, yet they are all accessible under the common service name my_web.

In a multi-host Docker Swarm cluster, the overlay network driver extends service discovery across multiple hosts. When services are deployed within an overlay network, Docker ensures that containers can communicate seamlessly. Here's how you create an overlay network and deploy services:

```
docker network create --driver overlay my_overlay_network
docker service create --name db_service --network my_overlay_network mysql:5.7
docker service create --name api_service --network my_overlay_network
      my_api_image
```

The overlay network ensures that the services db_service and api_service can discover and communicate with each other across different hosts in the Swarm.

Effective service discovery is crucial for microservices and distributed applications, enabling dynamic scaling and inter-service communication. By leveraging Docker's built-in mechanisms and tools like Docker

Compose and Docker Swarm, one can build scalable and resilient applications with ease.

5.11 Docker Network Security

Docker network security encapsulates various methodologies to safeguard containerized applications and communications from potential threats and vulnerabilities. Ensuring robust security mechanisms in Docker environments is paramount to prevent unauthorized access, data breaches, and other malicious activities. This section highlights pivotal security practices, network configurations, and tools that can be employed to secure Docker networks effectively.

One critical aspect of Docker network security involves understanding and managing network communication between containers. Docker provides multiple isolation techniques to control and restrict network access. Employing these techniques can mitigate risks associated with unverified network traffic and potential exploits.

Role-based Access Control (RBAC)

Implementing role-based access control is essential in managing who can create, modify, or delete networks and services within a Docker environment. Docker integrates with various authentication systems to enforce RBAC. Docker Enterprise Edition (EE) provides enhanced RBAC features through Docker Trusted Registry (DTR) and Universal Control Plane (UCP). These tools allow administrators to define granular access policies based on user roles and permissions.

Network Isolation

Docker networks can be configured to provide isolation between containers. Using separate Docker networks for different application components can limit the blast radius in case of a security incident. The main types of network isolation techniques include:

- **Bridge Networks:** By default, Docker creates a bridge network for containers, ensuring they can communicate internally but are isolated from external networks. Configuring bridge networks with custom iptables rules can further restrict traffic.
- **Overlay Networks:** Primarily used in Docker Swarm for multi-host communication, overlay networks also provide built-in encryption options (–opt encrypted) to secure data in transit.

- **Macvlan Networks:** By assigning unique MAC addresses, macvlan networks provide layer 2 isolation, which can be beneficial for isolating workloads that require direct network visibility.

Network Policies

Docker integrates with network plugins like Calico and Cilium, which enable the creation and enforcement of network policies. These policies govern the ingress and egress traffic for containers, defining which services can communicate with each other. Calico, for instance, uses a declarative policy model where rules can be defined in YAML format. Below is a sample Calico policy in YAML:

```
apiVersion: projectcalico.org/v3
kind: NetworkPolicy
metadata:
  name: allow-tcp-traffic
  namespace: default
spec:
  selector: all()
  ingress:
    - action: Allow
      protocol: TCP
  egress:
    - action: Allow
      protocol: TCP
  types:
    - Ingress
    - Egress
```

Firewalls and iptables

Firewalls and iptables rules can be employed to control network traffic at the host level. Docker integrates with the host's iptables to manage NAT and filter table rules effectively. Custom iptables configurations can block unauthorized access and allow only specific traffic. For instance, the following iptables rule restricts all incoming traffic except SSH:

```
iptables -P INPUT DROP
iptables -A INPUT -p tcp --dport 22 -j ACCEPT
```

Securing Docker Daemon

The Docker daemon is a critical component that needs to be secured to prevent unauthorized remote access. Configuring the Docker daemon to use TLS for all communications ensures that all traffic between the Docker client and daemon is encrypted. Here is an example of configuring Docker daemon with TLS:

```
dockerd --tlsverify \
    --tlscacert=/path/to/ca.pem \
    --tlscert=/path/to/server-cert.pem \
    --tlskey=/path/to/server-key.pem
```

Network Scanning Tools

Regularly scanning Docker networks for vulnerabilities is a proactive measure to identify and mitigate potential security threats. Tools like nmap and Docker Bench for Security can be used to assess the security posture. Docker Bench for Security checks for common best practices and misconfigurations:

```
docker run -it --net host --pid host --cap-add audit_control \
  --label docker_bench_security \
  docker/docker-bench-security
```

Intrusion Detection Systems (IDS)

Integrating an Intrusion Detection System (IDS) like Snort or Suricata with Docker can monitor and analyze network traffic for suspicious activity. These systems can be configured to work within Docker containers, ensuring thorough monitoring of containerized applications.

Securing Inter-Container Communication

Encrypting inter-container communication is essential when sensitive data is transmitted over the network. Docker Swarm mode provides an option to encrypt container communication using IPSec. For non-Swarm setups, setting up a VPN such as Weave or using service mesh solutions like Istio with mutual TLS (mTLS) can secure communication channels.

Regular Updates and Patches

Ensuring that Docker software, as well as the host operating system, is regularly updated with the latest security patches is vital. Vulnerabilities in Docker or the underlying host can expose an entire ecosystem to risks. Automating updates using tools like Watchtower can streamline this process.

By comprehensively applying these security measures, Docker networks can achieve a heightened level of security. Each layer of protection serves to fortify the environment against a wide array of potential cyber threats, ensuring robust and resilient containerized deployments.

5.12 Troubleshooting Docker Networking Issues

Diagnosing and resolving Docker networking issues requires a systematic approach, leveraging both Docker's built-in tools and standard network troubleshooting techniques. This section focuses on common problems and their solutions, using practical examples to elucidate each step.

1. Verifying Network Configuration

Before diving into complex troubleshooting, ensure the basic network configuration is correct. Start by listing all Docker networks:

```
docker network ls
```

This command displays all available Docker networks along with their types and drivers. Check if the network in question exists and is of the expected type.

Next, inspect the detailed configuration of a specific network:

```
docker network inspect <network_name>
```

This command returns a JSON output detailing the network's configuration, including connected containers, IP address ranges, options, and driver-specific settings. Anomalies in this output can signal configuration errors or conflicts.

2. Confirming Container Connectivity

To check if containers can communicate within the network, you can utilize both Docker CLI and container utilities like ping and curl. For instance, to test connectivity between two containers, first identify their IP addresses using:

```
docker inspect -f '{{range .NetworkSettings.Networks}}{{.IPAddress}}{{end}}' <
    container_id>
```

Once the IP addresses are known, execute a ping or curl command from within one container targeting the other:

```
docker exec -it <source_container_id> ping <target_container_ip>
```

If the ping fails, it suggests network isolation issues. For HTTP-based services, a curl command might be more insightful, revealing application-specific details:

```
docker exec -it <source_container_id> curl http://<target_container_ip>:<port>
```

3. Checking DNS Resolution

Docker uses an embedded DNS server to provide service discovery for containers. Failures in DNS resolution can prevent containers from finding each other by name. To troubleshoot DNS issues, verify the /etc/resolv.conf inside the container:

```
docker exec -it <container_id> cat /etc/resolv.conf
```

The output should include Docker's embedded DNS server (usually the gateway IP of the container's default network). If this is misconfigured, containers will fail to resolve names. Also, test DNS resolution directly:

```
docker exec -it <container_id> nslookup <service_name>
```

If DNS queries fail, restarting the Docker daemon can often resolve embedded DNS server issues:

```
sudo systemctl restart docker
```

4. Diagnosing Network Driver Issues

Different Docker networks utilize different drivers (e.g., bridge, overlay, macvlan). These drivers can sometimes introduce issues specific to their implementation. For example, in overlay networks, issues might arise from misconfigured or unreachable Docker Swarm nodes. To troubleshoot overlay network issues, inspect the state of the Swarm:

```
docker node ls
```

Ensure all nodes are active and reachable. For bridge networks, verify iptables rules:

```
sudo iptables -L -n -v
```

This command lists the current iptables rules, which Docker manipulates to allow container traffic. Misconfigurations here can prevent proper network communication.

5. Analyzing Logs for Errors

Docker and container logs can provide indispensable insights. For Docker daemon logs, use:

```
sudo journalctl -u docker
```

Search for any errors or warnings that might indicate underlying network issues. For individual container logs, utilize:

```
docker logs <container_id>
```

Look for application-level errors that might hint at network problems, such as connection timeouts or failures.

6. Monitoring Network Traffic

Advanced network troubleshooting may require monitoring network traffic to and from the containers. Tools like tcpdump and Wireshark are invaluable for this purpose. For example, to capture all traffic on a container's interface:

```
docker exec -it <container_id> tcpdump -i eth0
```

This command captures real-time traffic, which can then be analyzed to spot issues such as dropped packets, malformed packets, or unexpected network behavior.

By following these detailed troubleshooting steps, you can systematically diagnose and resolve various Docker networking issues, ensuring robust container communication and network integrity.

Chapter 6

Docker Storage and Volumes

This chapter examines Docker storage solutions, focusing on volumes and bind mounts. It covers creating, managing, and mounting volumes to containers, as well as the use of volume drivers and plugins. Techniques for backing up and restoring volumes, sharing data between containers, and optimizing storage performance are also discussed. The chapter includes insights into persistent storage in Docker Swarm and troubleshooting storage-related issues.

6.1 Introduction to Docker Storage

Docker provides several methodologies for managing storage within containerized environments. The fundamental purpose of Docker storage is to enable efficient data persistence and facilitate data sharing among containers while maintaining isolation and detachment from the container lifecycle. This section lays the groundwork for understanding various Docker storage paradigms by detailing the core concepts and mechanisms underpinning Docker's storage architecture.

At the heart of Docker storage are two principal forms: volumes and bind mounts. While both serve to associate storage with containers, their applications and functionalities exhibit distinct differences. Docker volumes are managed by Docker itself and are the preferred mechanism for persisting data and sharing data between containers. Bind mounts, on the other hand, rely directly on the host filesystem.

- **Volumes** – Volumes are fully managed by Docker and are the preferred mechanism for persisting data. They are stored in a part of the host filesystem which is managed by Docker (/var/lib/docker/volumes/ on Linux). Volumes are more flexible than bind mounts because they can be named and can be used by multiple containers simultaneously. Volume drivers enable volumes to persist data on remote storage systems and even across clusters.
- **Bind Mounts** – Bind mounts map a host directory or file to a container directory or file. This means that the source directory or file is defined by its absolute path on the host system. Bind mounts are typically used when one needs to share configuration files between the host and the container or for accessing resources that are either required by or produced by the container.

One of the pivotal properties of container storage solutions is their ability to separate the concerns of persistent data management from ephemeral container instances. This separation is critical to maintaining the stateless nature of containers while still allowing stateful applications to be elegantly containerized.

When a container is created, it utilizes a union filesystem for its filesystem. This union filesystem typically consists of multiple layers derived from the base image. Any data written to the container that is not stored within mounted volumes or bind mounts is considered ephemeral, meaning it will be destroyed when the container is removed. To ensure data persists beyond the lifecycle of a single container instance, coupling containers with external storage solutions like volumes is imperative.

The docker volume command provides capabilities for creating, inspecting, listing, removing, and pruning volumes. Understanding how to effectively leverage this command is essential for manipulating Docker volumes:

```
docker volume create my_volume
```

The command above creates a new Docker volume named my_volume. To verify the creation and inspect its details, one can utilize the following:

```
docker volume inspect my_volume
```

The output will detail the volume's properties and its mountpoint on the host filesystem, providing insight into the location where the data will be persisted.

To list all volumes available on the Docker host, the command is as follows:

```
docker volume ls
```

This command enumerates all volumes, making it convenient to track and manage the storage assets within the Docker environment.

Deleting a volume when it is no longer needed is executed using:

```
docker volume rm my_volume
```

This deletion is permanent, underscoring the importance of ensuring data within the volume is no longer required or has been properly backed up prior to removal.

Another integral concept in Docker storage is the management of volume drivers. Volume drivers expand the capability of Docker volumes by allowing the usage of external storage solutions such as cloud-based storage arrays or networked filesystems. This feature is particularly advantageous in orchestrating containers across distributed systems and in scenarios requiring high-availability and durable storage solutions. Configuring volume drivers typically requires specifying additional options during volume creation, an example being:

```
docker volume create --driver local --opt device=/dev/sda1 my_local_volume
```

This command utilizes the local driver to create a volume tied to a specific device on the host machine.

Understanding and effectively implementing Docker storage solutions is foundational to leveraging containers for diverse applications that demand data persistence, consistency, and robust sharing capabilities. With this groundwork established, further exploration into the creation, management, and optimization of Docker volumes, as well as utilizing advanced features like volume drivers and plugins, becomes vastly simplified and coherent.

6.2 Understanding Docker Volumes

Docker volumes offer a robust mechanism for managing container data, providing a flexible and performant solution for handling storage requirements. Unlike traditional approaches that store data directly on the container's writable layer, Docker volumes support a more persistent and efficient way to manage data.

Volumes are designed specifically to handle data persistence, making them particularly useful for scenarios where container data needs to outlive the container itself. This attribute is particularly beneficial for applications that require long-term storage, such as databases or stateful services.

Docker volumes are managed by Docker, abstracting away the complexity of underlying storage management. This abstraction enables developers to focus on application development without worrying about the specific details of filesystem operations.

To create a volume, the docker volume create command is used. The basic syntax is:

```
docker volume create <volume_name>
```

For example, to create a volume named my_volume, the following command is executed:

```
docker volume create my_volume
```

Upon creation, the volume can be inspected using the docker volume inspect command. This command provides detailed information about the volume, such as its creation time, mount point, and associated driver.

```
docker volume inspect my_volume
```

```
[
    {
        "CreatedAt": "2023-09-20T12:34:56Z",
        "Driver": "local",
        "Labels": {},
        "Mountpoint": "/var/lib/docker/volumes/my_volume/_data",
        "Name": "my_volume",
        "Options": {},
        "Scope": "local"
    }
]
```

Volumes are not tied to a specific path in the container. Instead, they can be mounted to any directory inside the container. This flexibility allows developers to organize their containerized applications' storage in a manner that best suits their requirements.

Mounting a volume to a container is achieved using the -v or –mount flag with the docker run command. The -v flag provides a shorthand method for volume mounting:

```
docker run -d -v my_volume:/app/data my_app_image
```

This command runs a container in detached mode (-d) from the image my_app_image, mounting the volume my_volume to the /app/data directory within the container.

Alternatively, the –mount flag offers a more verbose and flexible way to define mounts. It supports various options such as read-write permissions and volume drivers. An equivalent command using the –mount flag is:

```
docker run -d --mount source=my_volume,target=/app/data my_app_image
```

Volumes support several key use cases, including:

- **Data Persistence:** By persisting data independently of the container lifecycle, volumes are invaluable for stateful applications like databases. When a container is deleted and recreated, the volume retains its data.
- **Data Sharing:** Volumes can be shared between multiple containers. This feature is useful for scenarios where different services require access to the same data.
- **Efficient Storage Management:** Volumes are managed by Docker and optimized for performance, reducing the overhead associated with container storage management.
- **Backup and Recovery:** Volumes can be easily backed up and restored, facilitating disaster recovery and data migration strategies.

Volumes can be backed by different drivers, with the default being the local driver. Other drivers support network-attached storage solutions, such as NFS or cloud storage services. Choosing the appropriate volume driver depends on the use case and the storage requirements of the application.

The following command demonstrates how to create a volume using a named volume driver:

```
docker volume create --driver=local --opt type=tmpfs --opt device=tmpfs --opt o=size
    =100m my_tmpfs_volume
```

This command creates a volume named my_tmpfs_volume using the local driver with specific options that set it up as a tmpfs (RAM-backed filesystem) storage type with a size limit of 100 megabytes.

Understanding Docker volumes and their management is crucial for effectively leveraging Docker's storage capabilities. Mastery of these concepts ensures that applications are robust, performant, and scalable, capable of meeting diverse and demanding storage requirements.

6.3 Creating and Managing Volumes

Volumes in Docker are primarily used to enable the persistence of data generated by containers. They facilitate data sharing among multiple containers and offer a solution for managing stateful applications, which require data to outlive the containers themselves. This section explores how to create, inspect, and manage Docker volumes with precision and clarity.

To begin with, Docker volumes are created using the docker volume create command. This command initializes a new volume that can subsequently be attached to one or multiple containers. By default, volumes are managed by Docker, which ensures that their lifecycle is independent of the containers using them.

```
docker volume create my_volume
```

The above command creates a new volume named my_volume. To verify its creation, you can list all available volumes using:

```
docker volume ls
```

This command provides a list of all volumes, including my_volume, confirming its creation. To obtain more detailed metadata about a specific volume, use the docker volume inspect command:

```
docker volume inspect my_volume
```

The output of this command provides comprehensive information about the volume, including its mount point on the host system, creation time, and driver type:

```
[
  {
    "CreatedAt": "2023-10-01T12:34:56Z",
    "Driver": "local",
    "Labels": {},
    "Mountpoint": "/var/lib/docker/volumes/my_volume/_data",
    "Name": "my_volume",
    "Options": {},
    "Scope": "local"
  }
]
```

Volumes can be removed when they are no longer needed using the docker volume rm command. This command should be used with caution, as deleting a volume will result in the permanent loss of all data stored within it:

```
docker volume rm my_volume
```

In some cases, you may wish to remove all unused volumes that are not currently referenced by any container. This can be achieved using the docker volume prune command, which facilitates efficient clean-up of unused storage:

```
docker volume prune
```

The output prompts for confirmation to ensure that only unneeded volumes are deleted. This command is particularly useful for maintaining a clean and efficient storage environment, removing residual volumes left by deleted containers.

It is essential to understand that volumes persist data even when containers are stopped or removed. This makes them ideal for scenarios where data persistence is critical, such as databases, application configurations, and user-generated content. When creating volumes, Docker employs the default "local" volume driver to manage data storage locations and methods. However, advanced use cases may call for custom volume drivers, which provide greater flexibility and control over storage implementations. These custom drivers are discussed in-depth in later sections of this chapter.

To attach a volume to a container, the -v or –mount flag is used during container creation. The -v flag takes the format <volume-name>:<container-path>:

```
docker run -d -v my_volume:/data my_image
```

This command launches a container from my_image, mounting my_volume to the /data directory inside the container. Data written to /data will be persisted in my_volume on the host system. For more complex configurations, the –mount flag provides additional options such as read-write permissions and volume-driver specifications:

```
docker run -d --mount source=my_volume,target=/data,my_volume
```

Understanding the nuances of creating and managing volumes ensures that data persistence in Docker is handled effectively, guaranteeing that applications remain robust and resilient. With this knowledge, users can confidently employ Docker volumes to meet the demands of diverse and sophisticated use cases, ranging from simple data retention to complex, distributed storage solutions.

Next, the book will delve deeper into the art of mounting volumes to containers, further enriching the reader's understanding of Docker's storage capabilities.

6.4 Mounting Volumes to Containers

Mounting volumes to containers is a fundamental practice in Docker for ensuring persistent data storage, as well as for sharing data between the host machine and the container environment. This process involves linking a storage volume to a specific directory within a Docker container, allowing data to be stored persistently even when the container itself is deleted. Here, we will delve into the specifics of this process, examining key commands and configurations, and highlighting best practices.

To begin with, volume mounting can be accomplished using the docker run command with the -v or –mount flag. The -v flag follows a simplified syntax, whereas the –mount flag offers greater flexibility with advanced options.

A typical example using the -v flag might look like this:

```
docker run -d -v <volume\_name>:<container\_path> <image\_name>
```

Here, <volume_name> is the name of the Docker volume to be mounted, <container_path> is the path within the container where the volume will be accessible, and <image_name> specifies the Docker image from which to create the container.

For a more complex use case requiring additional configuration, the –mount flag is more suitable. The syntax is slightly more verbose but provides clarity:

```
docker run -d --mount type=volume,src=<volume\_name>,dst=<container\_path> <
    image\_name>
```

In this command, the type parameter specifies the type of mount, src (or source) indicates the volume name, and dst (or destination) specifies the container path.

Consider an example in which we have an application container that requires a persistent storage for its configuration files. We might use the following command:

```
docker run -d --name app-container --mount type=volume,src=app-config,dst=/app/
    config my\_application\_image
```

Upon executing this command, Docker creates or uses the existing volume named app-config and mounts it to the /app/config directory within the container named app-container.

Using these methods ensures the data persists beyond the lifecycle of the container, achieving data durability. It also simplifies data backup and restoration processes.

Testing the volume mounting can be achieved by entering the container and interacting with the mounted volume directly. This can be done using the docker exec command:

```
docker exec -it app-container /bin/bash
```

Once inside the container, navigating to the mounted volume path (/app/config) should reveal the data files. This validates that the mounting process has been successful.

Furthermore, mounting volumes can be beneficial when updating applications. You can spin up a new container version while linking it to the same volume, ensuring a seamless transition without data duplication.

An important consideration when mounting volumes is understanding how Docker manages desktop environments compared to cloud services or self-hosted instances. For desktop deployments, paths must follow the local system's file structure, e.g., C:\ on Windows or /Users on macOS. Network shares or cloud storage interfaces might require additional plugins or drivers.

Volume mounting also supports multiple containers accessing the same volume, making it ideal for collaborative environments. However, it is crucial to manage concurrency to prevent race conditions or conflicts over data access.

For illustrative purposes, consider a scenario where two containers share the same data volume:

```
docker run -d --name container1 --mount type=volume,src=shared-data,dst=/data my\
    _image
docker run -d --name container2 --mount type=volume,src=shared-data,dst=/data my\
    _image
```

Both container1 and container2 have access to the shared-data volume mounted at /data, allowing them to read from and write to the same data set.

In special cases, volume drivers can augment the mounting process with functionalities such as encryption or backup management. When invoking a volume driver, the command structure is:

```
docker run -d --mount 'type=volume,src=<volume\_name>,dst=<container\_path>,
    volume-driver=<driver\_name>'
```

In all scenarios, it is essential to track volume usage and manage volume lifecycle effectively to avoid orphaned or unused volumes occupying disk space. Regular auditing and cleanup can be performed through commands, such as:

```
docker volume ls
docker volume rm <volume\_name>
```

Finally, remember to provide adequate permissions on mounted volumes to prevent unauthorized access or data breach, respecting security best practices.

Incorporating these techniques and paying close attention to their configurations will immensely improve the robustness and reliability of your Docker deployments by ensuring data persistence and accessibility across container lifecycles.

6.5 Using Bind Mounts

Bind mounts are a fundamental aspect of Docker that offer a powerful mechanism for managing persistent data. Unlike Docker volumes, which are managed by Docker itself, bind mounts allow data persistence by linking a specific directory on the host machine to a directory in the container. This linkage provides numerous advantages, especially for scenarios that require frequent updates or interaction with the host's filesystem.

To utilize bind mounts, the essential command syntax in Docker is as follows:

```
docker run -v /path/on/host:/path/in/container my_image
```

In the above command, /path/on/host is the directory on the host machine you want to bind to /path/in/container inside the container.

Consider a practical example where we want to bind mount a local directory containing web content to an Nginx container. Assuming the local directory is /srv/web-data and it contains the necessary HTML files:

```
docker run --name webserver -v /srv/web-data:/usr/share/nginx/html:ro -d nginx
```

Here, the ro (read-only) option ensures that the container can read from but not write to the bound directory, preserving the integrity of the host data.

It is crucial to understand that bind mounts bypass Docker's volume management, directly linking the specified directory into the container. This has valid use cases but also potential security implications because the container gains access to the host filesystem. Henceforth, it is recommended to use bind mounts only when necessary and with the appropriate directory permissions and options.

One of the compelling reasons to use bind mounts is during the development process. Developers often need to sync code updates directly into the running container to test changes without rebuilding the container image repeatedly. Consider the scenario of developing a Node.js application:

1. Create the project directory and initialize the project:

```
mkdir mynodeapp
cd mynodeapp
npm init -y
```

2. Create a simple index.js file with the following Node.js code:

```
const http = require('http');

http.createServer((req, res) => {
  res.writeHead(200, {'Content-Type': 'text/plain'});
  res.end('Hello World\n');
}).listen(8080);
```

```
console.log('Server running at http://127.0.0.1:8080/');
```

3. Run the container with bind mount:

```
docker run -it --name mynodeapp -v "$(pwd)":/usr/src/app -w /usr/src/app node:
    latest node index.js
```

In this example: - -v "$(pwd)":/usr/src/app binds the current directory (containing index.js) to /usr/src/app inside the container. - -w /usr/src/app sets /usr/src/app as the working directory inside the container. - node index.js runs the Node.js application.

This setup allows for real-time updates to index.js on the host to be immediately reflected in the running container, significantly enhancing development process efficiency.

When working with bind mounts, it is also important to be cognizant of path references and potential differences between host and container environments. For instance, path configurations and file permissions on the host might differ from those expected inside the container. Ensuring consistency in permissions and understanding how paths are resolved in both contexts is vital for avoiding runtime errors and permissions issues.

For explicit control and to examine the containers using bind mounts, you can inspect the bind mount configuration with the following command:

```
docker inspect container_name
```

This command reveals detailed information about the container, including Mounts, where you can verify the source and destination of bind mounts along with any options like read-only access. An illustrative output from docker inspect provides clarity:

```
"Mounts": [
    {
        "Type": "bind",
        "Source": "/srv/web-data",
        "Destination": "/usr/share/nginx/html",
        "Mode": "ro",
        "RW": false,
        "Propagation": "rprivate"
    }
]
```

To ensure secure and effective use of bind mounts, adhere to the following best practices: - Employ least privilege by using read-only mounts whenever feasible. - Validate directories and file permissions on the host. - Limit the scope of bind mounts to avoid exposing sensitive host directories.

Properly utilized, bind mounts offer a robust solution for directory sharing and real-time data access between Docker containers and the host filesystem.

6.6 Volume Drivers and Plugins

Volume drivers and plugins extend Docker's storage capabilities, enabling advanced and specialized storage solutions beyond the default functionality. These drivers interact with external storage systems, providing consistent storage management across various environments and integrating seamlessly with Docker's orchestration tools.

Understanding the architecture and functionality of volume drivers and plugins is critical for effectively managing Docker storage in a production environment.

Understanding Volume Drivers

Volume drivers are software components that interface between Docker and storage backends. They enable Docker to manage storage across different storage solutions, including cloud storage services, distributed filesystems, and networked storage. This flexibility allows Docker containers to leverage existing infrastructure and maintain data persistency across container lifecycle events.

Docker uses the volume plugin extension mechanism to support external volume drivers. The extension mechanism allows drivers to dynamically add or remove volumes, offering high versatility in storage management. The built-in local driver, used when no driver is specified, stores volume data on the host filesystem.

To interact with a specific volume driver, the –driver flag is used with volume-related commands. For example, to create a volume with a custom driver:

```
docker volume create --driver custom_driver my_volume
```

This command instructs Docker to use the custom_driver for managing the volume my_volume.

Common Volume Drivers

Several volume drivers are available, each optimized for different storage systems and requirements. Some commonly used volume drivers include:

- **local**: The default driver, storing volumes on the local filesystem of the Docker host.
- **nfs**: Interfaces with Network File System (NFS) for network-based storage solutions.
- **aws**: Integrates with Amazon Web Services (AWS) for using Elastic Block Store (EBS) volumes.
- **glusterfs**: Interacts with GlusterFS for distributed storage solutions.
- **portworx**: Provides high availability and data redundancy for containers.
- **ceph**: Integrates with Ceph's distributed storage architecture.

Each driver caters to specific use cases and storage requirements, facilitating container deployments with scalable and persistent storage backends.

Installing and Using Volume Plugins

Volume plugins are typically distributed through the Docker Engine or via external repositories. To manage plugins, Docker provides a set of docker plugin commands to install, enable, and configure them. To install a volume plugin, the following command is used:

```
docker plugin install plugin_name
```

For instance, installing the Portworx volume plugin can be done as follows:

```
docker plugin install portworx/pxd:latest
```

After installation, the plugin needs to be enabled, if it isn't already enabled by default:

```
docker plugin enable portworx/pxd
```

Once the plugin is enabled, it can be specified during volume creation:

```
docker volume create --driver=portworx my_pxd_volume
```

Configuration and Options

Volume drivers may offer various configuration options to fine-tune operational parameters. These options are supplied during volume creation using the -o flag. For example, configuring an NFS volume might look like this:

```
docker volume create --driver=nfs -o share=192.168.1.1:/path/to/share my_nfs_volume
```

Here, the -o flag specifies the NFS share location with the share option.

Listing and Managing Volumes

To list volumes and see the driver associated with each, the following command can be executed:

```
docker volume ls
```

The output will include columns such as DRIVER and VOLUME NAME, making it clear which driver manages each volume. For instance:

```
DRIVER          VOLUME NAME
local           my_local_volume
nfs             my_nfs_volume
portworx        my_pxd_volume
```

Detailed inspection of a specific volume is available through:

```
docker volume inspect my_volume
```

Volume Life Cycle Management

Managing the lifecycle of volumes is crucial in maintaining storage hygiene and optimizing resources. Unused volumes can be removed to free up space using the following command:

```
docker volume rm my_volume
```

This command removes the volume my_volume, ensuring that the data managed by the associated driver is also appropriately handled.

Developing Custom Volume Plugins

Docker's plugin system supports the development of custom volume drivers tailored to specific needs. Plugins are generally developed in languages such as Go and must adhere to Docker's plugin API. A typical development workflow includes:

- Defining the plugin specification in the config.json file.
- Implementing the volume driver interface with essential methods:

Create, Remove, Path, Mount, and Unmount.

- Testing the plugin with different workloads to ensure robustness.

```
// Example Skeleton of a Go-based Volume Driver
package main

import (
    "net/http"
    "github.com/docker/go-plugins-helpers/volume"
)

type myVolumeDriver struct{}

func (d *myVolumeDriver) Create(req *volume.CreateRequest) error {
    // Implementation
    return nil
}

func main() {
    d := &myVolumeDriver{}
    h := volume.NewHandler(d)
    http.ListenAndServe(":8080", h)
}
```

Best Practices and Security Considerations

When using volume drivers and plugins, adhere to best practices to ensure security and efficiency. These include:

- Regularly updating plugins to leverage security patches and feature updates.
- Limiting volume driver access based on the principle of least privilege.
- Monitoring volume usage and performance metrics to proactively manage storage requirements.

Volume drivers and plugins significantly enhance Docker's storage capabilities, supporting the deployment of robust and scalable containerized applications. By understanding and effectively utilizing these components, one can achieve a sophisticated and resilient storage architecture.

6.7 Backing Up and Restoring Volumes

Data backup and recovery are fundamental practices to ensure data integrity and availability in containerized applications. Backing up Docker volumes allows administrators to safeguard against data loss due to container failures, hardware malfunctions, or other catastrophic events. Concurrently, the ability to restore volumes guarantees data recovery and continuity of services. This section elaborates on the methods and best practices for effectively backing up and restoring Docker volumes.

A common approach for managing backups involves using tools like tar and Docker's native docker cp command to transfer data between containers and host systems.

Backing Up Volumes using tar

One of the most straightforward methods to back up a Docker volume is by creating a compressed archive of the volume's contents. This method leverages the tar command within a temporary container. Here's how you can achieve this:

```
# Create a temporary container and use the tar command to back up the volume
docker run --rm -v my_volume:/volume_data -v $(pwd):/backup_dir alpine \
    sh -c "tar czf /backup_dir/my_volume_backup.tar.gz -C /volume_data ."
```

In this example, the –rm flag ensures that the temporary container is removed after execution. The volume my_volume is mounted at /volume_data within the container, and the current working directory on the host is mounted at /backup_dir. The tar command creates a compressed archive of the volume data and stores it in my_volume_backup.tar.gz within the host's working directory.

Restoring Volumes from a Backup

Restoring data from a backup archive requires extracting the contents of the tar file into the desired volume. This process is analogous to the backup procedure but in reverse:

```
# Create a temporary container and use the tar command to restore the volume
docker run --rm -v my_volume:/volume_data -v $(pwd):/backup_dir alpine \
    sh -c "tar xzf /backup_dir/my_volume_backup.tar.gz -C /volume_data"
```

In this script, the tar command extracts (xzf) the contents of my_volume_backup.tar.gz located in the host's working directory (/backup_dir) into the Docker volume mounted at /volume_data.

Automating Backups with Docker and Cron

While manual backup processes are effective, automating backups ensures regular data protection without human intervention. This can be achieved by scheduling backup tasks using cron jobs within the host system.

First, create a shell script to perform the backup:

```
#!/bin/bash
# Define backup file name
backup_file="backup_$(date +%F_%T).tar.gz"
# Execute Docker command to perform backup
docker run --rm -v my_volume:/volume_data -v $(pwd):/backup_dir alpine \
    sh -c "tar czf /backup_dir/$backup_file -C /volume_data ."
```

Make the script executable:

```
chmod +x backup_script.sh
```

Next, schedule the script using cron. Edit the crontab file:

```
crontab -e
```

Add a cron job entry to run the script at a specified interval, e.g., daily at midnight:

```
0 0 * * * /path/to/backup_script.sh
```

Best Practices for Volume Backups

To ensure robust backups and avoid potential issues:

- **Consistency**: Ensure that backups are taken during periods of low activity or after stopping containers to avoid inconsistencies caused by write operations. Utilize container pause capabilities or application quiescence to stabilize data before backup.
- **Retention and Rotation**: Implement a backup retention policy that defines how long backups are stored and when older backups are purged. Automated rotation strategies help manage storage space.
- **Testing Restorations**: Periodically test the restoration process to verify the integrity and reliability of backup files, ensuring that data can be recovered without issues.
- **Incremental Backups**: For large datasets, consider using incremental backups to reduce storage requirements and backup times. Tools like rsync or specialized backup solutions can support incremental backups.

With careful implementation of these backup and recovery procedures, Docker volumes can be safeguarded against data loss, ensuring continuity and reliability of containerized applications.

6.8 Sharing Data Between Containers

In a Docker-based infrastructure, sharing data between containers is a common requirement to ensure seamless communication and data coherence. Containers can share data through mounted volumes, enabling persistent storage that transcends the lifecycle of individual containers. This section explores the mechanisms by which data sharing can be achieved, with a focus on creating and managing shared volumes and understanding the best practices for maintaining data integrity and consistency.

To share data between containers, one can utilize Docker Volumes. Volumes are ideally suited for this purpose as they are independent of the container's lifecycle and can be mounted into multiple containers simultaneously. This process begins with the creation of a volume that will serve as the shared datastore.

```
$ docker volume create shared_data
```

With the shared volume created, it can be mounted to multiple containers. The following examples illustrate how to launch two containers, each mounting the shared_data volume to a specific directory within their filesystem. This configuration allows both containers to read and write to the same datastore.

```
$ docker run -d --name container1 -v shared_data:/app/data busybox
$ docker run -d --name container2 -v shared_data:/app/data busybox
```

In this setup, both container1 and container2 have the shared volume mounted at /app/data. Consequently, any file created in /app/data by one container is directly accessible to the other container.

Suppose container1 writes a file to the shared volume:

```
$ docker exec container1 sh -c 'echo "Hello from container1" > /app/data/shared.txt'
```

We can now verify that the file shared.txt is accessible from container2:

```
$ docker exec container2 cat /app/data/shared.txt
```

Execution of the above command in container2 should output:

```
Hello from container1
```

This confirms that the data written by container1 is available to container2, showcasing effective data sharing via Docker Volume.

To optimize this setup for more complex scenarios, Docker supports named volumes, which provide a more persistent and easily manageable method for defining storage. Named volumes, as demonstrated in the example above, benefit from Docker's built-in volume driver enhancements.

In some advanced use cases, additional configuration may be required to handle file permissions and concurrent access appropriately. While Docker manages basic access control, certain applications and workloads may necessitate more precise synchronization mechanisms and data integrity checks.

When scaling applications using Docker Compose, the same principles of shared volumes apply but with additional declarative power. Here's an example of a docker-compose.yml file that sets up two services sharing the same volume:

```
version: '3.8'
services:
  service1:
    image: busybox
    volumes:
      - shared_data:/app/data
    command: sh -c 'echo "Service1 running" && tail -f /dev/null'

  service2:
    image: busybox
    volumes:
      - shared_data:/app/data
    command: sh -c 'echo "Service2 running" && tail -f /dev/null'
volumes:
  shared_data:
```

Executing docker-compose up with the above configuration provisions both services with the shared volume, allowing them to use /app/data for inter-service communication and data exchange.

Finally, it is essential to monitor and manage the lifecycle of shared volumes, particularly when dealing with large-scale deployments or sensitive data. Regular backups, access monitoring, and thorough data orchestration practices are recommended.

By adequately leveraging Docker Volumes and the associated tooling, you can efficiently share data between containers, enabling cohesive and performant multi-container applications.

6.9 Persistent Storage in Docker

Persistent storage in Docker ensures that the data generated and used by containers is retained and remains accessible even after the containers are stopped or removed. This concept is vital for stateful applications where data persistence between sessions is necessary. Unlike ephemeral storage, which gets deleted with the container, persistent storage solutions in Docker provide a means to maintain data longevity.

Docker offers several approaches to managing persistent storage, primarily through volumes and bind mounts. Volumes are Docker-managed and are entirely managed by Docker Volumes API, while bind mounts rely on the host machine's filesystem. Understanding the characteristics and appropriate scenarios for each method is crucial for effective data management in containerized applications.

A volume in Docker can be created using the following command:

```
docker volume create my_volume
```

This command creates a new volume named my_volume. Once created, this volume can be mounted to one or more containers to provide persistent storage. Here is an example of using my_volume with a Docker container:

```
docker run -d --name my_container -v my_volume:/data busybox
```

In this example, the volume my_volume is mounted to the /data directory inside the container my_container. The files written to /data will persist even if the container is stopped or removed.

Volumes are ideal when you require persistent storage that is abstracted from the host filesystem, allowing for easier data portability across different environments. Volumes are stored in a part of the host filesystem which is managed by Docker (/var/lib/docker/volumes on Linux). This separation enhances security and makes it easier to manage storage.

Bind mounts, on the other hand, allow containers to access specific paths on the host filesystem. This method is useful when you need to persist data using directories outside of Docker's managed storage. Bind mounts are created by referencing directories or files on the host when starting containers. For example:

```
docker run -d --name my_container -v /path/on/host:/data busybox
```

In this example, the host directory /path/on/host is mounted to the container's /data directory. Any changes made within /data will directly affect the host's /path/on/host directory, and vice versa.

For distributed and stateful applications running on a Docker Swarm, the use of persistent storage becomes more complex. Docker Swarm utilizes volume drivers to manage persistent storage across the cluster. Volume drivers are plugins that extend Docker's volume functionality, enabling support for third-party storage solutions and cloud storage services. These drivers help in provisioning, mounting, and managing storage across different nodes in a Swarm.

When deploying services in Swarm mode, specifying the volume driver is essential. Here is an example of deploying a service with a named volume using a specified driver:

```
docker service create --name my_service --replicas 3 --mount type=volume,source=
    my_volume,target=/data,volume-driver=custom_driver busybox
```

In this example, custom_driver refers to a third-party volume driver that manages my_volume. Using such drivers allows for advanced capabilities like replication, distributed storage, and cloud integration, ensuring data persistence and high availability in Docker Swarm environments.

Another important consideration for persistent storage is the need for data backup and restoration. Docker makes it straightforward to back up volumes for disaster recovery or data migration purposes. To backup a Docker volume, one can use the tar command as follows:

```
docker run --rm -v my_volume:/data -v $(pwd):/backup busybox tar czvf /backup/
    my_volume_backup.tar.gz -C /data .
```

This command creates a container that mounts my_volume and the current working directory, and then archives the data from /data into a tarball located in the current directory. Restoring the volume can be accomplished through:

```
docker run --rm -v my_volume:/data -v $(pwd):/backup busybox tar xzvf /backup/
    my_volume_backup.tar.gz -C /data
```

Maintaining persistent storage in Docker is essential for applications that require data to remain intact between different container lifecycles. By leveraging Docker volumes, bind mounts, volume drivers, and appropriate backup/restoration techniques, one can effectively manage data persistence in both standalone and clustered environments. This ensures data durability, high availability, and operational continuity for containerized applications.

6.10 Storage Options in Docker Swarm

Docker Swarm provides a robust platform for orchestrating and managing containerized applications across a cluster of Docker engines. Storage management is a critical aspect of deploying stateful applications in a Swarm cluster. There are several storage options available in Docker Swarm, each catering to different use cases and requirements.

Docker Swarm nodes can utilize local storage, shared storage, or cloud-based storage solutions. Local storage refers to the storage resources physically present on the Docker host. While it is simple and easy to use, it does not support data persistence across multiple nodes or provide high availability. Shared storage solutions, such as Network File System (NFS) or Clustered File System (CFS), allow multiple nodes in the Swarm cluster to access the same set of files. Cloud-based storage services offer scalable and highly available storage options for Docker Swarm clusters running in the cloud.

The primary storage abstractions in Docker Swarm include volumes, bind mounts, and tmpfs mounts. Each of these storage options has its characteristics and use cases, which will be discussed in detail below.

- **Volumes:** Volumes are the preferred mechanism for persisting data in Docker Swarm. Docker manages volumes, and they can be created using custom volume drivers or plugins. Volumes are not tied to the lifecycle of a container, allowing data to persist even after the container is removed. This property is crucial for stateful applications such as databases. When deploying applications in a Swarm cluster, volumes can be configured using the Docker Compose file, ensuring consistent volume usage across the cluster. A volume can be created and used with the following command in a Docker Compose file:

```
version: '3.7'
services:
  web:
    image: nginx:alpine
    volumes:
      - web-data:/var/www/html
volumes:
  web-data:
```

  In this example, the 'web-data' volume is created and mounted to the '/var/www/html' directory in the 'web' service container. This configuration ensures that the web content persists even if the 'web' container is recreated.

- **Bind Mounts:** Bind mounts allow users to mount a file or directory from the host filesystem into a container. With bind mounts, data can be shared between the host and the container, making them suitable for use cases where you need direct access to the host filesystem. Bind mounts are specified with an absolute path and can be configured in a Docker Compose file as follows:

```
version: '3.7'
services:
  web:
    image: nginx:alpine
    volumes:
      - /home/user/web-data:/var/www/html
```

  In this example, the '/home/user/web-data' directory on the host is mounted to the '/var/www/html' directory inside the container. Changes made in the host directory are immediately visible inside the container, and vice versa.

- **Tmpfs Mounts:** Tmpfs mounts use the host's memory to create a temporary filesystem that is removed when the container stops. They are useful for storing non-persistent data or data that requires high performance and low latency. Tmpfs mounts can be configured in a Docker Compose file as follows:

```
version: '3.7'
services:
  web:
    image: nginx:alpine
    tmpfs:
      - /var/www/html:rw
```

  In this example, a tmpfs mount is created and mounted to the '/var/www/html' directory in the container. The data stored in this directory will reside in the host's memory, providing high read-/write performance but will be lost when the container is stopped.

To further enhance storage capabilities in Docker Swarm, users can leverage volume drivers and plugins. Plugins add functionalities such as support for various storage backends, volume snapshotting, and remote storage options. For example, the REX-Ray plugin enables Docker Swarm to use storage from different providers, such as Amazon EBS, Google Persistent Disks, and OpenStack Cinder. Configuring a volume to use the REX-Ray plugin can be done in a Docker Compose file as follows:

```
version: '3.7'
services:
  database:
```

```
    image: postgres:latest
    volumes:
      - db-data:/var/lib/postgresql/data
volumes:
  db-data:
    driver: rexray
    driver_opts:
      size: "20"
      volume_type: "gp2"
```

In this example, the ‘db-data‘ volume is created using the REX-Ray plugin, and it is configured to use a 20GB Amazon EBS volume with the type ‘gp2‘. This setup ensures that the database data is stored on a scalable and highly available backend.

Properly managing storage in Docker Swarm is essential for deploying reliable and scalable stateful applications. By understanding and utilizing the various storage options available, users can ensure their applications persist data correctly, perform efficiently, and scale seamlessly across a Swarm cluster.

6.11 Optimizing Storage Performance

In Docker environments, optimizing storage performance is essential to ensure that containers run efficiently without becoming a bottleneck. Several strategies and best practices can be employed to achieve optimal storage performance.

Choice of Storage Driver: The choice of storage driver significantly impacts performance. Docker supports several storage drivers, including overlay2, aufs, and devicemapper. The overlay2 driver is generally recommended due to its improved efficiency and lower overhead. It can be configured in the Docker daemon configuration file (/etc/docker/daemon.json) as follows:

```
{
  "storage-driver": "overlay2"
}
```

Use of SSDs: Solid State Drives (SSDs) provide faster read and write speeds compared to traditional Hard Disk Drives (HDDs). Using SSDs for Docker storage can dramatically improve performance, particularly for applications requiring high I/O operations.

Configuring Docker for SSDs: To further enhance the performance when SSDs are used, Docker should be configured to leverage their capabilities. For example, ensuring that the file system is optimized for SSDs and that necessary trim operations are enabled can help maintain performance over time.

Managing Container Layer Size: Containers generate layers for write operations, and large container layers can degrade performance. Keeping container layers small by minimizing write operations and cleaning up unnecessary files and packages helps improve storage efficiency.

Data Volume Placement: Placing Docker volumes on the same disk as the Docker daemon can cause contention and reduced performance. It is advisable to place data volumes on separate disks, particularly for high-performance applications:

```
docker volume create --opt device=/mnt/disks/data my_data_volume
```

Volume Driver Optimization: Some volume drivers offer specific performance-tuning options. For example, when using the 'local' driver, the 'o' option can mount volumes with specified flags:

```
docker volume create --driver local \
  --opt o=size=100g,uid=1000,gid=1000 \
  --opt device=/home/user/data \
  myvolume
```

Here, 'size' specifies the initial volume size, 'uid' and 'gid' set the user and group ID, and 'device' specifies the path.

Automated Log Rotation: Logs can consume significant disk space and impact performance. Configuring log rotation ensures that logs do not grow indefinitely:

```
"logs": {
  "driver": "json-file",
  "options": {
    "max-size": "10m",
    "max-file": "5"
  }
}
```

This configuration in the 'daemon.json' file specifies a maximum size of 10MB per log file and retains up to 5 files.

Using tmpfs Mounts: For ephemeral data that does not need persistence, tmpfs mounts (in-memory file system) can be used for better performance:

```
docker run -d --name tmpfs-container \
  --mount type=tmpfs,destination=/app tmpfs-image
```

This reduces the I/O burden on the disk and can significantly boost performance for temporary data storage.

Monitoring and Maintenance: Regular monitoring and maintenance of Docker storage are crucial. Tools like Grafana and Prometheus can be used to monitor metrics and pinpoint performance issues. Periodic cleanup of unused images, containers, and volumes prevents unnecessary disk usage.

Backing Up and Restoring Efficiently: Efficiently managing backups ensures that storage performance remains optimal. Use of incremental backups and proper scheduling can minimize the I/O impact during backup and restore processes.

Configuring Read-Only Containers: For applications that do not require write operations, configuring containers in read-only mode can enhance security and performance by reducing the need for write operations:

```
docker run -d --name readonly-container \
  --read-only myreadonlyimage
```

Direct I/O Usage: In scenarios where bypassing the OS cache is beneficial, direct I/O can be employed. This is particularly useful for databases:

```
docker run -d --name directio-container \
  --device /dev/sdb:/dev/xvdc --privileged directio-image
```

This ensures that the application directly manages data transfers to the device.

Optimizing storage performance in Docker environments involves a combination of proper hardware selection, careful configuration of Docker settings, regular maintenance, and judicious use of storage features. By applying these methodologies, Docker storage can operate efficiently, ensuring that container-based applications perform reliably and at their best potential.

6.12 Troubleshooting Storage Issues

Storage issues in Docker can significantly affect container performance and reliability. Diagnosing and resolving these problems involve understanding different components of Docker's storage subsystem and the various points at which failures can occur. This section details common storage problems and how to address them.

One frequently encountered issue relates to volume mounting errors. A failure to properly mount a volume can originate from incorrect volume syntax or non-existent paths. When creating a container with mounted volumes, verify the syntax in the docker run command. For example:

```
docker run -v /host/path:/container/path mycontainer
```

Ensure that both /host/path and /container/path are valid directories. An invalid host path will result in Docker attempting to create a directory, which might not be the desired behavior.

Troubleshooting can be aided by examining the container logs:

```
docker logs <container_id>
```

If the logs point to permissions-related issues, verify and adjust permissions and ownership of the host directory being mounted. Use the chmod and chown commands to set appropriate permissions:

```
sudo chmod -R 755 /host/path
sudo chown -R user:group /host/path
```

Another common issue is related to disk space. Containers running out of disk space will fail to write to mounted volumes. This can be monitored using the df command to check disk space usage:

```
df -h
```

Alternatively, to inspect the storage driver details and check how space is used within Docker, use the docker system df command:

```
docker system df
```

In cases where Docker's underlying storage driver faces problems, it is prudent to inspect its configuration and logs. The common storage drivers include overlay2, aufs, and devicemapper. Storage driver issues may manifest as failure to start containers or corrupted data. Investigate logs located at /var/lib/docker and view kernel logs using:

```
dmesg | grep -i docker
```

Corrupted or outdated Docker volumes can also impair container functionality. Volumes that have been improperly managed or left mounted for prolonged periods could accumulate redundant data, leading to inefficiencies. Use the following commands to list and remove unused volumes:

```
docker volume ls
docker volume rm <volume_name>
docker volume prune
```

When resolving issues with volume drivers or plugins, it is crucial to ensure that drivers are correctly installed and configured. Unsupported or improperly maintained drivers can cause mount failures and data loss.

To verify the current volume driver in use and its configuration, inspect volume details:

```
docker volume inspect <volume_name>
```

For plugin issues, check the status of the plugin:

```
docker plugin ls
```

In the context of Docker Swarm, persistent storage-related issues might also arise from improper configuration of cluster nodes or inconsistent states across the swarm nodes. Check swarm node status using:

```
docker node ls
docker node inspect <node_name>
```

It is also good practice to validate the network configuration, as storage problems may sometimes intersect with networking issues, especially for distributed storage solutions.

Using these commands, systematically address and resolve storage issues, ensuring better performance and reliability of Docker containers. This approach to troubleshooting not only helps in immediate resolution but also prevents future occurrences through better system understanding and configuration optimization.

Chapter 7

Docker Compose and Multi-Container Environments

This chapter introduces Docker Compose, detailing its installation and the structure of Docker Compose files. It guides readers in creating and managing multi-container applications, defining services, and working with volumes and networks. The chapter covers scaling services, using environment variables, and leveraging Docker Compose for development, testing, and production. Best practices for managing Docker Compose lifecycle and using it with Docker Swarm are also discussed.

7.1 Introduction to Docker Compose

Docker Compose is a tool for defining and running multi-container Docker applications. It simplifies the process of orchestrating multiple services necessary for the operation of complex applications by using a YAML file to configure the application's services. Through a single command, you can create and start all the services from the configuration. This cohesive approach addresses the need for seamless and efficient management of containerized applications, which are often composed of several interconnected services.

Docker Compose offers several key functionalities:

- **Configuration Management:** The YAML file allows for the declarative specification of services, their configuration, networks, and volumes.
- **Orchestration:** Compose manages the lifecycle of the application by handling the start-up, shutdown, and scaling of services.
- **Environment Customization:** It supports defining environment variables, which can be used to customize the behavior of services with ease.
- **Reusable Definitions:** Configuration files can be versioned and shared, supporting collaboration and reproducibility of environments.

Compose projects are usually structured as follows:

- docker-compose.yml: The primary configuration file where services, networks, and volumes are defined.
- Dockerfile: For each service that needs a custom image build, a Dockerfile is included.
- Environment Configuration Files: Optionally included to define environment-specific parameters.

A typical docker-compose.yml might define multiple services using the following structure:

```
version: '3.8'
services:
  web:
    image: nginx:alpine
    ports:
      - "80:80"
  redis:
    image: redis:alpine
```

In this example, the Compose file is using version 3.8 of the Compose file format. It defines two services, web and redis, each using images specified from Docker Hub. The web service defines a port mapping, exposing port 80 of the host to port 80 of the container.

To start the application defined by the Compose file, use the following command:

```
docker-compose up
```

The docker-compose up command starts all the services defined in the Compose file, creating and starting containers as needed. By default, it looks for a file named docker-compose.yml in the current directory.

Compose also provides commands for managing and troubleshooting applications:

- docker-compose ps: Lists the status of containers.
- docker-compose logs: Displays logs from services.
- docker-compose stop: Stops running services.
- docker-compose down: Stops services and removes containers, networks, and volumes created by docker-compose up.

For example, after running your services, you might want to check their status:

```
docker-compose ps
```

An output similar to the following will be shown:

```
   Name              Command                State      Ports
--------------------------------------------------------------------
example_web_1    /docker-entrypoint.sh ngin ...   Up    0.0.0.0:80->80/tcp
example_redis_1  docker-entrypoint.sh redis ...   Up    6379/tcp
```

Logs from all services can be fetched using:

```
docker-compose logs
```

This command consolidates logs from all participating containers, which can be invaluable for debugging and monitoring.

It is worth noting that Docker Compose has different behaviors based on the defined version. As of version 3 and above, it includes additional features and syntax improvements tailored for compatibility with Docker Swarm mode. This versioning allows Docker Compose to align closely with enhancements in Docker itself.

Docker Compose enables consistent development environments, reducing the friction of environment setup and discrepancies between development, staging, and production setups. This advantage makes it a cornerstone tool in modern DevOps practices, facilitating agile development, continuous integration, and continuous deployment.

Lastly, it is important to ensure that Docker Compose is installed in your environment. Installation procedures differ based on operating systems, and it typically requires Docker Engine to be installed as a prerequisite. The nuanced capabilities of Docker Compose discussed in subsequent sections will build upon these foundational concepts, illustrating its multifaceted utility in managing comprehensive multi-container applications.

7.2 Installing Docker Compose

Docker Compose is an essential tool for managing multi-container Docker applications. In this section, we will provide a step-by-step guide for installing Docker Compose on various operating systems, including Linux, macOS, and Windows. We will ensure that the installation process is clear and concise, enabling users to quickly get Docker Compose up and running.

Prerequisites: Before proceeding with the installation, ensure that Docker is already installed and running on your system. Docker Compose relies on Docker to manage containers, so having Docker set up is a prerequisite.

Installing Docker Compose on Linux: To install Docker Compose on a Linux system, follow these steps:

1. Download the Docker Compose binary from the official GitHub repository. This can be done using the curl command:

```
sudo curl -L "https://github.com/docker/compose/releases/download/1.29.2/
    docker-compose-$(uname -s)-$(uname -m)" -o /usr/local/bin/docker-
    compose
```

2. Make the binary executable by setting the appropriate permissions:

```
sudo chmod +x /usr/local/bin/docker-compose
```

3. Verify the installation by checking the version of Docker Compose:

```
docker-compose --version
```

   The output should resemble:

```
docker-compose version 1.29.2, build 5becea4c
```

Installing Docker Compose on macOS: Installing Docker Compose on macOS can be done via Homebrew, a popular package manager for macOS:

1. Update Homebrew to ensure you have the latest version of the package database:

```
brew update
```

2. Install Docker Compose using Homebrew:

```
brew install docker-compose
```

3. Verify the installation by checking the version of Docker Compose:

```
docker-compose --version
```

   The expected output:

```
docker-compose version 1.29.2, build 5becea4c
```

Installing Docker Compose on Windows: Docker Compose comes pre-installed with Docker Desktop for Windows. Ensure Docker Desktop is installed and follows these steps:

1. Open Docker Desktop and navigate to the "Settings" menu.
2. Under "General," ensure that the "Use the WSL 2 based engine" is enabled if you are using Windows Subsystem for Linux 2.
3. Open a command prompt and verify the installation by checking the version of Docker Compose:

```
docker-compose --version
```

   The output should be:

```
docker-compose version 1.29.2, build 5becea4c
```

Upgrading Docker Compose: To ensure you are using the latest features and security updates, it's crucial to keep Docker Compose up to date. The upgrade process varies slightly depending on the operating system.

On Linux:

1. Download the latest Docker Compose binary:

```
sudo curl -L "https://github.com/docker/compose/releases/download/<latest-
    version>/docker-compose-$(uname -s)-$(uname -m)" -o /usr/local/bin/
    docker-compose
```

2. Make the binary executable:

```
sudo chmod +x /usr/local/bin/docker-compose
```

3. Verify the updated installation:

```
docker-compose --version
```

   Confirm the output reflects the latest version.

```
docker-compose version <latest-version>, build <build-hash>
```

On macOS:

1. Use Homebrew to upgrade Docker Compose:

```
brew upgrade docker-compose
```

2. Verify the updated installation:

```
docker-compose --version
```

   Ensure the output shows the latest version.

```
docker-compose version <latest-version>, build <build-hash>
```

On Windows:

1. Open Docker Desktop and check for updates.
2. Install the available updates for Docker Desktop, which includes Docker Compose.
3. After restarting Docker Desktop, verify the updated installation:

```
docker-compose --version
```

   Confirm the output shows the latest version.

```
docker-compose version <latest-version>, build <build-hash>
```

Properly installing Docker Compose across different operating systems is crucial for managing multi-container Docker applications effectively. By following these instructions, users can ensure a seamless setup, thus paving the way for leveraging Docker Compose's full capabilities.

7.3 Understanding the Docker Compose File Structure

The Docker Compose file, typically named docker-compose.yml, is a YAML file used for defining and running multi-container Docker applications. This file contains configurations for the services, networks, and volumes that make up a Docker application. It is essential to understand the structure of the Compose file to effectively utilize Docker Compose.

YAML Basics

YAML (YAML Ain't Markup Language) is a human-readable data serialization standard that is often used for configuration files. It uses indentation to indicate hierarchy and structure, making it crucial to maintain consistent indentation levels. Key-value pairs, lists, and nested elements are common in YAML syntax.

Version

The version of the Compose file format is specified at the top of the docker-compose.yml file. Different versions define different sets of features and capabilities.

```
version: '3.8'
```

This line specifies that the Compose file adheres to version 3.8 of the Docker Compose file format.

Services

Services are the primary concept in Docker Compose. Each service configuration specifies the Docker image to use, the commands to run, ports to expose, and other settings. Services are defined using a dictionary under the services key.

```
services:
  web:
    image: nginx:latest
    ports:
      - "80:80"
```

In this example, a service named web is defined using the nginx:latest image and exposing port 80.

Images

The image attribute specifies the Docker image used by the service. If the image is not available locally, Docker Compose pulls it from the registry.

```
image: nginx:latest
```

Build

The build attribute specifies the context and the Dockerfile to build an image if an image doesn't exist locally or is not used directly from a registry.

```
build:
  context: .
  dockerfile: Dockerfile
```

The context specifies the build context (usually the path to the directory containing the Dockerfile), and the dockerfile specifies the file to use.

Ports

The ports attribute maps ports from the host to the container, defining which ports should be exposed and available for external access.

```
ports:
  - "80:80"
```

This maps port 80 of the host to port 80 of the container, making the container's web service accessible on the host machine's port 80.

Volumes

Volumes provide a mechanism for persisting data and sharing data between containers. The volumes key within a service definition specifies how directories on the local filesystem map to directories inside the container.

```
volumes:
  - ./data:/var/lib/mysql
```

This line mounts the local directory ./data to /var/lib/mysql within the container.

Environment Variables

Environment variables can be specified directly in the Compose file or via an environment file. They provide a way to pass configuration parameters into containers.

```
environment:
  MYSQL_ROOT_PASSWORD: example
```

This sets the MYSQL_ROOT_PASSWORD environment variable to example.

Networks

Networks define the communication paths between containers. By default, Compose sets up a single network for the application, but additional networks can be specified if needed.

```
networks:
  frontend:
  backend:
```

In this example, two networks, frontend and backend, are defined. Services can be connected to these networks as needed.

Deploy

The deploy key is used for specifying deployment settings for the services when using Docker Swarm.

```
deploy:
  replicas: 3
```

This configuration ensures that three replicas of the service are deployed.

Complete Sample

Here is a complete example of a docker-compose.yml file that illustrates a multi-container setup:

```
version: '3.8'

services:
  web:
    image: nginx:latest
    ports:
      - "80:80"
    networks:
      - frontend

  app:
    build:
      context: .
      dockerfile: Dockerfile
    ports:
      - "3000:3000"
    volumes:
      - .:/usr/src/app
    networks:
      - frontend
      - backend
    environment:
      - NODE_ENV=production

  db:
```

```
    image: mysql:5.7
    volumes:
      - db-data:/var/lib/mysql
    networks:
      - backend
    environment:
      MYSQL_ROOT_PASSWORD: example

networks:
  frontend:
  backend:

volumes:
  db-data:
```

This configuration defines three services: web, app, and db. The web service uses the nginx:latest image and connects to the frontend network. The app service is built from a Dockerfile in the current directory, connected to both frontend and backend networks, and includes environment variables for the application configuration. The db service uses the mysql:5.7 image, stores data in a named volume db-data, and connects to the backend network.

This thorough understanding of the Docker Compose file structure enables defining and managing multi-container Docker applications effectively, simplifying deployments, and maintaining application configurations.

7.4 Creating Your First Docker Compose File

A Docker Compose file is a YAML file that defines how multi-container applications are configured. This file is typically named docker-compose.yml, and it outlines the services, networks, and volumes necessary for the application. The file structure adheres to the YAML syntax, which means it is indentation-sensitive and structured hierarchically.

We will create a simple example, a multi-container application comprising an Nginx web server and a Redis database. The primary purpose of this section is to demonstrate the essential components and the syntax required to get a basic application up and running using Docker Compose.

Step 1: Creating the Project Directory

Begin by creating a directory for your project. This directory will contain the docker-compose.yml file and any other files required for your application.

```
mkdir my-docker-compose-app
cd my-docker-compose-app
```

Step 2: Defining Services in docker-compose.yml

Create a new file named docker-compose.yml in the project directory. This file will define the services that make up your application. In this example, we will define two services: web and redis.

Open the docker-compose.yml file in your preferred text editor and add the following content:

```
version: '3.8'

services:
  web:
    image: nginx:latest
    ports:
      - "80:80"
  redis:
    image: "redis:alpine"
```

Let's break down the content of this file: - **version: '3.8'**: Specifies the version of the Docker Compose file format. Using 3.8 ensures compatibility with features available in this version. - **services**: A top-level key under which all individual service definitions are nested. - **web**: This is the name of the first service. It uses the Nginx image from the Docker Hub. The ports key maps port 80 on the host to port 80 on the container. - **redis**: This is the second service, using the official Redis image tagged with alpine. The image keyword specifies the image to use for the container.

Step 3: Running Docker Compose

To start the application, navigate to the project directory and run the following command:

```
docker-compose up
```

This command will download the specified images (if not already available locally) and start the containers. The output will be displayed in the terminal, and you should see logs from both the Nginx and Redis services.

The server will be accessible at http://localhost:80.

Step 4: Stopping the Services

To stop the services, run:

```
docker-compose down
```

This command stops and removes all the containers defined in the docker-compose.yml file. It also removes any networks created by Docker Compose during the up process.

Environment Variables and Configuration Options

Docker Compose files can be configured further using environment variables. For instance, an environment variable can define a parameter, and this can be used within the docker-compose.yml file for flexibility.

```
version: '3.8'

services:
  web:
    image: nginx:latest
    ports:
      - "${WEB_PORT:-80}:80"
  redis:
    image: "redis:alpine"
```

In this example, the port mapping for the web service uses the WEB_PORT environment variable, with a default value of 80 if the variable is not set.

External Configuration Files

To keep the docker-compose.yml file clean and manageable, configuration options can be stored in a separate external file and referenced within the YAML.

Create a new file named config.env:

```
WEB_PORT=8080
```

Modify the docker-compose.yml to reference this configuration file:

```
version: '3.8'

services:
  web:
    image: nginx:latest
    ports:
      - "${WEB_PORT}:80"
    env_file:
      - config.env
  redis:
    image: "redis:alpine"
```

Using the env_file directive, Docker Compose now loads the environment configuration from config.env, allowing for better separation of configuration from the core Compose file.

The docker-compose.yml file is a powerful tool for managing multi-container Docker applications. By defining services, their configurations, and dependencies within a single file, it simplifies the orchestration of complex deployments. The flexibility to use environment variables and external configuration files allows for scalable and maintainable setups.

7.5 Building and Running Multi-Container Applications

In this section, we will delve into the process of building and running multi-container applications using Docker Compose. Multi-container applications are essential when different components of a software system need to run in isolation yet work together as a cohesive unit. Docker Compose provides a straightforward mechanism to manage these applications.

The primary tool for defining, visualizing, and running these applications is the docker-compose.yml file. This file uses YAML format to describe the services, networks, and volumes that comprise the application. Let us examine the structure and setup required to build and run a typical multi-container application.

Example Multi-Container Application: A Web Application

Consider a simple web application consisting of three services:

- A web server running NGINX
- An application server running Flask (a Python web framework)
- A database service running PostgreSQL

The docker-compose.yml file for this setup might look like the following:

```
version: '3'
services:
  web:
    image: nginx:latest
    ports:
      - "80:80"
    depends_on:
      - app

  app:
```

```
    build: ./app
    volumes:
      - .:/code
      - ./logs:/logs
    ports:
      - "5000:5000"
    depends_on:
      - db

  db:
    image: postgres:latest
    volumes:
      - db-data:/var/lib/postgresql/data
    environment:
      POSTGRES_DB: exampledb
      POSTGRES_USER: exampleuser
      POSTGRES_PASSWORD: examplepass

volumes:
  db-data:
```

Building the Application

To build the application, ensure you have Docker and Docker Compose installed on your machine. Navigate to the directory containing the docker-compose.yml file. Depending upon whether the services are built from images on DockerHub or custom Dockerfiles, use the following commands:

- If services are built from DockerHub images:

```
docker-compose up
```

- If services include custom Dockerfiles:

```
docker-compose up --build
```

Running docker-compose up starts the services defined in the docker-compose.yml file. The –build flag ensures that any service defined with a build instruction in the docker-compose.yml file is built before starting.

Inter-service Communication

Docker Compose handles network setups automatically. By default, all services in a Docker Compose application are connected to a common network, allowing them to communicate using service names defined in the docker-compose.yml. For instance, the Flask-based application server can connect to the PostgreSQL database using the service name db.

Here is an example configuration in the Flask application to connect to the PostgreSQL database:

```
import psycopg2

conn = psycopg2.connect(
    dbname="exampledb",
    user="exampleuser",
    password="examplepass",
    host="db" # Service name defined in docker-compose.yml
)
```

Persisting Data with Volumes

Data persistence is crucial, particularly for databases. In our docker-compose.yml file, we defined a volume db-data for the PostgreSQL service. This configuration ensures that data persists even if the container restarts. To illustrate:

- Volume declaration under the db service:

  ```
  volumes:
    - db-data:/var/lib/postgresql/data
  ```

  ensures that the data directory of PostgreSQL inside the container maps to a Docker-managed volume named db-data.

- Volume persistence setup in the volumes section:

  ```
  volumes:
    db-data:
  ```

  This directive creates and manages the volume.

Inspecting and Managing Containers

Once services are running, you may need to inspect logs, enter containers, or manage running containers. Docker Compose provides a suite of commands for these purposes:

- View running services:

  ```
  docker-compose ps
  ```

  This command lists the status of each container managed by Docker Compose.

- View logs:

  ```
  docker-compose logs -f
  ```

  The -f flag streams live logs, useful for debugging.

- Enter a specific container:

```
docker-compose exec <service\_name> /bin/bash
```

  Replace <service_name> with the name of the service you wish to access. For example:

```
docker-compose exec app /bin/bash
```

Scaling Services

Docker Compose allows you to scale services to handle increased load. For instance, you may want to run multiple instances of the application server. Use the scale command as follows:

```
docker-compose up --scale app=3
```

This command runs three instances of the app service. Docker Compose will ensure proper load balancing across these instances.

Shutting Down and Cleaning Up

To gracefully stop the application and remove containers, networks, and volumes associated with it, use:

```
docker-compose down
```

If you wish to remove named volumes declared in the volumes section of the docker-compose.yml file, use the -v flag:

```
docker-compose down -v
```

This command ensures a clean slate, suitable for running subsequent deployments without leftover artifacts.

Integrating these components effectively will scaffold your multi-container applications, enabling robust, scalable, and maintainable setups.

7.6 Defining Services in Docker Compose

In Docker Compose, a service is an abstraction that defines how a containerized application is deployed and configured. This encompasses the container image, environment variables, volumes, and network settings, among other parameters. The docker-compose.yml file serves as the blueprint for these services. Understanding how to define services effectively within this file is crucial to building robust, scalable, and maintainable multi-container applications.

A typical docker-compose.yml file follows a hierarchical structure where each service is a key under the services root node. Below is an example to illustrate the definition of multiple services:

```
// Sample docker-compose.yml File
version: '3.8'
services:
  app:
    image: myapp:latest
    build: .
    ports:
      - "8080:8080"
    volumes:
      - .:/app
    environment:
      - DATABASE_URL=mysql://db:3306/mydb
    networks:
      - app-network

  db:
    image: mysql:5.7
    volumes:
      - db-data:/var/lib/mysql
    environment:
      - MYSQL_ROOT_PASSWORD=rootpwd
      - MYSQL_DATABASE=mydb
    networks:
      - app-network

volumes:
  db-data:

networks:
  app-network:
```

- version: '3.8': Specifies the version of the Docker Compose file format. The version determines the features and attributes available. The latest recommended version is often used to take advantage of the newest features.
- services:: The root element under which individual services are defined.
- app:: Name of the first service, could be any identifier meaningful within the context of your application.
  - image: myapp:latest: Specifies the Docker image to use for this service.
  - build: .: Indicates that the Docker image should be built from the current directory (where the Dockerfile is located).

  - ports:: Map ports from the host to the container. "8080:8080" exposes port 8080 on the host machine to port 8080 inside the container.
  - volumes:: Mount host paths or named volumes. .:/app mounts the current directory to /app inside the container.
  - environment:: Set environment variables. DATABASE_URL is passed to specify the database connection string.
  - networks:: Define which networks the service is part of.

- db:: Name of the second service.
  - image: mysql:5.7: Specifies the Docker image for the Mysql 5.7 service.
  - volumes:: db-data:/var/lib/mysql mounts a named volume to persist the database.
  - environment:: Set environment variables, including MYSQL_ROOT_PASSWORD and MYSQL_DATABASE, necessary for MySQL initialization.
  - networks:: Uses the same network as the app service to ensure communication.

- volumes:: Named volumes that can be shared between services. db-data enables MySQL data persistence.

- networks:: Define custom networks. app-network is a user-defined network facilitating communication between services.

A more detailed explanation of each section is essential to understand nuances:

Service Definition Key Components:

1. **Image and Build Context**: The image key specifies the Docker image to pull from Docker Hub or another registry. Meanwhile, the build key provides a context for building an image from a Dockerfile. They are typically mutually exclusive within a service definition. If both are defined, Compose will use the local build instructions.

```
app:
  build: .
  image: myapp:latest
```

2. **Ports:** This maps the host machine's port to the container's port using the host:container syntax. This is crucial for exposing services running inside the container to the outside world.

```
ports:
  - "8080:8080"
```

3. **Volumes:** Docker volumes are used to persist data generated by and used by Docker containers. They can be paths on the host file system, paths within the container, or Docker named volumes that Docker manages.

```
volumes:
  - .:/app
  - db-data:/var/lib/mysql
```

4. **Environment Variables:** Environment variables are used to pass dynamic configuration data to services. These can include, but are not limited to, database connection strings, service passwords, and configuration toggles.

```
environment:
  - DATABASE_URL=mysql://db:3306/mydb
  - MYSQL_ROOT_PASSWORD=rootpwd
  - MYSQL_DATABASE=mydb
```

5. **Networks:** Networks in Docker Compose facilitate communication between services. By default, Docker Compose creates a default network for the application but specifying custom networks helps in organizing and segmenting services securely.

```
networks:
  - app-network
```

Utilizing Docker Compose Features:

1. **Dependencies:** Docker Compose allows you to declare dependencies between services. This can be critical when you want, for example, a database service to be fully initialized before an application service starts. This is done using the depends_on key.

```
app:
  depends_on:
    - db
```

2. **Command Override:** You can override the default command that a container runs using the command key. This is useful for executing specific tasks within a container, such as running migrations or initializing configurations.

```
app:
  command: ["bundle", "exec", "rails", "server"]
```

3. **Health Checks:** Health checks ensure that your services are running correctly. You can define health checks using the healthcheck key, which contains conditions and retries to verify service health.

```
app:
  healthcheck:
    test: ["CMD", "curl", "-f", "http://localhost:8080"]
    interval: 1m30s
    timeout: 10s
    retries: 3
```

These components form the backbone of service definitions in Docker Compose, enabling complex, interdependent applications to be described and managed through a single, coherent configuration file.

7.7 Working with Volumes and Networks in Compose

Volumes and networks are fundamental to the functionality of Docker Compose as they enable containers to store persistent data and communicate with each other. Understanding how to work with volumes and networks effectively is crucial for managing multi-container applications.

Volumes allow data to persist even when containers are recreated, providing a way to store data outside of the container's filesystem. Docker manages the content of volumes efficiently and ensures data integrity. There are two types of volumes in Docker: named volumes and anonymous volumes. Named volumes are specified by a name within the Docker Compose file, allowing for easy reference across multiple containers. Anonymous volumes are created without a specific name and are typically used for temporary data storage.

```
version: '3.8'

services:
  web:
    image: nginx:latest
    ports:
      - "80:80"
    volumes:
      - web_data:/usr/share/nginx/html

volumes:
  web_data:
```

In the example provided, a named volume called web_data is created and mounted to the /usr/share/nginx/html directory inside the nginx container. This allows data within the /usr/share/nginx/html directory to persist even if the nginx container is destroyed and recreated.

A significant advantage of using named volumes is the ease of specifying volume drivers, which enable different backends such as NFS, cloud storage, or encrypted storage. This offers a versatile and robust solution for data management across diverse environments.

Another essential concept in Docker Compose is **networks**, which facilitate communication between different services within a multi-container application. By default, Docker Compose creates a default network for all the services defined in a Compose file. However, custom networks can be defined to provide greater control over communication policies and isolation between containers.

The following example illustrates a Docker Compose file with custom networks:

```
version: '3.8'

services:
  web:
    image: nginx:latest
    ports:
      - "80:80"
    networks:
      - frontend
      - backend

  database:
    image: mysql:latest
    environment:
      MYSQL_ROOT_PASSWORD: example
    volumes:
      - db_data:/var/lib/mysql
    networks:
      - backend

networks:
  frontend:
    driver: bridge
  backend:
    driver: bridge

volumes:
  db_data:
```

In this example, two custom networks are defined: frontend and backend. The nginx container is connected to both networks, allowing it to communicate with both frontend and backend services. The mysql container is only connected to the backend network, isolating it from direct access by other services connected to the frontend network.

Bridge is the default network driver and is suitable for most applications. However, other network drivers such as overlay, host, and macvlan can be used depending on the specific requirements and deployment architecture.

Overlay networks are used to enable communication across multiple Docker daemons, making them ideal for distributed systems and clustered environments with Docker Swarm. Host networks remove network isolation between the container and the Docker host, sharing the host's networking stack with the container. This provides a performance advantage at the cost of encapsulation. Macvlan networks allow containers to appear as separate physical devices on the network, providing independent MAC addresses for each container.

Integrating volumes and networks in Docker Compose files involves defining and referencing them appropriately across services. Consideration must be given to data persistence, security, and communication requirements when designing multi-container applications.

Persistent data can be shared between containers by mounting volumes at the required paths within containers. Inter-service communication is orchestrated by attaching services to required networks, ensuring containers can interact seamlessly. Properly managed volumes and networks are critical to maximizing the efficiency, scalability, and security of Docker-based applications.

In practice, effective use of volumes and networks can mitigate common pitfalls of containerized environments, such as data loss during container lifecycle events and communication challenges in complex, multi-container deployments.

7.8 Scaling Services with Docker Compose

Scaling services is an essential aspect of managing multi-container applications efficiently. Docker Compose provides a straightforward mechanism to scale services up or down to handle varying loads. This section details the process of scaling services using Docker Compose, explaining both the syntax and the implications of different scaling strategies.

The ability to scale services allows for dynamically adjusting the number of container instances running for each service. This feature is highly beneficial for handling spikes in demand, parallel processing, or high availability requirements.

To scale a service in Docker Compose, the docker-compose up command is employed with the –scale flag, followed by the <service>=<replica_count> syntax. Here, <service> refers to the name of the service defined in the docker-compose.yml file, and <replica_count> specifies the desired number of instances. The following example demonstrates scaling a web service to three instances:

```
docker-compose up --scale web=3
```

This command ensures that three instances of the web service are running, distributing workload across these instances.

Docker Compose YML File Configuration

To understand the intricacies of scaling, it's crucial to look at the docker-compose.yml configuration. Consider the following example of a docker-compose.yml file that defines two services: web and db.

```
version: '3'
services:
  web:
    image: web-app:latest
    ports:
      - "8080:80"
    depends_on:
      - db
  db:
    image: mysql:5.7
    environment:
      MYSQL_ROOT_PASSWORD: example
```

In this setup, the web service depends on the db service. By running the scaling command:

```
docker-compose up --scale web=3
```

Docker Compose launches three containers for the web service. Each of these containers will have the same port mappings and environment configurations as defined in the docker-compose.yml file.

Networking and Scaling

When scaling services, Docker Compose automatically integrates the additional container instances into the defined network. All instances of a scaled service share the same network, enabling them to communicate seamlessly. Given our example, the three web containers can communicate with the db container via the service name db, as all of them are part of the same network.

Load Balancing

Docker Compose itself does not provide built-in load balancing across the scaled instances of a service. It is typically the responsibility of the service's upstream component to distribute requests across the available instances. For example, when scaling a web service, a load balancer like Nginx or HAProxy can be configured to distribute incoming HTTP requests evenly across the multiple web instances.

Here is an example docker-compose.yml that includes an Nginx service for load balancing:

```
version: '3'
services:
  nginx:
    image: nginx:latest
    ports:
      - "80:80"
    volumes:
      - ./nginx.conf:/etc/nginx/nginx.conf
    depends_on:
      - web
  web:
    image: web-app:latest
    expose:
      - "80"
  db:
    image: mysql:5.7
    environment:
      MYSQL_ROOT_PASSWORD: example
```

In this example, the Nginx service is configured with a custom nginx.conf file that defines load balancing rules to distribute traffic to the web service instances.

Resource Allocation

When scaling services, monitoring and resource allocation become critical. Docker Compose facilitates resource constraints on services using the deploy key in your docker-compose.yml file. Setting resource limits ensures fair resource allocation among service instances, preventing any single container from monopolizing the host's resources.

```
version: '3'
services:
  web:
    image: web-app:latest
    deploy:
      resources:
        limits:
          cpus: '0.50'
          memory: '256M'
  db:
    image: mysql:5.7
    environment:
      MYSQL_ROOT_PASSWORD: example
```

This configuration limits each web service instance to a maximum of 0.5 CPU units and 256 MB of memory.

Considerations for Stateful Services

While scaling stateless services (like web servers) is relatively straightforward, scaling stateful services (like databases) requires careful consideration. Databases typically maintain state that needs to be coherent across all instances. Without appropriate mechanisms such as database clustering or replication, simply scaling a database service may lead to data inconsistency.

Practical Use Cases

Scaling services with Docker Compose is practical in numerous real-world scenarios:

- **Microservices Architecture**: In a microservices architecture, different components can scale independently based on load.
- **Testing and Development**: Simulate high-load scenarios by scaling services in a development environment.
- **Redundancy and Failover**: Improve fault tolerance by running multiple instances of critical services.

The ease of scaling services with Docker Compose significantly enhances its utility in both development and production environments, making it a vital tool in modern application deployment and management strategies.

7.9 Environment Variables in Docker Compose

Environment variables are an essential aspect of managing configuration within Docker containers. They provide a flexible way of injecting dynamic or sensitive data into containers without hardcoding values within the Docker images or Docker Compose files. This practice not only enhances security but also promotes a more maintainable and scalable application deployment strategy.

In Docker Compose, environment variables can be specified in multiple ways:

- Directly within the docker-compose.yml file.
- Through an external .env file.
- By passing them at runtime via the command line.

We will examine each method in detail.

Specifying Environment Variables in the docker-compose.yml File

One straightforward approach is to define environment variables directly in the docker-compose.yml file under the environment key of a service. Consider the following example where we define environment variables for a web service:

```
version: '3.8'
services:
  web:
    image: nginx
    environment:
      - NGINX_HOST=localhost
      - NGINX_PORT=80
```

In this example, the web service is configured to use the nginx image with two environment variables: NGINX_HOST and NGINX_PORT. The values for these variables are directly specified in the docker-compose.yml file.

Using an External .env File

For better management of environment variables, especially when dealing with multiple services or environments (e.g., development, testing, production), it is often preferable to use an external .env file. The .env file should be placed in the same directory as your docker-compose.yml file.

Contents of the .env file:

```
NGINX_HOST=localhost
NGINX_PORT=80
DATABASE_URL=mongodb://db:27017
```

The docker-compose.yml file can then reference these variables:

```
version: '3.8'
services:
  web:
    image: nginx
    environment:
      - NGINX_HOST
      - NGINX_PORT
  database:
    image: mongo
    environment:
      - DATABASE_URL
```

Docker Compose automatically loads variables from the .env file into the environment where they can be accessed by your services.

Passing Environment Variables at Runtime

Environment variables can also be passed directly via the command line when starting a Docker Compose application. This method is less common but can be useful for overriding values during runtime. For example:

```
NGINX_PORT=8080 docker-compose up
```

Handling Sensitive Information

Environment variables may contain sensitive information such as passwords, API keys, or database credentials. In such cases, it's crucial to handle them with care. Here are some best practices:

- Avoid hardcoding sensitive values in the docker-compose.yml file.
- Use an external .env file and ensure it is added to your .gitignore file to prevent it from being version-controlled.
- Consider using secrets management services like AWS Secrets Manager, HashiCorp Vault, or Docker secrets for critical information.

Examples of Real-World Usage

Here is a more comprehensive example demonstrating the use of environment variables in a multi-container setup involving a web service and a database:

```
version: '3.8'
services:
  web:
    image: my_web_app
    environment:
      - DATABASE_URL
    ports:
      - "8000:8000"
  database:
    image: postgres
    environment:
      - POSTGRES_USER=example_user
      - POSTGRES_PASSWORD=example_password
      - POSTGRES_DB=example_db
```

And the corresponding .env file:

```
DATABASE_URL=postgresql://example_user:example_password@database:5432/
    example_db
```

In the above setup, the web service connects to the database service using the DATABASE_URL environment variable defined in the .env file.

Interpolating Environment Variables in docker-compose.yml

Docker Compose supports variable substitution within the docker-compose.yml file using the ${VAR} syntax. For instance, you can define placeholders in your docker-compose.yml file and provide their values using an .env file or via the command line:

```
version: '3.8'
services:
  web:
    image: my_web_app
    environment:
      - DATABASE_URL=${DATABASE_URL}
    ports:
      - "${WEB_PORT}:8000"
```

By adopting best practices for using environment variables in Docker Compose, developers can maintain more secure, configurable, and adaptable multi-container applications.

7.10 Using Docker Compose for Development and Testing

In modern application development, employing a consistent development and testing environment is essential to maintaining the integrity and reliability of software projects across different stages of the software lifecycle. Docker Compose plays a crucial role in facilitating this by providing a means to define and manage multi-container applications. This section explores how to leverage Docker Compose in a development and testing context.

To begin with, Docker Compose supports the creation of isolated environments that mirror production setups closely. This isolation aids developers in simulating real-world scenarios without the overhead of managing VMs or alternative complex setups. Consider a typical scenario comprising a web application with a front end, a back end, and a database. Using Docker Compose, one can orchestrate the interaction between these components effortlessly.

To illustrate, let us consider a docker-compose.yml file tailored for development:

```
version: '3.8'

services:
  web:
    build: ./web
    ports:
      - "3000:3000"
    volumes:
      - ./web:/app
    environment:
      - NODE_ENV=development
    depends_on:
      - api

  api:
    build: ./api
    ports:
      - "5000:5000"
    volumes:
      - ./api:/app
    environment:
      - FLASK_ENV=development
    depends_on:
      - db

  db:
    image: postgres:13
    volumes:
      - pgdata:/var/lib/postgresql/data
    environment:
      - POSTGRES_USER=example
      - POSTGRES_PASSWORD=example
      - POSTGRES_DB=example_dev

volumes:
  pgdata:
```

This configuration defines three services: web, api, and db. Each service is configured with development-specific settings:

- **Volumes:** The volumes directive is configured to mount the local directories ./web and ./api into the corresponding containers. This facilitates live code reloading, a vital feature for efficient development.
- **Ports:** The ports configuration exposes the necessary ports, allowing accessibility to the services on the host machine.
- **Environment Variables:** The environment parameter sets the application to run in a development mode, enabling verbose logging and debugging-friendly settings.

When running docker-compose up, Docker Compose orchestrates the starting of these services, respecting the dependency order defined by depends_on.

Another essential aspect of leveraging Docker Compose in development is the use of overriding configuration files. Docker Compose allows for multiple configuration files to be merged. This is particularly useful for defining differing settings between development and production. For instance, consider an override file named docker-compose.override.yml:

```
version: '3.8'

services:
  web:
    environment:
      - NODE_ENV=development
    volumes:
      - ./web:/app

  api:
    environment:
      - FLASK_ENV=development
    volumes:
      - ./api:/app

  db:
    environment:
      - POSTGRES_DB=example_dev
```

By default, docker-compose up takes into account both docker-compose.yml and docker-compose.override.yml files. Overriding specific settings such as environment variables or volumes for development ensures that the base configuration remains applicable for production setups while providing flexibility for development.

For testing, it is often necessary to reset the state of the containers to reflect a pristine environment. Docker Compose provides the command:

```
docker-compose down -v
```

Executing this command removes the containers along with their associated volumes, ensuring that subsequent docker-compose up invocations start with a fresh state. This is useful for integration tests where a clean slate guarantees reproducibility and avoids side effects from previous tests.

Additionally, Continuous Integration (CI) workflows benefit immensely from Docker Compose. By including docker-compose commands in CI scripts, one can simulate the entire application environment, run tests, and ensure that the code changes integrate seamlessly.

Here is a sample snippet from a CI configuration file (e.g., .gitlab-ci.yml):

```
stages:
  - build
  - test

build:
  stage: build
  script:
    - docker-compose -f docker-compose.test.yml up --build -d
    - docker-compose exec -T web npm install
    - docker-compose exec -T api pip install -r requirements.txt

test:
  stage: test
  script:
    - docker-compose exec -T web npm test
    - docker-compose exec -T api pytest
    - docker-compose down -v
```

The CI script above includes two stages: build and test. In the build stage, Docker Compose spins up the necessary services with the test configuration file. The test stage executes tests within the web and api services and subsequently brings down the environment, ensuring a clean state for each run.

Effective Docker Compose implementation in development and testing phases significantly enhances productivity and ensures that the software behaves consistently across different environments.

7.11 Managing Docker Compose Lifecycle

Managing the lifecycle of Docker Compose involves understanding the various commands and their appropriate use cases to efficiently handle multi-container applications. Maintaining control over the lifecycle from build through deployment to decommissioning is vital for maintaining an operational and high-performing infrastructure.

The lifecycle can be broadly understood through activities such as starting, stopping, pausing, unpausing, restarting, and removing services. Each of these activities corresponds with specific Docker Compose commands that streamline interaction with containerized applications.

Starting Services

Starting services using Docker Compose is accomplished with the up command. This command discovers and initiates the defined services in your docker-compose.yml file.

```
docker-compose up
```

By default, docker-compose up runs in the foreground. To run it in the background, use the -d (detached mode) option:

```
docker-compose up -d
```

Running the command in detached mode is particularly useful for services that need to persist and operate independently of the terminal session.

Stopping Services

To halt running services, the down command is used:

```
docker-compose down
```

This command stops and removes the containers defined in the docker-compose.yml file. It also removes associated networks by default unless they are specified as external networks. One can selectively stop services without removing their containers using the stop command:

```
docker-compose stop
```

This is especially useful in situations where a temporary stop of services is necessary without the need for a complete teardown.

Pausing and Unpausing Services

Services can be paused and unpaused using the pause and unpause commands, respectively. These commands are valuable when you want to momentarily suspend the container processes without stopping them outright.

```
docker-compose pause
docker-compose unpause
```

Pausing is particularly useful for performing quick maintenance tasks on the host without stopping the services completely.

Restarting Services

Restarting services is simpler with the restart command, which can restart all services or specific ones as needed.

```
docker-compose restart
```

Service-specific restarts can be done by specifying the service name:

```
docker-compose restart <service_name>
```

Restarting allows for configurations and environments to be re-applied without tearing down the entire setup, beneficial during testing and debugging phases.

Removing Containers and Volumes

The down command is further enhanced with options to remove volumes and images.

```
docker-compose down --volumes
docker-compose down --rmi all
```

Including the –volumes flag ensures that any anonymous volumes are also removed, freeing up storage space. The –rmi all flag instructs Docker Compose to remove all images used by services in the Compose file, which can be particularly useful in CI/CD pipelines or when cleaning up development environments.

Checking Service Status

Determining the status of running services can be performed with the ps command, which lists all the containers running in the context of the Compose file.

```
docker-compose ps
```

This command provides information including container names, statuses, ports, and other metadata, essential for monitoring and managing services.

Logging

For effective troubleshooting, viewing the logs of running services is imperative. Docker Compose facilitates this with the logs command.

```
docker-compose logs
```

To tail logs in real-time and follow the log output, the -f option (follow mode) can be used:

```
docker-compose logs -f
```

It is also possible to view logs for individual services by specifying the service name.

```
docker-compose logs <service_name>
```

Building and Rebuilding Services

When changes are made to the code or configuration, rebuilding the services may be necessary. This is done using the build command.

```
docker-compose build
```

One can force a rebuild even if nothing has changed by adding the –no-cache option, ensuring the latest versions of dependencies are used:

```
docker-compose build --no-cache
```

For ease, the rebuild can also be combined with up:

```
docker-compose up --build
```

Managing dependencies across containers is a facilitated process using Docker Compose. These commands demonstrated here streamline lifecycle management, making oversight of application deployment and maintenance more intuitive and efficient. Through mastery of these commands, a developer can ensure that applications perform reliably and securely throughout their lifecycle within a Docker Compose orchestrated environment.

7.12 Using Compose with Docker Swarm

Docker Swarm Mode is an integral feature of Docker that allows you to manage a cluster of Docker engines, which can be run in Swarm Mode to host distributed applications. Utilizing Docker Compose in conjunction with Docker Swarm enables orchestrating multi-container environments effectively and with higher resilience. Detailed utilization of Docker Compose files with Docker Swarm unifies cluster management and application lifecycle operations even in complex microservice architectures.

The primary advantage of Docker Swarm Mode is its native clustering functionality, enabling services expansion across various nodes while maintaining the simplicity of Docker Compose syntax. Understanding this powerful combination begins with deploying a Docker Swarm cluster and subsequently orchestrating the deployment with a Docker Compose file.

1. Initializing Docker Swarm

Starting a Docker Swarm cluster requires initializing the primary manager node. On this node, execute the following command:

```
docker swarm init --advertise-addr <MANAGER-IP>
```

```
Swarm initialized: current node (qwer1234abcd) is now a manager.
```

The –advertise-addr option specifies the manager's IP address that other nodes will use to join the swarm.

2. Joining Worker Nodes to the Swarm

Additional nodes can join the swarm as worker nodes using the command generated at the time of initialization. For instance:

```
docker swarm join --token SWMTKN-1-4jhs2t1a4bfjsgfyt5l0'accueilz \
<MANAGER-IP>:2377
```

```
This node joined a swarm as a worker.
```

This structure enables a flexible and decentralized system wherein tasks can be distributed across multiple nodes.

3. Deploying Services Using Docker Compose

Once the Swarm is initialized and worker nodes have joined, services can be deployed using a Docker Compose file. Docker Swarm leverages the Compose file structure for service definitions. A sample docker-compose.yml might look like the following:

```
version: '3.8'
services:
  web:
    image: nginx:alpine
    ports:
      - "80:80"
  redis:
    image: redis:alpine
    deploy:
      replicas: 3
      update_config:
        parallelism: 2
        delay: 10s
      restart_policy:
        condition: on-failure
    volumes:
      - redis_data:/data

volumes:
  redis_data:
```

The key capability here is that Swarm-specific configurations such as deploy parameters for service scaling, update configurations, and restart policies can be specified directly in the Compose file.

4. Deploying the Compose File to Swarm

Deploy the services defined in the docker-compose.yml file to the Swarm by employing the docker stack deploy command:

```
docker stack deploy -c docker-compose.yml <STACK-NAME>
```

```
Creating network <STACK-NAME>_default
Creating service <STACK-NAME>_web
Creating service <STACK-NAME>_redis
```

The -c flag specifies the Compose file, and <STACK-NAME> is the identifier for the collection of services being deployed as a stack.

5. Managing and Scaling Swarm Services

Services within the Swarm can be managed and scaled post-deployment using the docker service commands. To scale the Redis service defined previously, execute:

```
docker service scale <STACK-NAME>_redis=5
```

```
<STACK-NAME>_redis scaled to 5
overall progress: 5 out of 5 tasks
verify: Service converged
```

Swarm automatically manages the placement and lifecycle of these service instances, ensuring high availability and fault tolerance.

6. Updating Services in Swarm

Updating the application or configuration can be achieved seamlessly. For example, modifying the Compose file to update the NGINX image to a new version:

```
web:
  image: nginx:latest
```

Redeploy using the same docker stack deploy command:

```
docker stack deploy -c docker-compose.yml <STACK-NAME>
```

Swarm orchestrates a rolling update ensuring that service disruption is minimized by configuring update parameters defined under the deploy section.

7. Monitoring and Cleanup

Monitoring the state of the services and stack can be performed using the docker stack services and docker stack ps commands:

```
docker stack services <STACK-NAME>
docker stack ps <STACK-NAME>
```

Cleanup of the entire stack involves the command:

```
docker stack rm <STACK-NAME>
```

Utilizing Docker Compose with Docker Swarm enables robust multi-container application deployment in cluster environments. The combination allows for scalable, fault-tolerant applications managed through simplified configurations provided in Docker Compose files.

7.13 Best Practices for Docker Compose

Using Docker Compose efficiently in production environments requires adherence to best practices to ensure optimal performance, security, and maintainability of multi-container applications. Below are several recommendations that provide a structured approach for utilizing Docker Compose effectively.

Configuration Management

- **Use environment variables**: Environment variables should be utilized to manage environment-specific configurations. This practice facilitates the application's deployment across multiple environments (development, testing, production) without modifying the Docker Compose file. Store these variables in a .env file and reference them in the docker-compose.yml using ${VARIABLE_NAME} syntax.

```
version: '3.8'
services:
  app:
    image: myapp:latest
    environment:
      - APP_ENV=${APP_ENV}
```

- **Secret management**: Sensitive information, such as database credentials or API keys, should not be hard-coded in the docker-compose.yml. Instead, use Docker Swarm secrets or other secret management tools. Docker Compose provides an interface to securely manage these secrets.

```
version: '3.8'
services:
  app:
    image: myapp:latest
    secrets:
      - db_password

secrets:
  db_password:
    file: ./db_password.txt
```

- **Configuration separation**: Maintain separate Docker Compose files for distinct environments to manage configuration differences effectively. Use the docker-compose.override.yml for development configurations that can override the default settings.

```
docker-compose -f docker-compose.yml -f docker-compose.prod.yml up
```

Resource Management

- **Limit container resources**: Define resource constraints in the Docker Compose file to ensure fair resource allocation and to prevent any single container from monopolizing the host system's resources. This is achieved using the deploy.resources property.

```
version: '3.8'
services:
  app:
    image: myapp:latest
    deploy:
      resources:
```

```
        limits:
          cpus: '0.5'
          memory: 512M
```

- **Health checks**: Implement health checks to ensure that your services are running correctly. This helps in detecting and recovering from failures more effectively.

```
version: '3.8'
services:
  app:
    image: myapp:latest
    healthcheck:
      test: ["CMD", "curl", "-f", "http://localhost"]
      interval: 1m30s
      timeout: 10s
      retries: 3
```

Network Management

- **Use custom networks**: Define custom networks in Docker Compose to control the network topology and isolation between services. This ensures that only the necessary services can communicate with each other.

```
version: '3.8'
services:
  app:
    image: myapp:latest
    networks:
      - frontend

  db:
    image: mysql:5.7
    networks:
      - backend

networks:
  frontend:
  backend:
```

- **Network aliases**: Assign network aliases to services so that they can be accessed by these aliases within the network. This is useful for service discovery and maintaining clean and understandable service interactions.

```
version: '3.8'
services:
  cache:
    image: redis
    networks:
      backend:
        aliases:
```

```
      - redis-cache
```

Service Management

- **Use versioning for images**: Always tag your Docker images with explicit version tags (e.g., myapp:1.0.1) instead of using the latest tag. This practice assists in keeping track of which version of the service is running and helps in rollback scenarios if a deployment fails.
- **Leverage rolling updates**: In Docker Swarm and Kubernetes, leverage rolling updates to minimize downtime. Configure the deploy.update_config property to define how updates to services should be handled.

```
version: '3.8'
services:
  app:
    image: myapp:1.0.1
    deploy:
      update_config:
        parallelism: 2
        delay: 10s
```

- **Backup and recovery**: Implement strategies for backup and recovery, especially for stateful services such as databases. Ensure volumes used by these services are regularly backed up.

Logging and Monitoring

- **Centralized logging**: Use centralized logging systems (e.g., ELK stack, Fluentd) to aggregate and manage logs from all containers. Set up Docker logging drivers to send logs to these systems.

```
version: '3.8'
services:
  app:
    image: myapp:latest
    logging:
      driver: "json-file"
      options:
        max-size: "10m"
        max-file: "3"
```

- **Monitor container metrics**: Monitor performance metrics (CPU, memory, network usage) of your containers using monitoring tools like Prometheus and Grafana. This helps in proactive detection of any resource bottlenecks.

Security Best Practices

- **User permissions**: Avoid running containers as root. Use the user property to specify a non-root user.

```
version: '3.8'
services:
  app:
    image: myapp:latest
    user: "1000:1000"
```

- **Keep images up to date**: Regularly update your base images and application images to incorporate the latest security patches. Automate this process using CI/CD pipelines.
- **Set resource limits**: Define resource limits for your services to prevent Denial of Service (DoS) attacks and other forms of abuse.

Adopting these best practices ensures that Docker Compose applications remain efficient, manageable, and secure. By integrating environment-specific configurations, resource constraints, and proper logging and monitoring mechanisms, we achieve a robust orchestration system capable of handling complex multi-container deployments efficiently.

Security Best Practices

Chapter 8

Docker Kubernetes Integration

This chapter covers the integration of Docker with Kubernetes, explaining Kubernetes architecture and the process of setting up and deploying Docker containers on Kubernetes. It includes managing Kubernetes clusters, pods, and deployments, as well as networking, storage, and service discovery. Advanced topics such as using ConfigMaps and Secrets, scaling applications, monitoring and logging, and Kubernetes security best practices are also discussed.

8.1 Introduction to Kubernetes

Kubernetes, commonly abbreviated as K8s, is an open-source system for automating the deployment, scaling, and management of containerized applications. Developed initially by Google and now maintained by the Cloud Native Computing Foundation (CNCF), Kubernetes has become the de facto standard for container orchestration. It enables developers to deploy applications across a cluster of machines, abstracting the complexity of managing hardware resources and providing robust mechanisms for maintaining service availability.

To understand Kubernetes, it is vital to grasp its core concepts, architectural components, and the key terminology used throughout the system.

Kubernetes follows a declarative model, where the desired state of the system is defined, and the control plane works to match the current state to the desired state continuously.

Core Concepts

Cluster: A Kubernetes cluster is a set of node machines for running containerized applications. A cluster has one or more master nodes and a set of worker nodes.

Node: A node is a single machine in the Kubernetes cluster, which can be either a virtual or physical machine. Each node runs one or more pods.

Pod: A pod is the smallest, most basic deployable object in Kubernetes, representing a single instance of a running process in the cluster. Pods contain one or more containers and share the same network namespace, IP address, and storage.

Control Plane: The control plane consists of components that provide the cluster's management layer. The control plane makes global decisions about the cluster (e.g., scheduling) as well as detecting and responding to cluster events (e.g., starting up a new pod when a deployment's 'replicas' field is unsatisfied). Components of the control plane include the API server, controller manager, scheduler, and etcd storage.

API Server: The Kubernetes API server (kube-apiserver) is a component of the Kubernetes control plane that exposes the Kubernetes API. The API server is the front-end for the Kubernetes control plane.

Controller Manager: The controller manager runs controller processes. Controllers are responsible for noticing and responding when clusters lack the desired state. Example controllers include those handling replication, endpoints, and namespace management.

Scheduler: The Kubernetes scheduler (kube-scheduler) watches for newly created pods with no assigned node and selects a node for them to run on. The scheduler considers the available resources on each node to make efficient scheduling decisions.

etcd: etcd is a consistent and highly-available key-value store used by Kubernetes for all cluster data storage.

Kubelet: The kubelet is the primary "node agent" that runs on each node. It ensures that containers are running in a pod. The kubelet takes a set of PodSpecs provided through various mechanisms and ensures that the containers described in those PodSpecs are running and healthy.

Container Runtime: The container runtime is the software that is responsible for running containers. Kubernetes supports several container runtimes: Docker, containerd, CRI-O, and any implementation of the Kubernetes CRI (Container Runtime Interface).

Communication in Kubernetes

Kubernetes uses a tiered model of communication for efficient cluster management. The API server is central to all communications, facilitating interactions between various components within the control plane and the worker nodes.

Networking Model

Kubernetes defines a flat network structure where every pod can communicate with every other pod without using Network Address Translation (NAT). This model simplifies the network topology of clusters and provides flexibility in communication. To implement this networking, Kubernetes requires a Container Network Interface (CNI) plugin. Popular CNIs include Weave Net, Flannel, Calico, and Cilium.

Kubernetes clusters achieve network isolation through the use of namespaces, which partition network spaces within the same Kubernetes cluster. Network policies define how pods are allowed to communicate with each other and other network endpoints, enhancing security and control over inter-pod traffic.

Example Deployment

To practically illustrate Kubernetes deployment, consider the following example with a simple Nginx web server. The deployment YAML file defines a deployment with a 'replica' count of 3 for redundancy and load balancing.

```
apiVersion: apps/v1
kind: Deployment
metadata:
  name: nginx-deployment
spec:
  replicas: 3
  selector:
    matchLabels:
      app: nginx
  template:
    metadata:
      labels:
        app: nginx
    spec:
      containers:
      - name: nginx
        image: nginx:1.14.2
```

```
        ports:
        - containerPort: 80
```

To apply this deployment, one would use the 'kubectl' command-line tool:

```
kubectl apply -f nginx-deployment.yaml
```

The successful output will look like:

```
deployment.apps/nginx-deployment created
```

This deployment will automatically manage the desired number of pod replicas, ensuring that 3 instances of the Nginx container are running at all times.

In Kubernetes, the declarative configuration of the environment and applications, supported by robust automation, scalability, and high availability, fundamentally transforms the dynamic nature of managing containers. Understanding these foundational elements will facilitate comprehension of more advanced topics, such as scaling applications, managing configurations, and securing Kubernetes clusters, which will be covered in subsequent sections.

8.2 Understanding Kubernetes Architecture

Kubernetes architecture is built around a distributed system design aimed at managing containerized applications across multiple hosts. This architecture ensures high availability, scalability, and efficient resource utilization. The primary components of Kubernetes' architecture include the Control Plane and the Worker Nodes. Each plays a critical role in maintaining the desired state and operational functions of the cluster.

The Control Plane is responsible for providing the global state management and orchestration of the cluster. It consists of several key components: the API Server, etcd, the Scheduler, and the Controller Manager. These components collectively ensure that the application's desired state matches the cluster's actual state.

- **API Server**: The API Server acts as the front end for the Kubernetes Control Plane. It's the central management entity, through which all administrative tasks communicate with the cluster. The API Server exposes the Kubernetes API, which follows RESTful principles, and is utilized by kubectl (command-line tool), other API clients, and all Control Plane components.

```
curl -X GET http://<api-server-endpoint>/api/v1/nodes
```

```
Output:
{
  "kind": "NodeList",
  "apiVersion": "v1",
  "items": [...],
}
```

The API Server authenticates, authorizes, and processes REST requests, coordinating changes to shared resources.

- **etcd**: Kubernetes uses etcd as its consistent and reliable key-value store for all cluster data. etcd stores the entire configuration and state of the cluster. The strong consistency model of etcd is crucial for ensuring reliable state retrieval and updates across different nodes. It's also highly available and secures key-value data. Consistency in etcd is enforced via the Raft consensus algorithm, meaning all endpoints recognize the same source of truth.

```
etcdctl put /message "Hello, etcd"
etcdctl get /message
```

```
Output:
Hello, etcd
```

- **Scheduler**: The Scheduler ensures Pods are assigned to available nodes efficiently. It considers various factors such as resource requirements (CPU, Memory), combined assignments, and policies to best fit the Pods. The Scheduler continuously tracks resource utilization to make well-informed decisions on placing newly created or unscheduled Pods onto appropriate nodes.

```
apiVersion: v1
kind: Pod
metadata:
  name: resource-demo
spec:
  containers:
  - name: demo
    image: nginx
    resources:
      requests:
        memory: "64Mi"
        cpu: "250m"
      limits:
        memory: "128Mi"
        cpu: "500m"
```

- **Controller Manager**: The Controller Manager runs various controller processes to regulate state. A controller tracks the cluster's state via the API Server and takes action to drive the actual state towards the desired state. Controllers include Node Controller for managing nodes, Replication Controller for maintaining the correct number of pods, and Endpoint Controller for mapping services to pods.

Worker Nodes execute the workloads and host the running containers. Each Worker Node runs two essential agents: the Kubelet and the Kube-Proxy.

- **Kubelet**: The Kubelet ensures that containers are running in Pods. It receives Pod specifications from the API Server and executes the containers via container runtime, be it Docker, containerd, or another OCI-compliant runtime. The Kubelet interacts with the container runtime to pull images, start, stop, and manage container life cycles. It also reports the node's status and resource utilization back to the Control Plane.

```
kubectl get nodes
```

```
Output:
NAME        STATUS   ROLES    AGE   VERSION
worker-1    Ready    <none>   7d    v1.20.2
worker-2    Ready    <none>   7d    v1.20.2
```

- **Kube-Proxy**: The Kube-Proxy maintains network rules on each node. These rules allow network communication to Pods, allowing network sessions inside or outside the cluster. Kube-Proxy supports various modes such as Userspace, iptables, and IPVS to balance traffic between endpoints in a service.

```
kubectl get services
```

```
Output:
NAME         TYPE        CLUSTER-IP   EXTERNAL-IP   PORT(S)        AGE
kubernetes   ClusterIP   10.0.0.1     <none>        443/TCP        10d
nginx-svc    NodePort    10.0.0.2     <none>        80:30001/TCP   5d
```

Moreover, Kubernetes uses additional optional components such as add-ons to extend its functionality, including DNS, UI dashboards, monitoring (e.g., Prometheus), logging (e.g., ELK stack), and service meshes (e.g., Istio). These components must seamlessly integrate into the existing architecture to provide a robust and scalable container orchestration platform. Each added component integrates with the Kubernetes API Server, thereby accepting policies and modifications dynamically.

All interactions within a Kubernetes cluster leverage a modular and pluggable architecture. This ensures scalable, failure-resistant orchestration and management of distributed systems.

8.3 Setting Up Kubernetes with Docker

Setting up Kubernetes with Docker involves several steps, including installation of necessary tools and configuration of your environment. Docker provides a containerization platform, while Kubernetes offers container orchestration. Combining these technologies effectively allows you to manage, scale, and automate containerized applications.

First, ensure that Docker is installed and running on your system. Docker provides extensive documentation and installation guides suitable for different operating systems. For Linux-based systems, the command to add Docker's official GPG key and set up the stable repository is:

```
sudo mkdir -p /etc/apt/keyrings
curl -fsSL https://download.docker.com/linux/debian/gpg | sudo gpg --dearmor -o /etc/
    apt/keyrings/docker.gpg
echo \
  "deb [arch=$(dpkg --print-architecture) signed-by=/etc/apt/keyrings/docker.gpg]
      https://download.docker.com/linux/debian \
  $(lsb_release -cs) stable" | sudo tee /etc/apt/sources.list.d/docker.list > /dev/null
sudo apt-get update
sudo apt-get install docker-ce docker-ce-cli containerd.io docker-compose-plugin
sudo systemctl start docker
sudo systemctl enable docker
```

You can verify the Docker installation and its version with:

```
docker --version
```

```
Docker version 20.10.7, build f0df350
```

After installing Docker, the next step is to install 'kubectl', the Kubernetes command-line tool, which allows you to run commands against Kubernetes clusters. 'kubectl' can be installed using various package managers. For example, on a Debian-based system:

```
curl -LO "https://dl.k8s.io/release/$(curl -L -s https://dl.k8s.io/release/stable.txt)/bin
    /linux/amd64/kubectl"
chmod +x kubectl
sudo mv kubectl /usr/local/bin/
```

Verify that 'kubectl' is installed correctly:

```
kubectl version --client
```

```
Client Version: version.Info{Major:"1", Minor:"21", GitVersion:"v1.21.0", ...}
```

Next, install 'minikube', a tool that lets you run Kubernetes locally. Minikube runs a single-node Kubernetes cluster on your machine for development and testing purposes. Install Minikube using the following commands:

```
curl -LO https://storage.googleapis.com/minikube/releases/latest/minikube-linux-
    amd64
sudo install minikube-linux-amd64 /usr/local/bin/minikube
minikube start --driver=docker
```

The 'minikube start –driver=docker' command initiates a Kubernetes cluster using Docker as the driver. Confirm that Minikube is running:

```
minikube status
```

```
minikube
type: Control Plane
host: Running
kubelet: Running
apiserver: Running
kubeconfig: Configured
```

Minikube uses 'kubectl' for interacting with the cluster:

```
kubectl get pods -A
```

This command lists all running pods across all namespaces in the Minikube cluster. Initially, it will include system pods deployed by Kubernetes for core functionality.

Next, configure Docker to work with Minikube. Minikube creates a Docker environment that mimics production settings, however, it runs locally. To use the Docker daemon from Minikube in your environment, configure your shell:

```
eval $(minikube -p minikube docker-env)
```

Now, any Docker commands you run will use Minikube's Docker daemon. For example, you can build images inside the Minikube environment without pushing them to a registry:

```
docker build -t myk8sapp:v1 .
```

After building the Docker image, create a Kubernetes deployment to manage and scale your containerized application. Use the following 'kubectl' command to create a deployment:

```
kubectl create deployment myk8sapp --image=myk8sapp:v1
```

Verify that the deployment is successful by listing the pods:

```
kubectl get pods
```

```
NAME                        READY   STATUS    RESTARTS   AGE
myk8sapp-5b6f7d7b5b-mnkjz   1/1     Running   0          1m
```

Expose the deployment to the outside world as a service:

```
kubectl expose deployment myk8sapp --type=LoadBalancer --port=8080
```

You can access the service using the Minikube IP and assigned port. Retrieve the service URL using:

```
minikube service myk8sapp --url
```

Finally, clean up the resources to free up your environment. Delete the created service and deployment:

```
kubectl delete service myk8sapp
kubectl delete deployment myk8sapp
```

Stop Minikube to conserve system resources:

```
minikube stop
```

This section demonstrates the integration of Docker with Kubernetes using Minikube, setting up a local development environment capable of running and managing containerized applications.

8.4 Deploying Docker Containers on Kubernetes

Deploying Docker containers on Kubernetes involves several key steps, each requiring precise command execution and a deep understanding of the microservices architecture. This section will guide you through the entire process, ensuring that you gain the expertise needed to efficiently deploy and manage Docker containers in a Kubernetes environment.

1. Prerequisites

Before deploying Docker containers on Kubernetes, ensure that you have a functional Kubernetes cluster and the kubectl command-line tool configured to communicate with your cluster. Additionally, you should have Docker images ready to be deployed.

2. Creating Kubernetes Deployments

A Kubernetes deployment is a resource object that provides declarative updates to applications. To create a deployment, you need to define a YAML file that specifies the desired state, including the Docker image, number of replicas, and other configuration details.

Here is a sample YAML file named deployment.yaml:

```
apiVersion: apps/v1
kind: Deployment
metadata:
  name: my-docker-app
spec:
  replicas: 3
  selector:
    matchLabels:
      app: my-docker-app
  template:
    metadata:
      labels:
        app: my-docker-app
    spec:
      containers:
      - name: my-docker-app-container
        image: my-docker-app:latest
        ports:
        - containerPort: 8080
```

To create the deployment, execute the following command:

```
kubectl apply -f deployment.yaml
```

Upon execution, Kubernetes will pull the Docker image defined in the YAML file, create the specified number of replicas, and manage the deployment lifecycle.

3. Verifying Deployments

Verify that the deployment was successful by inspecting the deployment and pods:

```
kubectl get deployments
kubectl get pods
```

These commands list the current deployments and pods, respectively. The output should show the desired number of replicas running.

```
NAME            READY   UP-TO-DATE   AVAILABLE   AGE
my-docker-app   3/3     3            3           2m
```

4. Exposing Deployments

To allow external access to your application, create a service resource that maps a port on your cluster to a port on your pods. Define a service resource in a YAML file named service.yaml:

```
apiVersion: v1
kind: Service
metadata:
  name: my-docker-app-service
spec:
  selector:
    app: my-docker-app
  ports:
    - protocol: TCP
      port: 80
      targetPort: 8080
  type: LoadBalancer
```

Then, apply the service configuration:

```
kubectl apply -f service.yaml
```

This command creates a service of type LoadBalancer, which will expose your application externally. To obtain the external IP address of the service, use:

```
kubectl get services
```

The output will display the external IP address assigned to the service.

```
NAME                   TYPE           CLUSTER-IP   EXTERNAL-IP     PORT(S)        AGE
my-docker-app-service  LoadBalancer   10.96.0.1    <external-ip>   80:30622/TCP   1m
```

5. Managing and Updating Deployments

Kubernetes allows imperative and declarative management of deployments. To update the deployment, modify the YAML file and reapply it. For instance, to update the Docker image:

```
spec:
  containers:
  - name: my-docker-app-container
    image: my-docker-app:v2
```

Apply the updated YAML file:

```
kubectl apply -f deployment.yaml
```

Kubernetes will perform a rolling update, gradually replacing old instances with new ones, ensuring zero downtime.

6. Rolling Back Deployments

Should an update fail or introduce issues, you can rollback to a previous deployment version:

```
kubectl rollout undo deployment/my-docker-app
```

This command reverts the deployment to its previous state.

7. Scaling Deployments

Scaling deployments is pivotal for handling increased traffic or resource optimization. Modify the replicas field in the deployment YAML file, or scale imperatively using:

```
kubectl scale deployment my-docker-app --replicas=5
```

Kubernetes adjusts the deployment to the desired state.

Deploying Docker containers on Kubernetes involves creating deployment and service resources, verifying and managing deployments, updating and rolling back changes, and scaling applications. These operations form the cornerstone of Kubernetes container management, providing robustness, flexibility, and seamless scalability for modern applications.

8.5 Kubernetes Pods and Deployments

Kubernetes abstracts the complexity of managing containerized applications through defined constructs like Pods and Deployments. These constructs are integral to understanding and efficiently utilizing the Kubernetes ecosystem.

Pods are the smallest deployable units in Kubernetes and represent a single instance of a running process within your cluster. Each Pod encapsulates one or more containers, ensuring they are co-located on the same host machine and can share resources and dependencies. All containers in a Pod share the same network namespace, including the IP address and port space, enabling inter-container communication via localhost.

```
apiVersion: v1
kind: Pod
metadata:
  name: example-pod
spec:
  containers:
  - name: nginx
    image: nginx:1.17
    ports:
```

```
    - containerPort: 80
```

The above YAML configuration file defines a Pod named example-pod that runs an nginx container. Within the spec field, the Pod specifies the container's properties, such as the image and containerPort.

A Pod can pass through different lifecycle phases, such as Pending, Running, Succeeded, Failed, and Unknown. These phases collectively help in tracking the status and understanding the state of the application.

Deployments build on Pods, providing declarative updates to applications. A Deployment supervises the creation and management of a set of identical Pods and ensures that the defined number of Pods are running at all times. This is particularly beneficial for load balancing and scaling applications seamlessly.

```
apiVersion: apps/v1
kind: Deployment
metadata:
  name: example-deployment
spec:
  replicas: 3
  selector:
    matchLabels:
      app: nginx
  template:
    metadata:
      labels:
        app: nginx
    spec:
      containers:
      - name: nginx
        image: nginx:1.17
        ports:
        - containerPort: 80
```

The configuration file above defines a Deployment named example-deployment which maintains three replicas of an nginx Pod. Under the selector field, the Deployment manages Pods labeled with app: nginx, as specified under the template.metadata.labels.

In a Deployment, the specified number of replicas determines the desired state. Kubernetes continuously monitors the Deployment and adjusts the cluster to maintain the desired number of replicas, addressing issues like Pod failures, rescheduling, and offering rolling updates.

Deployments facilitate rolling updates with minimal downtime. When an update is triggered, the new Pods are created with the updated version, gracefully replacing the old Pods. This ensures the application remains accessible throughout the update process.

```
# Create the deployment
kubectl apply -f deployment.yaml

# Get status of the deployment
kubectl get deployments

# Scale the deployment to 5 replicas
kubectl scale deployment example-deployment --replicas=5

# Update the image in the deployment
kubectl set image deployment/example-deployment nginx=nginx:1.18

# View the rollout status
kubectl rollout status deployment/example-deployment

# Rollback the deployment to the previous stable state
kubectl rollout undo deployment/example-deployment
```

The above command set demonstrates common operations on a Deployment. The kubectl apply command initiates the deployment process described by the deployment.yaml file. Monitoring the deployment status, scaling, updating the image, checking rollout progress, and rolling back are achieved through straightforward kubectl commands, enhancing the manageability and efficiency of application deployments.

Understanding the interplay between Pods and Deployments is vital for effective application orchestration in Kubernetes. Pods serve as the atomic unit of deployment, encapsulating one or more containers to run an instance of an application. Deployments manage these Pods, ensuring desired states are met and providing the necessary mechanisms for scaling, updating, and ensuring application reliability.

8.6 Service Discovery and Networking in Kubernetes

Service discovery and networking are fundamental aspects of Kubernetes, enabling seamless communication between different components in a cluster. Kubernetes employs a comprehensive and flexible approach to networking that underpins the effective operation of services and the uniform management of pods' connectivity.

Service Discovery in Kubernetes

Kubernetes services enable the abstraction and grouping of a set of pods, allowing you to categorize these groups for logical structuring. A **Service** in Kubernetes provides an abstraction over the pods and supports service discovery by offering a stable endpoint, which remains consistent despite changes in the pod instances.

Kubernetes offers two primary service discovery mechanisms:

- **Environment Variables:** Kubernetes injects environment variables that contain service information into the pods when they start up. This approach, however, is static, and pods must be restarted to see changes.
- **DNS:** Kubernetes cluster includes a DNS server that tests each service and creates DNS records for them. DNS is much more dynamic compared to environment variable injection.

The following example demonstrates the creation of a service that exposes a set of pod replicas:

```
apiVersion: v1
kind: Service
metadata:
  name: my-service
spec:
  selector:
    app: MyApp
  ports:
    - protocol: TCP
      port: 80
      targetPort: 9376
```

This YAML configuration file creates a service named my-service that matches all pods labeled app=MyApp, and forwards incoming traffic on port 80 to the target port 9376 on the corresponding pods.

Networking in Kubernetes

Kubernetes networking design principles emphasize the ease of communication within the cluster by assuming a flat, non-isolated network model. Each pod receives a unique IP address, enabling direct inter-pod communication. Kubernetes enforces the following network model constraints:

- Pods on a node can communicate with all pods on all other nodes without Network Address Translation (NAT).
- Agents and services in the Kubernetes core can communicate with all pods without NAT.
- Network policies enable control over the communication flows inside the cluster.

Kubernetes Networking Model

The model comprises different layers and components, including:

- **Container-to-Container Networking:** Containers in the same pod share the same IP address and port space. They communicate with each other via the localhost network interface.
- **Pod-to-Pod Networking:** Pods communicate using their unique IP addresses. Kubernetes networking plugins, such as Flannel, Weave, and Calico, typically manage this layer.
- **Pod-to-Service Networking:** Services have a fixed IP that abstracts and load-balances to the backend pods. Within a namespace, Kubernetes DNS resolves the service name to the service IP.

Network Plugins

Several third-party network plugins comply with Kubernetes' Container Network Interface (CNI) specifications:

- **Flannel:** Implements a simple overlay network suitable for small to medium-sized clusters.
- **Calico:** Provides network policy and security enforcement with performance-optimized routing.
- **Weave Net:** Focuses on simplicity and quick setup, supporting multi-cloud and hybrid deployments.

Here is an example of defining network policies to control pod access:

```
apiVersion: networking.k8s.io/v1
kind: NetworkPolicy
metadata:
  name: allow-same-namespace
  namespace: default
spec:
  podSelector:
    matchLabels:
      role: db
  policyTypes:
  - Ingress
  - Egress
  ingress:
  - from:
    - podSelector:
        matchLabels:
          role: frontend
```

```
egress:
- to:
  - podSelector:
      matchLabels:
        role: backend
  ports:
  - protocol: TCP
    port: 3306
```

This policy defines ingress rules such that only pods with the label role:frontend can communicate with pods labeled role:db within the same namespace. Similarly, it allows egress traffic from db pods to backend pods on TCP port 3306.

Load Balancing

Kubernetes also supports various forms of load balancing. At the simplest level, the Kubernetes Service is a basic load balancer across pods. For external traffic, Kubernetes integrates with cloud providers and on-premises load balancers.

ClusterIP: The default type of service, providing an internal IP address accessible only within the cluster.

NodePort: Exposes a service on each node's IP at a static port, which requires manual configuration of external load balancers.

LoadBalancer: Automatically configures an external load balancer, integrating with cloud provider APIs to expose services publicly.

```
apiVersion: v1
kind: Service
metadata:
  name: my-loadbalanced-service
spec:
  type: LoadBalancer
  selector:
    app: MyApp
  ports:
    - port: 80
      targetPort: 9376
```

The above example deploys a LoadBalancer service, integrating with the cloud provider to expose a public IP for accessing the application.

As Kubernetes continues to evolve, enhancements in networking and service discovery are expected to offer even more flexibility, power, and simplicity in managing clustered environments. The comprehensive understanding of these concepts is crucial for efficient and reliable application deployment in Kubernetes orchestrated environments.

8.7 Managing Storage with Kubernetes

Efficient and reliable data storage is critical for containerized applications, especially with stateful applications that require persistent storage across the lifecycle of containers. Kubernetes provides a comprehensive and flexible set of storage solutions to address these needs, allowing applications to persist data reliably while retaining the benefits of container orchestration. This section delves into the various storage options within Kubernetes, their configuration, and management techniques.

Kubernetes abstracts storage through several key concepts: Volumes, PersistentVolumes (PVs), PersistentVolumeClaims (PVCs), and StorageClasses. Each of these components plays a crucial role in the Kubernetes storage architecture, and understanding their interplay is essential for effective storage management.

Volumes in Kubernetes are directories accessible to containers in a Pod. Unlike traditional storage in Docker, Kubernetes Volumes are lifecycle-bound to the Pod itself, meaning the volume data persists as long as the Pod exists. There are various types of volumes, such as emptyDir, hostPath, configMap, and secret. Each volume type serves different use cases, from temporary storage (emptyDir) to accessing host machine directories (hostPath), or for storing configuration data (configMap and secret).

An example of a Pod spec defining an 'emptyDir' volume and using it in a container is shown below:

```
apiVersion: v1
kind: Pod
metadata:
  name: my-pod
spec:
  containers:
  - name: my-container
    image: busybox
    volumeMounts:
    - mountPath: /usr/share/nginx/html
      name: my-storage
  volumes:
  - name: my-storage
    emptyDir: {}
```

This setup ensures that the directory at /usr/share/nginx/html in the container will have an emptyDir volume mounted to it, which exists for the lifetime of the Pod.

PersistentVolumes (PVs) are a Kubernetes resource that abstracts physical storage. They provide a mechanism to assign storage resources to the cluster independently of how they are consumed. PVs are cluster-scoped and represent real storage. They can be provisioned dynamically or statically, based on the defined StorageClasses.

An example of a PersistentVolume definition:

```
apiVersion: v1
kind: PersistentVolume
metadata:
  name: pv-example
spec:
  capacity:
    storage: 1Gi
  accessModes:
    - ReadWriteOnce
  persistentVolumeReclaimPolicy: Retain
  hostPath:
    path: "/mnt/data"
```

This PV declares a 1GiB storage capacity using a host path at /mnt/data, with an accessMode of ReadWriteOnce, making it accessible by a single node.

PersistentVolumeClaims (PVCs) are resource requests for storage by a user. A PVC specifies the storage size and access modes needed by a Pod. The Kubernetes control plane matches and binds the PVC to an appropriate PV based on the request's attributes and constraints.

An example of a PersistentVolumeClaim definition:

```
apiVersion: v1
kind: PersistentVolumeClaim
metadata:
  name: pvc-example
spec:
  accessModes:
    - ReadWriteOnce
  resources:
    requests:
      storage: 1Gi
```

In this PVC example, a request for 1GiB of storage with single-node read/write access is made. If a suitable PV is available, Kubernetes binds the PVC to it.

StorageClasses define different classes or profiles of storage based on performance, cost, or other characteristics. They facilitate dynamic provisioning of PVs, automatically supplying storage when PVCs are created. StorageClasses encapsulate the details of storage provider configurations.

An example of a StorageClass definition:

```
apiVersion: storage.k8s.io/v1
kind: StorageClass
metadata:
  name: standard
provisioner: kubernetes.io/aws-ebs
parameters:
  type: gp2
  zone: us-west-2a
reclaimPolicy: Delete
```

This StorageClass named standard uses the AWS EBS provisioner to dynamically allocate GP2-type storage in the us-west-2a zone, with a reclaim policy of Delete.

Dynamic Provisioning leverages StorageClasses for automatic PV creation to satisfy PVCs without manual intervention. This is highly efficient in cloud environments where underlying infrastructure supports such operations through APIs.

A PVC leveraging dynamic provisioning with a StorageClass:

```
apiVersion: v1
kind: PersistentVolumeClaim
metadata:
  name: pvc-dynamic-example
spec:
  storageClassName: standard
  accessModes:
    - ReadWriteOnce
  resources:
    requests:
      storage: 5Gi
```

When this PVC is created, Kubernetes uses the standard StorageClass to provision the required 5GiB storage dynamically.

Access Modes determine how a volume can be accessed once mounted to a Pod. These modes include ReadWriteOnce (mounted as read-write by a single node), ReadOnlyMany (mounted as read-only by multiple nodes), and ReadWriteMany (mounted as read-write by multiple nodes).

Effectively managing storage with Kubernetes involves selecting appropriate volume types and provision strategies, understanding the lifecycle of volumes, and ensuring the correct access modes for application requirements. This serves to build resilient, scalable stateful applications that fully leverage Kubernetes' capabilities.

8.8 Configuring and Managing Kubernetes Clusters

Configuring and managing Kubernetes clusters is a critical aspect of using Kubernetes effectively. This section will cover the various components, tools, and best practices for setting up, maintaining, and optimizing Kubernetes clusters, ensuring a reliable and performant environment for running containerized applications.

A Kubernetes cluster comprises both the control plane and a set of worker nodes. The control plane manages the Kubernetes cluster while the worker nodes run the containerized applications.

Control Plane Components The control plane components ensure that the desired state of the cluster matches the actual state. These components include:

- **etcd**: A distributed key-value store that stores the cluster configuration data and state information.
- **kube-apiserver**: The API server that exposes the Kubernetes API. It is the front-end to the Kubernetes control plane.
- **kube-scheduler**: Responsible for scheduling pods on available nodes based on resource requirements.
- **kube-controller-manager**: Runs controller processes, such as the node controller, replication controller, and endpoints controller.
- **cloud-controller-manager**: Integrates with cloud provider APIs to manage cloud-specific resources.

Worker Node Components Worker nodes run the applications in pods. The critical components on each worker node are:

- **kubelet**: An agent that runs on each node, ensuring that containers are running as expected.
- **kube-proxy**: A network proxy that maintains network rules on nodes, allowing communication between different Kubernetes services.

- **Container Runtime**: Software responsible for running containers, such as Docker.

Setting Up a Kubernetes Cluster Setting up a Kubernetes cluster involves installing and configuring these components on the appropriate nodes. The choice of installation methods may vary depending on whether it is a local development environment, a production setup, or a cloud-based deployment. Some popular tools and methods include:

- **Minikube**: Suitable for local development and testing, Minikube creates a single-node Kubernetes cluster on a local machine.
- **kubeadm**: Provides a straightforward and flexible way to set up a production-ready Kubernetes cluster. It covers the installation of control plane and worker node components.
- **Managed Kubernetes Services**: Cloud providers such as Google Kubernetes Engine (GKE), Amazon Elastic Kubernetes Service (EKS), and Azure Kubernetes Service (AKS) provide fully managed Kubernetes clusters, abstracting much of the complexity.

Here is an example of using kubeadm to set up a Kubernetes cluster:

```
# Initialize the Kubernetes control plane
sudo kubeadm init --pod-network-cidr=10.244.0.0/16

# Set up local kubeconfig for kubectl
mkdir -p $HOME/.kube
sudo cp -i /etc/kubernetes/admin.conf $HOME/.kube/config
sudo chown $(id -u):$(id -g) $HOME/.kube/config

# Install a network plugin, e.g., Flannel for pod networking
kubectl apply -f https://raw.githubusercontent.com/coreos/flannel/master/
    Documentation/kube-flannel.yml

# Join worker nodes to the cluster using the token and IP provided by kubeadm init
    command
kubeadm join <master-ip>:<port> --token <token> --discovery-token-ca-cert-hash <
    hash>
```

Cluster Configuration Management After initial setup, effective configuration management is essential. Kubernetes configurations can be managed using:

- **kubectl**: The primary command-line tool for interacting with the Kubernetes API server.

- **YAML/JSON Configuration Files**: Declarative configuration files defining the desired state for Kubernetes objects such as pods, services, and deployments.
- **Helm**: A package manager for Kubernetes, enabling the deployment of pre-configured applications using Helm charts.

Here is an example YAML configuration file for a simple deployment:

```
apiVersion: apps/v1
kind: Deployment
metadata:
  name: nginx-deployment
spec:
  replicas: 3
  selector:
    matchLabels:
      app: nginx
  template:
    metadata:
      labels:
        app: nginx
    spec:
      containers:
      - name: nginx
        image: nginx:1.14.2
        ports:
        - containerPort: 80
```

To apply this configuration:

```
kubectl apply -f nginx-deployment.yaml
```

Monitoring and Managing Resources Monitoring and managing resources help maintain cluster health and performance:

- **Resource Quotas and Limits**: Define the maximum compute resources a namespace can consume to prevent a single application from exhausting cluster resources.
- **Horizontal Pod Autoscaler (HPA)**: Automatically scales the number of pod replicas based on observed CPU utilization or other application-provided metrics.
- **Cluster Autoscaler**: Automatically adjusts the number of nodes in the cluster based on the current workload.

To create a Horizontal Pod Autoscaler for the nginx-deployment:

```
kubectl autoscale deployment nginx-deployment --cpu-percent=50 --min=1 --max=10
```

Upgrading Kubernetes Clusters Regularly upgrading a Kubernetes cluster ensures that you benefit from the latest features, improvements, and security patches. The upgrade process typically involves:

- Upgrading the control plane components.
- Upgrading worker nodes.
- Updating any custom or third-party components.

Upgrading using kubeadm involves the following steps:

```
# Upgrade the control plane components
sudo kubeadm upgrade plan
sudo kubeadm upgrade apply <version>

# Upgrade kubelet and kubectl on the master node
sudo apt-get update && sudo apt-get install -y kubelet=<version> kubectl=<version>
sudo systemctl restart kubelet

# Upgrade kubelet and kubectl on worker nodes
sudo apt-get update && sudo apt-get install -y kubelet=<version> kubectl=<version>
sudo systemctl restart kubelet
```

Regular monitoring, controlled resource consumption, and timely upgrades are essential parts of cluster management, ensuring the cluster is always available and serving its purpose effectively.

8.9 Using Kubernetes ConfigMaps and Secrets

ConfigMaps and Secrets are essential components in Kubernetes that manage configuration data and sensitive information separately from application code. This approach promotes a clean separation of concerns, enabling greater flexibility and security in managing applications.

ConfigMaps are used for storing non-confidential key-value pairs, such as configuration files, command-line arguments, or environment variables. Secrets, on the other hand, are specifically designed to handle sensitive information, such as passwords, OAuth tokens, and SSH keys. Both ConfigMaps and Secrets can be injected into pods as environment variables or mounted as files in a volume.

To create a ConfigMap from a literal value, the following kubectl command can be utilized:

```
kubectl create configmap example-config --from-literal=key1=value1 --from-literal=key2
    =value2
```

To verify the creation and view the details of the ConfigMap:

```
kubectl get configmaps example-config -o yaml
```

This command outputs the ConfigMap in YAML format, illustrating the stored key-value pairs:

```
apiVersion: v1
kind: ConfigMap
metadata:
  name: example-config
data:
  key1: value1
  key2: value2
```

Similarly, a Secret can be created using the kubectl command:

```
kubectl create secret generic example-secret --from-literal=password=my-password --
    from-literal=username=my-username
```

To view the details of the Secret, use:

```
kubectl get secrets example-secret -o yaml
```

The output will resemble the following:

```
apiVersion: v1
kind: Secret
metadata:
  name: example-secret
data:
  password: bXktcGFzc3dvcmQ=
  username: bXktdXNlcm5hbWU=
```

The values in the data field are base64 encoded, which is a method to ensure the plain text is not exposed directly, though it is important to note that base64 is not a secure encryption technique.

ConfigMaps and Secrets can be incorporated into a pod either as environment variables or as volumes. The following example demonstrates injecting a ConfigMap as environment variables in a pod definition:

```
apiVersion: v1
kind: Pod
metadata:
  name: configmap-pod
spec:
  containers:
  - name: mycontainer
    image: busybox
    env:
    - name: KEY1
      valueFrom:
```

```
        configMapKeyRef:
          name: example-config
          key: key1
    - name: KEY2
      valueFrom:
        configMapKeyRef:
          name: example-config
          key: key2
```

For Secrets, the process is similar:

```
apiVersion: v1
kind: Pod
metadata:
  name: secret-pod
spec:
  containers:
  - name: mycontainer
    image: busybox
    env:
    - name: PASSWORD
      valueFrom:
        secretKeyRef:
          name: example-secret
          key: password
    - name: USERNAME
      valueFrom:
        secretKeyRef:
          name: example-secret
          key: username
```

Both ConfigMaps and Secrets can also be utilized as volumes, allowing files within these objects to be mounted into a pod's file system. The following example illustrates mounting a ConfigMap as a volume:

```
apiVersion: v1
kind: Pod
metadata:
  name: configmap-volume-pod
spec:
  containers:
  - name: mycontainer
    image: busybox
    volumeMounts:
    - name: config-volume
      mountPath: /etc/config
  volumes:
  - name: config-volume
    configMap:
      name: example-config
```

In a similar manner, a Secret can be mounted as a volume:

```
apiVersion: v1
kind: Pod
metadata:
  name: secret-volume-pod
spec:
  containers:
```

```
  - name: mycontainer
    image: busybox
    volumeMounts:
    - name: secret-volume
      mountPath: /etc/secrets
  volumes:
  - name: secret-volume
    secret:
      secretName: example-secret
```

ConfigMaps and Secrets provide flexible ways to manage application configuration and sensitive data securely and efficiently. They ensure configurations are decoupled from the container images and enable dynamic updates without the need to rebuild or redeploy images. Optimizing utilization of these Kubernetes components can significantly enhance the manageability and security of containerized applications in a Kubernetes environment.

8.10 Scaling Applications in Kubernetes

Scaling applications in Kubernetes can be efficiently managed using the built-in mechanisms provided by Kubernetes, enabling a seamless response to varying demands. The primary objective of scaling is to adjust the number of replicas of an application to match the workload. This section delves into the scaling capabilities within Kubernetes, including horizontal and vertical scaling, and the use of autoscalers.

Horizontal scaling, also referred to as scaling out, involves adding more instances (replicas) of a Pod to distribute the load. Vertical scaling, or scaling up, means adjusting the resource limits of a container, such as CPU and memory, to meet the application's requirements.

Horizontal Pod Autoscaler (HPA)

The Horizontal Pod Autoscaler automatically scales the number of Pods in a deployment, replication controller, or replica set based on observed CPU utilization or other select metrics. The HPA is an API resource in Kubernetes that continually checks the resource consumption and adjusts the number of replicas accordingly.

Consider the following manifest for configuring an HPA:

```
apiVersion: autoscaling/v2beta2
kind: HorizontalPodAutoscaler
metadata:
  name: myapp-hpa
spec:
  scaleTargetRef:
```

```
    apiVersion: apps/v1
    kind: Deployment
    name: myapp
  minReplicas: 1
  maxReplicas: 10
  metrics:
  - type: Resource
    resource:
      name: cpu
      target:
        type: Utilization
        averageUtilization: 50
```

In this example, the manifest defines an HPA that scales the replicas of the deployment named myapp between 1 and 10 based on the CPU utilization. If the observed CPU usage exceeds 50

To create and apply this HPA, use:

```
kubectl apply -f hpa.yaml
```

Once applied, you can monitor the status of the HPA using:

```
kubectl get hpa
```

Kubernetes will then take care of adjusting the number of Pods as needed.

Vertical Pod Autoscaler (VPA)

The Vertical Pod Autoscaler adjusts the resource limits and requests for containers in a Pod. This is useful for applications where the load can change significantly but the application can benefit from more resources instead of more replicas. The VPA can operate in three modes: Off, Initial, and Auto. In Auto mode, the VPA will recommend and adjust resources to an optimal size.

Example manifest for VPA:

```
apiVersion: autoscaling.k8s.io/v1
kind: VerticalPodAutoscaler
metadata:
  name: myapp-vpa
spec:
  targetRef:
    apiVersion: "apps/v1"
    kind: Deployment
    name: myapp
  updatePolicy:
    updateMode: "Auto"
```

Apply the VPA configuration with:

```
kubectl apply -f vpa.yaml
```

The VPA will continually monitor the resource utilization and make recommendations or adjust the resource limits of Pods.

Cluster Autoscaler

While HPA and VPA are concerned with scaling the Pods, the Cluster Autoscaler is responsible for scaling the number of nodes in a cluster. This is particularly useful in cloud environments where the infrastructure can dynamically add or remove nodes based on the requirements.

The Cluster Autoscaler works with cloud provider APIs to adjust the number of nodes. For example, when using Google Kubernetes Engine (GKE), the following command configures the autoscaler:

```
gcloud container clusters update <cluster-name> \
    --enable-autoscaling --min-nodes 1 --max-nodes 10 \
    --zone <zone>
```

The Cluster Autoscaler adds nodes when Pods fail to schedule due to insufficient resources, and removes nodes when resources are underutilized.

Scaling Deployment using kubectl

kubectl also offers direct commands for scaling a deployment manually. To scale a deployment named myapp to 5 replicas, execute:

```
kubectl scale deployment myapp --replicas=5
```

Best Practices for Scaling

1. **Monitor Resource Usage:** Constantly monitor the resource usage of your applications to set appropriate thresholds for scaling. 2. **Use Resource Requests and Limits:** Define resource requests and limits for your containers to ensure the scheduler can make appropriate decisions. 3. **Testing Autoscalers:** Test the configurations of your autoscalers in a staging environment to ensure they behave as expected under different load scenarios. 4. **Logging and Monitoring Tools:** Integrate proper logging and monitoring tools such as Prometheus and Grafana to have insights into how the application is scaling and performing. 5. **Combining HPA and VPA:** Use both horizontal and vertical pod autoscalers for optimal scaling. The HPA will handle the replica count, and the VPA will manage resource allocation per Pod.

Example Scenario

Consider an e-commerce application where traffic spikes during sales events. An appropriate scaling policy involves both HPA to handle the surge in HTTP requests and VPA to manage backend databases requiring more CPU and memory during these peaks.

Firstly, define the HPA for the front-end:

```
apiVersion: autoscaling/v2beta2
kind: HorizontalPodAutoscaler
metadata:
  name: frontend-hpa
spec:
  scaleTargetRef:
    apiVersion: apps/v1
    kind: Deployment
    name: frontend
  minReplicas: 3
  maxReplicas: 50
  metrics:
  - type: Resource
    resource:
      name: cpu
      target:
        type: Utilization
        averageUtilization: 70
```

Next, define the VPA for the backend database:

```
apiVersion: autoscaling.k8s.io/v1
kind: VerticalPodAutoscaler
metadata:
  name: backend-vpa
spec:
  targetRef:
    apiVersion: "apps/v1"
    kind: Deployment
    name: backend
  updatePolicy:
    updateMode: "Auto"
```

By configuring these autoscalers, the front-end service dynamically scales based on traffic, while the backend adapts to the increased data processing requirements.

The provided concepts and configurations encapsulate the scaling methodologies in Kubernetes. Kubernetes' autoscaling capabilities are vital for maintaining application performance and resource efficiency in diverse production environments.

8.11 Monitoring and Logging in Kubernetes

Effective monitoring and logging are crucial for maintaining the health, performance, and security of applications deployed in Kubernetes. These practices provide insights into the system's behavior, aiding in diagnostics and performance tuning.

The Kubernetes environment inherently supports monitoring and logging through various open-source tools and integrations. Common tools include Prometheus for monitoring and Elasticsearch, Fluentd, and Kibana (the EFK stack) for logging.

Monitoring involves collecting, processing, storing, and analyzing metrics. Metrics provide quantitative data about the state of a system at a certain point in time. Key metrics to monitor in Kubernetes include CPU usage, memory consumption, pod availability, and network traffic.

The Prometheus and Grafana stack is a widely-used solution for monitoring in Kubernetes. Prometheus is responsible for scraping and storing metrics, while Grafana provides a visualization interface that allows users to build dashboards for monitoring purposes. To set up Prometheus and Grafana in a Kubernetes cluster, the following steps can be followed:

```
# Create a namespace for monitoring
kubectl create namespace monitoring

# Apply Prometheus manifest
kubectl apply -f https://raw.githubusercontent.com/prometheus-operator/kube-
    prometheus/main/manifests/prometheus-prometheus.yaml -n monitoring

# Apply Grafana manifest
kubectl apply -f https://raw.githubusercontent.com/grafana/helm-charts/main/charts/
    grafana/templates/deployment.yaml -n monitoring

# Check the status of Prometheus and Grafana pods
kubectl get pods -n monitoring
```

Once deployed, Prometheus automatically collects metrics from the Kubernetes nodes, pods, and services. These metrics can be accessed through the Prometheus web UI, which runs on a specified port, generally port 9090. To expose the Prometheus UI, port forwarding can be used:

```
kubectl port-forward -n monitoring prometheus-prometheus-0 9090:9090
```

Access the Prometheus UI by navigating to http://localhost:9090 in a web browser. Similarly, Grafana can be accessed by forwarding the respective port and navigating to the provided URL. Dashboards in Grafana can be imported from predefined templates or created from scratch, linking to the metrics collected by Prometheus.

Logging in Kubernetes involves collecting and storing logs generated by applications and the Kubernetes system itself. Logs are essential for tracing and identifying errors and understanding the behavior of a system over time.

The EFK stack is a popular solution for logging in Kubernetes. Elasticsearch stores logs, Fluentd collects and forwards logs, and Kibana provides an interface for log search and visualization.

To deploy the EFK stack, the following manifests can be applied:

```
# Create a namespace for logging
kubectl create namespace logging

# Apply Elasticsearch manifest
kubectl apply -f https://raw.githubusercontent.com/elastic/cloud-on-k8s/1.5.0/config/
    samples/elasticsearch/elasticsearch.yaml -n logging

# Apply Fluentd daemonset manifest
kubectl apply -f https://raw.githubusercontent.com/fluent/fluentd-kubernetes-
    daemonset/v1.11.2/deployment/fluentd-daemonset-elasticsearch.yaml -n logging

# Apply Kibana manifest
kubectl apply -f https://raw.githubusercontent.com/elastic/cloud-on-k8s/1.5.0/config/
    samples/kibana/kibana.yaml -n logging

# Check the status of Elasticsearch, Fluentd, and Kibana pods
kubectl get pods -n logging
```

Fluentd runs as a daemonset, ensuring that an instance runs on each Kubernetes node, thereby collecting logs from all workloads and forwarding them to Elasticsearch. Kibana connects to Elasticsearch and provides a powerful interface for querying and visualizing logs. Port forwarding for Kibana allows UI access as follows:

```
kubectl port-forward -n logging kibana-kb-0 5601:5601
```

Navigating to http://localhost:5601 provides access to the Kibana interface, where logs can be queried and visualized using built-in features and dashboards.

Kubernetes also supports native logging through kubectl logs command, which retrieves logs for a specific pod. Example usage includes:

```
kubectl logs -f <pod-name> -n <namespace>
```

For long-term log storage and more sophisticated searching capabilities, integrating with a full logging stack like EFK is preferable.

It's essential to implement monitoring and logging from the initial stages of application development to ensure system robustness and security. Efficient use of these tools helps in proactive monitoring, quick incident response, and continuous performance tuning. Regular reviews and adjustments to the monitoring and logging setup are recommended to adapt to the evolving system and application complexity.

8.12 Kubernetes Security Best Practices

Kubernetes security is a critical aspect that ensures the integrity, availability, and confidentiality of containerized applications. By adhering to security best practices, organizations can protect their Kubernetes environments from various threats, such as unauthorized access, data breaches, and malicious attacks. This section delves into several best practices, outlining measures for securing the different components and aspects of Kubernetes.

One of the foundational measures in securing a Kubernetes cluster is ensuring secure access to the cluster. Access to the Kubernetes API server should be restricted and controlled using Role-Based Access Control (RBAC). RBAC allows fine-grained control over permissions and can be configured by defining roles and bindings. For example, the following YAML configuration defines an RBAC policy that grants read-only access to a specific user:

```
apiVersion: rbac.authorization.k8s.io/v1
kind: Role
metadata:
  namespace: default
  name: read-only-role
rules:
- apiGroups: [""]
  resources: ["pods"]
  verbs: ["get", "list"]
---
apiVersion: rbac.authorization.k8s.io/v1
kind: RoleBinding
metadata:
  name: read-only-binding
  namespace: default
subjects:
- kind: User
  name: john-doe
  apiGroup: rbac.authorization.k8s.io
roleRef:
  kind: Role
  name: read-only-role
  apiGroup: rbac.authorization.k8s.io
```

This setup grants the user "john-doe" read-only permissions to the pods in the "default" namespace. Implementing RBAC policies helps in minimizing the risk of unauthorized actions within the cluster.

Another crucial component of Kubernetes security is securing the communication between different components. For securing data in transit, it is recommended to use Transport Layer Security (TLS) to encrypt the communication channels. This can be achieved by configuring the API server, etcd, and other components to use TLS certificates. Below is an example of configuring the Kubernetes API server with TLS:

```
kube-apiserver \
  --advertise-address=<API_SERVER_IP> \
  --tls-cert-file=/etc/kubernetes/pki/apiserver.crt \
  --tls-private-key-file=/etc/kubernetes/pki/apiserver.key \
  --client-ca-file=/etc/kubernetes/pki/ca.crt
```

Sensitive data within the cluster, such as passwords, tokens, and keys, should be stored securely. Kubernetes provides Secrets for handling such data securely. Secrets should be used instead of ConfigMaps for managing sensitive information. Here is an example of creating a Secret:

```
apiVersion: v1
kind: Secret
metadata:
  name: my-secret
type: Opaque
data:
  username: YWRtaW4=
  password: MWYyZDFlMmU2N2Rm
```

In this example, the username "admin" and password "1f2d1e2e67df" are base64 encoded. Applications can then access these secrets securely without exposing sensitive information in configuration files.

Applying security patches and updates timely is essential for maintaining the security of a Kubernetes environment. Regularly updating Kubernetes components, including the container runtime and node OS, helps mitigate known vulnerabilities. It is advisable to subscribe to security advisories and monitor the official Kubernetes release notes.

Network policies play a vital role in controlling the traffic flow between pods. Kubernetes supports network policies that allow specifying how pods can communicate with each other and other network endpoints. Here is an example of a network policy that allows incoming traffic only from pods within the same namespace:

```
apiVersion: networking.k8s.io/v1
kind: NetworkPolicy
metadata:
  name: allow-same-namespace
  namespace: default
spec:
  podSelector: {}
  policyTypes:
  - Ingress
  ingress:
  - from:
    - podSelector: {}
```

Properly configured network policies can greatly reduce the attack surface by limiting unnecessary exposure of services.

Container security is another key aspect. It's essential to follow best practices for building and deploying containers. This includes using minimal base images, avoiding running applications as root, and scanning images for vulnerabilities. Tools such as Aqua, Twistlock, and Clair can be used for vulnerability scanning of container images. An example of a Dockerfile using a minimal base image and a non-root user:

```
FROM alpine:3.12
RUN addgroup -S appgroup && adduser -S appuser -G appgroup
USER appuser
COPY app /app
CMD ["./app"]
```

Auditing and logging are integral parts of Kubernetes security. Enabling audit logging provides a record of all requests made to the API server and helps in detecting anomalous activities. An example of enabling audit logging can be seen below:

```
kube-apiserver \
  --audit-log-path=/var/log/kubernetes/audit.log \
  --audit-log-maxage=30 \
  --audit-log-maxbackup=10 \
  --audit-log-maxsize=100
```

By setting up audit logs, administrators can track user activities and API server interactions, facilitating the identification and investigation of potential security incidents.

Adhering to Kubernetes security best practices involves multiple layers and aspects, from secure RBAC policies and TLS configuration to managing secrets, applying updates, defining network policies, ensuring container security, and maintaining comprehensive logging and auditing. These practices collectively strengthen the security posture of Kubernetes environments and help in safeguarding containerized applications against various threats.

8.13 Upgrading and Maintaining Kubernetes Clusters

When operating Kubernetes clusters in a production environment, maintaining the system's integrity involves carefully planned upgrades and comprehensive maintenance procedures. This section delves into the best practices and methodologies for upgrading and maintaining Kubernetes clusters, ensuring seamless operations with minimal disruptions.

Upgrading a Kubernetes cluster is a multi-step process that requires attention to detail at every stage. The upgrade involves updating the Kubernetes control plane components, such as the API server, controller manager, and scheduler, as well as the worker nodes running the kubelet and kube-proxy. It is crucial to follow a systematic approach, starting with backups and testing in a staging environment.

1. Backup and Test: Before initiating any upgrade, backup the current state of the cluster. Use tools like etcdctl for backing up etcd, Kubernetes' key-value store for all cluster data. Ensure you have the latest snapshots to avoid any data loss during the upgrade. Testing the upgrade process in a staging environment that mirrors the production setup helps identify potential issues and minimizes risks.

2. Upgrade Control Plane: Begin the upgrade with the Kubernetes control plane by updating the components in a well-defined order:

```
# Upgrade kube-apiserver
sudo apt-get update && sudo apt-get install -y kube-apiserver=1.21.0

# Upgrade kube-controller-manager
sudo apt-get update && sudo apt-get install -y kube-controller-manager=1.21.0

# Upgrade kube-scheduler
sudo apt-get update && sudo apt-get install -y kube-scheduler=1.21.0
```

Monitor the control plane components for any errors post-upgrade by checking the logs and ensuring that the API server is responsive.

3. Upgrade Worker Nodes: Once the control plane is successfully upgraded, proceed with the worker nodes. Drain the nodes one by one:

```
# Drain the node to move workloads
kubectl drain <node-name> --ignore-daemonsets
```

Upgrade the kubelet and kube-proxy on the drained node:

```
# Upgrade kubelet
sudo apt-get update && sudo apt-get install -y kubelet=1.21.0

# Upgrade kube-proxy
sudo apt-get update && sudo apt-get install -y kube-proxy=1.21.0

# Restart kubelet
sudo systemctl restart kubelet
```

After upgrading and verifying the node's functionality, uncordon it to return it to the cluster:

```
# Uncordon the node
kubectl uncordon <node-name>
```

Repeat the process for each worker node.

4. Verify System Health: Post-upgrade, thoroughly verify the cluster's health. Check the Kubernetes components with:

```
# Check node status
kubectl get nodes

# Verify all pods are running
kubectl get pods --all-namespaces
```

Also, inspect etcd health and data integrity.

5. Upgrade Add-ons and Applications: Finally, upgrade Kubernetes add-ons, such as CoreDNS and the container network interface (CNI), to versions compatible with the new Kubernetes version. Update application deployments to leverage any new functionalities provided by the upgrade.

Maintenance Practices: Maintaining Kubernetes clusters involves ongoing monitoring, regular backups, and proactive updates to ensure security and performance.

1. Monitoring and Logging: Implement robust monitoring with tools like Prometheus and Grafana to visualize metrics related to cluster performance and health. Ensure comprehensive logging using solutions like Fluentd or the ELK stack (Elasticsearch, Logstash, Kibana) for centralized logs.

```
# Example Prometheus query for node health
up{job="node"} == 1
```

2. Regular Backups: Schedule regular backups of etcd and cluster resources. Automated tools such as Velero can be used to manage backups and restores efficiently.

3. Security Patching: Keep the Kubernetes components and underlying OS patched with the latest security updates. Use tools such as Kube-bench to regularly check for compliance with Kubernetes security best practices.

By following these best practices for upgrading and maintaining Kubernetes clusters, administrators can ensure high availability, reliability, and performance of their containerized environments, while minimizing the risk of downtime and data loss.

Chapter 9

Docker Best Practices and Security

This chapter outlines best practices for optimizing Dockerfile instructions, image size reduction, and container resource management. It covers implementing health checks, logging best practices, and Docker security measures such as running containers with least privilege, isolating containers, and network security. The chapter also discusses using Docker Bench for security, managing secrets, and ensuring regular updates and compliance auditing.

9.1 Introduction to Docker Best Practices

Docker has revolutionized the way we develop, package, and deploy applications. Its lightweight containerization technology promotes rapid development cycles and consistent runtime environments. However, as with all technologies, it is imperative to adopt best practices to maximize efficiency, security, and maintainability. This section addresses core principles and methodologies that should be adhered to while working with Docker, setting the stage for more detailed discussions in subsequent sections.

When developing with Docker, the Dockerfile is the blueprint for creating Docker images. Writing Dockerfiles can be deceptively simple, but it is essential to follow disciplined practices to avoid common pitfalls. A well-structured Dockerfile ensures that the final image is lean, secure, and efficient. Docker best practices revolve around several key areas: efficiency in building images, maintaining security standards, optimizing performance, and ensuring resource constraints.

Version Pinning and Base Image Selection

One fundamental best practice is to begin with an appropriate base image. The choice of a base image impacts the resultant image's size and security posture. It is advisable to use minimal base images such as alpine or scratch when possible. These images contain fewer packages, thereby reducing the surface area for potential vulnerabilities.

```
FROM alpine:3.12
# Minimal Alpine base image example
```

Moreover, version pinning helps maintain consistency across different environments. By specifying exact versions of the base image and dependencies, developers can ensure that the image behaves consistently, reducing the risk of discrepancies between development, testing, and production environments.

```
FROM python:3.8.5-slim
# Version pinned to ensure compatibility and consistency
```

Layering and Command Chaining

Docker builds images in layers, and each instruction in a Dockerfile creates an intermediate layer. Efficient layering can lead to significant gains in build time and image size. Combining related commands into single lines via command chaining with && and utilizing multi-stage builds can help minimize the number of layers and reduce redundancy.

```
RUN apt-get update && apt-get install -y \
    curl \
    vim \
    && apt-get clean && rm -rf /var/lib/apt/lists/*
# Combining commands reduces the number of layers created in the image
```

Multi-stage builds are another powerful technique for optimizing the final image size. By splitting the build process into multiple stages, developers can discard intermediary artifacts, retaining only the essential components in the final image.

```
FROM golang:1.15 AS builder
WORKDIR /app
COPY . .
RUN go build -o myapp
```

```
FROM alpine:3.12
COPY --from=builder /app/myapp /usr/local/bin/
ENTRYPOINT ["myapp"]
# Multi-stage build to keep the final image lean
```

Minimizing Layers and Reducing Image Size

It is advisable to minimize the number of layers by grouping multiple commands within single RUN instructions. Moreover, avoiding large image layers and reducing the number of included files can significantly decrease the image size. For instance, always include a .dockerignore file to prevent unnecessary files from being added to the image, akin to .gitignore in git.

```
# .dockerignore
node_modules
*.log
*.md
```

The COPY command should also be used judiciously to include only essential files. Reducing the size and number of artifacts copied to the image is crucial for maintaining a lean final image.

```
COPY requirements.txt .
RUN pip install -r requirements.txt
COPY . .
# Copying requirements first to leverage Docker layer caching
```

Security Considerations

Security is a paramount concern in containerized environments. It is necessary to run containers with the least privilege required. Avoid running applications as the root user within the container. Instead, create and use a non-root user.

```
RUN adduser --disabled-password --gecos "" appuser
USER appuser
# Create and use non-root user for increased security
```

Additionally, signing and scanning images for vulnerabilities should become a regular part of the build pipeline. Tools such as Docker Content Trust and image scanning services can be integrated to automate these checks.

Documentation and Maintainability

Proper documentation within Dockerfiles is often overlooked. Comments must be used to explain non-trivial instructions and reasoning behind specific choices. This practice enhances the maintainability of Dockerfiles and aids peers and future maintainers in understanding the structure and modifications made.

```
# Set base image to Python 3.8 slim
FROM python:3.8-slim

# Set work directory to /app
WORKDIR /app

# Copy requirements file and install dependencies
COPY requirements.txt .
RUN pip install --no-cache-dir -r requirements.txt

# Copy application code
COPY . .

# Use non-root user for security
RUN adduser --disabled-password --gecos "" appuser
USER appuser

# Specify default command to run
CMD ["python", "app.py"]
```

Efficiency in Build Context

Performance during the image build process can be enhanced by minimizing the build context. The build context is the set of files located in the specified PATH or URL when initiating a Docker build. By limiting the number of files in the context, the build process can transfer and process data more efficiently.

Container Initialization

Initiation of container entry points should be lean and efficient. The use of lightweight initialization systems such as tini can manage orphaned zombie processes, which are crucial in long-running services.

```
FROM python:3.8-slim
# Install tini
RUN apt-get update && apt-get install -y tini

# Initialize with Tini
ENTRYPOINT ["/usr/bin/tini", "--"]
CMD ["python", "app.py"]
```

Adherence to these best practices from the outset aids significantly in creating robust, secure, and maintainable Dockerized applications. As you progress through the subsequent sections, these foundational concepts will be expanded upon and tied into more complex scenarios and configurations.

9.2 Optimizing Dockerfile Instructions

Efficient and optimized Dockerfile instructions are essential for creating small, secure, and efficient Docker images. Not only do these optimizations reduce build times, but they also improve the performance and maintainability of the images. This section details various strategies for optimizing Dockerfile instructions.

A fundamental aspect of optimizing Dockerfile instructions is the careful selection and order of commands. Docker implements a layer-based filesystem, where each instruction in the Dockerfile creates a new layer. Hence, understanding and optimizing these instructions helps in minimizing the number of layers and their size.

Minimize the Number of Layers

Every Dockerfile instruction (such as RUN, COPY, and ADD) creates a new layer. Since each layer adds to the image size, it is prudent to minimize their number. One effective method is combining multiple RUN instructions into a single one. For instance, instead of:

```
RUN apt-get update
RUN apt-get install -y python
```

Combine them into:

```
RUN apt-get update && apt-get install -y python
```

This approach reduces the number of layers created and ensures a smaller and more efficient image.

Order of Instructions

Place commands that change less frequently at the top of the Dockerfile. By positioning stable commands first, Docker can leverage its cache more effectively, reducing the build time when the less frequently changed instructions remain untouched. For example:

```
FROM ubuntu:20.04

# Install base packages
RUN apt-get update && apt-get install -y \
      curl \
      wget

# Copy application source code
COPY . /app

# Install application dependencies
RUN pip install -r /app/requirements.txt
```

In this example, apt-get update and apt-get install run infrequently compared to changes in the application source code. Therefore, it is advantageous to place them at the top to maximize cache usage.

Reduce the Size of Instructions' Output

The size of layers can be further reduced by cleaning up after installing packages or downloading files. For instance, when using package managers like apt, use the –no-install-recommends option and remove cached files:

```
RUN apt-get update && apt-get install -y --no-install-recommends \
    python \
    && rm -rf /var/lib/apt/lists/*
```

This practice helps to remove unnecessary files, significantly reducing the image size.

Use .dockerignore File

A .dockerignore file is akin to a .gitignore file, specifying files and directories to be excluded from the build context. Including unnecessary files increases the image's size and build time. Hence, defining a .dockerignore file to exclude items such as temporary files, build artifacts, and source control metadata is beneficial:

```
# .dockerignore
*.tmp
*.swp
*.log
.git
```

This reduces the number of files sent to the Docker daemon, leading to faster builds and smaller images.

Optimize COPY and ADD Instructions

When copying files, use COPY instead of ADD unless necessary to leverage ADD's specific features like extracting archives. COPY is more transparent in its behavior, and its simplicity often results in better optimization.

For instance:

```
COPY . /app
```

Use absolute paths over relative paths, particularly when copying single files, to avoid copying unnecessary files.

Avoid Using Root User

Running instructions as the root user can pose security risks. Therefore, specify a non-root user to run the application's processes. First, create a user using the USER instruction and assign file permissions appropriately:

```
RUN useradd -m myuser
USER myuser
```

This not only provides better security but also conforms to the principle of least privilege.

Layer Caching

Docker's cache mechanism accelerates image builds by reusing existing layers from previous builds. As discussed, leveraging caching by ordering instructions based on their change frequency reduces rebuild times. Be cautious when modifying layers prone to frequent changes, as this can invalidate the cache and force a rebuild of subsequent layers.

Leverage Multi-Stage Builds

Multi-stage builds help in creating minimal and optimized image sizes by separating the build environment from the runtime environment. This approach allows copying only the necessary artifacts from the build stage to the final image, discarding development dependencies and intermediate files that are unneeded:

```
# Stage 1: Build environment
FROM golang AS builder
WORKDIR /app
COPY . .
RUN go build -o myapp

# Stage 2: Runtime environment
FROM alpine
WORKDIR /app
COPY --from=builder /app/myapp .
ENTRYPOINT ["./myapp"]
```

In this example, the Go application is built in a golang environment and then copied over a minimal alpine image, ensuring the final image is lean and contains only necessary runtime dependencies.

By meticulously following these strategies, Dockerfiles can be optimized to build secure, efficient, and maintainable images.

9.3 Image Size Reduction Techniques

Efficient management of Docker image sizes is crucial to optimize performance, reduce storage consumption, and enhance deployment speed. Several methodologies can be employed to systematically reduce the size of Docker images. Here, we will explore techniques focusing on leveraging multi-stage builds, minimizing the number of layers, using smaller base images, and removing unnecessary files.

Multi-Stage Builds

Multi-stage builds are a feature introduced in Docker 17.05 that enables the creation of Docker images in stages, allowing intermediate stages to be discarded, thus resulting in a smaller final image. This technique is especially beneficial for applications requiring a complex build process but only necessitate a small runtime environment.

```
FROM golang:1.16 AS builder
WORKDIR /app
COPY . .
RUN go build -o myapp

FROM alpine:latest
WORKDIR /root/
COPY --from=builder /app/myapp .
CMD ["./myapp"]
```

In this example, the golang:1.16 image is used for the building stage where the application is compiled. The second stage, based on the alpine:latest image, only contains the compiled binary, significantly reducing the image size.

Minimizing the Number of Layers

Each command in a Dockerfile creates a new layer. To reduce image size, it is essential to minimize the number of layers by chaining multiple commands together. This can be accomplished using the && operator in Unix-based systems.

```
FROM ubuntu:20.04
RUN apt-get update && apt-get install -y \
    curl \
    wget \
    && apt-get clean \
    && rm -rf /var/lib/apt/lists/*
```

In this Dockerfile, a single RUN instruction performs multiple operations, resulting in only one additional layer. This practice not only reduces the image size but also decreases build time.

Using Smaller Base Images

Starting from a smaller base image inherently reduces the final image size. Alpine Linux, for example, is a popular minimalist image that provides a suitable base for many applications.

```
FROM alpine:latest
RUN apk add --no-cache python3 py3-pip
COPY . .
CMD ["python3", "app.py"]
```

In contrast to larger OS images like ubuntu or debian, alpine is significantly smaller and often suffices for lightweight applications or microservices.

Removing Unnecessary Files

During the build process, it is common to generate temporary files or include unnecessary directories. Ensuring these files are excluded from the final image can yield substantial size savings.

```
FROM python:3.9-slim
WORKDIR /app
COPY requirements.txt .
RUN pip install --no-cache-dir -r requirements.txt && \
    rm -rf /root/.cache/pip
COPY . .
CMD ["python", "app.py"]
```

Including a .dockerignore file can further help in excluding files and directories that are not needed in the Docker image.

```
*.pyc
__pycache__/
.env
tests/
```

The .dockerignore file ensures that files matching the specified patterns are not included in the build context, thus streamlining the final image.

Effective use of these techniques requires a strategic approach tailored to the specific application and environment. Each method contributes to a more efficient and performance-optimized Docker image, fostering smoother deployments and operational environments.

9.4 Container Resource Management

Effective container resource management is crucial for maintaining optimal performance, preventing resource contention, and ensuring fair resource distribution among containers. Docker provides a variety of tools and options to manage resources such as CPU, memory, storage, and network. This section delves into these mechanisms in detail.

CPU Resource Management

Docker allows fine-grained control over the CPU resources allocated to containers. The primary options available for managing CPU resources include:

- –cpu-shares
- –cpus
- –cpu-period and –cpu-quota
- –cpuset-cpus

–cpu-shares is used to set up relative CPU weight, which defines the proportion of CPU cycles the container should receive. For example:

```
docker run -d --name container1 --cpu-shares=512 nginx
docker run -d --name container2 --cpu-shares=1024 nginx
```

In this scenario, container2 will receive twice as much CPU time as container1 when both are running.

–cpus can be used to set an absolute number of CPUs that a container can use. A decimal value can also be specified:

```
docker run -d --name container3 --cpus=1.5 nginx
```

This limits container3 to use no more than 1.5 CPU cores.

–cpu-period and –cpu-quota work together to control CPU bandwidth. –cpu-period defines the CPU period in microseconds, and –cpu-quota is the total available CPU time in the same period. For instance, to ensure a container uses half of CPU time, you can configure as follows:

```
docker run -d --name container4 --cpu-period=100000 --cpu-quota=50000 nginx
```

–cpuset-cpus allows you to assign specific CPUs to a container, enhancing performance by reducing context-switching overhead:

```
docker run -d --name container5 --cpuset-cpus="0,1" nginx
```

This restricts container5 to use only CPU 0 and CPU 1.

Memory Resource Management

Memory constraints can be imposed on containers to ensure stable performance and to prevent a single container from hogging memory resources. The primary options include:

- –memory
- –memory-swap
- –memory-reservation
- –oom-kill-disable

–memory sets an absolute limit on the maximum memory usage:

```
docker run -d --name container6 --memory=512m nginx
```

This restricts container6 to 512 MB of memory.

–memory-swap sets the total amount of swap space and physical memory a container can use. If –memory is set to 512 MB, and –memory-swap is set to 1 GB, then the container can use 512 MB of memory and 512 MB of swap:

```
docker run -d --name container7 --memory=512m --memory-swap=1g nginx
```

–memory-reservation sets a soft limit, which Docker tries to retain for the container, but it will allow overages:

```
docker run -d --name container8 --memory-reservation=256m nginx
```

–oom-kill-disable prevents Docker from killing the container when it runs out of memory, which can be critical for fault-tolerant applications:

```
docker run -d --name container9 --memory=256m --oom-kill-disable nginx
```

This will prevent the OOM (Out Of Memory) killer from terminating the container when its memory usage exceeds the limit.

Storage Limits

Storage management ensures that containers do not exhaust the host filesystem storage. Docker provides two primary ways to manage storage:

- –storage-opt

- –tmpfs

–storage-opt is used to set storage driver-specific options. For instance, configuring overlay2 driver with a size limit:

```
docker run -d --name container10 --storage-opt size=1g nginx
```

This restricts container10 to use a maximum of 1 GB of storage.

–tmpfs mounts a temporary filesystem in memory, constrained by the main memory limits:

```
docker run -d --name container11 --tmpfs /tmp:size=100m nginx
```

This makes a tmpfs mount at /tmp limited to 100 MB.

Network Performance

Network performance can be managed using network modes and traffic control. Docker's network modes are:

- bridge
- host
- none
- container:<name|id>

The bridge mode isolates container network, the host mode makes the container use the host's network stack, and none disables networking. The container mode allows a container to share another container's network namespace.

Docker uses tc (traffic control) to limit bandwidth. You can directly apply Linux tc commands to control traffic. For instance, limiting upload bandwidth:

```
tc qdisc add dev eth0 root tbf rate 1mbit burst 32kbit latency 400ms
```

Remember to manage iptables rules to filter and manipulate traffic packets as needed across Docker networks.

Further configuring resource limits ensures smooth operation of containers, reduces the likelihood of resource contention, and aligns with the best practices for container management.

9.5 Using Health Checks

Health checks are a fundamental aspect of maintaining the reliability and resilience of Docker containers. They enable the Docker engine to periodically examine the state of a running container, ensuring that it meets the expected operational criteria. This can help in automating recovery actions, alerting, and ensuring high availability of services. A well-configured health check can assist in identifying failing or misbehaving containers, enabling the orchestration layer to take appropriate actions such as restarting the container or alerting operators.

In Docker, health checks are defined within a Dockerfile using the HEALTHCHECK instruction. This instruction supports configuration of both the command to be run and several timing parameters. The following is an example of a typical HEALTHCHECK instruction in a Dockerfile:

```
HEALTHCHECK --interval=30s --timeout=10s --start-period=30s --retries=3 \
  CMD curl -f http://localhost/health || exit 1
```

In the example above:

- –interval=30s: Specifies that the health check should be performed every 30 seconds.
- –timeout=10s: Sets a timeout of 10 seconds for the health check command to complete.
- –start-period=30s: Defines an initial start period of 30 seconds after the container starts, during which health checks will not be attempted.
- –retries=3: Denotes that the health check will be retried up to 3 times before the container is marked as unhealthy.

The command CMD curl -f http://localhost/health || exit 1 is the actual health check command:

- curl -f http://localhost/health: Uses the curl command to fetch the endpoint /health from the local server.
- || exit 1: Ensures that if the curl command fails (non-zero exit status), the health check reports a failure.

When a health check fails, Docker updates the container's status to "unhealthy". This status can be queried programmatically or via tools such as Docker CLI. For example, to inspect the health status of a running container, you can use:

```
docker inspect --format='{{json .State.Health}}' <container_id>
```

The output will be in JSON format, reflecting the health status and details of the last few health checks performed. An example of such output is:

```
{
  "Status": "healthy",
  "FailingStreak": 0,
  "Log": [
    {
      "Start": "2023-04-14T11:52:32.736254092Z",
      "End": "2023-04-14T11:52:32.945539539Z",
      "ExitCode": 0,
      "Output": "HTTP/1.1 200 OK"
    },
    ...
  ]
}
```

Several key best practices should be adhered to when configuring health checks:

- **Use Lightweight Commands**: Health checks should minimize resource consumption. Utilize lightweight commands that accurately reflect the container's health without imposing significant overhead.
- **Timeout Configuration**: Ensure that the –timeout parameter is set appropriately to prevent long-running health checks from delaying subsequent checks.
- **Meaningful Endpoints**: When utilizing HTTP-based health checks, employ endpoints that give a true indication of the service state. Avoid endpoints that could be healthy while the actual service is not.
- **Consider Application-Specific Factors**: Tailor health checks to the specific characteristics of your application. For instance, if the application has a slow startup time, extend the –start-period to avoid false negatives during the initial phase.

Additionally, it is essential to understand the orchestration behavior regarding health statuses. In a distributed orchestration system like

Docker Swarm or Kubernetes, an unhealthy status may trigger actions such as container restart or re-scheduling. Consequently, ensuring accurate and reliable health check configurations becomes paramount to maintain service stability and provide quick recovery mechanisms.

Startup probes in Kubernetes offer further refinements, allowing delayed health check initiation for containers with particularly lengthy startup sequences. This further emphasizes the importance of customizing health check strategies to closely align with the operational characteristics of each service.

For advanced implementations, consider that health checks can be externalized via sidecar containers, which can perform in-depth health examinations of the primary container. This is particularly useful for complex applications where internal health metrics and external factors need assessment before determining overall container health.

Optimal health check configurations facilitate early detection of issues, reduce downtime through automated recovery, and contribute to robust, self-healing Docker deployments, critical for maintaining service uptime and reliability.

9.6 Docker Logging Best Practices

Effective logging in Docker is crucial for monitoring, troubleshooting, and maintaining applications within containers. Proper logging practices ensure that essential information is captured and can help in diagnosing issues rapidly. In this section, we delve into various best practices for Docker logging to enhance the reliability and manageability of containerized applications.

1. Use the Correct Logging Driver

Docker supports multiple logging drivers, and choosing the appropriate driver based on the infrastructure needs is essential. The default logging driver is 'json-file', but other drivers like 'syslog', 'journald', 'fluentd', 'gelf', 'awslogs', and 'splunk' might be more suitable for different environments.

```
docker run --log-driver=syslog <image-name>
```

Each logging driver has specific parameters and configurations. For instance, to use the syslog driver, configure the syslog-address:

```
docker run --log-driver=syslog --log-opt syslog-address=tcp://192.168.0.42:123 <image-
    name>
```

2. Centralize Logs

Centralizing logs can help in managing logs from multiple containers and services efficiently. Tools like ELK (Elasticsearch, Logstash, Kibana) or EFK (Elasticsearch, Fluentd, Kibana) stacks are commonly used.

```
@type forward
bind 0.0.0.0
port 24224

<match **>
  @type copy
  <store>
    @type stdout
  </store>
  <store>
    @type elasticsearch
    host localhost
    port 9200
  </store>
</match>
```

3. Structure Your Logs

Using structured logging formats like JSON facilitates parsing and searching logs. Docker's default helps you achieve this, but you can also customize log outputs from your application.

```
{
  "timestamp":"2023-10-05T12:34:56.789Z",
  "level":"INFO",
  "message":"User login successful",
  "user_id":1234
}
```

```
docker run --log-driver=json-file --log-opt max-size=10m --log-opt max-file=3 <image-
    name>
```

4. Limit Log Size

To prevent log files from consuming too much disk space, set limits on the size and number of log files.

```
docker run --log-opt max-size=5m --log-opt max-file=3 <image-name>
```

5. Enable Log Rotation

Log rotation ensures that log files do not grow indefinitely, which is crucial for disk space management and log file usability.

```
{
```

```
"log-driver": "json-file",
"log-opts": {
  "max-size": "10m",
  "max-file": "3"
 }
}
```

6. Separate Application Logs from Docker Logs

Keep application logs separate from Docker logs to avoid confusion and ensure application logs are easily accessible.

```
docker run -v /path/to/app/logs:/app/logs <image-name>
```

7. Use Logging Tags

Tags can help identify logs from specific containers or services, making filtering and searching in centralized logging systems more straightforward.

```
docker run --log-driver=syslog --log-opt tag="{{.Name}}/{{.ID}}" <image-name>
```

8. Monitor and Analyze Logs

Regularly monitor and analyze logs to identify patterns, detect anomalies, and maintain the health of your applications. Use tools integrated with centralized logging setups to visualize and query logs efficiently.

9. Secure Log Data

Ensure log data is secure both in transit and at rest. Use encryption and secure logging mechanisms to protect sensitive data within logs. For example, when using Fluentd, you can enable secure connections.

```
<source>
  @type forward
  port 24224
  bind 0.0.0.0
  secure yes
</source>
```

10. Adhere to Compliance Requirements

Ensure that your logging practices comply with relevant regulations and standards, such as GDPR, HIPAA, or PCI-DSS. Logs should contain necessary information for auditing while ensuring no sensitive information is exposed inadvertently.

Implementing these best practices within Docker environments helps maintain robust, manageable logging systems that support efficient application monitoring and troubleshooting.

9.7 Implementing Docker Security Best Practices

Docker security is a multifaceted domain encompassing numerous aspects ranging from container isolation to secret management. By adhering to recommended security practices, one can significantly reduce vulnerabilities and ensure robust protection for containerized applications. This section delves into critical security practices that should be implemented to fortify Docker environments.

One fundamental practice is to use the minimal base image necessary for the application. Large and bloated images introduce unnecessary attack surfaces. Preferably, lightweight images such as 'alpine' should be employed:

```
FROM alpine:latest
RUN apk add --no-cache python3
CMD ["python3"]
```

Regularly updating images is crucial to mitigate known vulnerabilities. Automated systems for image scanning and updates should be integrated within CI/CD pipelines. Tools such as 'Trivy' or Docker's native image scanning can be instrumental in identifying vulnerabilities. Example command for Trivy:

```
trivy image your_image:tag
```

A key practice is running containers with the principle of least privilege. Containers should run with the least necessary permissions and should not be executed as the root user. Modify the Dockerfile to specify a non-root user:

```
FROM alpine:latest
RUN adduser -D myuser
USER myuser
CMD ["sh"]
```

Containers should also be configured with restrictive capabilities to limit their system-wide privileges. The '–cap-drop' flag in 'docker run' can be used to remove capabilities:

```
docker run --cap-drop=ALL --cap-add=NET_BIND_SERVICE my_image
```

Network security is another critical facet. Segregating network traffic by using Docker's network modes or creating custom networks can hinder unauthorized communications. To isolate containers, create a custom network and connect containers only as necessary:

```
docker network create my_custom_network
docker run --network my_custom_network my_image
```

Implementing security through the use of 'seccomp' and 'AppArmor' profiles is advised. These mechanisms restrict the system calls and capabilities available to containers, further narrowing potential attack vectors. A basic 'seccomp' profile example restricting system calls looks like:

```
{
  "defaultAction": "SCMP_ACT_ERRNO",
  "syscalls": [
    {
      "names": ["execve"],
      "action": "SCMP_ACT_ALLOW"
    }
  ]
}
```

To apply this 'seccomp' profile:

```
docker run --security-opt seccomp=profile.json my_image
```

Secret management must be conducted outside of the container environment. Docker Swarm and Kubernetes provide mechanisms for managing secrets securely. Create and use Docker secrets as follows:

```
echo "my_secret" | docker secret create my_secret -
docker service create --name my_service --secret my_secret my_image
```

Consistent monitoring and logging are vital. Integrating solutions like 'Sysdig', 'Falco', or native Docker logs can assist in real-time tracking of security events. Configure Docker daemon to use secure logging drivers:

```
{
  "log-driver": "json-file",
  "log-opts": {
    "max-size": "10m",
    "max-file": "3"
  }
}
```

Regular compliance auditing should be performed using tools like 'Docker Bench for Security', which inspects hosts and Docker configurations against best practices:

```
docker run -it --net host --pid host --cap-add audit_control \
    --label docker_bench_security \
    docker/docker-bench-security
```

Ultimately, by adhering to these best practices, a robust defense mechanism for Docker environments can be established, thereby mitigating potential threats and ensuring the security of containerized applications.

9.8 Running Containers with Least Privilege

Running Docker containers with least privilege is a crucial strategy to mitigate security risks. This practice involves granting containers only the minimum privileges necessary for their operation, thereby restricting the potential impact of a compromised container. By adhering to the principle of least privilege, one can significantly reduce the attack surface and limit the scope of potential exploits.

To implement least privilege effectively, several strategies and configurations can be employed. The steps and best practices to achieve this include:

- **Avoid Running Containers as Root**

  By default, Docker containers run as the root user, which possesses all administrative privileges. Running as root presents substantial security risks as any vulnerability within the application could grant an attacker root access to the host system. It is critical to configure the Dockerfile to use a non-root user wherever possible.

  In the Dockerfile, use the USER directive to specify a non-root user:

  ```
  # Create a non-root user and group
  RUN groupadd -r appuser && useradd -r -g appuser appuser

  # Switch to the new user
  USER appuser
  ```

  This command creates a new user and group, and then switches to that user. It's essential to ensure that the non-root user has appropriate permissions to perform necessary tasks without elevating privileges inappropriately.

- **Limit Container Capabilities**

  Docker containers, by default, are granted a broad set of capabilities. Capabilities are Linux kernel features that allow for fine-grained control over process permissions. Reducing these capabilities can further constrain a container's potential to perform harmful actions.

To run a container with only the necessary capabilities, use the –cap-drop and –cap-add flags with the docker run command. For example, to drop all capabilities and then add only those that are strictly required:

```
docker run --cap-drop=ALL --cap-add=NET_BIND_SERVICE --cap-add=
    SYS_ADMIN mycontainer
```

In this example, the container is stripped of all capabilities and then granted only the NET_BIND_SERVICE and SYS_ADMIN capabilities. Careful consideration is needed to identify the exact set of capabilities required.

- **Use Read-only Filesystems**

  Mounting container filesystems in read-only mode is another effective method to minimize risk. This prevents any unauthorized writes to the filesystem, ensuring that even if an application is compromised, the attacker cannot modify, delete, or add files.

  To create a read-only filesystem, use the –read-only flag:

```
docker run --read-only mycontainer
```

  If the application requires writable paths, consider mounting specific directories as writable:

```
docker run --read-only -v /path/to/writable/dir mycontainer
```

- **Minimize Network Permissions**

  Controlling network access is another layer of security to enforce least privilege. Docker's network mode and configurations can be adjusted to restrict container network connectivity. For instance, a container can be run with no network access:

```
docker run --network none mycontainer
```

  For more fine-grained controls, Docker's user-defined networks can be used to isolate containers or enforce specific network policies.

- **Utilize Docker's Seccomp Profiles**

  Seccomp (secure computing mode) provides mechanisms to restrict system calls a process can make, thus limiting the kernel surface exposed to a container. Docker provides a default seccomp profile, but custom profiles can offer more restrictive controls.

To run a container with a strict seccomp profile:

```
docker run --security-opt seccomp=profile.json mycontainer
```

The profile.json file contains the seccomp rules, specifying which system calls are permitted or denied. Crafting these profiles requires a thorough understanding of the application's system call requirements.

- **Configure AppArmor and SELinux**

  Linux Security Modules (LSMs) such as AppArmor and SELinux provide mandatory access controls. These can be applied to Docker containers to enforce least privilege policies.

  To run a container with an AppArmor profile:

  ```
  docker run --security-opt apparmor=profile_name mycontainer
  ```

  Similarly, for SELinux, appropriate labels can be used to restrict the container's access:

  ```
  docker run --security-opt label=type:my_type mycontainer
  ```

  Creating and refining these security policies involves understanding the security requirements and behaviors of the containerized applications.

- **Limit Resource Usage**

  Restricting resources such as CPU and memory can prevent runaway processes and denial-of-service conditions. Use the –cpu-shares, –cpus, and –memory flags to limit resource allocation:

  ```
  docker run --cpu-shares=512 --cpus=1 --memory=512m mycontainer
  ```

  These mechanisms help control the resources a container can consume, ensuring a fair distribution among multiple containers and reducing the potential impact of a compromised container.

By meticulously configuring these settings, containers operate with the minimum privileges necessary, enhancing the overall security posture of the Docker environment.

9.9 Isolating Containers

Isolating containers is a fundamental aspect of strengthening the security and robustness of Docker applications. Container isolation ensures that applications running within a Docker container are confined to a certain extent, thus reducing the risk of unwanted interactions between containers and the host system. This isolation also aids in fault tolerance, making sure that an error or a breach in one container does not affect others. The key methods for achieving isolation involve leveraging namespaces, control groups (cgroups), capabilities, and user namespaces.

Namespaces are a Linux kernel feature that partitions kernel resources to provide processes with an isolated view of the system. Docker uses several types of namespaces to isolate various aspects of a container's environment.

- **PID Namespace:** Each container gets its own process ID (PID) namespace, meaning processes within the container have PIDs independent of those outside it.
- **Network Namespace:** This isolates a container's network interfaces, IP addresses, port numbers, and routing tables.
- **Mount Namespace:** Each container has its own filesystem mount points. Changes to mount points within a container do not affect the host system or other containers.
- **UTS Namespace:** This provides isolation of the hostname and domain name.
- **IPC Namespace:** This isolates inter-process communications resources, such as System V IPC and POSIX message queues.
- **User Namespace:** This allows root inside the container to be mapped to a non-root user outside the container, enhancing security.

For illustration, let's consider creating a container with user namespaces enabled. This requires configuring Docker daemon with user namespaces. The following configuration snippet can be added to your Docker daemon configuration file, typically located at /etc/docker/daemon.json:

```
{
  "userns-remap": "default"
}
```

After updating the configuration, restart the Docker daemon:

```
$ sudo systemctl restart docker
```

The **control groups (cgroups)** are another kernel feature used by Docker to limit and prioritize the resource usage (CPU, memory, disk I/O, etc.) of containerized applications. With cgroups, you can ensure that no single container consumes excessive system resources.

To limit the memory usage of a container to 256MB and CPU usage to 50

```
$ docker run -d --memory="256m" --cpus=".5" nginx
```

Linux **capabilities** define a fine-grained set of privileges that can be assigned to a process. By default, Docker drops many Linux capabilities to minimize the potential attack surface. However, you might need to explicitly add or drop capabilities based on the application requirements. For example, to drop all capabilities except the ones explicitly needed, you can use the –cap-drop and –cap-add options:

```
$ docker run -d --cap-drop=ALL --cap-add=NET_ADMIN nginx
```

User namespaces are an advanced isolation technique where each container can have its own set of user and group IDs that are distinct from the host system. This means root in the container is not root on the host, which significantly enhances security. Users can remap their UIDs and GIDs to different values within the container compared to the host, minimizing the risk of privilege escalation attacks.

Another aspect of isolation is **network isolation**. Docker provides several network drivers for different use cases:

- bridge: Default network driver for containers, providing isolation on the same Docker host.
- host: Containers share the host system's network stack, no network isolation.
- none: Completely disables networking for the container.
- overlay: Enables communication between Docker Daemons across hosts.

- macvlan: Assigns a unique MAC address to each container, appearing as a physical device on the network.

To isolate container communication, you can configure network access rules using Docker's firewall settings or network policies in orchestrators like Kubernetes. Docker's iptables integration can be used to safeguard which containers can communicate with each other and the outside world. Here's an example of configuring an isolated network:

```
$ docker network create --driver bridge isolated_network
$ docker run --network=isolated_network --name container1 alpine
$ docker run --network=isolated_network --name container2 alpine
$ docker run --network=isolated_network --name container3 nginx
```

In this example, container1, container2, and container3 are all on a custom bridge network called isolated_network. This provides an isolated network environment where only these containers can communicate directly with each other.

Lastly, it is prudent to employ **security profiles** to enforce mandatory access controls. Docker supports integration with security modules like AppArmor and SELinux, which can be used to create policies restricting what containers can and cannot do. For example, using AppArmor:

```
$ docker run --security-opt apparmor=your_profile_name ubuntu
```

Integrating these techniques ensures that each container is as isolated as practical, reducing the risk surface and enhancing the overall security and stability of the Docker environment.

9.10 Network Security in Docker

Network security is an essential component in the deployment of Docker containers. Ensuring that containers can communicate securely, both among themselves and with external networks, involves understanding the Docker networking model and employing various security measures.

Docker provides several network drivers to manage networking aspects including bridge, host, overlay, and macvlan drivers. Each of these drivers has its own security considerations.

Bridge Networks

Bridge networks are the default type of networks created by Docker.

Containers connected to the same bridge network can communicate with each other directly. To secure these networks:

- Utilize firewall rules to control traffic to and from the containers.
- Implement user-defined bridge networks to isolate groups of containers, reducing the chance of unintended communication.
- Use internal networks to avoid exposing the network to external access.

Host Networks

Host networks allow containers to share the host's networking namespace. This means that containers will have access to the host's network interfaces. Securing host networks involves:

- Limiting the use of host networking as it exposes the containers to the host's network.
- Configuring iptables rules on the host to restrict inbound and outbound traffic.
- Ensuring that containers running on host networks do not run with unnecessary privileges.

Overlay Networks

Overlay networks enable the deployment of services across multiple Docker daemons, forming a single network shared among all participating nodes. To secure overlay networks:

- Use IPsec (Internet Protocol Security) to secure the data plane.
- Encrypt network traffic between containers using TLS (Transport Layer Security).
- Regularly audit and rotate certificates used for securing the communication.

Macvlan Networks

Macvlan networks allow containers to have their own MAC address and appear as physical devices on the network. Security measures include:

- Segmenting the network using VLANs to isolate container traffic.
- Configuring proper ARP (Address Resolution Protocol) settings to prevent spoofing attack.
- Implementing access control lists (ACLs) to limit communication based on policies.

Securing Communication

Ensuring secure communication between Docker containers also involves:

- Enabling mutual TLS authentication between containers.
- Managing and protecting sensitive data such as network certificates and keys using Docker Secrets.
- Regularly updating software to mitigate the risk of vulnerabilities.
- Employing container-level network policies, using third-party tools such as Calico or Cilium, to enforce security rules at the container level.

Controlling External Access

Restricting external access to containers minimizes potential attack vectors:

- Configure firewall rules to limit access to only necessary ports.
- Utilize the Docker firewall chains (DOCKER-USER) for setting custom rules.
- Leverage reverse proxies like Nginx or Traefik to manage inbound traffic securely.
- Ensure that only required services are exposed, and run container-specific services on non-standard ports when possible.

Monitoring and Logging

The security state of Docker networks should be continuously monitored to detect and respond to any incidents promptly:

- Use network monitoring tools such as Wireshark or tcpdump to analyze traffic.
- Employ centralized logging solutions to collect and analyze network logs.
- Set up alerts for unusual network activities that could indicate a potential security breach.

Best Practices

Implementing best practices for Docker network security includes:

- Regularly audit network configurations and container settings.
- Apply the principle of least privilege by limiting container access to only what is necessary.
- Use network namespaces to isolate network resources.
- Employ mutual TLS authentication to establish trust between communicating entities.
- Stay updated with the latest security patches and Docker releases.

Example Configuration

To illustrate, consider a Docker Compose file example where services are defined to use a user-defined bridge network with secured settings:

```
version: '3.8'
services:
  web:
    image: nginx:latest
    networks:
      - front-tier
    ports:
      - "80:80"
  db:
    image: postgres:latest
    networks:
      - back-tier
    environment:
      POSTGRES_DB: exampledb
      POSTGRES_USER: exampleuser
      POSTGRES_PASSWORD: securepassword
networks:
  front-tier:
    driver: bridge
    ipam:
      config:
```

```
      - subnet: 192.168.1.0/24
  back-tier:
    driver: bridge
    internal: true
```

In this example, the 'web' service is connected to the 'front-tier' network which is externally accessible on port 80, whereas the 'db' service resides in the 'back-tier', which is internal and restricted. This setup ensures that the database is not directly accessible from the outside, adhering to the security best practices.

By implementing these strategies, ensure the Docker networking environment remains secure, reducing potential risks associated with containerized applications. These configurations should be tested and continuously monitored to adapt to any emerging threats or changes in the deployment environment.

9.11 Using Docker Bench for Security

Docker Bench for Security is an essential tool designed to automate the process of security auditing against the Docker Engine. It consists of a script that checks for dozens of common best practices using the CIS (Center for Internet Security) Docker Benchmark guidelines. This section will explore the installation, configuration, execution, and interpretation of Docker Bench for Security outputs.

Docker Bench can be executed on any system where Docker is installed. The primary purpose is to evaluate the host environment's security against established benchmarks and provide actionable recommendations. Before proceeding with the installation, ensure that the Docker environment is correctly set up and running without issues.

Installation: To begin using Docker Bench for Security, clone the repository from the official Docker GitHub account. This can be done using the following command:

```
git clone https://github.com/docker/docker-bench-security.git
```

Once cloned, navigate to the directory containing the Docker Bench for Security script:

```
cd docker-bench-security
```

Execution: Docker Bench for Security can be executed directly using a

Unix shell, or alternatively, it can be run as a Docker container. Running it as a container encapsulates the execution environment, thereby eliminating discrepancies related to host environment dependencies. The following command executes Docker Bench directly from the shell:

```
sh docker-bench-security.sh
```

To run Docker Bench inside a Docker container, execute:

```
docker run -it --net host --pid host --userns host --cap-add audit_control \
    -v /var/lib:/var/lib \
    -v /var/run/docker.sock:/var/run/docker.sock \
    -v /etc:/etc --label docker_bench_security \
    docker/docker-bench-security
```

Configuration: The script can be customized to suit specific needs by modifying its configuration files. This includes adjusting the list of checks performed or altering parameters as per organizational security policies. The configuration settings are located within the tests directory. Each test file corresponds to a set of checks, which are annotated for easy understanding.

Output Interpretation: Upon execution, Docker Bench for Security generates detailed output that indicates pass or fail status against each benchmark. The results are categorized based on sections from the CIS Docker Benchmark.

The output format typically resembles:

```
[INFO] 1 - Host Configuration
[WARN] 1.1  - Ensure a separate partition for containers has been created
[PASS] 1.2  - Ensure that the Docker daemon is configured to use TLS for both
              client and server authentication
```

INFO indicates a non-critical check, WARN denotes potential issues that should be addressed, and PASS indicates compliance with the benchmark.

Key areas covered by Docker Bench include but are not limited to:

- Host Configuration: Ensures the host environment is appropriately configured for running Docker securely.
- Docker Daemon Configuration: Verifies if the Docker daemon is operating securely, including TLS usage.
- Container Images and Build File: Checks the security practices in Dockerfile and image management.
- Container Runtime: Ensures containers are running with configurations enhancing security.

- Docker Security Operations: Validates the ongoing security operations practices within the Docker context.

Recommendations: Based on the output, take the following actions to comply with best practices:

- Address WARN and INFO items by implementing measures such as network segmentation, appropriate user privileges, and enforcing encryption.
- Schedule regular runs of Docker Bench for Security as part of a continuous security assessment routine.
- Integrate Docker Bench into CI/CD pipelines to ensure any developments align with security benchmarks before deployment.

Docker Bench for Security provides a robust foundation for maintaining a secure Docker environment, ensuring compliance with industry standards. Regular implementation and addressing the recommendations help prevent vulnerabilities associated with misconfigurations and outdated practices.

9.12 Managing Secrets in Docker

Effective management of secrets in Docker is crucial for maintaining the security and integrity of applications. Secrets can include passwords, API keys, SSL certificates, and other sensitive information. This section delves into methodologies and tools for securely handling secrets within Docker environments without compromising their confidentiality.

Docker provides dedicated mechanisms for managing secrets, particularly through Docker Swarm. In a Swarm, secrets are stored in in-memory file systems, ensuring they are encrypted at rest and only available to the nodes that need them. However, there are also strategies for managing secrets outside of Swarm mode, which will be discussed.

Creating and Using Secrets in Docker Swarm

The docker secret command allows for creating, managing, and deploying secrets in a Docker Swarm. Consider the following steps to create and use a secret.

- **Create a Secret**: Assume we need to handle a database password securely. First, create the secret:

```
echo "my_db_password" | docker secret create db_password -
```

- **Deploy Services with Secrets**: When deploying a stack or service, secrets can be included in the deployment specifications:

```
version: '3.1'
services:
  db:
    image: mysql:latest
    secrets:
      - db_password
secrets:
  db_password:
    external: true
```

In this configuration, the secret db_password is made available to the database service. The secret file is mounted as /run/secrets/db_password within the container, and the application can read it directly.

- **Accessing Secrets**: Inside the container, secrets are accessible as files in the /run/secrets directory. For example, to read the secret in an application:

```
with open('/run/secrets/db_password', 'r') as secret_file:
    db_password = secret_file.read().strip()
```

Managing Secrets Outside Docker Swarm

In scenarios where Docker Swarm is not used, managing secrets requires alternative approaches:

- **Environment Variables**: While not the most secure, environment variables are commonly used to pass secrets into containers. This method introduces risks, as environment variables can be accessed relatively easily. An example configuration can be seen below:

```
version: '3.3'
services:
  app:
    image: myapp:latest
    environment:
      - DB_PASSWORD=${DB_PASSWORD}
```

Usage of environment variable files can reduce exposure:

```
docker run --env-file ./env.list myapp:latest
```

- **Mounted Volumes**: Volumes can be used to pass secret files into containers. This approach is slightly more secure than environment variables but requires careful handling:

```
version: '3.3'
services:
  app:
    image: myapp:latest
    volumes:
      - ./secrets:/run/secrets
```

  Ensure the ./secrets directory contains appropriately secured files, as these will be mounted into the container.

- **Third-Party Secret Management Tools**: Tools like HashiCorp Vault, AWS Secrets Manager, or Azure Key Vault provide more robust mechanisms to manage and inject secrets:

```
# HashiCorp Vault example
vault kv put secret/db_password value=my_db_password
export DB_PASSWORD=$(vault kv get -field=value secret/db_password)
docker run -e DB_PASSWORD=$DB_PASSWORD myapp:latest
```

  Here, secrets are securely stored and retrieved as needed, limiting their exposure within the container environment.

Best Practices for Managing Secrets

To safeguard secrets effectively, adhere to these best practices:

- **Least Privilege Principle**: Ensure secrets are only accessible by the services that require them.
- **Encryption at Rest and Transit**: Always encrypt secrets when stored and during transmission.
- **Frequent Rotation**: Regularly rotate secrets to minimize the risk associated with secret compromise.
- **Audit and Monitoring**: Implement logging and monitoring to detect unauthorized access to secrets.

Managing secrets in Docker requires implementing these security measures to mitigate risks and maintain the integrity of sensitive data. Adopting the right strategies and tools ensures that secrets remain protected within containerized environments.

9.13 Regular Updates and Patch Management

Regular maintenance and timely updates stand as pillars of maintaining a secure and efficient Docker environment. Effective patch management ensures that vulnerabilities are mitigated, system performance is optimized, and compliance with security policies is maintained. This section elucidates the critical aspects of handling updates and patches in a Dockerized infrastructure.

Importance of Regular Updates: Frequent updates are imperative for the following reasons:

- **Security Vulnerabilities**: Security patches are released to fix vulnerabilities discovered in Docker itself, the host operating system, or the applications running within containers.
- **Performance Enhancements**: Updates may include improvements that enhance the performance and stability of the Docker environment.
- **Compatibility**: Keeping components updated ensures compatibility with other software and services, reducing the risk of unexpected failures.

Understanding the Docker Release Cycle: Docker releases updates on a regular cycle, which includes stable, edge, and nightly builds. It is crucial to understand each type of release to make informed decisions:

- **Stable Releases**: These are thoroughly tested and are suitable for production environments.
- **Edge Releases**: These include the latest features and fixes but might not be fully tested for production readiness.
- **Nightly Builds**: These contain the most recent changes but are highly experimental and should not be used in critical environments.

Automating Updates with Continuous Integration/Continuous Deployment (CI/CD): For seamless updates, integrating Docker updates into the CI/CD pipeline is effective. Example configuration using Jenkins:

```
pipeline {
    agent any
    stages {
        stage('Build') {
            steps {
                script {
                    dockerImage = docker.build("myapp:${env.BUILD_ID}")
                }
            }
        }
        stage('Test') {
            steps {
                script {
                    dockerImage.inside {
                        sh 'make test'
                    }
                }
            }
        }
        stage('Deploy') {
            steps {
                script {
                    dockerImage.push()
                }
            }
        }
    }
    post {
        always {
            cleanWs()
        }
    }
}
```

Monitoring Security Advisories: Subscribing to Docker security advisories and utilizing tools such as CVE databases can help in staying informed about new vulnerabilities. The following command subscribes to security notifications:

```
# Subscribe to Docker Security Advisories
curl -O https://docker.com/security/advisories
```

Applying Patches to Docker Engine and Components: Updating the Docker engine can be done using package managers. Ensure the Docker daemon and associated components are updated regularly:

```
# Update Docker Engine on Ubuntu
sudo apt-get update
sudo apt-get install docker-ce docker-ce-cli containerd.io
```

Updating Base Images: Base images should be regularly updated to incorporate the latest security patches. Automate the rebuilding of images:

```
# Automated Rebuild of Docker Images
docker build -t myimage:latest .
```

```
docker push myimage:latest
```

Version Pinning: To ensure consistency and prevent breaking changes in the environment, version pinning is advisable. Pinning ensures that the specified versions of images and dependencies are used:

```
# Dockerfile with version pinning
FROM ubuntu:18.04
RUN apt-get update && apt-get install -y nginx=1.14.0-0ubuntu1.7
```

Container Orchestration Update Strategies: In a Kubernetes environment, updates can be managed with rolling updates or blue-green deployments to ensure zero downtime:

```
# Kubernetes Rolling Update
kubectl set image deployment/myapp myapp=myimage:latest
```

These methodologies provide an organized framework for maintaining and updating Docker environments. By embedding these practices into the operational workflow, Docker users can maintain a secure, efficient, and compliant infrastructure.

9.14 Auditing and Compliance with Docker

Auditing and compliance are critical components for maintaining the security and operational integrity of Docker environments. Ensuring compliance not only helps in adhering to legal and organizational standards but also mitigates risks associated with security breaches, data loss, and system vulnerabilities. This section delves into the various aspects of auditing Docker environments and achieving compliance with industry standards.

To effectively audit and maintain compliance, a multifaceted approach should be employed. This includes regularly reviewing container configurations, monitoring activity within containers and hosts, and validating that containers are operating under the least privilege principle. Additionally, ensuring that Docker configurations meet organizational policies and relevant regulatory requirements is paramount.

1. Configuration Auditing

Configuration auditing involves periodically reviewing the current settings of Docker hosts and containers to ensure they comply with recommended security practices and organizational policies.

```
$ docker run -it --net host --pid host --cap-add audit_control \
  -v /var/lib:/var/lib -v /var/run/docker.sock:/var/run/docker.sock \
  --label docker_bench_security \
  docker/docker-bench-security
```

Docker Bench for Security is a script that checks for dozens of common best practices around deploying Docker containers in production. It includes checks for:

- Ensuring that Docker is updated to the latest version.
- Monitoring Docker daemon configurations.
- Verifying that only trusted users have Docker access.
- Ensuring that sensitive directories are not mounted.

2. Activity Monitoring and Logging

Logging and monitoring the activities within Docker containers and the Docker daemon are crucial for security and compliance. This allows administrators to detect unauthorized activities, potential breaches, and system performance issues.

```
$ sudo mkdir -p /etc/systemd/system/docker.service.d
$ sudo tee /etc/systemd/system/docker.service.d/override.conf <<-'EOF'
[Service]
ExecStart=
ExecStart=/usr/bin/dockerd --log-level=info
EOF

$ sudo systemctl daemon-reload
$ sudo systemctl restart docker
```

Monitoring tools such as Prometheus, Grafana, and ELK (Elasticsearch, Logstash, Kibana) stack can be integrated with Docker to provide real-time insights and historical data analysis. These tools help identify anomalies and maintain a comprehensive log of all activities.

```
$ docker run -d --name kibana -p 5601:5601 --link elasticsearch:elasticsearch \
  -e ELASTICSEARCH_URL=http://elasticsearch:9200 \
  docker.elastic.co/kibana/kibana:7.10.0
$ docker run -d --name logstash -p 5044:5044 --link elasticsearch:elasticsearch \
  -e xpack.monitoring.elasticsearch.url=http://elasticsearch:9200 \
  docker.elastic.co/logstash/logstash:7.10.0
```

3. Policy Compliance and Regular Audits

Ensuring containers and Docker daemon configuration adherence to organizational policies and industry standards like CIS Benchmarks,

GDPR, HIPAA, etc., is essential. Regular audits should be scheduled to verify compliance continually.

Utilize tools like OpenSCAP, an auditing tool that provides compliance checklists and vulnerability management features, to automate and streamline this process.

```
$ sudo oscap-docker image YOUR_IMAGE_ID/NAME --profile xccdf_org.ssgproject.
    content_profile_pci-dss scan | tee results.xml
```

The output of the OpenSCAP scan provides a detailed report indicating compliance status and actionable items to address any non-compliant configurations.

```
<results>
  <rule-result idref="xccdf_org.ssgproject.content_rule_dockerfile_config">
    <result>fail</result>
  </rule-result>
  ...
</results>
```

4. Continuous Compliance and Automated Checks

Establishing continuous compliance involves integrating security and compliance checks into the Continuous Integration and Continuous Deployment (CI/CD) pipeline. By doing so, each new code commit and deployment is vetted against compliance standards automatically.

```
stages:
  - build
  - test
  - scan

build:
  stage: build
  script:
    - docker build -t myapp .

test:
  stage: test
  script:
    - docker run -d --name myapp_test myapp
    - docker exec myapp_test pytest

scan:
  stage: scan
  image: docker.io/openscap/scap-workbench
  script:
    - docker run --rm -v $(pwd):/mnt myapp oscap xccdf eval --profile pci-dss --results /
        mnt/results.xml --report /mnt/report.html /mnt/compliance_content.xml
  artifacts:
    paths:
      - results.xml
      - report.html
```

With the integration of scanning and compliance checks in CI/CD pipelines, relevant stakeholders receive immediate feedback, allowing for quicker remediation actions and maintaining ongoing compliance.

5. Documentation and Reporting

Maintaining comprehensive documentation of Docker configurations, policies, and audit reports is essential for auditing and compliance. This allows for transparency and provides a historical record of compliance efforts.

Prepare and store documentation encompassing:

- Configuration guidelines.
- Audit logs and reports.
- Incident response plans.
- Security policies and best practices.

Implementing these measures and maintaining rigorous auditing and compliance processes ensures a secure, compliant Docker environment, aligning with best practices and regulatory standards.

Chapter 10

Advanced Docker Concepts and Techniques

This chapter delves into advanced Docker concepts such as daemon configuration, custom plugins, and multi-stage builds. It explores Docker networking internals, advanced volume management, and automating Docker with scripts. The chapter also covers integration with CI/CD pipelines, Docker Swarm advanced features, container orchestration strategies, performance tuning, and advanced monitoring and logging techniques.

10.1 Introduction to Advanced Docker Concepts

Advanced Docker concepts encompass a range of methodologies, configurations, and strategies designed to leverage Docker's full potential in complex environments. This section aims to provide a comprehensive foundation for understanding the extended capabilities and sophisticated techniques essential for proficient Docker usage.

Docker, inherently, is a versatile platform that streamlines the development, deployment, and operation of applications across containers. While basic Docker usage covers container creation, management, and fundamental networking, advanced concepts delve into granular control over the Docker daemon, customization via plugins, sophisticated build processes, intricate networking, and robust volume management.

Docker Daemon Configuration: The Docker daemon is a crucial background service running on the host machine, managing Docker components, including images, containers, networks, and storage. Advanced configuration allows fine-tuning of its behavior, resource usage, security settings, and logging. For example, configuring daemon.json provides control over logging drivers, storage drivers, and the setting of experimental features.

```
{
  "log-driver": "json-file",
  "log-opts": {
    "max-size": "10m",
    "max-file": "3"
  },
  "storage-driver": "overlay2",
  "experimental": true
}
```

Customizing Docker with Plugins: Plugins extend Docker's functionalities, providing modular capabilities for networking, storage, and volume management. Docker supports plugins for third-party services, enabling custom integrations without altering core components. These plugins are distributed as Docker images and can be installed and managed using the Docker CLI.

```
docker plugin install vieux/sshfs
```

Multi-Stage Builds for Production: Multi-stage builds optimize Docker image creation by using multiple "stages" within a single Dockerfile. This approach allows different dependencies and build environments to be isolated and managed efficiently. Multi-stage builds result in smaller, production-ready images by excluding development dependencies.

```
# First stage: builder
FROM golang:1.17 as builder
WORKDIR /app
COPY . .
RUN go build -o myapp

# Second stage: runner
FROM alpine:latest
RUN apk --no-cache add ca-certificates
WORKDIR /root/
COPY --from=builder /app/myapp .
CMD ["./myapp"]
```

Docker Networking Internals: Understanding Docker's networking infrastructure is pivotal for designing secure and high-performance network topologies. Docker provides several network drivers, including bridge, host, none, and overlay, each serving different purposes.

Bridge Network: By default, Docker creates a bridge network, connecting containers to the same network interface enabling inter-container communication. Custom bridge networks provide isolation between sets of containers.

```
docker network create --driver bridge my_custom_bridge
```

Host Network: Utilizes the host's network stack, providing high network performance but requiring careful management to avoid port conflicts.

```
docker run --network host nginx
```

Overlay Network: Used primarily in Docker Swarm mode for multi-host networking. It abstracts the underlying physical network, allowing seamless container communication across multiple Docker hosts.

```
docker network create --driver overlay my_overlay_network
```

Advanced Volume Management: Docker volumes provide a means to persist data generated by and used by Docker containers. Advanced volume management includes using named volumes, mounting host directories, and utilizing third-party volume plugins.

```
docker volume create my_volume
```

```
docker run -d -v my_volume:/data busybox
```

Understanding these advanced concepts equips users with the necessary tools to optimally configure Docker environments, ensuring performance, security, and scalability. Each technique discussed lays the groundwork for mastering Docker's expansive feature set, enabling sophisticated containerized application management.

10.2 Docker Daemon Configuration

The Docker daemon is a background service running on the host that manages Docker containers. It listens for Docker API requests and manages Docker objects such as images, containers, networks, and volumes. Configuring the Docker daemon properly is crucial for ensuring optimal performance, security, and reliability of your containerized applications.

To customize the Docker daemon, configuration files and command-line options can be used. The main configuration file for the Docker daemon is /etc/docker/daemon.json. This file allows you to specify various parameters that control the behavior of the Docker daemon. Below is an example of a typical daemon.json file:

```
{
    "storage-driver": "overlay2",
    "log-level": "info",
    "insecure-registries": ["myinsecure.registry.com:5000"],
    "default-runtime": "runc",
    "metrics-addr" : "127.0.0.1:9323",
    "experimental": true
}
```

Storage Driver: The storage-driver option specifies which storage driver the Docker daemon should use. The overlay2 storage driver is generally recommended for modern Linux distributions due to its efficiency and robust performance.

Log Level: Setting the log-level parameter controls the verbosity of logs generated by the Docker daemon. Possible values include debug, info, warn, error, and fatal.

Insecure Registries: The insecure-registries field is an array of URLs that Docker considers insecure. This is useful for testing purposes or when using self-signed certificates in a development environment.

Default Runtime: The default-runtime option specifies the runtime Docker will use by default to run containers. The default runtime, runc, is the standard for container operation, but other runtime options such as kata-runtime can be configured to provide enhanced security features.

Metrics Address: The metrics-addr configuration is used to specify the address bound to provide daemon metrics in Prometheus format. Example address format: "127.0.0.1:9323".

Experimental Features: Enabling the experimental flag allows access to Docker's experimental features, which are not yet stable but may provide cutting-edge capabilities.

After modifying the daemon.json file, the Docker daemon must be reloaded and restarted to apply the changes:

```
sudo systemctl daemon-reload
sudo systemctl restart docker
```

The docker daemon command, which is used to manually start the Docker daemon, also accepts various flags to customize its behavior. For instance, the following command starts the Docker daemon with a specific storage driver and log level:

```
dockerd --storage-driver=overlay2 --log-level=info
```

When configuring the Docker daemon, it is important to follow security best practices. Limiting access to the Docker daemon socket (/var/run/docker.sock) is essential to prevent unauthorized users from controlling Docker. Typically, only root and users in the docker group should have access to this socket.

Configuring secure communication with the Docker daemon involves using TLS certificates. The tlsverify flag enables TLS and verifies client certificates. First, ensure you have generated the required keys and certificates for your CA. Then, configure the Docker daemon to use these certificates:

```
dockerd --tlsverify \
        --tlscacert=/path/to/ca.pem \
        --tlscert=/path/to/server-cert.pem \
        --tlskey=/path/to/server-key.pem \
        -H=0.0.0.0:2376
```

In daemon.json, the corresponding configuration would be:

```
{
    "tlsverify": true,
    "tlscacert": "/path/to/ca.pem",
    "tlscert": "/path/to/server-cert.pem",
    "tlskey": "/path/to/server-key.pem",
    "hosts": ["tcp://0.0.0.0:2376"]
}
```

Proper logging and monitoring of the Docker daemon can provide insights into its performance and aid in diagnosing issues. Configuring a logging driver, such as json-file, syslog, or journald, ensures consistent logging. Below is an example of setting the logging driver and log options in daemon.json:

```
{
    "log-driver": "json-file",
    "log-opts": {
        "max-size": "10m",
        "max-file": "3"
    }
}
```

In scenarios where advanced logging mechanisms are necessary, such as aggregating logs from multiple nodes, using a log collector like

Fluentd or ELK stack is recommended. The Docker daemon supports direct integration with such tools through its logging drivers.

Docker daemon's performance can be tuned by adjusting resource limits and optimizing parameters such as max-concurrent-uploads and max-concurrent-downloads. These parameters control the number of concurrent layer uploads and downloads, respectively:

```
{
  "max-concurrent-uploads": 5,
  "max-concurrent-downloads": 10
}
```

Advanced users may leverage cgroups and namespaces configurations to fine-tune resource allocation and isolation, respectively. Ensuring that cgroups are configured appropriately on the host and that Docker is started with proper cgroup settings can help optimize resource usage and system stability.

Understanding and configuring the Docker daemon is paramount for administrators tasked with managing Docker in production environments. The daemon.json file offers a flexible and powerful way to customize the Docker daemon, ensuring that it meets the specific needs and constraints of the deployment environment.

10.3 Customizing Docker with Plugins

Docker plugins enhance the core functionality of Docker by allowing additional features and integrations to be added without altering the Docker source code. This concept allows for a more modular and extensible system, accommodating a wide range of use cases and environments. Docker plugins can be used for networking, volume storage, logging, authorization, and more. Understanding how to utilize and manage Docker plugins is essential for advanced Docker users.

The Docker plugin system is designed to be straightforward and versatile. Plugins are distributed as Docker images and must adhere to the Docker plugin API. Configuration and management are typically performed via the Docker CLI or Docker API, using commands such as docker plugin install and docker plugin enable.

To demonstrate, let us consider the steps for managing plugins in Docker.

```
docker plugin install vieux/sshfs
```

In this command, vieux/sshfs is the name of the plugin. Docker will pull the plugin image from Docker Hub or another Docker registry, if specified. The user may need to pass additional options or accept a license agreement depending on the plugin's requirements.

Post installation, plugins must often be explicitly enabled:

```
docker plugin enable vieux/sshfs
```

Enabling a plugin allows Docker to load it during the startup sequence, making its functionality available to containers. Conversely, a plugin can be disabled using the following command:

```
docker plugin disable vieux/sshfs
```

Docker plugins may be automatically updated or removed when necessary. To remove a plugin, the plugin must first be disabled, and then removed:

```
docker plugin rm vieux/sshfs
```

Plugin management ensures that only the necessary plugins are operational, helping to maintain system performance and security.

A practical application of Docker plugins is in networking. There are plugins available to support various networking frameworks and technologies that extend Docker's native networking capabilities. For example, the Weave plugin allows for software-defined networking (SDN) which simplifies network configuration across distributed Docker containers.

To install the Weave network plugin, the following command is used:

```
docker plugin install weaveworks/net-plugin:latest_release
```

After the plugin is installed and enabled, it can be used to create custom network configurations that facilitate container communication over complex topologies.

Another significant use case for Docker plugins is volume management. Docker provides basic volume management capabilities, but plugins enable integration with various storage backends. For instance, the RexRay plugin enables Docker volumes to interface with block storage solutions from cloud providers and storage platforms.

Consider the installation of the RexRay plugin for Amazon EBS:

```
docker plugin install rexray/ebs REXRAY_PREEMPT=true EBS_ACCESSKEY=
    your_access_key EBS_SECRETKEY=your_secret_key
```

This command installs the RexRay plugin and passes the required configuration options, such as access keys for Amazon EBS. The configured plugin can subsequently create and manage Docker volumes that leverage Amazon EBS.

```
$ docker volume create -d rexray/ebs --name my-aws-volume
my-aws-volume
```

The above command creates a Docker volume named my-aws-volume using the RexRay plugin. This volume can now be mounted and utilized by Docker containers in the same way as native Docker volumes, but with the added capability of interfacing with Amazon EBS.

Regarding observability, logging plugins are crucial as they allow Docker to integrate with external logging systems. For example, the fluentd plugin routes container logs to a Fluentd log collector.

To install and use the Fluentd plugin:

```
docker plugin install fluent/fluentd
```

Configure a container to use the Fluentd logging driver:

```
docker run -d --name my_app --log-driver=fluentd --log-opt fluentd-address=localhost
    :24224 my_app_image
```

The above command runs a container named my_app and directs its logs to a Fluentd instance running on localhost at port 24224.

In terms of security, authorization plugins offer a mechanism to control access to Docker functionalities according to defined policies. These plugins can enforce granular access controls, ensuring that users and applications have appropriate permissions.

For example, to install an authorization plugin:

```
docker plugin install cesanta/docker_auth:1.0
```

Enable the plugin to enforce access control policies:

```
docker plugin enable cesanta/docker_auth:1.0
```

The plugin will enforce policies defined in its configuration, guarding against unauthorized actions.

Combining these plugins unlocks advanced Docker capabilities, tailored to specific enterprise needs, ranging from enhanced networking and storage to robust logging and controlled access, thus facilitating the deployment and management of sophisticated containerized applications.

10.4 Multi-Stage Builds for Production

Multi-stage builds represent an optimized approach for constructing Docker images, particularly for production environments. This methodology leverages multiple FROM instructions within a single Dockerfile to create intermediate stages, thereby enabling the reduction of image size and enhancing build efficiency. The objective is to include only the necessary components in the final image, while utilizing intermediate containers for tasks such as compiling or setting up dependencies.

Overview of Multi-Stage Builds

The fundamental principle underpinning multi-stage builds is the utilization of multiple base images sequentially in a Dockerfile. A typical process involves different stages for compiling code, running tests, and packaging the final application. Each stage helps to ensure that only the minimal required files and dependencies are carried forward to subsequent stages, thus optimizing the final image used in production.

```
# First Stage: Build the Go program
FROM golang:1.16 as builder

WORKDIR /app

COPY . .

RUN go mod download
RUN go build -o app

# Second Stage: Minimal Image
FROM alpine:latest

WORKDIR /root/

COPY --from=builder /app/app .

CMD ["./app"]
```

In this example, the first stage uses the official Golang image to set up a Go environment, download necessary modules, and build the binary. The second stage initiates a minimal Alpine image, copying the compiled binary from the builder stage. This results in a significantly smaller final image as it contains only the compiled application and none of the build tools.

Advantages of Multi-Stage Builds

1. **Reduced Image Size**: By excluding build tools and unnecessary files from the final image, multi-stage builds substantially reduce the image size, leading to quicker deployment times and lower storage re-

quirements. 2. **Enhanced Security**: Limiting the final image to essential components minimizes attack vectors, thereby enhancing container security. 3. **Improved Build Efficiency**: Intermediate stages can cache specific layers, which optimizes rebuild times during iterative development cycles.

Multi-Stage Builds in Complex Applications

Multi-stage builds are particularly advantageous for complex application environments where multiple dependencies must be managed. For instance, a web application may require a compilation step with node.js and a server-side component with Python.

```
# Stage 1 - Build Frontend
FROM node:14 as frontend-builder

WORKDIR /frontend

COPY frontend/package*.json ./
RUN npm install
COPY frontend/ ./
RUN npm run build

# Stage 2 - Build Backend
FROM python:3.9 as backend-builder

WORKDIR /backend

COPY backend/requirements.txt ./
RUN pip install -r requirements.txt
COPY backend/ ./
RUN python setup.py install

# Stage 3 - Assemble Final Image
FROM nginx:alpine

COPY --from=frontend-builder /frontend/build /usr/share/nginx/html
COPY --from=backend-builder /backend/dist /app/

CMD ["nginx", "-g", "daemon off;"]
```

In this case, the first stage builds the frontend assets using Node.js, and the second stage sets up and installs the Python backend server. Finally, a minimal Nginx image is used to serve the static frontend files while also including the backend component. This structure ensures optimal organization and efficient resource utilization in the final production image.

Best Practices for Multi-Stage Builds

When employing multi-stage builds, several best practices should be observed to maximize benefits:

1. **Minimize the Number of Stages**: Limit the number of stages to

essential steps to reduce complexity and overhead. 2. **Use Appropriate Base Images**: Select lightweight, minimal base images for the final stage to ensure a compact production image. 3. **Cache Layers Effectively**: Take advantage of Docker's layer caching by structuring the Dockerfile to change infrequently modified layers first. 4. **Clean Up After Each Stage**: Remove unnecessary files and dependencies after each stage to maintain lean images.

Understanding and implementing multi-stage builds for production environments facilitates a more efficient, secure, and manageable Docker setup, pivotal for modern development workflows and continuous integration/continuous deployment (CI/CD) pipelines. The principles and practices outlined here are fundamental for leveraging Docker's full potential in a production context, driving effective resource management and operational excellence.

10.5 Docker Networking Internals

In Docker, networking is a critical aspect that ensures the connectivity of containers both to each other and to external networks. Understanding Docker networking internals involves delving into the various networking models, drivers, and namespaces that Docker provides. This section comprehensively discusses the fundamental networking concepts in Docker, including the overlay, bridge, host, and none networks, along with network namespaces and how Docker manages them.

The Docker networking model is built on a set of drivers that determine how networking is managed within and between containers. The default driver is the bridge driver, which creates a bridge network that containers can join. This network allows containers to communicate with each other while providing isolation from the host network. When a container is started, Docker automatically assigns it to a bridge network unless specified otherwise.

```
$ docker run -d --name webserver nginx
```

In this example, the container named webserver is connected to the default bridge network.

Exploring network namespaces is fundamental to understanding Docker networking. Network namespaces provide isolated network environments for containers, making it possible for each container to have its own network stack, including IP addresses, routing tables, and network devices. Docker leverages Linux namespaces to achieve this isolation, creating a new network namespace for each container.

When Docker creates a container, it assigns a pair of virtual Ethernet devices called veth pairs. One end of the veth pair is assigned to the container, while the other end is attached to the bridge network on the host. The veth device inside the container appears as eth0 and serves as the container's network interface.

```
$ sudo ip netns
```

Executing the above command lists all network namespaces currently available, showcasing the isolated network environments for each container. Each container can communicate with other containers on the same bridge network through these interfaces.

The overlay network driver is another critical aspect of Docker networking, especially in a multi-host Docker Swarm environment. Overlay networks enable the creation of a single virtual network that spans multiple hosts, allowing containers on different Docker hosts to communicate as if they are on the same network. This is integral for distributed applications that require communication between containers on different physical or virtual machines.

Creating an overlay network is straightforward and is typically done in the context of a Docker Swarm cluster:

```
$ docker network create --driver overlay my_overlay_network
```

Once the overlay network is created, services in the Docker Swarm can be attached to it, ensuring seamless communication across multiple hosts.

The host network driver allows a container to share the host's network stack. This means the container will not have its own network namespace, and all networking will be directly through the host. This can be useful for performance-sensitive applications where the overhead of virtualization needs to be minimized. Utilizing the host network provides no network isolation between the container and the host.

```
$ docker run --net host -d --name hostnet-container nginx
```

This command runs a container with nginx using the host's network stack, bypassing network isolation.

Lastly, the none network driver is used when no networking is required for a container. This completely disables networking for the container, which might be practical for certain resource-constrained applications or highly isolated security contexts.

```
$ docker run --net none -d --name isolated-container busybox
```

This snippet demonstrates starting a container without any network connectivity.

Docker also supports custom network drivers via community and third-party plugins. These drivers can be used to integrate Docker networking with existing enterprise network infrastructures, providing greater flexibility and advanced networking capabilities. Plugins can be installed and managed through the Docker CLI, and they extend Docker's networking beyond the built-in drivers.

Understanding the lifecycle of Docker networks is crucial. When a container is created, Docker performs several steps: it creates a network namespace for the container, a veth pair, and attaches one end of the veth pair to the bridge network. Additionally, Docker configures the container's IP address, routes, and other networking details based on the chosen network driver.

```
Creating a Docker container involves:
1. Creating a network namespace
2. Creating a pair of veth interfaces
3. Attaching one end of veth to bridge network
4. Assigning IP address and configuring routes
```

For containers on the same host, Docker's bridge network provides an efficient means of communication. For inter-host communication, the overlay network driver in a Docker Swarm setup ensures containers across different hosts can interact seamlessly. This distributed networking capability is fundamental for microservices architectures that require reliable and scalable inter-container communication.

Performance considerations in Docker networking involve understanding the overhead introduced by different network drivers. For instance, the bridge driver introduces some overhead due to packet forwarding, while the host driver minimizes overhead by sharing the host's network stack. Performance tuning may involve selecting the appropriate network driver based on the application's network performance requirements.

In essence, Docker networking internals span the basic bridge network to advanced distributed networking using overlay networks. The choice of network driver significantly impacts container communication and performance, making it essential to select the appropriate driver based on specific application needs. This intricate control over container networking is one of the many powerful features that Docker provides, enabling modern, containerized applications to function efficiently and effectively.

10.6 Advanced Volume Management

Advanced volume management in Docker is essential to efficiently manage persistent data storage across containers and services. By default, Docker volumes provide a mechanism to persist and share data among containers, but advanced management techniques extend these capabilities for improved scalability, security, and performance.

Volumes are essentially directories (or files) on the host machine that are mounted into containers. They are managed by Docker and can be created, listed, and removed using Docker CLI commands. The following commands cover basic volume operations:

```
# Create a new Docker volume
docker volume create my_volume

# List all Docker volumes
docker volume ls

# Inspect a specific Docker volume
docker volume inspect my_volume

# Remove a Docker volume
docker volume rm my_volume
```

While basic volume management commands are useful for straightforward scenarios, advanced needs can be met with the following capabilities: volume drivers, volume options, named volumes, volume backups, and data migration.

Volume Drivers:

Docker volume drivers allow volumes to be created and managed by external storage systems. Examples of volume drivers include 'local', 'azurefile', 'efs', and 'netapp'. Custom volume drivers can also be implemented using Docker's volume driver API, extending the storage capabilities to accommodate a variety of backend systems:

```
# Create a volume with a specific driver
docker volume create --driver local my_local_volume

# Create a volume using an external driver, e.g., Azure File Storage
docker volume create --driver azurefile --opt share=myshare my_azure_volume
```

The '–opt' flag allows passing driver-specific options during volume creation, tailoring the volume to specific use cases.

Named Volumes vs. Anonymous Volumes:

Named volumes are defined explicitly by a user, often attached to specific data repositories or services. In contrast, anonymous volumes are created by Docker dynamically and typically removed when the container is deleted. Named volumes provide easier data management and maintainability, especially in orchestrated environments.

```
# Create and use a named volume
docker run -d --name nginx --mount source=my_named_volume,target=/usr/share/
    nginx/html nginx:latest

# Use an anonymous volume
docker run -d --name nginx -v /usr/share/nginx/html nginx:latest
```

Backup and Restore Volumes:

Backing up and restoring Docker volumes is crucial for disaster recovery and migration purposes. This can be achieved using the 'docker run' command with tar utilities to create snapshots of data.

```
# Create a backup of a Docker volume
docker run --rm -v my_volume:/volume -v $(pwd):/backup busybox tar cvf /backup/
    backup.tar /volume

# Restore a Docker volume from a backup
docker run --rm -v my_volume:/volume -v $(pwd):/backup busybox tar xvf /backup/
    backup.tar -C /volume
```

Volume Binding and Propagation:

Volume binding allows mounting directories from the host file system into containers with control over access modes such as read-only ('ro') and read-write ('rw'). Propagation settings ('rshared', 'rslave', and 'rprivate') further control how mounts are shared between host and containers.

```
# Bind-mount a host directory into a container with read-only access
docker run -d --name nginx --mount type=bind,source=/host/path,target=/container/
    path,readonly nginx:latest

# Configure bind propagation
docker run -d --name nginx --mount type=bind,source=/host/path,target=/container/
    path,bind-propagation=rshared nginx:latest
```

Cross-host Volume Persistence:

In distributed environments like Docker Swarm and Kubernetes, ensuring data persistence across multiple hosts is critical. Networked storage solutions such as NFS, GlusterFS, and Ceph can be used in conjunction with Docker volume drivers to maintain data consistency and availability across nodes.

```
# Example of using NFS for Docker volumes in a Swarm setup
docker volume create \
  --driver local \
  --opt type=nfs \
  --opt o=addr=10.0.0.10,nolock,soft,rw \
  --opt device=:/path/to/volume \
  my_nfs_volume
```

Security Considerations:

Ensuring the security of Docker volumes is paramount. This includes setting appropriate file system permissions, leveraging encryption solutions for sensitive data, and isolating volumes between different tenants or applications to minimize risks.

For example, encrypting volumes using Linux Unified Key Setup (LUKS) can secure data at rest:

```
# Encrypt a Docker volume using LUKS (example assumes the volume is mounted at /
    dev/sdX)
sudo cryptsetup luksFormat /dev/sdX
sudo cryptsetup luksOpen /dev/sdX encrypted_volume
```

By implementing advanced volume management techniques, Docker environments can achieve greater resilience, enhanced performance, and improved data security. These strategies are essential for running production workloads with container-based applications.

10.7 Docker API and Client Libraries

The Docker API, along with its client libraries, provides an extensive mechanism for programmatically interacting with Docker. By leveraging these tools, developers can build sophisticated applications that automate and manipulate Docker containers, images, networks, and other core components. This section provides a deep dive into the Docker API, exploring its endpoints and usage patterns, and presents an overview of available client libraries that simplify interaction with the API in various programming languages.

The Docker API is a RESTful API, which means it adheres to the constraints of the REST architecture, providing resource-based interaction through standard HTTP methods. The primary HTTP methods used include GET for retrieving information, POST for creating resources, PUT for updating resources, and DELETE for removing resources.

The API endpoints are categorized based on the Docker components they manage, such as containers, images, volumes, networks, and services.

```
curl --unix-socket /var/run/docker.sock http://v1.41/containers/json
```

In the above example, the curl command queries the Docker API to list all containers. The unix-socket option specifies the Unix socket used for local Docker communications, and the URL http://v1.41/containers/json requests a list of containers in JSON format. The version number v1.41 refers to the API version.

The response from the API would be a JSON array containing details about each container:

```
[
    {
        "Id": "e90e34656806",
        "Names": ["/example"],
        "Image": "nginx",
        "ImageID": "sha256:xyz",
        "Command": "nginx -g 'daemon off;'",
        ...
    }
]
```

To enhance ease-of-use, Docker provides client libraries for several programming languages, abstracting the direct HTTP communication into more intuitive function calls.

Python Client Library

The Docker SDK for Python is widely used to interact with the Docker API. It facilitates seamless integration and provides a comprehensive set of methods for managing Docker resources.

To install the Docker SDK for Python, use the following command:

```
pip install docker
```

Once installed, the SDK can be used to interact with Docker. The following is an example of how to list all Docker containers using the Python client library:

```
import docker

client = docker.from_env()

for container in client.containers.list():
    print(container.id, container.name)
```

The docker.from_env() function initializes the client to connect to the Docker daemon. The client.containers.list() method retrieves a list of container objects, each representing a running container, which can be manipulated or queried further.

Go Client Library

The Docker client library for Go offers a robust and efficient way to interface with Docker, taking advantage of Go's performance and concurrency features.

To include the Docker client library in a Go project, use the following command:

```
go get github.com/docker/docker/client
```

Here is an example of listing all Docker containers using the Go client library:

```
package main

import (
    "context"
    "fmt"
    "github.com/docker/docker/api/types"
    "github.com/docker/docker/client"
)

func main() {
    cli, err := client.NewClientWithOpts(client.FromEnv, client.
        WithAPIVersionNegotiation())
    if err != nil {
        panic(err)
    }

    containers, err := cli.ContainerList(context.Background(), types.
        ContainerListOptions{})
    if err != nil {
        panic(err)
    }

    for _, container := range containers {
        fmt.Println(container.ID, container.Names[0])
    }
}
```

In this Go program, client.NewClientWithOpts initializes the Docker client using environment variables, while the cli.ContainerList method retrieves a list of containers. The context.Background() function provides a context for the API call, essential for managing request deadlines and cancellations in Go.

JavaScript Client Library

For developers working in Node.js, the dockerode library provides an elegant solution for interacting with the Docker API.

To install the dockerode library, use the following command:

```
npm install dockerode
```

The subsequent example illustrates how to list all Docker containers using dockerode:

```
const Docker = require('dockerode');
const docker = new Docker();

docker.listContainers((err, containers) => {
    if (err) {
        throw err;
    }
    containers.forEach(container => {
        console.log(container.Id, container.Names[0]);
    });
});
```

This JavaScript code initializes a Docker client instance and retrieves the list of containers using the listContainers method, printing each container's ID and name.

The Docker API, complemented by these client libraries, enables seamless and efficient automation and integration of Docker into various software environments. Understanding and leveraging these tools empower developers to create more dynamic and responsive applications that can fully utilize the capabilities of Docker.

By mastering the use of the Docker API and client libraries, one can automate complex workflows, integrate containerized applications into broader systems, and build robust, scalable solutions that are adaptable to evolving requirements in modern software development practices.

10.8 Automating Docker with Scripts

Automating Docker with scripts can significantly streamline container management tasks, making them more repeatable and less prone to human error. Shell scripting, especially with bash or sh, is a common and powerful approach to achieve automation. In this section, we will explore how to script common Docker operations, such as building, running, stopping, and removing containers, as well as automating complex workflows.

To begin, let us understand the basic structure of a shell script. A shell script is a file that contains a series of commands that are executed sequentially by the shell interpreter. These commands can include calls to Docker commands to automate container management.

Consider the following example, which demonstrates a simple script to build and run a Docker container:

```
#!/bin/bash

# Define variables
IMAGE_NAME="myapp"
CONTAINER_NAME="myapp_container"

# Build the Docker image
echo "Building Docker image..."
docker build -t $IMAGE_NAME .

# Run the Docker container
echo "Running Docker container..."
docker run -d --name $CONTAINER_NAME $IMAGE_NAME
```

This script begins with the #!/bin/bash shebang line, indicating that the script should be run using the Bash shell. The script defines the variables IMAGE_NAME and CONTAINER_NAME to store the names of the Docker image and container, respectively. It then builds the Docker image using the docker build command and runs the container using the docker run command.

More complex automation tasks often involve handling multiple containers, managing container networking, and dealing with container volumes. Below is an example of a script that automates the deployment of a multi-container application with a custom Docker network and attached volumes:

```
#!/bin/bash

# Define variables
NETWORK_NAME="mynetwork"
VOLUME_NAME="myvolume"
WEB_IMAGE="webserver"
DB_IMAGE="database"
WEB_CONTAINER="webserver_container"
DB_CONTAINER="database_container"

# Create custom Docker network
echo "Creating custom Docker network..."
docker network create $NETWORK_NAME

# Create Docker volume
echo "Creating Docker volume..."
docker volume create $VOLUME_NAME

# Build and run the database container
echo "Starting database container..."
docker run -d --name $DB_CONTAINER --network $NETWORK_NAME --volume
    $VOLUME_NAME:/data $DB_IMAGE
```

```
# Wait for database to initialize
echo "Waiting for database initialization..."
sleep 10

# Build and run the web server container
echo "Starting web server container..."
docker run -d --name $WEB_CONTAINER --network $NETWORK_NAME
    $WEB_IMAGE

# Display running containers
echo "Containers running:"
docker ps
```

In this script, a custom Docker network and volume are created using the docker network create and docker volume create commands, respectively. Next, it starts up the database container and attaches the volume to it. The script includes a pause (sleep 10) to allow the database to initialize before starting the web server container. Finally, the script lists the running containers using the docker ps command.

Error handling is an essential aspect of scripting for automation. This ensures that scripts can robustly handle failures without leaving the system in an inconsistent state. Below is an enhanced version of the previous script with basic error handling:

```
#!/bin/bash

set -e

# Define variables
NETWORK_NAME="mynetwork"
VOLUME_NAME="myvolume"
WEB_IMAGE="webserver"
DB_IMAGE="database"
WEB_CONTAINER="webserver_container"
DB_CONTAINER="database_container"

# Function to clean up resources
cleanup() {
  echo "Removing containers..."
  docker rm -f $WEB_CONTAINER $DB_CONTAINER || true
  echo "Removing network..."
  docker network rm $NETWORK_NAME || true
  echo "Removing volume..."
  docker volume rm $VOLUME_NAME || true
}

# Trap errors and clean up
trap cleanup EXIT

# Create custom Docker network
echo "Creating custom Docker network..."
docker network create $NETWORK_NAME

# Create Docker volume
echo "Creating Docker volume..."
docker volume create $VOLUME_NAME
```

```
# Build and run the database container
echo "Starting database container..."
docker run -d --name $DB_CONTAINER --network $NETWORK_NAME --volume
    $VOLUME_NAME:/data $DB_IMAGE

# Wait for database to initialize
echo "Waiting for database initialization..."
sleep 10

# Build and run the web server container
echo "Starting web server container..."
docker run -d --name $WEB_CONTAINER --network $NETWORK_NAME
    $WEB_IMAGE

# Display running containers
echo "Containers running:"
docker ps
```

In this script, the set -e command is used to make the script exit immediately if any command exits with a non-zero status. A cleanup function is defined to remove containers, network, and volume. The trap command is used to call the cleanup function upon the script's exit, ensuring that resources are properly cleaned up even if an error occurs.

Scripting automation with Docker can also involve scheduling tasks. Cron jobs can be used to schedule scripts to run at specific intervals. To schedule a script to run every day at midnight, add the following line to the crontab file using the crontab -e command:

```
0 0 * * * /path/to/script.sh
```

This line specifies that the script located at /path/to/script.sh will be executed every day at midnight.

By leveraging scripting techniques, Docker users can significantly improve efficiency and consistency in managing containers, ensuring that complex workflows are executed reliably and repeatably.

10.9 Integrating Docker with CI/CD Pipelines

Continuous Integration (CI) and Continuous Deployment (CD) are methodologies that enable software development teams to deliver code changes more frequently and reliably. Integrating Docker into CI/CD pipelines automates and streamlines the building, testing, and deployment processes. This section discusses the integration of Docker with popular CI/CD tools, highlighting practical techniques and considerations to enhance efficiency.

Firstly, let's consider a typical CI pipeline utilizing Docker. The primary steps include:

- Building Docker images.
- Running automated tests.
- Pushing the images to a registry.
- Deploying the application containers.

The choice of CI/CD tools varies, but the principles largely remain consistent. For demonstration purposes, Jenkins, GitLab CI, and GitHub Actions are considered.

Jenkins Integration Jenkins is a widely used open-source automation server. To integrate Docker with Jenkins:

- Install the required plugins: Docker plugin, Docker Pipeline plugin.
- Set up a Jenkins pipeline script utilizing Docker commands.

Below is an example of a Jenkins pipeline script (Jenkinsfile):

```
pipeline {
    agent { docker { image 'maven:3.6.3-jdk-8' } }
    stages {
        stage('Build') {
            steps {
                script {
                    docker.build('my-app')
                }
            }
        }
        stage('Test') {
            steps {
                script {
                    docker.image('my-app').inside {
                        sh 'mvn test'
                    }
                }
            }
        }
        stage('Deploy') {
            steps {
                script {
                    docker.withRegistry('https://myregistry.com', 'registryCredentials') {
                        docker.image('my-app').push('latest')
                    }
                }
```

```
            }
        }
    }
}
```

This script defines a Jenkins pipeline with three stages: Build, Test, and Deploy. It demonstrates utilization of the Docker agent, building and testing within Docker containers, and pushing the built image to a registry.

GitLab CI/CD Integration GitLab CI/CD offers integrated functionality for CI/CD processes within GitLab projects. Docker can be easily integrated through the use of a .gitlab-ci.yml file:

```
stages:
  - build
  - test
  - deploy

variables:
  DOCKER_TLS_CERTDIR: "/certs"

build:
  stage: build
  image: docker:19.03.12
  services:
    - docker:19.03.12-dind
  script:
    - docker build -t my-app .

test:
  stage: test
  image: docker:19.03.12
  services:
    - docker:19.03.12-dind
  script:
    - docker run my-app mvn test

deploy:
  stage: deploy
  image: docker:19.03.12
  services:
    - docker:19.03.12-dind
  script:
    - docker login -u "$CI_REGISTRY_USER" -p "$CI_REGISTRY_PASSWORD" "
        $CI_REGISTRY"
    - docker push my-app:latest
```

This example configures three stages: build, test, and deploy. Docker-in-Docker (dind) is used as a service to enable Docker commands within the GitLab CI/CD job runners.

GitHub Actions Integration GitHub Actions enables CI/CD workflows directly within GitHub repositories. The following example illustrates a workflow for building, testing, and deploying a Dockerized application:

```
name: CI Pipeline

on: [push]

jobs:
  build:
    runs-on: ubuntu-latest

    steps:
    - name: Checkout code
      uses: actions/checkout@v2

    - name: Set up Docker Buildx
      uses: docker/setup-buildx-action@v1

    - name: Login to Docker Hub
      uses: docker/login-action@v1
      with:
        username: ${{ secrets.DOCKER_USERNAME }}
        password: ${{ secrets.DOCKER_PASSWORD }}

    - name: Build and push Docker image
      uses: docker/build-push-action@v2
      with:
        context: .
        push: true
        tags: my-app:latest

  test:
    runs-on: ubuntu-latest

    steps:
    - name: Checkout code
      uses: actions/checkout@v2

    - name: Set up Docker Buildx
      uses: docker/setup-buildx-action@v1

    - name: Login to Docker Hub
      uses: docker/login-action@v1
      with:
        username: ${{ secrets.DOCKER_USERNAME }}
        password: ${{ secrets.DOCKER_PASSWORD }}

    - name: Run tests
      run: |
        docker run my-app mvn test
```

This script sets up a GitHub Actions workflow divided into two jobs: build and test. It uses Docker-related actions to manage the setup and execution of Docker commands.

Best Practices for Docker Integration in CI/CD When integrating Docker within CI/CD pipelines, consider the following best practices:

- Use Docker layers effectively to speed up the build process by minimizing image rebuilds.
- Securely manage secrets and credentials, utilizing specific CI/CD tool mechanisms to store and retrieve sensitive data.
- Monitor the performance and health of the CI/CD pipeline, leveraging Docker-specific metrics where possible.
- Implement automated rollbacks in case of deployment failures to ensure service continuity.
- Utilize multi-stage builds in Dockerfiles to create lean and efficient production images.

Automation and orchestration strategies involving Docker can significantly enhance the reliability and speed of software delivery workflows. By stringently following these practices and the provided configurations, development teams can achieve seamless integration of Docker with their CI/CD pipelines. Additionally, an emphasis on security, performance tuning, and monitoring will ensure robustness and resilience of the automated workflows.

10.10 Docker Swarm Advanced Features

Docker Swarm extends the capabilities of the Docker engine by providing native clustering functionality. It allows users to deploy and manage a cluster of Docker nodes as a single virtual system, simplifying orchestration and scaling. This section covers advanced features of Docker Swarm that enhance its functionality, making it suitable for complex production environments.

One core feature of Docker Swarm is **service discovery**. Swarm mode implements an internal DNS server that allows containers to discover each other by their service names. This means that when you deploy a service, it can be automatically discovered by other containers in the swarm through DNS resolution.

Example: Deploying a Service with Service Discovery

```
docker service create --name my-web-service --replicas 3 -p 8080:80 nginx
```

After deploying this service, containers can communicate using the name my-web-service. Swarm mode ensures availability of the service under the given name, despite container restarts, relocations, or scale adjustments.

Beyond basic discovery, Docker Swarm integrates powerful **load balancing** mechanisms. Each service deployed in swarm mode is available via a configurable endpoint. Requests to this endpoint are automatically distributed among the service's replicas, ensuring balanced resource utilization and redundancy.

Swarm employs both **internal** and **external load balancing**. Internal load balancing is handled by Swarm's DNS and iptables rules, directing traffic within the cluster. External load balancers can also be configured to distribute traffic to Swarm nodes. Integrating Swarm with an external load balancer involves configuring the external system to route traffic to Swarm's service ports.

Example: Sample External Load Balancer Configuration

```
backend my_web_service
    balance roundrobin
    server node1 192.168.1.2:8080 check
    server node2 192.168.1.3:8080 check
    server node3 192.168.1.4:8080 check
```

Docker Swarm also includes a sophisticated **routing mesh**. Swarm's routing mesh allows any node in the swarm to receive requests on the service ports, forwarding them to the appropriate service—regardless of which node the service runs on. This mechanism ensures seamless reachability for all services, simplifying network configuration.

Swarm's **overlay networking** extends these capabilities by providing a multi-host network option. Containers can be connected to the same network even when residing on different hosts, making service discovery and load balancing across the cluster straightforward. The seamless integration with overlay networks effectively isolates service traffic while allowing easy inter-service communication.

Example: Creating an Overlay Network

```
docker network create -d overlay my_overlay_network
```

Example: Using Overlay Network in a Service

```
docker service create --name db --network my_overlay_network mongo
docker service create --name web --network my_overlay_network nginx
```

Security within Docker Swarm is robust, featuring **automatic node management**, **secure certificate distribution**, and **encrypted communications**. When a new node joins the swarm, Swarm automatically handles the distribution and rotation of cryptographic certificates used for verifying node identity and securing communications. Additionally, service-to-service communication can be encrypted over overlay networks, ensuring data protection in transit.

Example: Encrypting Data on an Overlay Network

```
docker network create --opt encrypted -d overlay secure_network
```

Enhanced control over security policies is possible through **RBAC (Role-Based Access Control)**. Docker Enterprise Edition (EE) allows fine-grained control over user permissions, ensuring that only authorized users can perform specific actions within the swarm. This is crucial in multi-tenant environments where different teams might operate different services within the same cluster.

Example: Creating a Role with Permissions in Docker EE

```
docker enterprise role create --name my_role --description "Access to critical service"
docker enterprise role set-permission my_role --resource service=my-critical-service --
    permission read,update
docker enterprise user add-role --username user1 --role my_role
```

Swarm's **autoscaling** capabilities enable dynamic response to load changes. Although not natively supported as in Kubernetes, autoscaling can be implemented using external tools and custom scripts. Integration with monitoring tools can trigger scaling events based on predefined metrics, optimizing resource usage and maintaining service performance.

Example: Using Swarm API for Autoscaling Script

```
import docker
client = docker.from_env()

service = client.services.get('my-web-service')
current_replicas = service.attrs['Spec']['Mode']['Replicated']['Replicas']
# Scaling up example
if metrics_indicate_high_load():
    service.scale(current_replicas + 1)
# Scaling down example
elif metrics_indicate_low_load():
    service.scale(current_replicas - 1)
```

Swarm's support for **rolling updates** facilitates seamless deployment updates by replacing service tasks incrementally. Options include controlling the parallelism of the update, the timing between updates, and the failure action. This ensures minimal disruption and rollback capabilities in case of errors.

Example: Rolling Update Configuration

```
docker service update --image nginx:latest --update-parallelism 2 --update-delay 10s my-
    web-service
```

Lastly, Swarm provides feature-rich **logging and monitoring** integrations. Log drivers like json-file, syslog, and third-party tools enable comprehensive logging of service activity. Monitoring tools such as Prometheus and Grafana can be integrated to visualize metrics and set up alerting systems, thus ensuring operational transparency and responsiveness.

Example: Configuring a Service with a Custom Log Driver

```
docker service create --name my-service --log-driver syslog nginx
```

For a smooth integration of Docker Swarm's advanced features, consider these best practices:

- Regularly update node certificates and enforce encrypted communication
- Leverage built-in load balancing and routing mesh for efficient traffic management
- Utilize overlay networks for scalable and secure service connectivity
- Implement Role-Based Access Control to manage user permissions effectively
- Employ monitoring and alerting tools to maintain service health and performance

By adopting these strategies, the full potential of Docker Swarm's capabilities can be tapped, ensuring a highly available, scalable, and secure container orchestration environment.

10.11 Using Docker with Other Orchestration Tools

The ecosystem of container orchestration has expanded significantly, with multiple tools that complement Docker and cater to diverse deployment needs. Understanding how Docker integrates with other orchestration tools is crucial for advanced container management, allowing seamless scaling, automation, and resilience of applications. This section explores prominent orchestration tools like Kubernetes, Apache Mesos, and HashiCorp Nomad, discussing their interactions with Docker.

Kubernetes is one of the most widely adopted orchestration tools for containerized applications, known for its robust features and extensive community support. Kubernetes orchestrates Docker containers by grouping them into logical units for management and discovery, using a concept called *pods*, which are the smallest deployable units that can contain one or more containers.

The **Kubernetes architecture** consists of the following key components:

- **Master Node:** Manages the Kubernetes cluster and consists of several key components such as *etcd*, the API server, the controller manager, and the scheduler.
- **Worker Nodes:** These nodes run the application workloads and are managed by the master node. Each worker node runs a container runtime (Docker), a kubelet, and a kube-proxy.

To deploy a Docker container to a Kubernetes cluster, the general workflow involves the creation of **YAML configuration files** that define the desired state of the application, including resources such as pods, services, deployments, and config maps. Here is an example of a simple Kubernetes deployment running a Docker container:

```
apiVersion: apps/v1
kind: Deployment
metadata:
  name: my-app
spec:
  replicas: 3
  selector:
    matchLabels:
      app: my-app
  template:
```

```
metadata:
  labels:
    app: my-app
spec:
  containers:
  - name: my-app-container
    image: my-app-image:latest
    ports:
    - containerPort: 8080
```

kubectl is the command-line tool used to interact with the Kubernetes cluster. The following command applies the deployment configuration:

```
kubectl apply -f deployment.yaml
```

Apache Mesos serves as a distributed systems kernel, providing efficient resource isolation and sharing across distributed applications. Mesos enables fine-grained sharing of resources, dynamically allocating resources to applications running in Docker containers. Marathon, a container orchestration platform running on Apache Mesos, simplifies the deployment and management of Docker containers.

In a typical Apache Mesos setup, Marathon provides a REST API for deploying containers. Here is an example of a Marathon application definition to deploy a Docker container:

```
{
  "id": "my-app",
  "container": {
    "type": "DOCKER",
    "docker": {
      "image": "my-app-image:latest",
      "network": "BRIDGE",
      "portMappings": [
        { "containerPort": 8080, "hostPort": 0, "servicePort": 9000 }
      ]
    }
  },
  "cpus": 0.5,
  "mem": 256.0,
  "instances": 3
}
```

The Marathon UI or the command-line interface can be used to submit this application, enabling seamless orchestration of Docker containers on Mesos.

HashiCorp Nomad is a flexible, enterprise-grade cluster scheduler designed to support a broad range of workloads, including Docker. Nomad's single binary simplicity contrasts with the more extensive setups of tools like Kubernetes, making it suitable for smaller teams or simpler applications.

To deploy a Docker container using Nomad, a job specification file is defined. Here's an example of a Nomad job file for a Docker container:

```
job "example" {
  datacenters = ["dc1"]

  group "example" {
    task "server" {
      driver = "docker"

      config {
        image = "my-app-image:latest"
        port_map {
          http = 8080
        }
      }

      resources {
        cpu = 500
        memory = 256
      }

      service {
        name = "example-service"
        port = "http"
      }
    }
  }
}
```

This job file can be run using the Nomad CLI:

```
nomad job run example.nomad
```

Each of these orchestration tools integrates seamlessly with Docker, offering various advantages depending on the complexity and scale of the deployment requirements. While Kubernetes excels in large-scale, complex environments with its extensive features, Mesos provides efficient resource utilization across diverse systems. Nomad, on the other hand, offers simplicity and flexibility for a range of workloads.

10.12 Container Orchestration Strategies

Container orchestration is essential for managing the lifecycle of containers, especially in large-scale, microservices-based applications. A robust orchestration strategy ensures that containers are deployed, managed, and scaled efficiently. This section explores various container orchestration strategies, focusing on concepts, architecture, and best practices to optimize containerized applications.

Core Concepts and Components:

Container orchestration involves numerous components working in unison. The primary components include:

- **Scheduler:** Determines on which nodes/hosts the container instances should run.
- **Load Balancer:** Distributes network or application traffic across multiple containers.
- **Service Discovery:** Enables containers to find each other over the network.
- **Resource Manager:** Allocates CPU and memory resources to containers.
- **Cluster Manager:** Maintains the state of the container cluster, including node health and service availability.

Node Management:

Effective node management is critical. Nodes can be categorized as master and worker nodes. Master nodes manage the orchestration layer, including scheduling and API management. Worker nodes run applications. A recommended strategy is to ensure that master and worker nodes are isolated to prevent resource contention. Nodes should be monitored continuously, and faulty nodes should be automatically replaced.

Deployment Strategies:

Choosing the right deployment strategy depends on factors like application architecture, uptime requirements, and resource availability. Common deployment strategies include:

- **Rolling Updates:** Updates services iteratively, minimizing downtime by incrementally replacing instances.
- **Blue/Green Deployment:** Maintains two environments (blue and green); one serves live traffic while the other is updated.
- **Canary Deployment:** Gradually shifts traffic to the new version to minimize risk.
- **A/B Testing:** Directs a portion of traffic to a new version for testing purposes.

Scaling Strategies:

Scaling can be horizontal or vertical. Horizontal scaling adds more container instances, whereas vertical scaling involves adding more resources (CPU, memory) to existing instances. Horizontal scaling is usually preferred due to its efficiency and easy fault isolation.

```
# Scale a service to run 5 instances
$ docker service scale my_service=5
```

Service Discovery and Load Balancing:

For efficient container communication, service discovery is indispensable. DNS-based service discovery and key-value store-based discovery (like etcd or Consul) are prevalent methods. Load balancing distributes the traffic evenly, and can be accomplished using techniques like round-robin or least-connections.

High Availability and Fault Tolerance:

High availability (HA) ensures continuous operation without failure. Implementing HA involves multiple master nodes in an active-active setup, automatic failover mechanisms, and redundancies. Fault tolerance enables the system to continue functioning even when components fail. This can be achieved through self-healing processes where failed containers or nodes are automatically replaced.

Security Considerations:

Security is paramount in orchestration. Key strategies include:

- **Namespace Isolation:** Isolate containers using namespaces to ensure process and network separation.
- **RBAC (Role-Based Access Control):** Implement RBAC policies to control access to resources.
- **Network Policies:** Define policies to control communication between containers.
- **Image Scanning:** Regularly scan container images for vulnerabilities.

Logging and Monitoring:

Continuous logging and monitoring are vital. Tools like Prometheus for monitoring and Elasticsearch, Logstash, and Kibana (ELK) stack for logging are commonly used. These tools help in proactive issue detection and performance management.

```
# Query logs for errors
$ curl -XGET 'http://localhost:9200/_search' -H 'Content-Type: application/json' -d'
{
  "query": {
    "match": {
      "message": "error"
    }
  }
}
'
```

Integrating CI/CD Pipelines:

A well-defined CI/CD pipeline automates code integration, testing, and deployment, ensuring consistency and efficiency. Integration with orchestration tools allows for automated deployment and rollback capabilities.

By adhering to these strategies, container orchestration can be optimized for performance, reliability, and scalability, ensuring the smooth operation of containerized environments.

10.13 Performance Tuning for Docker

Performance tuning in Docker involves optimizing container performance, resource allocation, image build times, and runtime efficiency. This section elucidates techniques to fine-tune Docker environments, fostering enhanced performance across various dimensions including CPU, memory, I/O, and network utilization.

Effective performance tuning starts with understanding the Docker architecture, particularly its use of the host's kernel. Containers share the host OS kernel, segregating resources at the process level using namespaces and cgroups. Optimizing these resources directly impacts container performance.

Resource Constraints: Docker allows explicit control over CPU and memory allocation to containers using the –cpu and –memory flags in the docker run command. Limiting resource allocation ensures a balanced distribution across multiple containers.

```
docker run --cpus="1.5" --memory="512m" my_container
```

In this example, the container is allocated 1.5 CPU units and 512MB of memory. Fine-tuning these values based on application requirements can prevent resource contention and enhance performance.

CPU Shares and Quotas: Docker also supports specifying CPU shares using the –cpu-shares flag, allowing prioritization of CPU time for containers. A higher number denotes a higher priority.

```
docker run --cpu-shares=1024 my_container
```

Setting CPU quotas via the –cpu-quota flag defines the maximum CPU time a container can use within a period. This is useful for limiting CPU-intensive processes.

```
docker run --cpu-quota=50000 --cpu-period=100000 my_container
```

Here, the container can utilize 50% of the CPU time within a 100-millisecond period.

Memory Tuning: Apart from setting memory limits, Docker provides options to manage memory constraints more granularly. The –memory-swap flag controls the total memory usage, including swap space. Setting this flag to -1 enables unlimited swap, whereas setting it to 0 disables swap memory, restricting usage to physical RAM.

```
docker run --memory="512m" --memory-swap="1g" my_container
```

In this example, the container can use up to 512MB of RAM and an additional 512MB of swap space.

I/O Performance: For I/O-bound applications, tuning disk I/O performance is critical. Docker allows controlling block I/O (Blkio) weight using the –blkio-weight flag. This flag sets a relative weight for I/O bandwidth between containers, ranging from 10 to 1000.

```
docker run --blkio-weight=500 my_container
```

For more granular control, the blkio-weight-device and device-read-bps/write-bps flags can be utilized to specify I/O limits on particular devices.

```
docker run --device-read-bps /dev/sda:1mb --device-write-bps /dev/sda:1mb
    my_container
```

Network Performance: Optimizing network performance involves tuning the configuration of the Docker networking settings. Monitoring and adjusting network modes and parameters such as MTU (Maximum Transmission Unit) size can significantly impact performance, especially for high-traffic applications.

Consider using the host network mode for applications requiring high network throughput and low latency, as it eliminates the network namespace isolation overhead.

```
docker run --network host my_container
```

Another technique involves adjusting the MTU size to match the infrastructure's network settings, avoiding fragmentation. This can be configured by setting the –opt com.docker.network.driver.mtu=<value> option in custom bridge networks.

```
docker network create --driver bridge --opt com.docker.network.driver.mtu=1450
    my_network
```

Kernel Parameters: Tuning kernel parameters for Docker involves adjusting settings in the sysctl interface. Commonly tuned parameters include those for networking performance and process limits. For instance, increasing the value of vm.max_map_count is often necessary for applications such as Elasticsearch.

```
docker run --sysctl vm.max_map_count=262144 my_container
```

Parameters adjusted via the –sysctl flag apply only to specific containers, providing fine-grained control.

Image Optimization: Optimizing Docker images minimizes build times and enhances runtime performance. A multi-stage build approach reduces the image size by separating build dependencies from runtime dependencies.

```
FROM golang:alpine AS builder
WORKDIR /app
COPY . .
RUN go build -o myapp

FROM alpine:latest
WORKDIR /root/
COPY --from=builder /app/myapp .
CMD ["./myapp"]
```

In this Dockerfile, the build dependencies are defined in the first stage, and only the compiled binary is copied to the final image, resulting in a smaller, optimized image.

Reducing the number of layers in Docker images by combining commands with && and using .dockerignore to exclude unnecessary files and directories improves image build efficiency and performance.

Monitoring and Profiling: Continuous monitoring and profiling help identify bottlenecks and areas for improvement. Tools such as Docker stats, cAdvisor, Prometheus, and Grafana provide insights into container performance metrics.

```
docker stats
```

This command displays real-time metrics, including CPU, memory, network I/O, and block I/O usage for running containers. Integrating these metrics with monitoring solutions facilitates proactive performance management.

Handling High Workloads: In scenarios with high workloads, scaling containers horizontally using orchestration platforms like Docker Swarm or Kubernetes ensures optimal distribution of tasks across multiple nodes, leveraging the entire cluster's computational resources.

Commands to manage scaling in Docker Swarm:

```
docker service scale my_service=5
```

This command scales the specified service to 5 instances, distributing the load and improving performance.

Implementing these performance tuning techniques enhances the efficiency and reliability of Dockerized applications, ensuring they run optimally in various environments.

10.14 Monitoring and Logging Advanced Techniques

Monitoring and logging are critical components in the management of Docker-based environments. They enable administrators to maintain operational health, promptly detect anomalies, and perform root cause analyses. This section examines advanced techniques for monitoring and logging in Docker, emphasizing tools and practices that enhance observability and diagnostics.

Docker provides built-in capabilities for logging and monitoring, but advanced scenarios typically require integrating additional tools and services. We will explore how to leverage such tools to obtain comprehensive insights into containerized applications.

1. Monitoring with Prometheus and Grafana

Prometheus is an open-source systems monitoring and alerting toolkit designed for reliability and scalability. Combined with Grafana for visualizing the collected metrics, it provides a powerful monitoring solution.

First, ensure that the Prometheus Docker image is running:

```
docker run -d --name prometheus -p 9090:9090 prom/prometheus
```

Create a prometheus.yml file with the following configuration:

```
global:
  scrape_interval: 15s

scrape_configs:
  - job_name: ’docker’
    static_configs:
      - targets: [’<DOCKER_HOST_IP>:9323’]
```

The Docker Daemon needs to be configured to expose metrics on port 9323. This can be achieved by adding the following to the Docker Daemon's configuration file (/etc/docker/daemon.json):

```
{
  ”metrics-addr” : ”0.0.0.0:9323”,
  ”experimental” : true
}
```

After updating the configuration, restart the Docker service.

```
sudo systemctl daemon-reload
sudo systemctl restart docker
```

Next, run Grafana:

```
docker run -d --name=grafana -p 3000:3000 grafana/grafana
```

Configure Grafana to use Prometheus as a data source by accessing the Grafana UI at http://<HOST_IP>:3000, navigating to Configuration > Data Sources, and adding Prometheus with the URL http://<HOST_IP>:9090.

2. Logging with the ELK Stack (Elasticsearch, Logstash, Kibana)

The ELK stack provides a comprehensive and extensible logging solution. Follow these steps to set up each component.

Run the Elasticsearch container:

```
docker run -d --name elasticsearch -p 9200:9200 -e ”discovery.type=single-node”
     elasticsearch:7.10.1
```

Run the Logstash container and mount a configuration file with pipeline settings:

Create a file named logstash.conf:

```
input {
  tcp {
    port => 5044
    codec => "json"
  }
}

output {
  elasticsearch {
    hosts => "http://<ELASTICSEARCH_HOST>:9200"
    index => "docker-logs-%{+YYYY.MM.dd}"
  }
}
```

Then run Logstash:

```
docker run -d --name logstash -p 5044:5044 -v $(pwd)/logstash.conf:/usr/share/logstash
    /pipeline/logstash.conf logstash:7.10.1
```

Run the Kibana container:

```
docker run -d --name kibana -p 5601:5601 kibana:7.10.1
```

In the Docker Daemon configuration file (/etc/docker/daemon.json), configure the logging driver to send logs to Logstash:

```
{
  "log-driver": "json-file",
  "log-opts": {
    "max-size": "200m",
    "max-file": "3"
  },
  "log-driver": "syslog",
  "log-opts": {
    "syslog-address": "tcp://<LOGSTASH_HOST>:5044",
    "tag": "{{.Name}}"
  }
}
```

Restart the Docker service to apply these settings.

```
sudo systemctl daemon-reload
sudo systemctl restart docker
```

Logstash will now receive logs from Docker, process them, and send them to Elasticsearch. These logs can be visualized in Kibana by accessing the Kibana interface at http://<HOST_IP>:5601.

3. Performance Monitoring with cAdvisor

cAdvisor (Container Advisor) provides insights into the resource usage and performance characteristics of running containers.

Run cAdvisor container:

```
docker run -d \
  --name=cadvisor \
  -p 8080:8080 \
  --volume=/var/run/docker.sock:/var/run/docker.sock:ro \
  --volume=/sys:/sys:ro \
  --volume=/var/lib/docker/:/var/lib/docker:ro \
  gcr.io/cadvisor/cadvisor:latest
```

Access the cAdvisor interface at http://<HOST_IP>:8080 to visualize metrics on resource usage such as CPU, memory, network, and filesystem consumption.

4. Implementing Alerts with Prometheus

Prometheus supports alerting rules that can trigger notifications based on specified conditions. Configure alerting rules in the prometheus.yml file:

```
rule_files:
  - "alerts.yml"
```

Create an alerts.yml file with rules:

```
groups:
- name: example
  rules:
  - alert: HighMemoryUsage
    expr: process_resident_memory_bytes > 500 * 1024 * 1024
    for: 5m
    labels:
      severity: critical
    annotations:
      summary: "High memory usage"
      description: "Memory usage is above 500MB for more than 5 minutes"
```

Restart the Prometheus container to apply changes.

```
docker restart prometheus
```

Alerts will be visible in the Prometheus UI under the 'Alerts' tab and can be configured to send notifications via email, Slack, or other channels using Alertmanager.

The combination of these tools and configurations provides a robust monitoring and logging infrastructure for Docker environments. This setup enables comprehensive observability, facilitating proactive management and expedited troubleshooting.

Chapter 11

Troubleshooting Docker

This chapter focuses on diagnosing and resolving common Docker issues, including installation problems, container startup failures, and performance bottlenecks. It covers analyzing Docker logs, networking and storage troubleshooting, and addressing Docker Daemon failures. The chapter also provides guidance on debugging Dockerfiles, resolving build failures, and utilizing Docker's diagnostic tools.

11.1 Introduction to Docker Troubleshooting

The objective of Docker troubleshooting is to identify, diagnose, and resolve issues that can hamper the operation of Docker containers and the Docker platform. Troubleshooting Docker involves understanding the components and architecture of Docker, recognizing common problems, and employing systematic approaches to resolve them. This section lays the foundation for a detailed exploration of various troubleshooting techniques.

Docker, as a containerization platform, abstracts application environments into isolated containers. Each container includes the application, its dependencies, and configuration files. The separation from the host operating system allows containers to operate uniformly across diverse environments. Initial steps in troubleshooting involve distinguishing whether an issue originates from Docker itself, the application within a container, or the host operating system.

- **Docker Components:** A robust understanding of Docker's core components is essential. These include:
  - Docker Engine: The underlying client-server application consisting of the Docker daemon (dockerd), a REST API, and the Docker CLI (command-line interface).
  - Containers: Encapsulated environments for running applications.
  - Images: Immutable snapshots used to instantiate containers.
  - Volumes: Data storage mechanisms for persisting data created within containers.
  - Networks: Configurations that enable communication between containers and external systems.
- **Basic Troubleshooting Steps:** Troubleshooting typically begins with systematic steps such as:
  - Reviewing Docker logs using the docker logs command.
  - Inspect command execution results with docker inspect.
  - Monitoring real-time container statistics with docker stats.
- **Common Issues:** Problems frequently encountered include:
  - Installation failures, due to unmet dependencies or configuration errors.
  - Container startup issues, often related to incorrect configurations in Dockerfiles, network problems, or inadequate resources.
  - Performance bottlenecks, which might stem from resource constraints or inefficient application code.

Understanding Docker logs is a pivotal aspect of troubleshooting. Docker logs provide detailed insights into container operations and errors.

```
docker logs <container_id>
```

The output from the above command appears as follows:

```
2023-03-15T12:34:56.789Z INFO  [App] - Application starting
2023-03-15T12:35:01.123Z ERROR [App] - Database connection failed
2023-03-15T12:35:05.456Z INFO  [App] - Retrying database connection
```

The logs should be scrutinized for errors and messages that indicate where issues might originate. Patterns in the output, such as repeated retry attempts or specific error messages, can provide clues to underlying problems.

The Docker inspect command is integral for obtaining detailed information about Docker objects such as containers, images, volumes, and networks. For instance, inspecting a container yields comprehensive data including configuration, state, and network settings.

```
docker inspect <container_id>
```

An example of relevant fields in the output might be:

```
[
  {
    "Id": "3b1afa3c28e9",
    "State": {
      "Status": "running",
      "Running": true,
      "Paused": false,
      "Restarting": false
    },
    "HostConfig": {
      "CpuShares": 2,
      "Memory": 104857600
    }
  }
]
```

The State field reveals the current status of the container, while HostConfig provides details on resource allocation, which can be critical when diagnosing performance issues.

Real-time monitoring of container performance using docker stats aids in identifying resource bottlenecks. Key metrics such as CPU usage, memory usage, and network I/O are displayed.

```
docker stats <container_id>
```

Sample output is as follows:

```
CONTAINER ID   NAME    CPU %   MEM USAGE / LIMIT    NET I/O
3b1afa3c28e9   myapp   2.34%   50MiB / 100MiB       1.2MB / 1.1MB
```

Persistent issues likely require an examination of the container's environment and configurations. Dockerfiles, the blueprints for Docker images, need careful validation. Common pitfalls include misconfigured environment variables and incorrect instructions for adding dependencies.

When troubleshooting networking issues, verifying network configurations and connections between containers is crucial. Commands such as docker network ls and docker network inspect provide valuable information about existing networks and their configurations. Incorrect network modes or isolated containers can prevent communication, leading to functionality losses.

```
docker network inspect <network_name>
```

Example output:

```
[
  {
    "Name": "my_network",
    "Id": "7d4f1a4b80c2",
    "Driver": "bridge",
    "Containers": {
      "3b1afa3c28e9": {
        "Name": "myapp",
        "IPv4Address": "172.18.0.2"
      }
    }
  }
]
```

Analyzing the above output reveals container names and IP addresses, aiding in diagnosing connectivity problems.

Effective use of these diagnostic tools and commands enables the accurate identification and resolution of Docker-related issues, leading to more stable and predictable container environments.

11.2 Common Docker Installation Issues

Docker installation can present a variety of challenges, particularly due to the interaction between Docker and the underlying operating system. Understanding these common issues is essential to ensure a smooth installation process. This section explores several prevalent problems users may face, including permission errors, missing dependencies, unsupported operating systems, network configuration issues, and validation failures of the installation. Each scenario will be examined with possible diagnostic steps and resolutions.

Permission errors are frequently encountered during Docker installation, especially on Unix-based systems. Docker requires elevated privileges to access the Linux kernel features it depends on. Users often encounter errors when the appropriate permissions are not granted. Ensure that the user executing the Docker commands is part of the 'docker' group:

```
$ sudo usermod -aG docker $USER
$ newgrp docker
```

Non-reboot methods, such as using the 'newgrp' command, allow for immediate application without requiring a system reboot. If permission errors persist, verify Docker's installation path and execute commands with 'sudo' for elevated privileges:

```
$ sudo docker run hello-world
```

Dependencies play a crucial role in Docker's functionality. Missing or incompatible libraries and packages can result in failed installations. For instance, Docker relies on specific versions of libraries such as 'libc' and kernel modules. Check for system updates and install any missing dependencies as follows:

```
$ sudo apt-get update
$ sudo apt-get install apt-transport-https ca-certificates curl gnupg-agent software-
      properties-common
```

If an installation fails, examine the logs located at '/var/log/syslog' or '/var/log/docker.log' for detailed error messages. These logs can reveal unmet dependencies or conflicting packages.

Using an unsupported operating system is another common issue. Docker is designed for specific distributions and versions of Linux. Ensure your operating system is listed on Docker's support page. Attempting to install Docker on an unsupported OS may require building from source, which can introduce complexities. If Docker is incompatible with your system, consider using a supported distribution such as:

- Ubuntu
- CentOS
- Debian
- Fedora

Network configuration issues can hinder the installation process, particularly when external repositories or package sources are unreachable. Confirm network connectivity and the ability to reach Docker's installation repositories:

```
$ ping google.com
$ curl -fsSL https://download.docker.com/linux/ubuntu/gpg | sudo apt-key add -
```

Network proxies and firewalls might also block access. Configure proxy settings correctly and ensure firewall rules allow traffic on the relevant ports. For proxy setup, include environment variables in your shell configuration file:

```
export HTTP_PROXY="http://proxy.example.com:80"
export HTTPS_PROXY="http://proxy.example.com:443"
```

Lastly, validation failures during Docker installation might arise from misconfigured repositories or broken packages. Verify repository configurations and ensure they are correctly set up in sources lists. For Ubuntu, the repository should be added as follows:

```
$ sudo add-apt-repository \
  "deb [arch=amd64] https://download.docker.com/linux/ubuntu \
  $(lsb_release -cs) \
  stable"
```

After adding the repository, update the package index and install Docker:

```
$ sudo apt-get update
$ sudo apt-get install docker-ce docker-ce-cli containerd.io
```

Validating the installation ensures Docker correctly operates:

```
$ docker --version
Docker version 20.10.8, build 3967b7d
```

```
$ docker run hello-world
Hello from Docker!
This message shows that your installation appears to be working correctly.
```

By addressing these common issues—permissions, dependencies, unsupported operating systems, network configurations, and validation errors—users can successfully troubleshoot and resolve Docker installation problems.

11.3 Diagnosing and Resolving Container Startup Problems

Diagnosing and resolving container startup problems involves systematically analyzing the underlying causes preventing a Docker container from starting or running correctly. Correct identification of these causes can facilitate targeted and effective resolutions. The following methodologies and tools will be instrumental in this diagnostic process.

Firstly, inspecting the container's logs is essential. Logs provide a detailed account of the events leading up to and during the container's startup. Docker offers the docker logs command, which retrieves the logs generated by a specific container. It is crucial to emphasize that log analysis should be the first step in diagnosing startup issues.

```
docker logs <container_id>
```

For instance, if running docker logs my_container reveals errors such as "unable to connect to database", the problem likely lies in the container's environment variables or network configuration. Logs might also indicate issues such as missing or misconfigured dependencies, inadequate permissions, or syntax errors in scripts being executed.

Secondly, it is beneficial to review the Dockerfile if the container is built from a custom image. Examining the Dockerfile can reveal errors in instructions, misplaced files, or incorrect CMD or ENTRYPOINT specifications. For a container failing to start due to a misconfigured ENTRYPOINT, the Dockerfile might have:

```
ENTRYPOINT ["invalid/executable"]
```

Correcting the path or filename as per the actual executable located within the container is necessary.

Thirdly, it is important to ensure the container's network setup is appropriately configured. Sometimes, containers do not start because they cannot communicate with necessary services. Validating network connectivity between containers and services they depend on can be performed using the docker network command suite:

```
docker network ls
docker network inspect <network_name>
```

If issues are found, adjusting network settings or ensuring dependent services are operational might be required. For example, adding a container to the correct network can be accomplished as shown below:

```
docker network connect <network_name> <container_id>
```

Moreover, container resource allocation should be reviewed to rule out issues related to insufficient memory or CPU allocation. A container may fail to start if the host system lacks the required resources. Docker's docker stats command provides real-time resource usage of containers, aiding the diagnosis of resource exhaustion issues:

```
docker stats
```

Inspecting the resource constraints specified during container setup helps in such cases. These constraints are often specified using the –memory and –cpus flags:

```
docker run --memory="256m" --cpus="1" <image>
```

Ensuring adequate resources are allocated can resolve many startup issues.

Another critical area is checking for file system issues within the container. Containers rely on correct file paths and permissions. Debugging commands like docker exec allow attaching to a running container to inspect its file system:

```
docker exec -it <container_id> /bin/bash
```

Once attached, commands such as ls, cat, and chmod can confirm the existence, readability, and correct permissions of required files.

Configurations provided via environment variables and mounted volumes should also be verified. Misconfigured environment variables or missing volumes could lead to startup failures. Inspecting the container's environment with the docker inspect command can highlight misconfigurations:

```
docker inspect <container_id>
```

Lastly, the container's exit code can provide clues. Docker containers return an exit code upon termination, indicating success (0) or failure (non-zero error code). To obtain the exit code:

```
docker inspect <container_id> --format='{{.State.ExitCode}}'
```

Interpreting the exit code against standard exit codes can help isolate the problem. For instance, an exit code of 127 usually means a command was not found, indicating potential issues with CMD or ENTRYPOINT.

Resolutions should be guided by the diagnostics performed. If logs indicate dependency errors, addressing those specific dependencies is necessary. Correcting Dockerfile errors, verifying network configurations, adjusting resource allocations, fixing file system issues, and confirming the proper configuration of environment variables and volumes will collectively address and resolve most container startup problems effectively. Each step in this detailed diagnosis aims to provide a clear, methodical path to identify and fix the root cause of container startup failures, ensuring successful and stable container operation.

11.4 Managing Container Performance Issues

Performance issues in Docker containers can have significant impacts on application responsiveness and overall system efficiency. Effective management of these issues necessitates a comprehensive understanding of container resource allocation, monitoring tools, and optimization techniques.

Containers share the host system's resources, which often leads to resource contention if not properly managed. Docker provides mechanisms to allocate and limit resources for each container, including CPU, memory, and block I/O. Precise resource allocation ensures that critical containers receive sufficient resources while limiting the impact of less critical ones.

To allocate CPU resources, Docker supports two primary options: –cpus and –cpu-shares. The –cpus option specifies the number of CPUs available to the container:

```
docker run --cpus="2" mycontainer
```

In contrast, the –cpu-shares option adjusts the relative share of CPU time:

```
docker run --cpu-shares="512" mycontainer
```

It should be noted that –cpu-shares does not limit the CPU usage but prioritizes the usage among other containers.

Memory allocation is controlled using the –memory and –memory-swap options. The –memory option restricts the maximum amount of memory allocated to a container:

```
docker run --memory="256m" mycontainer
```

Additionally, the –memory-swap option can be used to allow swapping to disk, providing an extended memory area at the cost of performance:

```
docker run --memory="256m" --memory-swap="512m" mycontainer
```

Limiting block I/O performance is vital to avoid disk contention, which is managed via the –device-read-bps, –device-write-bps, –device-read-iops, and –device-write-iops options. These parameters can control the maximum read/write speed and input/output operations per second (IOPS) for a specific device:

```
docker run --device-read-bps /dev/sda:1mb mycontainer
```

Once resources are allocated optimally, monitoring container performance is crucial. Docker provides built-in tools like docker stats to observe real-time resource usage:

```
docker stats mycontainer
```

The output includes CPU, memory, network I/O, and block I/O statistics:

```
CONTAINER ID   NAME          CPU %    MEM USAGE / LIMIT   MEM %    NET I/O           BLOCK I/O    PIDS
1a2b3c4d5e6f   mycontainer   25.23%   50.7MiB / 256MiB    19.81%   1.23GB / 1.02GB   5MB / 2MB    10
```

For long-term performance analysis, integrating Docker with monitoring tools such as Prometheus and Grafana provides comprehensive insights. Docker includes metrics endpoints that can be scraped by Prometheus for detailed analysis. A sample configuration in prometheus.yml might include:

```
scrape_configs:
  - job_name: 'docker'
    static_configs:
      - targets: ['localhost:9323']
```

Grafana can then visualize this data, presenting trends and anomalies graphically.

Diagnosing performance bottlenecks often involves identifying specific issues like high CPU usage, excessive memory consumption, or disk I/O saturation. Each type of issue requires targeted strategies:

- **High CPU Usage:** Identify the processes within the container using excessive CPU via tools like htop or top. Optimize or refactor code to improve efficiency.
- **Excessive Memory Consumption:** Check for memory leaks or inefficient memory usage patterns. Use diagnostic tools like Valgrind or heap profilers.
- **Disk I/O Saturation:** Minimize disk writes, cache frequently accessed data in memory, and use faster storage solutions like SSDs.

In some cases, tuning the host system itself may be necessary. Adjusting kernel parameters, configuring appropriate filesystem options, and ensuring adequate physical resources can substantially enhance container performance.

Lastly, investigating the impact of container density—number of containers running on a single host—is crucial. Overloading a host with too many containers can lead to resource starvation and degrade performance. Proper orchestration tools like Kubernetes can help manage the placement and scaling of containers more effectively.

Managing container performance is an iterative and comprehensive process, demanding constant monitoring, prompt diagnosis, and ongoing optimization to maintain a balanced and efficient container ecosystem.

11.5 Analyzing Docker Logs for Troubleshooting

Effective troubleshooting often begins with a thorough analysis of Docker logs. Docker logs provide critical insights into the behavior and state of running containers as well as the daemon. This section explores the methodologies and tools necessary to interpret these logs, facilitating the identification and resolution of various issues.

Containers in Docker encapsulate applications and their dependencies. As these applications run, they generate log data that Docker can capture and expose. Two primary sources of log data in Docker are the container logs and the Docker daemon logs. Each plays a pivotal role in debugging and resolving issues.

The command docker logs is fundamental for accessing a container's logs. This utility reads the stdout and stderr streams of a specific container.

```
docker logs <container_id>
```

By using the <container_id> or the <container_name>, one can view the log output that would typically be written to the console if the application were running interactively. For instance, to view the logs of a container with ID abc123, the command would be:

```
docker logs abc123
```

Docker supports several options with the docker logs command to tailor the output based on the issue at hand. Notable options include:

- –follow, -f: Continuously outputs new log entries, similar to the tail -f command.

- –since: Displays logs generated after a specific time.
- –tail: Limits the number of log entries displayed to the most recent N lines.

For example, to follow logs in real-time and limit the start point to logs generated after 2021-08-01T00:00:00, one could use:

```
docker logs -f --since "2021-08-01T00:00:00" abc123
```

Moreover, for applications generating substantial log data, analyzing partial logs using –tail can be more efficient. Displaying only the last 100 lines of logs can be achieved via:

```
docker logs --tail 100 abc123
```

Applications might also generate structured logs in JSON format for better readability and automated parsing. Docker's logging drivers can be configured to capture these structured logs and redirect them appropriately. Configuration of logging drivers can be set in the /etc/docker/daemon.json file.

```
{
  "log-driver": "json-file",
  "log-opts": {
    "max-size": "10m",
    "max-file": "3"
  }
}
```

These settings ensure the log size is capped at 10MB and maintains a maximum of three log files before rotating. These options help manage disk usage and prevent logs from consuming excessive resources.

For daemon-level troubleshooting, examining the Docker daemon logs is imperative. These logs provide comprehensive details pertaining to the Docker service operations. The daemon logs are typically located at /var/log/docker.log on most Linux distributions, or available via the system's journal logs if Docker is managed as a systemd service.

To view the Docker daemon logs using systemd's journalctl, utilize:

```
sudo journalctl -u docker.service
```

Actions such as starting, stopping, and restarting containers or the daemon might bring specific issues to light in the daemon logs. For instance, to follow the daemon log output in real-time, the following command can be issued:

```
sudo journalctl -u docker.service -f
```

Sometimes issues are buried within a massive amount of log data. Employing filtering tools like grep to search for keywords or specific error messages can be highly efficient. Below is an example filtering for errors:

```
sudo journalctl -u docker.service | grep "error"
```

Comprehensive log entries often indicate root causes for many problems, including network failures, storage access problems, or configuration errors. Custom log drivers can redirect logs to external systems like Elasticsearch, Splunk, or various cloud log management solutions, enabling more sophisticated real-time analysis and dashboarding capabilities.

In certain scenarios, container-specific logs might not suffice for debugging distributed applications. Tools like docker-compose can aggregate multiple service logs:

```
docker-compose logs
```

The log output is combined, showcasing inter-service communication and synchronized behavior, crucial for diagnosing complex multi-container setups. Options similar to docker logs also apply to docker-compose logs, such as -f for follow mode and –tail for limiting log entries.

A methodical approach to log analysis, coupled with the powerful utilities that Docker provides, facilitates swift detection and resolution of issues that surface during container execution. This systematic examination not only aids in debugging but also ensures smooth and reliable containerized environments.

11.6 Networking Issues and Solutions

In Docker, networking is a fundamental aspect that connects containers, services, and external networks. Effective troubleshooting of networking issues requires a comprehensive understanding of Docker's networking model, which includes various drivers and configurations. Common networking problems can arise from misconfigured network settings, conflicts between containers, or firewall rules. Here, we explore typical networking issues and their resolutions, ensuring containers communicate seamlessly within the Docker environment.

Firstly, one must grasp the different Docker network types: bridge, host, none, and user-defined networks (both bridge and overlay). Each network type serves unique purposes and knowing their distinctions aids in pinpointing the root of networking issues.

- **Bridge Network:** Used by default and isolates containers into a private internal network on a single Docker host.
- **Host Network:** Removes network isolation between the container and the Docker host, making the container use the host's networking directly.
- **None Network:** Disables networking for the container.
- **User-Defined Networks:** Custom networks that offer more flexibility and control, including bridge and overlay types.

A common issue is containers unable to communicate with each other on a user-defined bridge network. This frequently arises from network misconfigurations. Below is an example of setting up a user-defined network and launching containers within it.

```
# Create a user-defined bridge network
docker network create --driver bridge my_custom_network
# Run containers in the user-defined network
docker run -dit --name container1 --network my_custom_network alpine
docker run -dit --name container2 --network my_custom_network alpine
```

Ensuring the containers are on the same network and can resolve each other by name can be verified using ping or similar network tools. A typical scenario might look like the following inside a container:

```
# Attach to container1
docker exec -it container1 sh
# Ping container2
ping container2
```

If the ping fails, verify network settings using docker inspect:

```
docker inspect container1
docker inspect container2
```

This output provides details such as the IP addresses assigned to the containers and their network configurations. Look for discrepancies that might prevent connectivity.

Firewalls on the host machine can also impede Docker network traffic. Ensure necessary ports are open and no rules are blocking Docker's bridge network. For instance, on Ubuntu systems using iptables:

```
sudo iptables -A INPUT -p tcp --dport 2376 -j ACCEPT
```

Ensure Docker's IP forwarding is enabled, which allows containers to communicate across networks. This can be verified and enabled in the sysctl settings:

```
# Check IP forwarding status
sysctl net.ipv4.ip_forward
# Enable IP forwarding if not already enabled
sudo sysctl -w net.ipv4.ip_forward=1
```

Another frequent network issue is related to DNS resolution failures within containers, which can stem from the Docker DNS server or external DNS misconfigurations. Containers use Docker's embedded DNS server, which can be overridden by setting custom DNS servers using the –dns flag:

```
docker run -dit --name dns_container --dns 8.8.8.8 --dns 8.8.4.4 alpine
```

For more complex network-related issues, Docker's network troubleshooting commands such as docker network ls, docker network inspect, and docker network connect prove invaluable. For example:

```
# List all networks to identify any anomalies or unexpected networks
docker network ls
# Inspect a specific network to detail its configuration and connected containers
docker network inspect my_custom_network
# Manually connect a running container to a different network
docker network connect my_custom_network container3
```

Lastly, diagnosing issues with overlay networks, typically used in Docker Swarm or Kubernetes environments, involves multiple hosts and ensuring that the Docker Engine is appropriately configured. Network plugins and configurations play a crucial role. Diagnose by confirming that the overlay network spans multiple hosts:

```
# Run on each Docker host part of the swarm or Kubernetes cluster
docker network inspect <overlay_network_name>
```

Understanding and resolving Docker networking issues requires examining both the Docker network configurations and the host's network setup. Incorporating systematic troubleshooting steps like inspecting configurations, verifying connectivity, and ensuring proper firewall settings significantly aids in rectifying these problems.

11.7 Storage and Volume Troubleshooting

Storage issues in Docker environments often stem from the complexities of managing persistent data across ephemeral containers. Addressing these issues requires a strong understanding of how Docker manages data storage and the mechanisms it provides for persistency and volume management. This section delves into the common problems encountered with Docker storage and volumes, their diagnostics, and proven resolution strategies.

Docker provides multiple ways to manage data, with volumes being the most commonly used method due to their flexibility and ease of use. Other methods include bind mounts and tmpfs mounts. Understanding the difference between these modes is critical for efficient troubleshooting.

- **Volumes:** Managed by Docker, volumes are stored in a part of the host filesystem, usually under $/var/lib/docker/volumes/$.
- **Bind mounts:** Allow data sharing between the host and container, enabling containers to directly access files on the host system.
- **Tmpfs mounts:** Stored in the host memory, they are non-persistent and lose their data upon container shutdown.

Common Issues with Docker Volumes:

- **Volume Not Found:** Often occurs when the volume name is misspelled or the volume is not created.
- **Permission Issues:** These can arise when the container user does not have adequate permissions to access the volume.
- **Data Inconsistency:** Arises due to improper volume management or concurrent access by multiple containers.
- **Disk Space Exhaustion:** Happens when the host system runs out of storage.

Volume Not Found:

The error usually occurs during the container start-up. Diagnosing this problem involves ensuring the volume exists and is correctly referenced in the Docker run command or Docker Compose file.

```
docker volume ls
```

The above command lists all the volumes managed by Docker. Misnaming can be verified, and the appropriate corrections can be made in the Docker command or Compose file.

```
docker volume create my_volume
```

```
docker run -d -v my_volume:/app/data my_image
```

Creating the missing volume using the docker volume create command and ensuring the volume is correctly attached to the container can resolve many issues related to volume not found errors.

Permission Issues:

Addressing permission issues involves analyzing the file permissions and ownership both on the host and within the container.

```
ls -l /var/lib/docker/volumes/my_volume/_data/
```

The above command inspects the file permissions and ownership in the host's volume directory. Files and directories that the container user must access should have the correct permissions.

When a container is configured to run as a non-root user, ensure that this user has the necessary permissions to access the desired files. Files may need to be chown'ed appropriately.

```
sudo chown -R user:group /var/lib/docker/volumes/my_volume/_data/
```

Data Inconsistency:

Such issues often arise from improper use of volumes across multiple containers. Each container access to the volume needs careful planning and synchronization mechanisms to prevent write conflicts.

For databases and other stateful applications, wherein data consistency is critical, using Docker volumes should be approached with caution. Containers should ideally perform isolated data operations, or appropriate locking mechanisms should be incorporated.

```
docker run -d --name db-server -v dbdata:/var/lib/mysql mysql
```

```
docker run --rm --volumes-from db-server -it busybox
```

In the above scenario, 'dbdata' volume is shared among the MySQL server and a BusyBox container, necessitating precise control over access times and operations to prevent data corruption.

Disk Space Exhaustion:

A frequent issue in long-running Docker deployments arises when the host system runs out of storage due to unbound data accumulation in volumes.

Initial diagnostics involve verifying the host's available storage:

```
df -h
```

If /var/lib/docker/volumes/ or the Docker root directory is consuming significant space, intervention is required. You can clear unwanted volumes using:

```
docker volume prune
```

```
WARNING! This will remove all local volumes not used by any container.
Are you sure you want to continue? [y/N] y
```

Use the volume prune command cautiously, especially in production environments. Regular monitoring and automated clean-up mechanisms can mitigate the risk of disk space saturation.

Addressing these common storage and volume issues promptly and methodically ensures stable and efficient Docker container operations. Understanding the underlying principles of Docker's volume management system empowers administrators to resolve problems effectively and maintain persistent data integrity across container lifecycles.

11.8 Dealing with Docker Daemon Failures

Docker Daemon is the core background service responsible for managing Docker containers on a host machine. Failures in the Docker Daemon can lead to substantial operational disruptions. This section delves into common Docker Daemon failure scenarios, diagnostic methods, and potential resolutions.

Firstly, one must ensure that the Docker service is active and running.

On Linux systems, the status of the Docker Daemon can be checked using the following command:

```
sudo systemctl status docker
```

This command provides an overview of the service state. A healthy service typically shows active (running). If the service is not running, it can be started with:

```
sudo systemctl start docker
```

If the Docker Daemon fails to start, the journal logs should be inspected to identify specific errors. This can be achieved by examining the journal entries using:

```
sudo journalctl -u docker.service
```

This log provides comprehensive error details that can pinpoint the precise cause of the failure. Common issues involve deprecated flags, misconfigurations in /etc/docker/daemon.json, or conflicts with other services.

Configuration File Issues:

The /etc/docker/daemon.json file contains critical settings for the Docker Daemon. Any syntactical errors or misconfigurations within this file can prevent the Docker Daemon from starting. An example of a correctly formatted daemon.json is:

```
{
  "storage-driver": "overlay2",
  "log-level": "error",
  "iptables": false
}
```

Errors can be identified when the Daemon refuses to start after editing daemon.json. Ensure that proper JSON syntax is maintained, and there are no extraneous commas or mismatched braces. Invalid configurations can be corrected or the file can be reverted to a known working backup.

Deprecation and Compatibility Problems:

As Docker evolves, certain features and flags may become deprecated or incompatible with the current version. Ensure that the Docker Engine and all related components are up to date. Updating Docker can be performed using:

```
sudo apt-get update
```

```
sudo apt-get install --only-upgrade docker-ce
```

Compatibility issues often emerge when the kernel or underlying operating system libraries are outdated. Compatibility matrix documentation provided by Docker can be referred to for verifying supported versions.

Resource Constraints:

Resource allocation, particularly memory and CPU limits, can impact the Docker Daemon's stability. Low system resources may cause the service to fail sporadically or under high load. Monitoring system resources using tools like free and top offers insights into whether the failures stem from resource limitations.

```
free -m
top
```

Corruption in Docker Data:

Corrupt state information within Docker's operational directories, such as /var/lib/docker, can lead to failures. If corruption is suspected, these directories should be inspected and cleared cautiously. Backing up critical data before performing any deletions is recommended. For a quick but drastic measure:

```
sudo systemctl stop docker
sudo rm -rf /var/lib/docker
sudo systemctl start docker
```

This resets Docker to its default state, resolving issues related to corrupted data at the expense of losing current container states and images.

Docker Daemon Options:

Docker runs with certain command-line options that define its behaviour. These options are typically configured in the service unit file located at /lib/systemd/system/docker.service. Misconfigured options in this file can prevent Docker from starting as expected. For example, modifying the service file to include custom options:

```
ExecStart=/usr/bin/dockerd --iptables=false
```

After making changes to this file, it is necessary to reload the systemd manager configuration and restart Docker:

```
sudo systemctl daemon-reload
sudo systemctl restart docker
```

Permission and Ownership Issues:

Docker requires specific permissions to function correctly. Ensure that the Docker Daemon and its related directories have the correct ownership and permission settings. Incorrect permissions can cause the Daemon to fail due to access issues. To set the right permissions:

```
sudo chown root:root /var/run/docker.sock
sudo chmod 666 /var/run/docker.sock
```

Append additional steps by inspecting firewall rules. Docker relies on appropriate network configurations. Conflicts or overly restrictive firewall settings can block Docker functionalities. Listing and understanding the current iptables rules help to diagnose such issues:

```
sudo iptables -L -v
```

By addressing these common failure points systematically, one can diagnose and mitigate Docker Daemon failures effectively, ensuring a robust operational environment.

11.9 Debugging Dockerfile Issues

Analyzing and fixing Dockerfile issues is a critical skill for anyone aiming to master Docker. A well-constructed Dockerfile ensures that your containerized applications run efficiently and correctly. Debugging Dockerfile issues can involve identifying syntax errors, understanding the build context, resolving dependencies, and optimizing the image layers.

Identifying Syntax Errors

Syntax errors are among the most common issues encountered when writing a Dockerfile. To identify syntax errors, carefully review the Dockerfile and compare it against Docker's reference documentation. Docker's build process will typically fail with a clear error message indicating the problematic line. Here, a good practice is to use docker build with the –no-cache option to ensure the entire Dockerfile is processed afresh, allowing any syntax errors to surface:

```
docker build --no-cache -t myimage .
```

Understanding Build Context

The build context refers to the set of files at the directory level that Docker has access to during the build process. Misunderstandings about the build context can lead to errors such as files not being found or incorrect files being included in the image. Ensure all necessary files are within the build context, typically the directory where the Dockerfile is located. For example, if the Dockerfile attempts to copy a file that is not present in the build context, the build will fail:

```
COPY myapp/ /usr/src/myapp/
```

If the myapp/ directory does not exist in the build context, Docker will raise an error. Confirm the directory structure and working directory are correctly configured:

```
docker build -t myimage /path/to/build/context
```

Resolving Dependencies

Automating the installation of dependencies is a key aspect of Dockerfile usage. However, failing to ensure all dependencies are correctly installed can lead to runtime errors. For example, missing libraries or wrong versions of packages can cause an application to crash. One way to preemptively address these issues is by adding checks and ensuring you are using the correct package management commands. For example, in a Python-based application, you might include the following in your Dockerfile:

```
RUN pip install -r requirements.txt
```

Ensure that requirements.txt specifies all the necessary packages and their versions. For verbose error logging during the build process, the –progress=plain flag can be used:

```
docker build --progress=plain -t myimage .
```

Optimizing Image Layers

Each instruction in a Dockerfile creates a new layer in the Docker image. Unnecessary layers can bloat the image size and increase build time. To debug and optimize image layers, carefully order the instructions and minimize the number of layers created by combining RUN commands where feasible:

```
RUN apt-get update && apt-get install -y \
    package1 \
    package2 && \
    apt-get clean && \
    rm -rf /var/lib/apt/lists/*
```

Using multi-stage builds can also significantly reduce the final image size by isolating the build dependencies and including only the necessary runtime dependencies in the final image. Example of a multi-stage build for a Go application:

```
# Stage 1: Build the application
FROM golang:1.16 as builder
WORKDIR /app
COPY . .
RUN go build -o myapp

# Stage 2: Copy only the necessary data from Stage 1
FROM alpine:latest
WORKDIR /usr/local/bin
COPY --from=builder /app/myapp .
CMD ["myapp"]
```

Debugging RUN Commands

The output from RUN commands during the image build process can be critical in understanding what is causing a failure. Redirecting output to log files or using verbose logging can assist in diagnosing issues within RUN commands. For instance:

```
RUN pip install -r requirements.txt > install.log 2>&1
```

This will redirect both standard output and error messages to install.log, which can be inspected after the build process fails. Additionally, consider using interactive shell commands within the Dockerfile for debugging:

```
RUN /bin/bash -c "if [ ! -f /path/to/file ]; then echo 'File missing'; fi"
```

By following these practices and understanding the common pitfalls outlined, developers can effectively debug Dockerfile issues, leading to more reliable and efficient Docker images.

11.10 Resolving Docker Build Failures

Docker build failures can stem from various reasons, ranging from syntax errors in the Dockerfile to network issues during image creation. Identifying the root cause is essential to effectively resolve these failures and achieve a successful build. This section delves into common causes of Docker build failures and provides systematic strategies to troubleshoot and resolve them.

Syntax and Configuration Errors

Incorrect syntax and configuration in the Dockerfile are frequent reasons for build failures. Ensure your Dockerfile syntax adheres to Docker's official documentation. During the build process, Docker provides error messages that can pinpoint the exact line where the problem lies. For example, a missing backslash in a multi-line command or a misplaced instruction keyword can cause an immediate failure.

```
FROM python:3.8-slim-buster
WORKDIR /app
COPY . /app

RUN apt-get update && apt-get install -y \
    build-essential \
    libssl-dev \
    && rm -rf /var/lib/apt/lists/*

CMD ["python", "app.py"]
```

In the above Dockerfile, if there is a syntax error, Docker will typically indicate the line number and the nature of the error, guiding you to correct it.

Dependency and Network Issues

Network-related issues, such as failed dependencies and timeout errors, also commonly cause Docker build problems. External dependencies, such as packages from remote repositories, require a stable internet connection during the build process. Transient network issues or misconfigured proxy settings can lead to failures when fetching these dependencies.

Consider the following scenario where dependency installation fails due to network issues:

```
RUN pip install -r requirements.txt
```

If the network is unstable, you might encounter errors like:

```
ERROR: Could not fetch URL https://pypi.org/simple/...: There was a problem
confirming the ssl certificate: HTTPSConnectionPool(host='pypi.org',
port=443): Max retries exceeded with url: /simple/... (Caused by
SSLError(SSLContext(...)))
```

To resolve such issues, ensure you have a reliable network connection and appropriate proxy configurations if needed.

IAM Roles, Permissions, and Quotas

In cloud environments, insufficient permissions or exhausted quotas can impede Docker build processes. Ensure you have appropriate IAM roles and permissions configured, especially when accessing private repositories or deploying images to container registries. Additionally, verify that your cloud resource quotas, such as CPU, memory, or storage, are not exceeded during the build.

Multi-Stage Builds and Caching

Multi-stage builds are employed to reduce image size and separate build environments from runtime environments. However, misconfigurations in multi-stage builds can lead to failures. Ensure each stage is correctly referenced, and the artifacts needed for subsequent stages are properly handled.

```
FROM golang:1.16 as builder
WORKDIR /go/src/app
COPY . .
RUN go build -o myapp

FROM alpine:latest
WORKDIR /root/
COPY --from=builder /go/src/app/myapp .
CMD ["./myapp"]
```

In this example, if the *builder* stage fails due to a missing dependency or compilation error, the subsequent stages will inevitably fail. It is beneficial to examine the logs of each stage individually.

Docker supports build caching to expedite the build process. However, cache-related issues may arise if the cache becomes invalid or corrupt. Forcefully clearing the build cache can sometimes resolve unexplained build problems.

```
docker build --no-cache -t myapp:latest .
```

Debugging Techniques and Tools

Utilizing Docker's build flags such as –progress and –target can facilitate troubleshooting. The –progress flag helps provide more detailed output, while –target allows building up to a specific stage to isolate the error.

```
docker build --progress=plain -t myapp:latest .
docker build --target builder -t builder-stage .
```

docker image history can visualize the layers and identify where the failure occurs:

```
docker image history myapp:latest
```

```
IMAGE          CREATED         CREATED BY                                          SIZE
<image-id>     1 minute ago    /bin/sh -c #(nop)  CMD ["./myapp"]                  0B
<image-id>     1 minute ago    /bin/sh -c COPY --from=builder /go/src/app...       12.8MB
...
```

By examining the history, you can trace back through the image layers generated during the build process.

Effective diagnosis and resolution of Docker build failures necessitate careful analysis of Dockerfile syntax, network stability, dependency management, and leveraging debugging tools. Identifying the root cause through systematic troubleshooting ensures builds complete successfully, resulting in efficient and reliable Docker workflows.

11.11 Troubleshooting Docker Compose Deployments

Docker Compose is a tool that simplifies multi-container Docker applications. Issues may arise when deploying services using Docker Compose, requiring a structured approach to diagnose and resolve. Knowledge of common errors, proper logging, and understanding underlying Docker mechanisms are essential for effective troubleshooting.

When troubleshooting Docker Compose deployments, start by verifying the 'docker-compose.yml' file for syntax errors and configuration issues. The 'docker-compose.yml' file orchestrates multi-container deployments, specifying service definitions, environment variables, networks, and volumes.

```
docker-compose config
```

Executing the above command checks for syntax correctness and standardizes the configuration output. Ensuring no configurations errors exist helps narrow down potential issues.

If the configuration is valid but services are not starting as expected, examine the output and exit codes of Docker Compose.

```
docker-compose up --verbose
```

This invocation provides detailed information about the deployment process, aiding in identifying which services fail to start and why. Common errors like conflicting port assignments, network misconfigurations, and missing environment variables often surface here.

Container logs are critical for understanding service failures. Using Docker Compose, aggregate logs from all containers with:

```
docker-compose logs
```

Examining logs can reveal errors like dependency failures, misconfigurations, or runtime exceptions that cause services to malfunction. If a specific service log is needed, tailor the command:

```
docker-compose logs <service_name>
```

Network issues often affect service communication in Docker Compose. Use the 'docker network ls' and 'docker network inspect' commands to verify network creation and configuration, identifying connectivity problems between services.

Example:

```
docker network ls
docker network inspect <network_name>
```

Volumes also play a significant role in Docker Compose deployments. Persistent data issues can arise if volumes are not correctly defined or mounted. Inspect and debug volumes by listing them and examining usage:

```
docker volume ls
docker volume inspect <volume_name>
```

Additionally, if Docker Compose services are not behaving as expected, restarting services can help. Here, 'docker-compose down' followed by 'docker-compose up' ensures a clean start:

```
docker-compose down
docker-compose up
```

Verify that all services are up and running with:

```
docker-compose ps
```

This command provides a summary of running services, their states, and port mappings. Ensure all required services are active, and no unintentional exits have occurred.

If services continuously restart or fail to deploy, delve into resource constraints. Ensure the host machine has adequate resources (memory, CPU, disk space) by monitoring:

```
docker stats
```

Review the resource consumption of containers to identify bottlenecks or excessive usage contributing to failures.

Finally, Docker Compose deployments sometimes face issues with differing file version compatibility or system configurations. Verify the versions of Docker and Docker Compose in use, ensuring they meet the project's requirements. Update to the latest compatible versions when necessary:

```
docker --version
docker-compose --version
```

Many issues can be resolved by aligning service definitions with updated configurations and ensuring compatibility with the host system's resources and configurations. Implementing these steps methodically aids in diagnosing and resolving deployment issues in Docker Compose, stabilizing multi-container applications efficiently.

11.12 Using Docker Inspect and Other Diagnostic Tools

The effective management and troubleshooting of Docker containers often necessitate precise and detailed information about the state and configuration of the various components involved. docker inspect is a powerful tool for retrieving comprehensive details about Docker objects such as containers, images, networks, and volumes. This section will explore how to utilize docker inspect effectively, alongside other diagnostic tools pivotal for resolving complex issues.

The docker inspect command retrieves low-level information about Docker objects in JSON format. For example, to obtain details about a specific container, one would execute:

```
docker inspect <container_id_or_name>
```

The output is extensive, encompassing numerous fields that detail the container's configuration, state, network settings, and more. A typical truncated output may look as follows:

```
[
  {
    "Id": "e90e34656806",
    "Created": "2021-01-01T12:00:00.000000000Z",
    "Path": "/bin/bash",
    "Args": [],
    "State": {
      "Status": "running",
      "Running": true,
      "Paused": false,
      "Restarting": false,
      "OOMKilled": false,
      "Dead": false,
      "Pid": 12345,
      "ExitCode": 0,
      "Error": "",
      "StartedAt": "2021-01-01T12:00:05.000000000Z",
      "FinishedAt": "2021-01-01T12:00:00.000000000Z"
    },
    "Image": "sha256:e9d1...",
    "ResolvConfPath": "/var/lib/docker/containers/e90e34656806/resolv.conf",
    "HostnamePath": "/var/lib/docker/containers/e90e34656806/hostname",
    "HostsPath": "/var/lib/docker/containers/e90e34656806/hosts",
    "LogPath": "/var/lib/docker/containers/e90e34656806/log.json",
    ...
    "NetworkSettings": {
      ...
      "Networks": {
        "bridge": {
          "IPAMConfig": null,
          "Links": null,
          "Aliases": null,
          "NetworkID": "02e...",
          "EndpointID": "3aa...",
          "Gateway": "172.17.0.1",
          "IPAddress": "172.17.0.2",
          "IPPrefixLen": 16,
          "IPv6Gateway": "",
          "GlobalIPv6Address": "",
          "GlobalIPv6PrefixLen": 0,
          "MacAddress": "02:42:ac:11:00:02"
        }
      }
    }
  }
]
```


One significant advantage of docker inspect is its ability to filter output using the -f or –format flag. This is particularly useful for extracting specific fields without parsing the entire JSON. For instance, to get just the container's IP address:

```
docker inspect -f '{{ .NetworkSettings.Networks.bridge.IPAddress }}' <
    container_id_or_name>
```

Other diagnostic tools supplement docker inspect by offering various functionalities critical for debugging. These include:

Docker Logs: Examining logs is essential for understanding container runtime issues. Use the docker logs command to fetch logs for a container:

```
docker logs <container_id_or_name>
```

The -f flag can be used to follow log output as it is generated, and –tail flag to view the most recent lines.

Docker Events: Monitoring Docker events allows the observation of real-time activities within the Docker engine, aiding in the diagnosis of issues arising from specific actions:

```
docker events
```

This command provides a stream of events, which can be filtered by type, container, image, etc., using the –filter option.

Docker Stats: Real-time statistics about container resource usage can be crucial for diagnosing performance bottlenecks:

```
docker stats
```

This yields dynamic utilization metrics such as CPU, memory, and network I/O for active containers.

Docker Top: Extracting process-level information running within containers aids in identifying misbehaving processes:

```
docker top <container_id_or_name>
```

This command displays the same information as the ps command on Linux systems.

Docker Diff: Investigating changes in a container's filesystem can help pinpoint configuration changes or unanticipated modifications:

```
docker diff <container_id_or_name>
```

This lists changes to the container's filesystem since it started.

Container Networking Commands: Tools such as docker network inspect provide insights into Docker networks:

```
docker network inspect <network_id_or_name>
```

This command reveals details about Docker networks, including the containers connected to them and their respective IP addresses.

These diagnostic commands form a crucial part of the Docker troubleshooting toolkit, providing granular insights into the behavior and state of various Docker components. Leveraging these tools effectively can significantly simplify the process of diagnosing and resolving issues.

11.13 Reporting and Seeking Help for Docker Issues

When encountering Docker issues that you cannot resolve independently, reporting the problem and seeking external assistance becomes necessary. This section provides a structured approach for effectively reporting issues and seeking help within the Docker community and related support channels. Thoroughly documenting your problem and communicating it clearly is vital to receiving useful and timely responses.

Documenting the Problem

Accurate and comprehensive documentation of the issue you are facing is the first step towards seeking help. The following guidelines can assist in documenting the problem effectively:

- **Describe the issue explicitly**: Provide a clear and concise description of the problem. Avoid vague statements such as "Docker is not working."
- **Include relevant context**: Mention the environment in which you are running Docker, including the operating system, Docker version, and any other relevant software or configuration details.
- **List the steps to reproduce the issue**: Document the exact steps you took before encountering the problem. This allows others to replicate the issue and diagnose it accurately.
- **Provide error messages and logs**: Include any error messages, logs, or stack traces that are pertinent to the issue. Wrap shell commands and their outputs in the appropriate LaTeX environments for clarity.
- **Describe any troubleshooting steps already taken**: Outline what you have attempted to resolve the issue, including the results of those efforts.

Example of a Well-documented Issue

Description: Container fails to start with a "no such file or directory" error.

Environment:

- **Operating System:** Ubuntu 20.04
- **Docker Version:** 20.10.7
- **Docker Compose Version:** 1.29.2

Steps to Reproduce:

1. Define the following Dockerfile:

```
FROM python:3.8-slim-buster
WORKDIR /app
COPY . /app
CMD ["python", "app.py"]
```

2. Build the Docker image:

```
docker build -t my-python-app .
```

3. Run the image:

```
docker run my-python-app
```

Error Message:

```
python: can't open file 'app.py': [Errno 2] No such file or directory
```

Troubleshooting Steps Taken:

- Verified that app.py exists in the current directory.
- Checked the Docker image contents to ensure app.py is copied:

```
docker run --rm -it my-python-app ls /app
```

- Output of the above command shows that app.py is indeed missing.

Seeking Help from the Docker Community

After documenting the issue, the next step is to seek help. Docker has a vast and active community where you can ask questions and report problems. Some useful platforms include:

- **GitHub Issues**: For reporting bugs or requesting features, the official GitHub repositories (e.g., https://github.com/docker/docker) are appropriate. Ensure you search existing issues to avoid duplicates. When creating a new issue, provide detailed information following the template.

- **Docker Forums**: The Docker community forums (https://forums.docker.com/) are excellent for asking questions and sharing experiences. Engage with a broad spectrum of Docker users and experts.
- **Stack Overflow**: Tag your question with docker and provide detailed context (https://stackoverflow.com/questions/tagged/docker). Stack Overflow is beneficial for code-related inquiries and best practices.
- **Slack and IRC**: Various Docker user groups and channels are available on Slack and IRC for real-time communication. These platforms facilitate direct interaction with community experts.
- **Community Meetups**: Participating in Docker community meetups, either virtually or physically, provides opportunities to share problems and learn from others' experiences.

Best Practices for Seeking Help

When asking for help, adhere to the following best practices to ensure effective communication and problem resolution:

- **Be specific and concise**: Clearly articulate your issue without unnecessary details. Focus on the key points that are essential for understanding the problem.
- **Be respectful and patient**: Community members are volunteers who assist in their spare time. Respect their contributions and allow adequate time for responses.
- **Follow up with updates**: If you resolve the issue independently or identify further details, update your posts or issue reports to help others who might face similar problems.
- **Express gratitude**: Acknowledge and appreciate the assistance you receive, promoting a positive and collaborative community environment.

Effective reporting and seeking help for Docker issues facilitate quick resolutions and contribute to a collaborative and thriving Docker community. The next section will cover a fundamental aspect of Docker's diagnostic tools, such as docker inspect, empowering you to troubleshoot issues independently.

Chapter 12

Real-World Docker Use Cases

This chapter explores practical applications of Docker across various domains, including development environments, CI/CD pipelines, and microservices architectures. It covers Docker's use in database management, legacy application support, data science, big data, web hosting, and IoT applications. The chapter also discusses cloud deployments, multi-cloud environments, and presents case studies of successful Docker implementations.

12.1 Introduction to Real-World Docker Use Cases

Docker is designed to facilitate the use of containers as a method of software distribution, deployment, and isolation. In this section, we examine the practical applications that have led to its widespread adoption across various domains.

Development Environments

Developers benefit significantly from Docker's ability to create isolated and reproducible environments. This advantage ensures consistency across different development machines, mitigating the well-known "works on my machine" problem. Docker images encapsulate all necessary dependencies, libraries, and runtime environments, making it straightforward to replicate a development setup. The following Dockerfile demonstrates setting up a basic Python development environment:

```
FROM python:3.8-slim-buster

WORKDIR /app

COPY requirements.txt requirements.txt
RUN pip install -r requirements.txt

COPY . .

CMD ["python", "app.py"]
```

Once the image is built, developers can start containers and be confident that the environment is consistent with those used by their colleagues.

Continuous Integration/Continuous Deployment (CI/CD)

Docker streamlines the CI/CD pipeline by providing a consistent build and deploy process. Its integration with popular CI/CD tools like Jenkins, GitLab CI, and CircleCI simplifies the creation of repeatable and reliable builds. The uniform environment ensures that tests run identically in local development and build servers. Here is an example of how Docker can be integrated into a GitLab CI pipeline:

```
stages:
  - build
  - test
  - deploy

build:
  stage: build
  image: docker:latest
  services:
    - docker:dind
  script:
    - docker build -t my-app .

test:
  stage: test
  image: docker:latest
  services:
    - docker:dind
  script:
    - docker run my-app pytest

deploy:
  stage: deploy
  image: docker:latest
  services:
    - docker:dind
  script:
    - docker run my-app deploy-script.sh
```

This setup benefits from Docker's ability to manage dependencies and runtime versions, ensuring consistency and eliminating discrepancies between environments.

Microservices Architecture

Docker's containerization technology is pivotal in microservices architectures. Containers provide the necessary isolation and resource control, enabling independent development, deployment, and scaling of microservices. Each service runs in its own container, interacting with others through well-defined APIs. A simple illustration of a microservice deployment using Docker Compose:

```
version: '3'

services:
  db:
    image: postgres:12
    environment:
      POSTGRES_DB: mydatabase
      POSTGRES_USER: user
      POSTGRES_PASSWORD: password
  web:
    build: ./web
    ports:
      - "5000:5000"
    depends_on:
      - db
  auth:
    build: ./auth
    ports:
      - "5001:5001"
    depends_on:
      - db
```

In this configuration, each microservice – the database, web server, and authentication service – runs in its own container. Scalability and availability can be enhanced by managing replicas and load balancers through orchestrators like Kubernetes or Docker Swarm.

Database Management

Containers assist in the consistency and reproducibility of database environments, making them indispensable in development and testing. Docker allows quick provisioning of database instances, leveraging the same version and configuration across various stages of the deployment lifecycle. For example, to start a MySQL container:

```
docker run --name mydb -e MYSQL_ROOT_PASSWORD=root -e
    MYSQL_DATABASE=mydatabase -d mysql:latest
```

Database images on Docker Hub cover a wide array of popular choices, offering pre-configured setups for rapid deployment.

Legacy Applications

Legacy applications often operate on outdated runtime environments or dependencies, presenting challenges in modern infrastructure. Docker alleviates these issues by encapsulating the complete runtime environment of such applications, ensuring they run consistently regardless of the underlying host OS. A Dockerfile for a legacy Java application might look like:

```
FROM openjdk:8-jre-alpine

WORKDIR /app

COPY legacy-app.jar .

CMD ["java", "-jar", "legacy-app.jar"]
```

This containerization isolates legacy dependencies, permitting the execution of old applications on contemporary infrastructure without conflicts.

Data Science and Machine Learning (ML) Workflows

Docker images help standardize data science environments, incorporating necessary libraries, tools, and runtime dependencies, thus guaranteeing reproducibility. A typical Dockerfile for a data science project using Jupyter Lab and TensorFlow might be:

```
FROM tensorflow/tensorflow:latest-gpu-jupyter

WORKDIR /notebooks

COPY requirements.txt /notebooks/
RUN pip install -r requirements.txt

EXPOSE 8888
CMD ["jupyter", "lab", "--ip=0.0.0.0", "--allow-root"]
```

By sharing the Docker image, data scientists and ML engineers ensure that models and experiments can be replicated accurately across different systems.

Big Data Applications

Big data frameworks like Hadoop, Spark, and Kafka can be daunting to configure and manage. Docker simplifies the setup and scaling of these frameworks, providing isolated environments for complex workflows. The example below configures a simple Hadoop environment using Docker Compose:

```
version: '3'
```

```
services:
  namenode:
    image: bde2020/hadoop-namenode:2.0.0-hadoop2.7.4-java8
    environment:
      - CLUSTER_NAME=test
    ports:
      - "9870:9870"
  datanode:
    image: bde2020/hadoop-datanode:2.0.0-hadoop2.7.4-java8
    environment:
      - SERVICE_PRECONDITION=namenode:9870
```

Such configurations enable seamless creation and management of big data environments, facilitating efficient development and testing pipelines.

Web Hosting

Web applications benefit from Docker's ability to encapsulate the web server stack, including the application server, database, and other necessary services. The isolation provided by containers ensures predictable behavior across different stages, from development to production. For instance, a basic NGINX server setup in Docker:

```
FROM nginx:latest

COPY ./html /usr/share/nginx/html

EXPOSE 80

CMD ["nginx", "-g", "daemon off;"]
```

Deployers can use Docker Compose to manage more comprehensive web hosting stacks, including additional services like TLS termination and load balancing.

Internet of Things (IoT)

Docker assists in IoT applications by providing lightweight containers deployable on resource-constrained devices. By standardizing the deployment process, Docker ensures consistent environment settings across all devices. An illustrative Dockerfile for an IoT application using MQTT:

```
FROM python:alpine

WORKDIR /app

COPY . .

RUN pip install paho-mqtt

CMD ["python", "iot_client.py"]
```

This encapsulation simplifies the deployment of IoT applications, promoting consistency and reliability in distributed environments.

Cloud Deployment

Docker's containerization facilitates cloud deployments, streamlining the process of packaging and deploying applications to various cloud providers. It provides a consistent layer atop different infrastructure providers, enabling smooth transitions between development and production environments. An example of deploying a container to AWS Elastic Container Service (ECS) is:

```
# ECS Task Definition
{
  "containerDefinitions": [
    {
      "name": "my-app-container",
      "image": "my-app-image:latest",
      "cpu": 256,
      "memory": 512,
      "essential": true,
      "portMappings": [
        {
          "containerPort": 80,
          "hostPort": 80
        }
      ]
    }
  ],
  "family": "my-app-task",
  "networkMode": "awsvpc",
  "requiresCompatibilities": ["FARGATE"]
}
```

Docker's compatibility with various orchestration tools simplifies multi-cloud deployments, further enhancing flexibility and resilience.

Multi-Cloud Environments

Multi-cloud strategies leverage Docker for consistent operations across different cloud platforms. Docker, combined with orchestrators like Kubernetes, facilitate the deployment, scaling, and management of applications in multi-cloud environments. A Kubernetes deployment configuration for a multi-cloud setup demonstrates this versatility:

```
apiVersion: apps/v1
kind: Deployment
metadata:
  name: my-app
spec:
  replicas: 3
  selector:
    matchLabels:
      app: my-app
  template:
    metadata:
```

```
    labels:
      app: my-app
  spec:
    containers:
    - name: my-app
      image: my-app-image:latest
      ports:
        - containerPort: 80
```

Managing applications across multiple cloud providers enhances fault tolerance and service availability, proving especially valuable in large-scale environments.

These use cases demonstrate Docker's versatile and powerful capabilities, which have catalyzed its adoption in diverse real-world scenarios, driving efficiency, consistency, and scalability in modern application deployment practices.

12.2 Docker for Development Environments

Utilizing Docker for development environments provides a consistent and isolated setup that replicates the production environment as closely as possible. This alignment helps mitigate the common issue of "works on my machine" syndrome, ensuring consistency across different stages of software development. Docker images can encapsulate all dependencies, libraries, and configurations required for the application, allowing developers to work in a standardized environment regardless of their local setup.

A typical use case involves the creation of a Dockerfile, which contains instructions on how to build a Docker image for the development environment. Here is an example of a Dockerfile for a Node.js application:

```
# Use an official Node.js runtime as a parent image
FROM node:14

# Set the working directory in the container
WORKDIR /usr/src/app

# Copy the package.json and package-lock.json files
COPY package*.json ./

# Install the dependencies
RUN npm install

# Copy the source code into the container
COPY . .

# Expose the port the app runs on
EXPOSE 3000
```

```
# Command to run the application
CMD ["npm", "start"]
```

This Dockerfile starts with a base image of Node.js version 14. It sets the working directory to /usr/src/app, copies the package configuration files, installs the dependencies using npm install, and finally, copies the rest of the application code. The specified port 3000 is exposed, and the application is started using npm start.

Running a development container can be accomplished with the following command:

```
docker build -t my-node-app .
docker run -it --rm -p 3000:3000 -v $(pwd):/usr/src/app my-node-app
```

In this command, docker build creates the Docker image from the Dockerfile, tagging it as my-node-app. The docker run command starts a container from this image, with the -it flag for interactive mode and terminal access, –rm to automatically remove the container when it stops, -p to bind the container's port 3000 to the host's port 3000, and -v to mount the current directory into the container's working directory. This allows the code within the container to reflect changes made on the host machine immediately.

To streamline development workflows, Docker Compose can be used for defining and running multi-container Docker applications. Here's an example docker-compose.yml file for the same Node.js application, including a MongoDB service:

```
version: '3.8'

services:
  db:
    image: mongo
    volumes:
      - mongo-data:/data/db
    ports:
      - "27017:27017"

  app:
    build:
      context: .
    ports:
      - "3000:3000"
    volumes:
      - .:/usr/src/app
    depends_on:
      - db

volumes:
  mongo-data:
```

In this docker-compose.yml file, two services are defined: db, which runs a MongoDB container, and app, which builds and runs the Node.js application defined in the same context (the current directory). The volumes directive is used to persist data across container restarts for MongoDB, and mount the project directory for live code updates in the development container. The depends_on directive in the app service ensures that the database service is started before the application.

With the Docker Compose setup in place, the development environment can be started using:

```
docker-compose up
```

Developers can stop and remove the containers with:

```
docker-compose down
```

One of the key benefits of such a setup is the ability to mirror the production environment closely. This setup allows teams to define their entire application's environment with versioned infrastructure as code, bringing consistency across development, staging, and production environments.

Additionally, Docker for development environments supports collaborative workflows. Developers can create and share Docker images, ensuring that every team member or new hire can replicate the exact development environment with minimal setup. This lowers the barriers to entry and accelerates onboarding processes.

From an integration standpoint, Docker also plays well with various CI/CD tools, which allows for automated builds and tests in environments identical to those used in local development. This consistency enhances the reliability of the software being developed.

Using Docker for development not only ensures environment consistency but also enables testing and debugging in a controlled, reproducible setup. It empowers developers to concentrate on coding and problem-solving without being bogged down by environment configuration issues, thus enhancing productivity and code quality. This chapter continues to explore Docker's applications across other critical areas, each leveraging its inherent ability to provide isolated, consistent, and reproducible environments.

12.3 Docker in Continuous Integration/Continuous Deployment (CI/CD)

Continuous Integration (CI) and Continuous Deployment (CD) are crucial components of modern software development practices, aimed at enhancing code quality, reducing integration issues, and accelerating delivery cycles. Docker streamlines CI/CD processes by providing a consistent and isolated environment for building, testing, and deploying applications. This section delves into the integration of Docker with CI/CD pipelines, illustrating its implementation and benefits.

A typical CI/CD pipeline consists of several stages: code integration, automated testing, building, and deployment. Docker can be utilized at each stage to improve efficiency and reliability. Consider a simple pipeline configuration:

1. **Code Integration**: Developers push their code changes to a version control system (e.g., Git). Docker images can serve as the base environment for code integration. 2. **Automated Testing**: Test suites are executed within Docker containers to ensure that the code changes do not introduce new bugs or break existing functionality. 3. **Building**: Docker containers package the application, along with its dependencies, into immutable images. 4. **Deployment**: The Docker images are deployed to various environments (staging, production) using orchestrators such as Kubernetes or Docker Swarm.

```
pipeline {
    agent any
    stages {
        stage('Build') {
            steps {
                script {
                    dockerImage = docker.build("my-app:${env.BUILD_ID}")
                }
            }
        }
        stage('Test') {
            steps {
                script {
                    dockerImage.inside {
                        sh 'pytest tests/'
                    }
                }
            }
        }
        stage('Deploy') {
            steps {
                script {
                    docker.withRegistry('https://my-registry.com', 'registryCredentials')
                        {
                        dockerImage.push("${env.BUILD_ID}")
```

```
                    dockerImage.push('latest')
                }
            }
        }
    }
  }
}
```

In the above example, Jenkins, a popular CI/CD tool, orchestrates the pipeline. The Build stage creates a Docker image of the application. The Test stage runs the test suite inside a container derived from this image. Finally, the Deploy stage pushes the tagged image to a Docker registry.

Advantages of Docker in CI/CD:

- **Consistency**: Docker ensures consistency across development, testing, and production environments. Since the same Docker image is used throughout the pipeline, the risk of environment-related issues is minimized. - **Isolation**: Docker containers encapsulate applications and their dependencies, providing an isolated environment for each build and test run. This isolation prevents conflicts between different application versions or dependency sets. - **Reproducibility**: Using Docker images makes builds reproducible. If a build fails, developers can reconstruct the exact environment in which the failure occurred by using the corresponding image. This reproducibility aids in debugging and issue resolution. - **Scalability**: Docker can easily scale CI/CD pipelines. Containers can be spawned, executed, and destroyed rapidly, allowing parallel processing of multiple builds and tests, which reduces overall pipeline execution time.

Consider a more detailed Dockerfile for a Python-based application, used within a CI pipeline:

```
# Base image
FROM python:3.9-slim

# Set environment variables
ENV PYTHONDONTWRITEBYTECODE=1 \
    PYTHONUNBUFFERED=1

# Install dependencies
COPY requirements.txt .
RUN pip install --no-cache-dir -r requirements.txt

# Set work directory
WORKDIR /usr/src/app

# Copy application source code
COPY . .

# Run application
```

```
CMD ["python", "app.py"]
```

In the CI process, this Dockerfile ensures that each build uses a consistent Python environment defined by the Python 3.9 Slim base image. The application's dependencies are installed using the requirements.txt file, and the source code is copied into the container's file system. The final command runs the application.

For a comprehensive understanding of Docker's role in CI/CD, it is essential to explore integration with various CI/CD tools, such as GitLab CI, Travis CI, and CircleCI. Each tool has its configuration syntax and capabilities but embraces Docker for environment consistency.

For example, in GitLab CI, the .gitlab-ci.yml configuration might look like this:

```
stages:
  - build
  - test
  - deploy

variables:
  DOCKER_DRIVER: overlay2

build:
  stage: build
  script:
    - docker build -t my-app:$CI_COMMIT_SHA .

test:
  stage: test
  script:
    - docker run my-app:$CI_COMMIT_SHA pytest tests/

deploy:
  stage: deploy
  script:
    - docker login -u $CI_REGISTRY_USER -p $CI_REGISTRY_PASSWORD
        $CI_REGISTRY
    - docker push $CI_REGISTRY/my-app:$CI_COMMIT_SHA
    - docker push $CI_REGISTRY/my-app:latest
```

This setup reflects a similar structure to the Jenkins pipeline, with stages for building, testing, and deploying the Dockerized application.

Docker's compatibility with various CI/CD systems underscores its flexibility and utility in streamlining software delivery processes. The consistent, isolated, and reproducible environments Docker offers make it an invaluable tool in modern CI/CD pipelines, facilitating faster, more reliable software releases.

12.4 Microservices Architecture with Docker

Microservices architecture is a design paradigm that structures an application as a collection of loosely coupled services. Each of these services is independently deployable, self-contained, and performs a specific function within the overall system. Docker facilitates the implementation of microservices by providing lightweight, portable, and consistent runtime environments.

A significant advantage of using Docker in a microservices architecture is the ability to encapsulate each microservice in a Docker container. This encapsulation ensures that the microservice has all the necessary dependencies bundled within the container, making it supremely portable across various environments, from development to production.

Consider a simple e-commerce application composed of the following microservices:

- **User Service:** Manages user accounts and authentication.
- **Product Service:** Handles product listings, details, and searches.
- **Order Service:** Processes customer orders and maintains order histories.
- **Payment Service:** Manages payment processing and transactions.
- **Inventory Service:** Tracks inventory levels and updates stock information.

Each microservice can be containerized using Docker. Below is the Dockerfile for the Product Service, illustrating how dependencies are included and the service is configured to run.

```
FROM node:14

# Create app directory
WORKDIR /usr/src/app

# Install app dependencies
COPY package*.json ./
RUN npm install

# Bundle app source
COPY . .

# Expose port
```

```
EXPOSE 8080

# Run the service
CMD [ "node", "product_service.js" ]
```

In this Dockerfile:

- We start by pulling the Node.js base image (FROM node:14).
- We set the working directory inside the container (WORKDIR /usr/src/app).
- We copy the dependency files and install them (COPY package*.json ./ followed by RUN npm install).
- We copy the rest of the application source code into the container (COPY . .).
- We expose a port (EXPOSE 8080) that the service will listen on.
- We define the command to run the service when the container starts (CMD ["node", "product_service.js"]).

Once the Dockerfiles are defined for each microservice, we can use docker-compose to manage them collectively. A docker-compose.yml file helps in defining and running multi-container Docker applications. Below is a sample docker-compose.yml file for our e-commerce application:

```
version: '3'

services:
  user-service:
    build: ./user-service
    ports:
      - "5000:5000"
    networks:
      - ecommerce-network

  product-service:
    build: ./product-service
    ports:
      - "8080:8080"
    networks:
      - ecommerce-network

  order-service:
    build: ./order-service
    ports:
      - "9000:9000"
    networks:
      - ecommerce-network
```

```
  payment-service:
    build: ./payment-service
    ports:
      - "7000:7000"
    networks:
      - ecommerce-network

  inventory-service:
    build: ./inventory-service
    ports:
      - "6000:6000"
    networks:
      - ecommerce-network

networks:
  ecommerce-network:
    driver: bridge
```

In this docker-compose.yml file:

- Each microservice is defined under the services section.
- build: specifies the directory containing the Dockerfile for the service.
- ports: maps the internal container ports to the host machine ports for accessibility.
- networks: assigns each service to a custom network named ecommerce-network.
- The networks: section at the bottom defines the custom network configuration.

While setting up microservices using Docker, inter-service communication is critical. Docker networks provide a robust mechanism for this. By placing all services on the same network (in this case, ecommerce-network), Docker ensures that services can discover and communicate with each other via service names.

Docker Compose simplifies orchestration during development, but in production environments, container orchestration platforms like Kubernetes are often employed. Kubernetes provides advanced features such as automated deployment, scaling, load balancing, and self-healing capabilities.

A Kubernetes representation of the same microservices can be achieved through Deployment and Service YAML manifests. Below are brief examples for the Product Service:

```yaml
apiVersion: apps/v1
kind: Deployment
metadata:
  name: product-service
spec:
  replicas: 3
  selector:
    matchLabels:
      app: product-service
  template:
    metadata:
      labels:
        app: product-service
    spec:
      containers:
      - name: product-service
        image: product-service:latest
        ports:
        - containerPort: 8080
```

```yaml
apiVersion: v1
kind: Service
metadata:
  name: product-service
spec:
  type: ClusterIP
  selector:
    app: product-service
  ports:
  - port: 8080
    targetPort: 8080
```

In the Kubernetes Deployment manifest:

- We define how many replicas of the service should run (replicas: 3).
- We specify the Docker image to use (image: product-service:latest).
- We define the ports exposed by the container (ports: - containerPort: 8080).

In the Kubernetes Service manifest:

- We create a Service resource to expose the Deployment.
- The selector matches the Pods defined by the Deployment, routing traffic to them.
- The ports section maps the service port to the container port.

Utilizing Docker and Kubernetes, microservices architectures are not only easier to develop and maintain but also highly scalable and resilient to failures. The containerization of each service provides consistency across various environments and isolates the services, reducing complexities related to dependency management.

12.5 Docker for Database Management

Leveraging Docker for database management provides several advantages, including environment consistency, scalability, and seamless integration. By containerizing databases, developers and database administrators (DBAs) can effortlessly create, deploy, and maintain database instances. This section details methods and best practices for using Docker to manage various types of databases, covering relational and NoSQL databases, backup and restore procedures, and performance optimization.

Relational Databases

Relational databases, such as PostgreSQL, MySQL, and MariaDB, can be efficiently managed with Docker. To illustrate, let's take PostgreSQL as an example and demonstrate the process of setting up and managing a PostgreSQL database container.

To begin, you need to pull the PostgreSQL image from Docker Hub:

```
docker pull postgres
```

Once the image is downloaded, you can run a container and specify necessary configurations, such as environment variables for the username and password:

```
docker run --name postgres-container -e POSTGRES_PASSWORD=mysecretpassword
    -d postgres
```

This command will create and start a PostgreSQL container named 'postgres-container' with the specified password. To verify that the container is running, use the following command:

```
docker ps
```

The output will indicate the status of the PostgreSQL container:

```
CONTAINER ID   IMAGE      COMMAND                  CREATED         STATUS
NAMES
d0e7e1b1a9d3   postgres   "docker-entrypoint.s..."   2 seconds ago   Up 5 seconds
postgres-container
```

To interact with the PostgreSQL database, you can use the 'psql' command-line tool. First, access the running container:

```
docker exec -it postgres-container bash
```

Then, switch to the PostgreSQL user 'postgres' and open the 'psql' shell:

```
psql -U postgres
```

NoSQL Databases

NoSQL databases like MongoDB and Redis are also easily managed within Docker containers. For instance, to set up a MongoDB container, start by pulling the appropriate image from Docker Hub:

```
docker pull mongo
```

Next, run the container:

```
docker run --name mongo-container -d mongo
```

To connect to the MongoDB database, you can use the MongoDB client tool 'mongo'. First, shell into the container:

```
docker exec -it mongo-container bash
```

Then, start the MongoDB client:

```
mongo
```

Backup and Restore Procedures

One of Docker's notable strengths is simplifying backup and restore operations. For relational databases, you can use built-in tools. For instance, to back up a PostgreSQL database, execute the following command by attaching to the running PostgreSQL container:

```
docker exec -t postgres-container pg_dumpall -c -U postgres > db_backup.sql
```

To restore a PostgreSQL database from a backup file:

```
cat db_backup.sql | docker exec -i postgres-container psql -U postgres
```

Similarly, for MongoDB, you can utilize 'mongodump' and 'mongorestore' tools for backup and restore. To back up a MongoDB database:

```
docker exec mongo-container mongodump --archive=/data/db/dump.archive
docker cp mongo-container:/data/db/dump.archive dump.archive
```

To restore from the backup archive:

```
docker cp dump.archive mongo-container:/data/db/dump.archive
docker exec mongo-container mongorestore --archive=/data/db/dump.archive
```

Performance Optimization

Performance optimization in a containerized environment involves several considerations such as resource allocation, storage management, and network configurations. Docker allows you to limit resources like CPU and memory when running containers. For example, to limit a PostgreSQL container to use only 1 CPU and 512MB of memory:

```
docker run --name postgres-container -e POSTGRES_PASSWORD=mysecretpassword
    -d --cpus=".5" --memory="512m" postgres
```

For storage optimization, use Docker volumes to persist data outside the container's filesystem. This not only ensures data persistence across container restarts but also potentially improves I/O performance by using optimized storage drivers. Create a volume and use it in the PostgreSQL container:

```
docker volume create pgdata
docker run --name postgres-container -e POSTGRES_PASSWORD=mysecretpassword
    -d -v pgdata:/var/lib/postgresql/data postgres
```

Networking configurations can also impact performance. Properly configuring Docker networks can lead to efficient communication between database containers and other services. Typically, a user-defined bridge network is recommended for connecting containers in a more controlled environment:

```
docker network create my_custom_network
docker run --name postgres-container --network my_custom_network -e
    POSTGRES_PASSWORD=mysecretpassword -d postgres
```

Utilizing these techniques ensures that Docker containers hosting databases achieve optimal performance, reliability, and manageability.

12.6 Running Legacy Applications with Docker

Legacy applications are often essential to an organization's operations, yet running and maintaining these applications can pose significant challenges. These challenges include compatibility issues with modern infrastructure, difficulty in replicating development and production environments, and ensuring security and compliance. Docker provides a robust solution for encapsulating legacy applications, allowing them to run in isolated environments that mimic their original runtime conditions. This section delves into techniques and best practices for containerizing legacy applications using Docker, ensuring their longevity and operational stability.

Assessing Compatibility

Before containerizing a legacy application, it is crucial to conduct a thorough assessment of its components and dependencies. This includes the operating system, libraries, and middleware that the application depends on. Identifying these elements helps in creating a Docker environment that replicates the original runtime as closely as possible.

```
dpkg --get-selections | grep -v deinstall > installed-packages.txt
```

The above command generates a list of installed packages in a Debian-based system. A similar approach can be taken for other Linux distributions or even Windows environments. This package list serves as a valuable reference when constructing the Docker image.

Creating a Dockerfile for a Legacy Application

A Dockerfile is a script that contains a series of instructions on how to build a Docker image. For a legacy application, the Dockerfile should replicate the original environment as closely as possible. Begin by selecting a base image that matches the operating system and version the legacy application was initially built upon.

```
FROM ubuntu:14.04

# Set environment variables
ENV DEBIAN_FRONTEND noninteractive

# Install dependencies
COPY installed-packages.txt /tmp/
RUN xargs -a /tmp/installed-packages.txt apt-get install -y

# Copy application files
COPY legacy-app /opt/legacy-app
```

```
# Set working directory
WORKDIR /opt/legacy-app

# Expose necessary ports
EXPOSE 8080

# Run the application
CMD ["./start-legacy-app.sh"]
```

This Dockerfile uses Ubuntu 14.04 as the base image and installs the packages listed in the 'installed-packages.txt' file. It then copies the legacy application files into the image, sets the appropriate working directory, exposes necessary ports, and defines the command to run the application.

Addressing Dependency Resolution

Many legacy applications depend on specific versions of libraries or middleware. Pinning these dependencies within the Dockerfile ensures consistency. For instance, if a specific version of a library is required, it can be explicitly installed:

```
RUN apt-get update && apt-get install -y libxyz=1.2.3-4
```

If the legacy application relies on older versions of software that are no longer available in standard repositories, alternative methods such as custom repositories or direct downloads may be necessary.

Network and Connectivity Configuration

Networking and connectivity configurations are critical considerations when containerizing legacy applications. Ensure that all network endpoints and databases the application interacts with are accessible from within the Docker container. This may involve setting up Docker networks or modifying the application's configuration to use environment variables for dynamic setup.

```
# Set environment variables for network endpoints
ENV DB_HOST=db.internal
ENV DB_PORT=5432

# Run the application with environment configurations
CMD ["bash", "-c", "envsubst < /opt/legacy-app/config.template > /opt/legacy-app/
    config && ./start-legacy-app.sh"]
```

Testing and Validation

Rigorous testing is essential to validate that the containerized legacy application functions correctly. Create a comprehensive suite of tests encompassing unit tests, integration tests, and end-to-end tests. Utilize Docker Compose to simulate production-like environments during testing.

```
version: '3.8'
services:
  legacy-app:
    build: .
    ports:
      - "8080:8080"
    networks:
      - app-network

networks:
  app-network:
```

Run the tests to ensure the application behaves as expected within the container. Address any issues that arise, iterating on the Dockerfile and associated configurations as necessary.

Deployment and Maintenance

Once validated, the Docker image can be deployed to a production environment. Ongoing maintenance involves regular updates to the Docker image, ensuring the base image and dependencies are kept current with security patches. Automating the build and deployment process using CI/CD tools can streamline these updates.

Typical CI/CD pipelines include stages such as building the Docker image, running tests, and deploying the image to a container orchestrator such as Kubernetes.

```
# Build the Docker image
docker build -t my-legacy-app:latest .

# Run tests
docker run --rm -v $(pwd)/tests:/tests my-legacy-app:latest ./run-tests.sh

# Push the image to a registry
docker tag my-legacy-app:latest my-registry/my-legacy-app:latest
docker push my-registry/my-legacy-app:latest

# Deploy the image using Kubernetes
kubectl set image deployment/legacy-app legacy-app=my-registry/my-legacy-app:latest
```

By containerizing legacy applications with Docker, organizations can ensure the continued operational viability of these critical systems. Docker provides consistent, isolated environments that replicate the original runtime conditions, simplifying maintenance and deployment while enhancing security and compliance.

12.7 Docker for Data Science and ML Workflows

Containerization has emerged as a pivotal element in managing the intricate dependencies and environments required for data science and machine learning (ML) workflows. Docker, in particular, offers a streamlined solution for reproducibility, scalability, and collaboration in the data science ecosystem. This section delves into practical aspects and methodologies to leverage Docker effectively for data science and ML applications.

Data science projects often involve a myriad of software tools, libraries, and frameworks. Managing these dependencies can be cumbersome, especially when collaborating across different environments. Docker addresses this by encapsulating the entire environment, ensuring that the code runs consistently regardless of the underlying system. Consider a Python-based data science project that utilizes libraries such as NumPy, pandas, scikit-learn, and TensorFlow. By using Docker, we can create an isolated environment that includes all required dependencies.

```
FROM python:3.8-slim

# Set environment variables
ENV PYTHONUNBUFFERED=1

# Set the working directory
WORKDIR /app

# Copy the requirements file and install dependencies
COPY requirements.txt .
RUN pip install -r requirements.txt

# Copy the rest of the application code
COPY . .

# Command to run the application
CMD ["python", "main.py"]
```

In this Dockerfile, the base image python:3.8-slim provides a lightweight Python environment. The WORKDIR instruction sets the working directory inside the container to /app. The COPY instructions transfer the requirements.txt file and install the specified Python dependencies, followed by copying the application's code into the container.

This encapsulation is particularly useful in machine learning workflows where consistency is crucial. For instance, model training might be performed on a high-performance cloud instance, while inference could occur on an edge device. Docker ensures that the environment on both platforms is identical, mitigating any discrepancies due to differing library versions or system configurations.

Data science workflows often involve multiple stages, such as data preprocessing, model training, evaluation, and deployment. Each stage can be encapsulated within a Docker container, facilitating modularity and reusability.

```
FROM python:3.8-slim

# Set environment variables
ENV PYTHONUNBUFFERED=1

# Set the working directory
WORKDIR /preprocess

# Copy the requirements file and install dependencies
COPY requirements.txt .
RUN pip install -r requirements.txt

# Copy the preprocessing script
COPY preprocess.py .

# Command to run the preprocessing script
CMD ["python", "preprocess.py"]
```

The above example demonstrates a Dockerfile for the data preprocessing stage. Similar Dockerfiles can be created for subsequent stages like training and evaluation, each tailored to execute their specific tasks. This modular approach enhances clarity and simplifies debugging and updating individual stages.

One significant challenge in data science is ensuring reproducibility. Docker's advantage is evident here as it allows for environment versioning. By specifying the exact versions of the base image and dependencies, one can recreate the environment precisely. For example, a researcher can share a Docker image used for their experiments, allowing peers to replicate the results exactly:

```
# Build the Docker image from Dockerfile
docker build -t data-preprocess:latest .

# Run a container from the built image
docker run --rm data-preprocess:latest
```

The –rm flag ensures that the container is removed after execution, maintaining a clean system. This command sequence encapsulates the workflow environment, thus making it portable and reproducible.

For machine learning model deployment, Docker can integrate seamlessly into various deployment frameworks. For instance, deploying a trained neural network model using TensorFlow Serving in a Docker container involves the following Dockerfile:

```
FROM tensorflow/serving:latest

# Copy the model to be served
COPY models/my_model /models/my_model

# Set environment variables for TensorFlow Serving
ENV MODEL_NAME=my_model

# Expose the port TensorFlow Serving will run on
EXPOSE 8501

# Command to run TensorFlow Serving
CMD ["tensorflow_model_server", "--rest_api_port=8501", "--model_name=
    my_model", "--model_base_path=/models/my_model"]
```

With this configuration, TensorFlow Serving will launch within a container, making the model accessible via an HTTP REST API. This ensures that the deployment environment is consistent and can be easily scaled or updated.

Moreover, Docker's role extends to collaborative aspects of data science. Utilizing Docker Compose allows orchestration of multi-container setups where different services are interconnected. For a comprehensive ML pipeline, one can design a docker-compose.yml file that configures containers for data storage, preprocessing, training, and serving.

```
version: '3.8'

services:
  db:
    image: postgres:latest
    environment:
      POSTGRES_USER: user
      POSTGRES_PASSWORD: password
      POSTGRES_DB: data

  preprocess:
    build: ./preprocess
    volumes:
      - ./data:/data
    depends_on:
      - db

  train:
    build: ./train
    volumes:
      - ./data:/data
    depends_on:
      - preprocess

  serve:
    build: ./serve
    ports:
      - "8501:8501"
    depends_on:
```

```
  - train
```

This docker-compose.yml file defines a multi-container application where a PostgreSQL database container is used for data storage while other containers perform preprocessing, training, and serving tasks. This orchestration facilitates seamless transitions between different stages of the data science workflow.

When executed, the following command will initiate the entire pipeline:

```
docker-compose up
```

By utilizing Docker for data science and ML workflows, practitioners can achieve greater efficiency, consistency, and reproducibility. Docker not only simplifies environment management but also enhances collaboration, deployment, and scalability of data-driven applications.

12.8 Managing Big Data Applications with Docker

Docker provides a versatile framework for managing big data applications, offering foundational improvements in terms of scalability, reproducibility, and ease of deployment. Leveraging containerization, big data applications can be efficiently orchestrated and managed, enabling optimal resource utilization and mitigating common challenges associated with distributed data processing systems.

Big data applications inherently require high computational power and proficient data management strategies. Docker's lightweight containers enable the creation and deployment of scalable, isolated environments, which alleviates the resource constraints and dependency management issues that traditionally accompany big data initiatives.

Hadoop and Docker
Hadoop is a framework that allows distributed processing of large data sets across clusters of computers. Installing and configuring Hadoop can be complex due to its dependencies on various libraries and components. Utilizing Docker for Hadoop configurations simplifies this process.

Below is an example Dockerfile for setting up a Hadoop environment:

```
FROM ubuntu:20.04

# Install Java
```

```
RUN apt-get update && apt-get install -y openjdk-8-jdk

# Set environment variables
ENV JAVA_HOME=/usr/lib/jvm/java-8-openjdk-amd64
ENV HADOOP_VERSION=3.2.2
ENV HADOOP_HOME=/opt/hadoop

# Install Hadoop
RUN wget https://downloads.apache.org/hadoop/common/hadoop-
      $HADOOP_VERSION/hadoop-$HADOOP_VERSION.tar.gz \
   && tar -xzvf hadoop-$HADOOP_VERSION.tar.gz -C /opt \
   && ln -s /opt/hadoop-$HADOOP_VERSION /opt/hadoop \
   && rm hadoop-$HADOOP_VERSION.tar.gz

# Set Hadoop environment variables
ENV PATH=$PATH:$HADOOP_HOME/bin:$HADOOP_HOME/sbin

# Expose ports
EXPOSE 8088 8042 50070 50075
```

Once the Docker image is built from this Dockerfile, it can be instantiated to create multiple nodes in a Hadoop cluster.

Spark and Docker

Apache Spark is another prominent big data processing engine that benefits from Docker. Spark's ability to process data in-memory makes it an ideal candidate for containerized environments, which provide isolated and reproducible setups. Below is an example of Dockerfile for setting up a Spark environment:

```
FROM openjdk:8-jdk

# Define Spark version
ENV SPARK_VERSION=3.1.2
ENV HADOOP_VERSION=3.2

# Download and install Spark
RUN wget https://www.apache.org/dyn/closer.cgi/spark/spark-$SPARK_VERSION/
      spark-$SPARK_VERSION-bin-hadoop$HADOOP_VERSION.tgz \
   && tar -xvf spark-$SPARK_VERSION-bin-hadoop$HADOOP_VERSION.tgz -C /
         opt/ \
   && mv /opt/spark-$SPARK_VERSION-bin-hadoop$HADOOP_VERSION /opt/
         spark \
   && rm spark-$SPARK_VERSION-bin-hadoop$HADOOP_VERSION.tgz

# Set Spark environment variables
ENV SPARK_HOME=/opt/spark
ENV PATH=$PATH:$SPARK_HOME/bin

# Expose ports
EXPOSE 7077 8080
```

Container orchestration tools like Kubernetes can further enhance the deployment and management of Spark clusters, facilitating dynamic scaling and resource allocation based on demand.

Using Docker Compose for Big Data Stacks

Docker Compose simplifies multi-container Docker applications by defining services, networks, and volumes in a single YAML file. Below is a basic example of a Docker Compose file for orchestrating a Hadoop and Spark cluster:

```
version: '3'
services:
  hadoop-namenode:
    image: hadoop:3.2.2
    container_name: hadoop-namenode
    ports:
      - "50070:50070"
      - "8088:8088"

  hadoop-datanode:
    image: hadoop:3.2.2
    container_name: hadoop-datanode
    depends_on:
      - hadoop-namenode
    ports:
      - "50075:50075"
      - "8042:8042"

  spark-master:
    image: spark:3.1.2
    container_name: spark-master
    ports:
      - "7077:7077"
      - "8080:8080"

  spark-worker:
    image: spark:3.1.2
    container_name: spark-worker
    depends_on:
      - spark-master
    environment:
      - SPARK_MASTER=spark://spark-master:7077
```

By declaring services like hadoop-namenode, hadoop-datanode, spark-master, and spark-worker, this Docker Compose configuration enables the orchestration and scaling of a comprehensive big data stack with minimal manual intervention.

Benefits of Dockerizing Big Data Applications

Dockerizing big data applications provides several advantages:

- **Consistency:** Containers ensure that applications run the same way regardless of the environment, minimizing discrepancies between development, testing, and production.
- **Isolation:** Each container runs in its own isolated environment, reducing the risk of conflicts between applications.
- **Scalability:** Containers can be easily scaled horizontally by

adding more instances to meet increased demand.

- **Resource Efficiency:** Containers are lightweight and use system resources more efficiently compared to traditional virtual machines.

- **Simplified Dependency Management:** Docker images encapsulate all dependencies within the container, simplifying the setup process and eliminating the need to manage dependencies individually.

Monitoring and Maintenance

Effective monitoring and maintenance of big data applications are crucial for ensuring their reliability and performance. Tools such as Prometheus and Grafana can be integrated into Dockerized big data environments for robust monitoring solutions.

Consider the following Docker Compose configuration for adding Prometheus and Grafana to the stack:

```
version: '3'
services:
  prometheus:
    image: prom/prometheus:latest
    ports:
      - "9090:9090"
    volumes:
      - ./prometheus.yml:/etc/prometheus/prometheus.yml

  grafana:
    image: grafana/grafana:latest
    ports:
      - "3000:3000"
```

```
# prometheus.yml Configuration
global:
  scrape_interval: 15s

scrape_configs:
  - job_name: 'spark'
    static_configs:
      - targets: ['spark-master:8080', 'spark-worker:8081']
```

This setup deploys Prometheus and Grafana containers, enabling the monitoring of Spark components by scraping metrics from the Spark master and worker nodes.

Integration of Docker with big data applications not only simplifies deployment but also improves the scalability, reliability, and performance monitoring of these applications, ultimately making the management of large-scale data processing systems more efficient and effective.

12.9 Hosting Web Applications with Docker

When hosting web applications, Docker offers a versatile and efficient platform that addresses many of the challenges traditionally associated with deployment and scalability. This section delves into the practical aspects of using Docker to host web applications, covering containerization of web services, load balancing, network configurations, and continuous deployment strategies.

Docker simplifies the process of creating a consistent environment by encapsulating applications and their dependencies within containers. This approach ensures that web applications behave identically in development, testing, and production environments, greatly reducing the notorious "it works on my machine" problem. A fundamental step is to define a Dockerfile for the web application.

```
# Use the official Node.js image from the Docker Hub
FROM node:14

# Create and set the working directory
WORKDIR /usr/src/app

# Copy the package.json and package-lock.json files
COPY package*.json ./

# Install dependencies
RUN npm install

# Copy the rest of the application code
COPY . .

# Expose the port the app runs on
EXPOSE 3000

# Define the command to run the app
CMD ["node", "app.js"]
```

This Dockerfile outlines a multi-step process to build an image containing a Node.js application. It starts by using an official Node.js base image, sets up a working directory, copies dependency files, installs the dependencies, and finally copies the application code. The EXPOSE instruction indicates which port the container will listen on at runtime, and the CMD instruction specifies the command to start the application.

To build the Docker image from this Dockerfile, the following command is used:

```
docker build -t my-node-app .
```

Once the image is built, you can run a container using:

```
docker run -p 3000:3000 my-node-app
```

Here, the -p option maps port 3000 on the host to port 3000 in the container, making the web application accessible at http://localhost:3000.

One of Docker's strengths is its ability to easily orchestrate multi-container applications using docker-compose. A docker-compose.yml file can be used to define and manage multiple services. Below is an example for a web application with both a front-end service (Node.js) and a back-end service (MongoDB).

```
version: "3"
services:
  web:
    build: .
    ports:
      - "3000:3000"
    depends_on:
      - db

  db:
    image: mongo:4.2
    volumes:
      - data:/data/db

volumes:
  data:
```

In this configuration, docker-compose will build the web service from the Dockerfile and run a MongoDB container from an official image. The depends_on instruction ensures the web container starts after the database container is up and running. Data persistence for MongoDB is managed through Docker volumes, which are defined under the volumes key.

Executing the docker-compose configuration is straightforward:

```
docker-compose up
```

This command will bring up both the web application and the MongoDB database, with appropriate networking between them.

Additionally, for production environments where high availability and load balancing are crucial, Docker Swarm or Kubernetes can be employed. These orchestrators manage clusters of containers, distribute traffic, and handle failovers. A fundamental concept in load balancing involves distributing incoming requests across multiple instances of the application to ensure no single instance is overwhelmed.

Below is a simple Kubernetes deployment example that takes the previous web application and scales it across multiple pods:

```
apiVersion: apps/v1
kind: Deployment
metadata:
  name: web-deployment
spec:
  replicas: 3
  selector:
    matchLabels:
      app: web
  template:
    metadata:
      labels:
        app: web
    spec:
      containers:
      - name: web
        image: my-node-app:latest
        ports:
        - containerPort: 3000
```

This configuration file defines a Kubernetes Deployment for the web application, specifying that three replicas (pods) should be running. The selector matches the pods with the app: web label, and each pod runs the specified Docker image with the application exposed on port 3000.

To deploy this configuration, use:

```
kubectl apply -f web-deployment.yaml
```

For handling external traffic, Kubernetes Ingress or services will provide routing and load balancing.

```
apiVersion: v1
kind: Service
metadata:
  name: web-service
spec:
  type: LoadBalancer
  selector:
    app: web
  ports:
  - protocol: TCP
    port: 80
    targetPort: 3000
```

This Service configuration defines a LoadBalancer service that routes traffic from port 80 on the host to port 3000 on the pods labeled with app: web.

By integrating Docker with modern CI/CD pipelines, automated build, test, and deployment cycles can be created. This is facilitated by tools like Jenkins, GitLab CI/CD, and GitHub Actions. A typical CI/CD pipeline includes automated testing to ensure code quality, followed by containerization and deployment to staging or production environments. The following snippet illustrates a simplified GitLab CI/CD configuration for Docker:

```
stages:
  - build
  - test
  - deploy

build:
  stage: build
  script:
    - docker build -t my-node-app:latest .

test:
  stage: test
  script:
    - docker run --rm my-node-app:latest npm test

deploy:
  stage: deploy
  script:
    - docker push my-node-app:latest
    - kubectl apply -f web-deployment.yaml
```

This configuration defines a pipeline consisting of build, test, and deploy stages. The build stage builds the Docker image, the test stage runs tests inside a container, and the deploy stage pushes the image to a registry and applies Kubernetes deployment configurations.

The infrastructure capabilities provided by Docker make it an essential tool for hosting web applications, ensuring consistent and repeatable deployments, scalability, and operational efficiency.

12.10 Docker for IoT Applications

The integration of Docker technology within Internet of Things (IoT) applications has transformed how these systems are developed, deployed, and maintained. Docker provides significant advantages in terms of scalability, isolation, and resource efficiency. When it comes to IoT, these characteristics are essential due to the diverse and resource-constrained nature of many IoT devices.

IoT systems involve numerous devices that collect and transmit data, often requiring real-time processing and analysis. Docker containers are ideal for running these processing tasks due to their lightweight nature and rapid deployment capabilities. Furthermore, Docker's ability to encapsulate dependencies and application code into a single container ensures consistent behavior across different devices and platforms.

1. Simplifying Deployment on Edge Devices

Edge computing in IoT involves processing data near the source of data generation to reduce latency and bandwidth usage. Docker containers make it feasible to run complex applications on edge devices with limited resources. By containerizing applications, developers can ensure that the precise stack running on their development environment will function in the same manner on the edge devices.

```
# Build the Docker container image
docker build -t my-iot-app:latest .

# Run the Docker container on the edge device
docker run -d --name iot-container -p 8080:8080 my-iot-app:latest
```

In this example, the Docker container is built and then deployed to an edge device, enabling seamless execution of the application with all its dependencies encapsulated within the container.

2. Managing Microservices in IoT Solutions

IoT solutions often utilize microservices architectures to enhance modularity and scalability. Each microservice can be containerized, promoting isolation and efficient resource utilization. This approach allows for independent scaling, updating, and deployment of each service, catering specifically to the dynamic requirements of IoT applications.

```
version: '3'
services:
  sensor-data-service:
    image: sensor-data-service:latest
    ports:
      - "5000:5000"

  data-processing-service:
    image: data-processing-service:latest
    ports:
      - "5001:5001"

  alert-service:
    image: alert-service:latest
    ports:
      - "5002:5002"
```

Using the provided Docker Compose configuration, multiple microservices essential for an IoT application—such as sensor data handling, data processing, and alerting—can be easily orchestrated and managed.

3. Over-the-Air (OTA) Updates

Docker facilitates Over-the-Air (OTA) updates for IoT devices, simplifying the distribution of new features and security patches. Instead of updating individual dependencies or configuration files, a new version of the container image is pushed to the device.

```
# Pull the updated Docker container image
docker pull my-iot-app:latest

# Stop the currently running container
docker stop iot-container

# Remove the old container
docker rm iot-container

# Run the updated container
docker run -d --name iot-container -p 8080:8080 my-iot-app:latest
```

These commands demonstrate the simplicity of updating IoT devices by deploying a new Docker container image, thus minimizing system downtime and ensuring the device runs the latest version of the application.

4. Enhanced Security

IoT devices are particularly vulnerable to security breaches due to their widespread distribution and diverse operating environments. Docker ensures enhanced security through container isolation, reducing the attack surface by limiting each container's access to the host system.

```
# Run the Docker container with restricted privileges
docker run -d --name secure-iot-container --security-opt no-new-privileges:true my-iot-
    app:latest
```

The no-new-privileges option ensures that the processes running within the container cannot acquire additional privileges, enhancing the security of the IoT application.

5. Resource Optimization

IoT devices often have limited computational resources. Docker's lightweight nature allows for efficient utilization of CPU, memory, and storage. It enables multiple containers to run on a single device without significant overhead, meaning that IoT systems can handle more tasks simultaneously compared to traditional VM-based approaches.

```
# Display the resource usage of all running Docker containers
docker stats
```

The docker stats command provides a comprehensive view of the resource consumption of each running container, enabling continuous monitoring and optimization of the system's performance.

6. Data Aggregation and Analysis

Docker assists in the aggregation and analysis of data collected from multiple IoT devices. Containers can run data processing pipelines, machine learning models, and analytic tools necessary for deriving insights from the collected data.

```
# Deploy a containerized data aggregation service
docker run -d --name data-aggregator -p 6000:6000 data-aggregation-service:latest
```

A data aggregation service within a Docker container can continuously process incoming data from various IoT devices, making it easier to handle large-scale data streams and extract valuable information.

7. Edge and Cloud Synergy

Docker enables smooth interoperability between edge computing and cloud infrastructure, facilitating a hybrid approach to IoT application deployment. Containers can be moved seamlessly between local devices and cloud servers, optimizing where computational tasks are executed based on real-time requirements and resource availability.

```
# Tag and push the Docker container image to a cloud registry
docker tag my-iot-app:latest mycloudregistry/my-iot-app:latest
docker push mycloudregistry/my-iot-app:latest

# Pull and run the container image on an edge device
docker pull mycloudregistry/my-iot-app:latest
docker run -d --name iot-container -p 8080:8080 mycloudregistry/my-iot-app:latest

# Pull and run the container image on a cloud server
ssh user@cloud-server "docker pull mycloudregistry/my-iot-app:latest && docker run -d
      --name iot-container -p 8080:8080 mycloudregistry/my-iot-app:latest"
```

This example highlights the fluidity with which Docker containers facilitate the deployment of IoT applications across both edge devices and cloud environments.

Overall, the convergence of Docker with IoT applications unlocks unprecedented possibilities in terms of consistency, security, and scalability, revolutionizing how IoT systems are deployed and managed.

12.11 Cloud Deployment with Docker

Deploying Docker containers on cloud platforms enables developers to build, ship, and run distributed applications with high reliability and scalability. The cloud environment can provide autoscaling, load balancing, and managed services that are essential for production-grade applications. This section delves into the key aspects of leveraging Docker in cloud deployments, discussing various cloud providers, container orchestration platforms, and strategies for optimizing deployment.

Container orchestration is fundamental for managing containerized applications in the cloud. Kubernetes has emerged as the leading orchestration platform and integrates seamlessly with Docker. Most major cloud providers offer managed Kubernetes services, simplifying the deployment process. For example, Google Kubernetes Engine (GKE), Amazon Elastic Kubernetes Service (EKS), and Azure Kubernetes Service (AKS) provide automated Kubernetes clusters with integrated monitoring and logging capabilities. Utilizing these services allows for automated deployment, scaling, and operation of containerized applications.

To deploy Docker containers on a Kubernetes cluster, one must define Kubernetes objects such as Pods, Deployments, and Services. Below is an example of a Kubernetes Deployment YAML file that specifies a stateless application deploying a Docker container:

```
apiVersion: apps/v1
kind: Deployment
metadata:
  name: example-deployment
spec:
  replicas: 3
  selector:
    matchLabels:
      app: example
  template:
    metadata:
      labels:
        app: example
    spec:
      containers:
      - name: example-container
        image: example/image:latest
        ports:
        - containerPort: 80
```

This file describes a Deployment that ensures three replicas of the example-container are running at any given time, using the example/image:latest Docker image. Kubernetes automatically handles scaling and self-healing, restarting containers that fail or become unresponsive.

Networking in cloud deployments is managed through Services and Ingress resources. A Kubernetes Service enables communication between different components of an application, while an Ingress resource manages external access to the services, typically via HTTP or HTTPS. Below is the YAML for a Service and an Ingress resource:

```
apiVersion: v1
kind: Service
metadata:
  name: example-service
spec:
  selector:
    app: example
  ports:
    - protocol: TCP
      port: 80
      targetPort: 80
  type: LoadBalancer
---
apiVersion: networking.k8s.io/v1
kind: Ingress
metadata:
  name: example-ingress
spec:
  rules:
  - host: example.com
    http:
      paths:
      - path: /
        pathType: Prefix
        backend:
          service:
            name: example-service
            port:
              number: 80
```

In this configuration, the example-service is exposed as a LoadBalancer, allowing it to receive external traffic. The example-ingress defines a rule that directs traffic from example.com to the example-service at port 80. This setup is common in cloud deployments where managed load balancers are utilized.

Another critical aspect of cloud deployment with Docker is the integration with Continuous Integration/Continuous Deployment (CI/CD) pipelines. CI/CD tools such as Jenkins, GitLab CI, and GitHub Actions can automate the build, test, and deployment process. Docker images are built and pushed to a Docker registry, which can be public (Docker Hub) or private (AWS ECR, Google Container Registry). Below is an example of a Jenkins Pipeline script that builds and deploys a Docker image to a Kubernetes cluster:

```
pipeline {
  agent any
  environment {
    registry = "example/image"
    registryCredential = 'docker-hub-credentials'
    dockerImage = ''
  }
  stages {
    stage('Clone repository') {
      steps {
        git 'https://github.com/example/repository.git'
```

```
      }
    }
    stage('Build Docker Image') {
      steps {
        script {
          dockerImage = docker.build registry
        }
      }
    }
    stage('Push Docker Image') {
      steps {
        script {
          docker.withRegistry( '', registryCredential ) {
            dockerImage.push("${env.BUILD_NUMBER}")
            dockerImage.push("latest")
          }
        }
      }
    }
    stage('Deploy to Kubernetes') {
      steps {
        script {
          kubernetesDeploy(
            configs: 'k8s/deployment.yaml',
            kubeconfigId: 'kubeconfig-credentials'
          )
        }
      }
    }
  }
}
```

This Jenkins Pipeline performs several stages: cloning the repository, building the Docker image, pushing the image to Docker Hub, and deploying it to a Kubernetes cluster using a pre-configured kubeconfig.

Monitoring and logging are integral components of managing Docker deployments on the cloud. Prometheus and Grafana are popular tools for monitoring Kubernetes clusters, providing insights into application performance and resource utilization. Fluentd or ELK (Elasticsearch, Logstash, and Kibana) stacks are often used for log aggregation and analysis. Below are the configurations to deploy Prometheus and Grafana on Kubernetes:

```
apiVersion: apps/v1
kind: Deployment
metadata:
  name: prometheus
spec:
  replicas: 1
  selector:
    matchLabels:
      app: prometheus
  template:
    metadata:
    labels:
      app: prometheus
```

```
    spec:
      containers:
      - name: prometheus
        image: prom/prometheus:latest
        ports:
        - containerPort: 9090
---
apiVersion: v1
kind: Service
metadata:
  name: prometheus
spec:
  selector:
    app: prometheus
  ports:
    - protocol: TCP
      port: 9090
      targetPort: 9090
---
apiVersion: apps/v1
kind: Deployment
metadata:
  name: grafana
spec:
  replicas: 1
  selector:
    matchLabels:
      app: grafana
  template:
    metadata:
      labels:
        app: grafana
    spec:
      containers:
      - name: grafana
        image: grafana/grafana:latest
        ports:
        - containerPort: 3000
---
apiVersion: v1
kind: Service
metadata:
  name: grafana
spec:
  selector:
    app: grafana
  ports:
    - protocol: TCP
      port: 3000
      targetPort: 3000
```

These configurations deploy Prometheus and Grafana as single-instance Deployments with corresponding Services. Prometheus scrapes metrics from various endpoints and Grafana visualizes these metrics, allowing administrators to create dashboards for monitoring system and application performance.

Efficient cloud deployment with Docker also involves using Infrastructure as Code (IaC) tools such as Terraform or AWS CloudFormation.

These tools manage cloud infrastructure environments in a consistent manner, enabling version control and automated deployments. Below is a simple Terraform configuration to create an Amazon EKS cluster:

```
provider "aws" {
  region = "us-west-2"
}

resource "aws_eks_cluster" "eks_cluster" {
  name = "example-cluster"
  role_arn = aws_iam_role.eks_role.arn

  vpc_config {
    subnet_ids = [aws_subnet.subnet1.id, aws_subnet.subnet2.id]
  }
}

resource "aws_iam_role" "eks_role" {
  name = "eks-role"
  assume_role_policy = <<EOF
{
  "Version": "2012-10-17",
  "Statement": [
    {
      "Action": "sts:AssumeRole",
      "Principal": {
        "Service": "eks.amazonaws.com"
      },
      "Effect": "Allow",
      "Sid": ""
    }
  ]
}
EOF
}
```

This Terraform script configures an EKS cluster with the necessary IAM role and VPC settings. By utilizing IaC, one can reproduce and modify cloud environments programmatically, ensuring consistency across development, testing, and production stages.

These aspects form the backbone of deploying Docker containers on the cloud, leveraging container orchestration, CI/CD, monitoring, and IaC. This comprehensive approach ensures efficient, scalable, and reliable applications.

```
deployment.apps/example-deployment created
service/example-service created
ingress.networking.k8s.io/example-ingress created
deployment.apps/prometheus created
service/prometheus created
deployment.apps/grafana created
service/grafana created
aws_eks_cluster.example-cluster: Creation complete after 12m
```

12.12 Docker in Multi-Cloud Environments

As organizations increasingly seek agility and resilience in their IT infrastructure, the adoption of multi-cloud strategies has become a significant trend. A multi-cloud environment involves the use of multiple cloud computing services from different providers, enabling organizations to leverage the strengths and capabilities of each while mitigating the risks of vendor lock-in. Docker, with its containerization technology, plays a pivotal role in facilitating the deployment, management, and orchestration of applications across these diverse cloud ecosystems.

Advantages of Multi-Cloud Deployments

A multi-cloud strategy offers several key advantages:

- **Resilience and Redundancy:** By distributing workloads across multiple cloud providers, organizations can enhance their resilience against service outages and disruptions. This redundancy ensures continuous availability and mitigates risks associated with single points of failure.

- **Cost Optimization:** Different cloud providers offer varying pricing models and cost structures. Multi-cloud environments allow organizations to optimize costs by strategically deploying workloads to the most cost-effective provider.

- **Regulatory Compliance:** Certain regions and industries have specific compliance requirements that can be better addressed by using local cloud providers. Multi-cloud strategies facilitate adherence to these regulations by enabling data storage and processing in compliant regions.

- **Best-of-Breed Services:** Different cloud providers excel in different areas. A multi-cloud approach enables organizations to leverage the best services from each provider, such as advanced AI capabilities from one and superior storage solutions from another.

- **Avoidance of Vendor Lock-In:** Relying on a single cloud provider can lead to dependency on their services and technology stack. Multi-cloud strategies mitigate this risk by ensuring that applications are portable and compatible with multiple environments.

Docker's Role in Multi-Cloud Environments

Docker containers encapsulate applications and their dependencies in a lightweight, portable format, which significantly simplifies the deployment and management of applications across different cloud environments. Docker's portability ensures that containers can run consistently regardless of the underlying infrastructure or cloud provider, thus enabling true multi-cloud compatibility.

Deployment Strategies

There are several strategies for deploying Docker containers in multi-cloud environments:

- **Direct Deployment:** Containers are directly deployed to the infrastructure of different cloud providers using Docker tools. For example, using Docker Compose to orchestrate multi-container applications across clouds.
- **Container Orchestration:** Tools like Kubernetes, Swarm, and Mesosphere can manage containerized applications across multiple cloud environments. These orchestration tools abstract away the complexities of managing containers at scale, such as load balancing, auto-scaling, and service discovery.

A common example of deploying Docker in a multi-cloud environment involves the use of Kubernetes, an open-source container orchestration platform. Kubernetes supports multi-cloud deployments by providing a consistent layer of abstraction over the underlying infrastructure, enabling seamless management of containerized applications across various providers.

```
apiVersion: apps/v1
kind: Deployment
metadata:
  name: nginx-deployment
  labels:
    app: nginx
spec:
  replicas: 2
  selector:
    matchLabels:
      app: nginx
  template:
    metadata:
      labels:
        app: nginx
    spec:
      containers:
      - name: nginx
        image: nginx:1.14.2
        ports:
        - containerPort: 80
```

In the example above, an Nginx deployment is defined in a Kubernetes manifest file, which can be deployed to multiple Kubernetes clusters running on different cloud providers. The same manifest file can be applied uniformly across clouds, ensuring consistent deployment and operation.

Networking in Multi-Cloud Deployments

Networking is a critical aspect of multi-cloud deployments. Interconnecting multiple cloud environments involves dealing with various networking challenges, such as handling different subnet configurations, ensuring low-latency communication, and maintaining secure connections.

Docker and Kubernetes support several networking solutions to address these challenges:

- **VPN Gateways:** Establish secure connections between different cloud environments using VPN gateways. This approach provides encrypted communication channels between distributed services.
- **Service Mesh:** Implement a service mesh to manage and secure communication between microservices. Tools like Istio and Linkerd provide advanced networking features, such as traffic management, load balancing, and security policies.
- **Cloud-Native Networking:** Leverage cloud providers' native networking solutions, such as AWS VPC, Azure Virtual Network, and Google Cloud VPC, to ensure reliable and scalable connectivity between services.

Data Management Challenges

Data management is another key consideration in multi-cloud environments. Ensuring data consistency and availability across geographically dispersed cloud data centers can introduce complexity.

Several strategies can help:

- **Data Replication:** Implement data replication mechanisms to ensure that data is synchronized across different cloud environments, providing high availability and fault tolerance.
- **Distributed Databases:** Utilize distributed databases that natively support multi-cloud deployments, such as Cassandra, CockroachDB, and Google Cloud Spanner.

- **Centralized Data Services:** Store data in a centralized location accessible from multiple clouds, using solutions like Amazon S3 or Google Cloud Storage.

Security Considerations

Security in multi-cloud environments requires a comprehensive approach to protect containerized applications and data across different cloud platforms. Key considerations include:

- **Identity and Access Management (IAM):** Implement robust IAM policies to control access to resources and services across cloud providers.
- **Encryption:** Ensure data is encrypted both at rest and in transit using industry-standard encryption protocols.
- **Security Policies:** Apply consistent security policies across environments, leveraging tools such as Kubernetes Network Policies and Docker Content Trust.

Logging and Monitoring

Effective logging and monitoring are essential to maintain visibility and manageability in multi-cloud environments. Standardized logging and monitoring solutions help ensure consistent observability across clouds.

Popular solutions include:

- **Prometheus:** An open-source monitoring system that integrates seamlessly with Kubernetes, providing powerful metrics gathering and querying capabilities.
- **ELK Stack:** Elasticsearch, Logstash, and Kibana can be used to aggregate and visualize logs from containers deployed across multiple clouds.
- **Grafana:** A versatile dashboard and visualization tool that can integrate with various data sources, providing real-time monitoring and analytics.

```
global:
  scrape_interval: 15s
```

```
scrape_configs:
  - job_name: "kubernetes"
    kubernetes_sd_configs:
      - role: node
```

The Prometheus configuration file provided above demonstrates how to scrape metrics from Kubernetes nodes. This setup can be extended to multiple Kubernetes clusters running across different cloud providers to centralize monitoring data.

Using Docker in multi-cloud environments empowers organizations to build resilient, cost-effective, and optimized application architectures. By leveraging containerization, orchestration, networking, data management, security, and monitoring best practices, organizations can successfully navigate the complexities of multi-cloud deployments and capitalize on the benefits they offer.

12.13 Case Studies: Successful Docker Implementations

Organizations across various industries have effectively leveraged Docker to enhance their workflows, improve resource utilization, and reduce operational overhead. This section illustrates concrete examples of Docker implementations, highlighting the challenges addressed, the solutions devised, and the outcomes achieved. These case studies demonstrate Docker's versatility and its value in solving diverse problems in real-world scenarios.

Case Study 1: A FinTech Startup Enhances CI/CD with Docker

A rapidly growing FinTech startup faced issues with prolonged release cycles and inconsistent development environments. To overcome these obstacles, the startup implemented Docker for their continuous integration/continuous deployment (CI/CD) workflows.

The startup's original CI/CD pipeline was marred by environment discrepancies across development, staging, and production stages. Developers often encountered the "it works on my machine" problem, resulting in delayed release cycles and increased debugging effort.

The team adopted Docker to containerize all application components, including the backend services written in Python, the frontend application built using React, and the PostgreSQL database. Docker Compose files were created to define multi-container Docker applications, ensuring that each developer's environment replicated the production setup.

```
# Dockerfile for backend service
FROM python:3.8-slim

WORKDIR /app
COPY requirements.txt requirements.txt
RUN pip install -r requirements.txt
COPY . .
CMD ["python", "app.py"]
```

```
# Dockerfile for frontend service
FROM node:14

WORKDIR /app
COPY package.json package.json
RUN npm install
COPY . .
CMD ["npm", "start"]
```

```
# docker-compose.yml
version: '3.8'

services:
  backend:
    build: ./backend
    ports:
      - "5000:5000"
    environment:
      - DATABASE_URL=postgresql://db:5432/service_db
    depends_on:
      - db

  frontend:
    build: ./frontend
    ports:
      - "3000:3000"

  db:
    image: postgres:13
    environment:
      POSTGRES_USER: user
      POSTGRES_PASSWORD: password
      POSTGRES_DB: service_db
    volumes:
      - postgres_data:/var/lib/postgresql/data

volumes:
  postgres_data: {}
```

The introduction of Docker led to significant improvements:

- Consistent development environments: By using Docker, each developer worked in an isolated and uniform environment, eliminating discrepancies and reducing the time spent on debugging environment-specific issues.

- Reduced CI/CD pipeline times: Docker's lightweight containers allowed for quicker provisioning and teardown of testing environments, reducing overall pipeline execution times.
- Streamlined deployment process: The use of Docker in staging and production ensured that the environment was consistent and reliable, which minimized deployment failures and rollback instances.

Case Study 2: An E-commerce Platform Migrates Legacy Applications with Docker

An established e-commerce company aimed to modernize its legacy monolithic applications built on Java and running on outdated hardware. The objective was to minimize downtime, improve scalability, and reduce infrastructure costs.

The company opted to containerize its legacy applications using Docker. They began with lift-and-shift, encapsulating the entire monolithic applications inside Docker containers to run them on modern cloud infrastructure.

Their process involved creating Dockerfiles for each service in the legacy system and gradually splitting the monolith into microservices. This allowed individual services to be independently developed, tested, and deployed.

```
# Dockerfile for legacy service
FROM openjdk:8-jre

COPY target/legacy-service.jar app.jar
ENTRYPOINT ["java", "-jar", "/app.jar"]
```

During the migration, the company leveraged Docker Compose to manage the multiple containers and adopted Kubernetes for orchestration to ensure high availability and scalability.

```
# docker-compose.yml for legacy application
version: '3.8'

services:
  legacy_service:
    build: ./legacy_service
    ports:
      - "8080:8080"
    environment:
      - DATABASE_URL=postgresql://db:5432/legacy_db

  db:
    image: postgres:13
    environment:
      POSTGRES_USER: user
```

```
      POSTGRES_PASSWORD: password
      POSTGRES_DB: legacy_db
    volumes:
      - postgres_data:/var/lib/postgresql/data

volumes:
  postgres_data: {}
```

The transition led to numerous benefits:

- Enhanced scalability: By containerizing applications and using Kubernetes orchestration, the company could scale individual services in response to demand, optimizing resource utilization and performance.
- Reduced infrastructure costs: Running containers on cloud infrastructure reduced reliance on outdated hardware, resulting in cost savings on maintenance and upgrades.
- Improved deployment speed: The ability to deploy containers rapidly in cloud environments enabled faster iteration and updates, leading to quicker feature rollouts and bug fixes.

Case Study 3: A Healthcare Analytics Company Optimizes Data Science Workflows with Docker

A healthcare analytics company faced challenges with the reproducibility and scalability of their data science projects. Consistency between development and production environments was often disrupted by library incompatibilities and dependency hell.

To address these issues, the company harnessed Docker to create portable, consistent environments for their data science workflows. Each project included Dockerfiles to specify the necessary dependencies and configurations, ensuring reproducibility across different stages.

```
# Dockerfile for data science environment
FROM jupyter/scipy-notebook:latest

WORKDIR /home/jovyan
COPY requirements.txt requirements.txt
RUN pip install -r requirements.txt
COPY . .
CMD ["start-notebook.sh"]
```

For complex workflows involving multiple interacting components, Docker Compose was utilized to define and manage the full stack.

```
# docker-compose.yml for data science project
```

```
version: '3.8'

services:
  jupyter:
    build: ./jupyter
    ports:
      - "8888:8888"
    volumes:
      - ./notebooks:/home/jovyan/notebooks

  db:
    image: postgres:13
    environment:
      POSTGRES_USER: user
      POSTGRES_PASSWORD: password
      POSTGRES_DB: analytics_db
    volumes:
      - postgres_data:/var/lib/postgresql/data

volumes:
  postgres_data: {}
```

The implementation yielded notable benefits:

- Enhanced reproducibility: Docker enabled exact replication of environments, ensuring that analyses and model training performed the same regardless of the machine or platform.
- Streamlined collaboration: Data scientists could share Docker images, facilitating collaboration and preventing "works-on-my-machine" issues.
- Scalability: By containerizing the computational tasks, the company could easily scale processing power horizontally using a cloud-based infrastructure.

These case studies are illustrative of Docker's robust capabilities to address real-world challenges. By providing a consistent, scalable, and efficient environment, Docker has empowered diverse organizations to achieve technical and operational excellence.

Made in the USA
Monee, IL
05 November 2026

67814338R00243